Language Learning, Teaching and Testing
A Companion

V. D. Singh

FOUNDATION®
B O O K S

Delhi • Bangalore • Mumbai • Kolkata • Chennai • Hyderabad

Published by
Cambridge University Press India Pvt. Ltd.
under the Foundation Books imprint
Cambridge House, 4381/4 Ansari Road, Daryaganj
New Delhi 110002

Cambridge University Press India Pvt. Ltd.
C-22, C-Block, Brigade M.M., K.R. Road, Jayanagar
Bangalore 560 070
Plot No. 80, Service Industries, Shirvane, Sector-1, Nerul
Navi Mumbai 400 706
10 Raja Subodh Mullick Square, 2nd Floor, **Kolkata** 700 013
21/1 (New No. 49), 1st Floor, Model School Road, Thousand Lights
Chennai 600 006
House No. 3-5-874/6/4, (Near Apollo Hospital), Hyderguda, **Hyderabad** 500 029

© Cambridge University Press India Pvt. Ltd.
First Published 2008

ISBN 978-81-7596-593-5

Typeset at Sanchauli Image Composers, New Delhi.

Published by Manas Saikia for Cambridge University Press India Pvt. Ltd. and printed at Sanat Printers, Kundli.

This work has been possible with the blessings of
Guruji Maharaj Pandit Krishna Gopal Vyas (1915–2002)
to whose memory it is dedicated.

Preface

This book has grown out of my long years of teaching and research in the field of language education. It began as a teacher's response to the difficulties novices felt comprehending technical terms used in the books and lectures on the subject. Language education being an inter-disciplinary field has, for explication in its discourse, drawn from neighbouring disciplines such as linguistics, psychology and sociolinguistics. Specialists in the field (of language education) often assume their readers' familiarity with the terms they use or their accessibility to the references they cite. The gap between the assumed and the actual causes difficulties the *Companion* seeks to address.

Innovation and theorising in the domain especially of second language education have brought with them a host of new terms. The need to fine-tune their discourse has led writers to exploit the resources of the lexicon to invest words with new signification. They have often resorted to the devices of metaphor leading them to create expressions such as 'the surrender value,' 'the affective filter'

and a 'syncopated approach.'

Inter-blending education, ideology and critical awareness has further spurred terminological inventiveness so that the term 'literacy,' for example, has come to acquire new meanings.

Scholars and teachers in the field of language education often need mediation to access the meaning and import of the terms used in the literature on the subject. An attempt has been made in this book to fulfil that need.

In putting the book together, I have taken the help from many of my colleagues at the erstwhile Central Institute of English and Foreign Languages (now renamed English and Foreign Languages University) in Hyderabad. I owe them a debt of thanks. My thanks also go to the editing and the production teams at the Cambridge University Press India Private Limited, New Delhi, for giving this book the form it has.

Special thanks to Lalita for her patience and support, and to Lalit and Siddhartha for help with the frequently-occurring glitches.

V. D. Singh

How to use the book

Locating the Term

To find the term you are looking for, either scan through the items listed under the relevant heading(s) in the *Subject Index,* or go directly to its alphabetical place in the entries. The entries are arranged alphabetically, as in a dictionary.

If you are not sure of the exact term (a word or a phrase), you may take a look at the subject headings in the Index to locate the area(s) that relate(s) the term/topic you have in mind, and then scan through the items listed under them.

Cross-referencing

Words and phrases in the text of an entry printed in SMALL CAPITALS cross-refer to other entries in the *Companion.*

Further cross-referencing is done by asking the user, where necessary, to *See/See also* some other entry.

Defining the Headword

Following the Headword in **Boldface**, is a brief definition of the term. What follows in the rest of the entry is the exposition. In cases where a term is used in more than one context, the definition and exposition are numbered 1, 2 , 3 and so on.

Conventions

LEARNER. Following the practice in the writings on language learning and teaching, the word 'learner' has been used for the pupil. The Learner, however, need not be a formally enrolled one for instruction. For adult learners, the word 'student' has generally been preferred.

SECOND LANGUAGE/FOREIGN LANGUAGE. To save space, the abbreviated form SL has been used to refer to both 'second language' and 'foreign language.' The abbreviated form FL is used where the reference is specifically to 'foreign language.'

SHE and HER. To avoid sexism in usage, the pronouns 'she' and 'her' have been preferred over *s/he* or *he,* and *her/his* or *his/her* or *his.*

Examples. Since the book is written in English, the examples are drawn from it.

Subject Index

Note:
(i) The entries listed under a heading are those that *relate* to the broad area indicated by it.
(ii) In some cases, though the relationship between the heading and an entry listed under it is not a direct one, the latter has been included keeping in view the diverse needs of the users, and the inter-connectedness of the topics/entries.
(iii) Some entries are listed under more than one heading.

Associative learning; Attention; Avoidance behaviour/strategy; Awareness; Bottom-up; Bottom-up processing; Catenizing; Challenge; Cognitive; Cognitive approaches to language teaching; CALP; Closure-oriented style of learning; Cloze; Cognitive-code learning theory; Cognitive learning strategies; Cognitive perspectives on learning; Cognitive styles; Communication strategies; Communicational teaching project; Communicative language learning; Communicative language teaching; Concept map; Conceptual strategies; Construct; Constructivism; Contiguity learning; Creative-construction hypothesis; Creative thinking; Data-driven processing; Declarative knowledge; Discovery; Double translation; Equilibrium; Field dependence/independence; Forgetting; General ability; Generalization; Guessing; Heuristic; Heuristic approaches in LT; Hypercorrection 2; Hypothesis 2; Hypothesis-testing; Ideation; Incorporation strategy; Induction; Inductive learning; Inferencing; Input; Intake; Integrative reconciliation; Intelligence; Interdependency hypothesis; Interdependency principle; Jigsaw task; Knowledge; Knowledge about language; Knowledge structures; Laddering; Language acquisition device; Lateral thinking; Learning strategies; Learning style; Listening comprehension strategies; Mediation; The Mediation theory; Memorisation; Memory; Mental age; Mentalism; Metacognition; Metacognitive strategies; Mind-map; Miscue; Mnemonic devices; The modularity view; Module 2; Monitoring; Motivation; Noticing; Open questions; Output; Overgeneralization; Parallel thinking; Perception; Problem-based learning; Problem-posing; Problem-solving; Processing; Production strategy; Reading miscues; Reading strategies; Reading with response; Reflection 1; Reflective learning; Scaffolding; Schema/schemata; Schema theory; Social constructivism; Strategy; 'Studial methods;' Study approaches; Styles of learning; Synectics; Task; Task-based learning; Thinking; Thinksheet; Top down 1; Zone of proximal development.

COMMUNICATION. (*See also* **Language use.**). Acceptability; Accommodation 2; Achievement behaviour; Adjustment; Appropriateness; Avoidance strategy; Bilingual processes; Book language; Careful style; Circumlocution; Code; Code mixing/switching; Coherence; Cohesion; Cohesive ties; Colloquial speech; Commercialese; Communication; Communication accommodation theory; Communication process; Communication strategies; Communicative; Communicative approaches to language teaching; Communicative competence; Communicative efficiency; Communicative function; Communicative language learning; Communicative language teaching; Communicative language testing; Communicative orientations of language teaching; Communicative stress; Context; The Co-operative principle; Dialogue journals; Discourse competence; Discourse management; Discourse repair; Exchange; Extralinguistic; Face-to-face communication: Feedback 3; Fluency; Focus; Func-

attention hypothesis; Self-assessment; Self-direction; Self-esteem; Self-image; Self-evaluation/Self-assessment; Self-instructed/self-(managed) learning; Self-rating; Semanticising; Semantic map; Silent period; Skill; Social constructivism; Social learning theory; Social strategies; Speaking practice; Specific practice; The Stereotype hypothesis; The S-R theory; Strategy; Street learning; Stress; 'Studial methods;' Study approaches; Style 2;Styles of learning; Styles vs strategies; Substitution drills; Substitution tables; Suggestopedia; Sunburn method; System revision; *Tabula rasa;* Tandem learning; Task-based learning; Terminal behaviour; The three Ps of SLT; 'Time-on-task'; Tolerance of ambiguity 1; Topic method; Transfer; Transfer of skills; Transfer of training; Uptake 1; Workshop; Zone of proximal development.

Factors in language learning. Accommodation; Acculturation; Achievement behaviour; Acquisition-poor environment; Acquisition-rich environment; Adaptation; Affect; Affective factors; Affiliation motive; Age; Alienation; Anxiety; Aptitude; Attention; Attitude 1; Autonomy; Chronological age; Challenge; Channel capacity; Closure-oriented styles of learning; Cognition; Creativity; Discovery; Enrichment; Extroversion/ introversion; Field dependence/independence; Fossilization; The Good language learner; Heuristic; Ideation; Individual learner differences; Input; Introspection; Language learning aptitude; Learner beliefs; Learner characteristics; Learner support; Learner training; Learner

typology; Learning strategies; Motivation; Natural setting; Perception; Personality; Risk-taking; Self-esteem; Stress; Tolerance of ambiguity.

LANGUAGE LEARNING EXERCISES, GAMES, & TASKS. Action chain; Amplification; Anagram; Analogy games; Analysis 1; Articulation exercises; Assignment; Authentic task; Awareness-raising; Brainstorming; Chaining; The Chorus 'method'; Command cards; Comprehension; Conditioned substitution tables; Conversion; Co-operative task; Declamation; Dictation; Dicto-comp.; 'Double translation'; 'Dramatic method'; Dramatisation; Drill; Elliptical exercises; Elocution; Essay; Exchange journals; Expansion 1, 2; Fixed-choice items; Forced-choice items; Folk tales; Frame 1; Free composition; Group work; Homework; *Imitatio;* Information gap; Information transfer; Integrative; Jigsaw task; Language games; Language through actions; Listen and repeat; The Look-and-listen exercise; The Look-and-say exercise; Matching tables; Matching-type item; *Metaphrasis;* Mind-map; Note-making; Note-making and note-taking; Oral composition; Oral drill tables; Pair practice; Pair work; Paraphrase; Parsing; Passive listening; Pattern drill/pattern practice drill; Pedagogic task; Peer review; Picture cards; Picture composition; Picture vocabulary; Practice; Précis-making; Pretence in language teaching; Project; Puppetry; Read-and-listen exercises; Reading aloud; Reading syndicate; Recitation 1; Reproduction 1; Reverse interpretation; Role play 1; Sentence completion task; Simulation; Speaking

SOCIOLINGUISTICS/SOCIOLOGY.

RESEARCH and LANGUAGE EDUCATION.

ability. Mental capacity to perform a task.

ability grouping. Dividing learners into groups according to ability level. The idea of dividing learners into groups is to form homogeneous groups for smooth teaching. However, such grouping may have disadvantages. Learners placed in the low track may develop a sense of inferiority, and this could be psychologically detrimental to their learning. *See also* STREAMING.

abridgement. Shortening the length of a book [novel, biography, etc.] without sacrificing the quality and effect of the original. Abridged versions are used as SUPPLEMENTARY READERS on language courses for learners who are not so proficient as to be able to read the originals comfortably. Supplementary readers are usu. both abridged and simplified. *Cf.* SIMPLIFICATION.

academic literacy. Ability to use LANGUAGE FOR (formal) ACADEMIC PURPOSES.

academic skills. Language skills particularly relevant to pursuing higher studies. These skills include the ability to use a FORMAL (1) variety of the language in scholarly contexts, academic styles of writing [papers and dissertations], STUDY SKILLS and oral presentation skills. Some of the skills needed in particular are those of introducing a topic, concluding a discussion; arguing, defining, comparing and contrasting, explaining, exemplifying, and interpreting data. These may be needed in creating both the oral and the written discourse.

academic writing. Writing usually in the context of one's education and study at the college/university level. It includes writing of ASSIGNMENTS, papers, ESSAY-EXAMINATIONS, PRÉCIS, SUMMARIES, SEMINAR-reports, and materials for academic publications. Some skills specific to academic writing are those of arguing, analysing, defining, comparing, and evaluating. Academic writing is usually GENRE-SPECIFIC (relating to form, format and LANGUAGE VARIETY). It is usually of the expository type, and formal in style. Advanced Academic writing, as in research, calls for the ability to write abstracts and hypotheses, the method and procedure section(s), findings, conclusions and summary.

accent. 1. The prominence or emphasis with which an individual sound or a SYLLABLE in a word, or a word within a phrase may be articulated. For example, in the word emphasis, the first syllable 'em' is accented. **2.** [Of a language] Particular way of speaking a language/DIALECT. The accent of a speaker may indicate her social and educational background, profession, native language, and the region or country she comes from. **3.** With reference to number 1 above, a sign or symbol used above letters in printed/written words to indicate accent, **Example**, 'emphasis'.

acceptability. Tolerability [by educated listeners/speakers] of features of USAGE and pronunciation. Several factors contribute to the tolerability of an utterance or a piece of writing.

1

Some of these are: INTELLIGIBILITY, COR-
RECTNESS 1, and APPROPRIATENESS to the
(social) context.

The norms of acceptability of usages
and pronunciations vary according to
the context such as social and educational.

accommodation. Adjustment. **1.** In
psychology, the process of our existing
knowledge getting modified in the light
of new information. In LL, a process of
SYSTEM REVISION. *Cf.* ASSIMILATION. *See
also* INTEGRATIVE RECONCILIATION. **2.** In
speech, adjusting one's pronunciation
and other features of speech to the
needs of the listener. In doing this,
one may have to speak slowly, repeat,
or rephrase certain expressions. Much
depends on the speaker's alertness to
the feedback from the listener. *See also*
SPEECH ACCOMMODATION.

acculturation. The process of becoming adjusted to a new CULTURE in learning a SL, which involves, among other
things, interaction with the TL community and readjustment of attitudes.
Acculturation is considered to promote
SL acquisition.

acculturation hypothesis. A theory
of L2 acquisition developed by Schumann (1978). Its main point is that
the process of ACCULTURATION aids the
acquisition of a SL. The greater the social and psychological distance of the
learner from the TL [and CULTURE], the
slower the pace of acquisition.

Schumann's theory is based on studies of SL acquisition by migrants to
a TL-speaking country, and is more
appropriately applicable to those situations.

accuracy. Correctness of language

– grammatical, lexical, and phonological. *See also* CORRECTNESS (1), and
FLUENCY.

accuracy order. *See* NATURAL ORDER
HYPOTHESIS.

achievement. Success in learning/
mastering something, usually following a course of instruction. *See also*
ACHIEVEMENT TESTS.

achievement behaviour. Stretching
one's communication-resources to
achieve communicative goals. The
behaviour consists of using achievement strategies of communication,
also known as compensatory strategies, which include APPROXIMATION,
CIRCUMLOCUTION, (LANGUAGE) TRANS-
FER, PARAPHRASE, and word coinage.
Achievement strategies are contrasted
with AVOIDANCE STRATEGIES AND REDUC-
TION STRATEGIES. *See also* COMMUNICA-
TION STRATEGIES.

achievement tests. Language tests
based on what has been taught on
a course of study. Examinations in
the educational context are typically achievement tests also known
as ATTAINMENT TESTS. Syllabus-based,
achievement tests could be FINAL, or
progress achievement tests often called
class tests. As different from achievement tests are PROFICIENCY TESTS.

acquaintance vocabulary. The
vocabulary one can recognise but not
easily recall for active use when speaking or writing. It is also known as one's
PASSIVE VOCABULARY.

acquisition device. *See* LANGUAGE
ACQUISITION DEVICE.

acquisition of language. The process
of learning a language, i.e., developing in oneself competence in using

the language for communication. This process could be a subconscious or a semi-conscious one as in the case of children learning their MT. Learning could also be through formal instruction received from tutors, or in educational institutions. Much SL learning is of this kind.

Some writers, notably S. Krashen (1982), distinguish between ACQUISITION and LEARNING treating them distinct processes: acquisition being implicit and LEARNING(2), deliberate and through instruction. The first leads to a fluent use of the acquired language and the second, to MONITORED performance. However, not many subscribe to this dichotomy. They take an INTERFACE POSITION.

acquisition order. *See* ORDER OF DEVELOPMENT.

acquisition-poor environment. Educational and social environment which offers learners severely limited exposure to the TL, and scant LL resource. *See also* ACQUISITION-RICH ENVIRONMENT.

acquisition-rich environment. An environment which provides learners plenty of opportunities to listen to the TL, and speak, read and write in it. A classroom that engages learners in such interactive processes, provides the environment. The social and academic milieu outside the classroom may also similarly be acquisition-rich.

action chain. A LL task that involves performance of a sequence of connected actions and verbalising while doing them. An example: the following chain of actions deals with making a telephone call. In full view and hearing of the class, the nominated student does the following and when doing so, says:
I lift the handset
I listen for the dial tone
I dial the number
I wait for the telephone to ring at the called number, and wait for a response. And so on

Before the learners are asked to perform the chain, the teacher demonstrates the actions saying at each point what she is doing. 'Then the pupils do the actions in small groups, the sentences being said in chorus by one of the small groups sitting down, or in turn by each pupil, or by the ones who are doing the actions.' (Gurrey: 1955) *See also* THE CHORUS METHOD.

action research. A form of research in which the key process is the researcher's (critical) REFLECTION on her own actions, performance, or practices in social situations including classroom teaching. Action research is undertaken with a view to finding solution to a problem the researcher has faced. In Action research done by teachers, the research practices are integral with their pedagogical practice, which the researchers seek to understand, evaluate, and improve on. Thus in the context of teaching, Action research becomes teacher research. *See also* TEACHER AS RESEARCHER.

active vocabulary. Words one can easily recall for use. Also known as PRODUCTIVE VOCABULARY, and contrasted with RECOGNITION vocabulary, active vocabulary consists of words that usually occur in an individual's speech and writing.

activity. Instructional actions involving learner participation. In a classroom, teachers typically control, guide, and engage learners in learning activities. Classroom activities have an almost unlimited variety: reading out aloud a sentence from the textbook to producing its explanation orally or in writing are all activities.

activity method. An approach to teaching that considers the learner as an active participant in learning rather than a passive recipient of knowledge. In it activities performed by learners replace much of the teacher-centred instruction. Of the many learner activities some are PROJECT WORK, GROUP WORK, topic activity (*See* TOPIC METHOD), and discussion.

actual developmental level. According to Vygotsky, the level in a child's cognitive development when she can complete a task on her own. *Cf.* ZONE OF PROXIMAL DEVELOPMENT.

adaptation. 1.[Of teaching materials] Making changes to AUTHENTIC TEXTS by shortening or simplifying them, by adding to them or deleting from them in order to make them suitable for pedagogic purposes, i.e., to make them easy to understand, to bring them in line with the course specifications, and make them suited to learner age, learner needs and learners' level of proficiency. Adaptation involves changes like restating meanings, simplifying and rearranging words, sentence structures, and the DISCOURSE structure of the original material. The process requires careful balance in handling the original so that its meaning and identity are not over-simplified, altered or distorted. **2.** [In language teaching] Modifying a given METHOD of teaching

in order to make it more suitable to the needs of learners, their age, LEARNING STYLES, etc. **3.** [In the development of intellect/cognition.] The process of ACCOMMODATION (1) and ASSIMILATION new perceptions into what one already knows. A child familiar only with chairs, first perceives a sofa as chair. After perceiving the difference, the child ADAPTS its cognitive structure to accommodate the knowledge of a new kind of seat, the sofa.

adaptive testing. Individualised, tailored testing [of language proficiency]. In it the test items are so selected as to match the test-taker's level.

additional language. The language opted for study in addition to the prescribed one(s) in the curriculum. In certain contexts, the term is preferred to 'SL' for its neutral connotation.

additive bilingualism. A speech situation where the learning and use of a SL does not (adversely) affect the learner/user's competence in the MOTHER TONGUE. The term carries contrast with subtractive bilingualism in which the use of a SL gradually leads to an erosion of competence in the MT.

adjustment. Co-operation in conversation/communication. The interlocutors in a communicative situation co-operatively negotiate the course of meaning by seeking clarifications, responding to the feedback received, filling in gaps, and guessing the intended meaning of their interlocutor.

advance organiser. A term used by the educational psychologist Ausubel, to refer to the conceptual aid provided to the learner in advance of the learning material itself to facilitate cognition. An advance organiser is a device to help learners to bridge the gap between their current knowledge and the new material that will be taught. 'The substantive content of a given organiser or a series of organisers is selected on the basis of their appropriateness for explaining, integrating, and interrelating the material they precede.' This strategy is used to enhance 'the organisational strength of cognitive structure.' Previewing questions, or pre-teaching of key words are some of the devices that can be used as aids.

affective factors. Factors related to one's feelings, emotions and experience. It is hypothesised that they play an important role in facilitating/ obstructing the holistic process of learning. Anxiety, feeling relaxed, SELF-ESTEEM, and sense of security are some of the factors associated with affect. A lot of importance is being attached to these factors in recent approaches to SL pedagogy. One of the hypotheses in S. Krashen's (1981) theory of SLA postulates that the SL learner needs to be affectively at ease to be able to make satisfactory progress in learning. Recognition of the role of affective factors in SL learning comes in the wake of the realisation that one of the shortcomings of some past practices has been the undue importance given to COGNITION and cognitive factors to the exclusion of the affective ones.

affective filter. A cognitive-affective mechanism that screens the learners' PERCEPTION, and does not allow their minds to cooperate with them in their learning of a SL. S. Krashen (after Dulay and Burt, 1977) in his theory of SLA [a set of hypotheses] postulates that for learning to succeed, learners need to be affectively relaxed during learning. To explain this, he uses the metaphorical expression AFFECTIVE FILTER, which is an adjustable mechanism. When the learners are in grip of anxiety and a lack of self-confidence, their affective filters are, so to say, in a raised state. When they feel motivated to learn, confident of themselves, and anxiety-free, their mental-affective filters get lowered. This psychological state, according to some, particularly S. Krashen, is the most conducive to learning.

affective reaction. Fear or anxiety caused in the learner. The reaction, i.e., the emotional STRESS may be caused by the learner's fear of such things as of poor performance in the class or at the exam., the stern attitude of the teacher, and the difficulty of the item to be learnt. The reasons for fear may include lack of self-confidence and an underrating of one's ability. Whatever the factor, the reaction affects the learner's performance.

affiliation motive. The need and desire to socialise with other people. When the motive relates to the TL community, it is considered to facilitate SL learning.

age. The period one has lived since one's birth. The period is one's chronological age. SLL is seen significantly related to age Many hold the view that as one's age advances, one's LANGUAGE ACQUISITION DEVICE becomes less efficient. From early infancy to puberty is the period most suited for SLA, and after this the plasticity of the human brain decreases. *See also* CRITICAL PERIOD HYPOTHESIS. In educational contexts, a distinction is drawn between one's CHRONOLOGICAL AGE and MENTAL AGE. The MENTAL AGE is a measure of one's intelligence and is calculated by using intelligence tests. *See* INTELLIGENCE QUOTIENT. EDUCATIONAL AGE refers to the level of the performance of a child in relation to a particular class, grade, or standard. The age is assessed by a STANDARDISED TEST.

age placement of teaching materials. Judging the suitability of teaching materials for a particular age-group. As learners in different age groups have different interests and different levels of linguistic proficiency, it is desirable that teaching materials match these.

aim. *See* OBJECTIVES.

alexia. Word blindness: partial or complete loss of ability to identify the printed word.

alienation. A feeling of separation from others. When in relation to the TL/SL community, it can be a hindrance to (S)LL *See also* ANOMIE (1), and OWNERSHIP.

alphabet. The set of letters used in the writing system of a language. English and some other languages use the Roman alphabet. Sometimes the term is used to refer to an individual letter of the alphabet.

alphabetic method. The method of teaching word-reading and word meaning by pronouncing the letters constituting the word. An example of young learners using this method to practice is:- g - a - t - e =/geit/. Gate means *pha:tak.* [in Hindi] The method is supposed to help memorise the spelling and the meaning of a word.

ambiguity. Imprecision of meaning making possible more than one meaning of a word/sentence. The word *fork* is an example of LEXICAL ambiguity, and the sentence *Visiting relatives can be a nuisance* of syntactic/grammatical ambiguity. These are instances of *potential* ambiguity, as the intended meaning would be clear from the context.

ambiversion. *See* EXTROVERSION.

ambilingual. Someone equally proficient in two languages. *See* BILINGUALISM.

amplification. Expansion, **example,** of an idea, a statement or a TOPIC SENTENCE. Amplification is primarily a writing task/an INTEGRATIVE test of writing ability.

anagram. A TASK in which letters are to be rearranged into words. An **Example,** *tesfro* – forest. The task has a variety of forms.

analogistic thinking. Thinking in terms of METAPHORS – a mode of creative thinking. In this, the learner discovers likenesses between two apparently dissimilar things such as dancing and the billowing of tree-branches. Analogistic thinking is supposed to be generative of ideas and original thinking.

analogy game. A LANGUAGE GAME in which the learner has to infer the relationship between two things/concepts. These two are supplied [often in an incomplete sentence]. A third concept also is mentioned for which the learner has to give the analogically related concept. **Example:** *A hat is to head as shoes are to –*

analysis. 1. Breaking down something, **Example**, a sentence into its component parts in order to study it. Formal and semantic analyses of words, phrases, sentences, and longer units are a key activity in formal grammar-based models of LT. **2.** The process of dividing and classifying in oral/written communication, esp. in EXPOSITORY WRITING. *See also* ANALYTICAL SKILL.

analytic scoring. Scoring in which separate marks are awarded for each of the specified components [or, the constituent TRAITS] of the skill being evaluated. **Example**, in analytic scoring of a written composition, the evaluators instead of arriving at a round score holistically, award separate scores for such (analytic) categories as accuracy, organisation, and coherence. *See* HOLISTIC SCORING.

The relative weighting for individual categories depends on the objective, priority, level, etc. of the Test. An advantage of such scoring is that the candidate's performance is reported in the form of a set of scores which can be used to build a PROFILE. Analytic scoring goes with CRITERION-REFERENCED TESTS and with COMMUNICATIVE LANGUAGE TESTING.

analytical skill. The skill of breaking up (and studying) a thing such as a piece of writing or speech into its constituent elements, and the faculty to see their inter-relationship. For example, it calls for analytical skill to see [and describe] how a speaker has introduced a topic, marshalled arguments[main and subsidiary] to support it and concluded the talk, or at which point(s) she digressed, repeated, or contradicted herself. Analytical skill includes more abilities than just that of breaking up. Probing a problem, examining its cause(s) and effect(s), being able to see the pros and cons of an issue would also involve analytical skill.

analytic syllabuses. SYLLABUSES that selectively include those areas and points of teaching that respond directly to the needs of the learners. Wilkins (1976) made a distinction between ANALYTIC and SYNTHETIC syllabuses, and claimed that his NOTIONAL-FUNCTIONAL SYLLABUS was of the former kind, a claim not acceptable to many. Incidentally, according to this distinction, synthetic syllabuses aim at teaching TL's lexis, syntax, morphology, phonology, etc. in a GENERAL-PURPOSE [LANGUAGE COURSE] way, 'incrementally.'

andragogy. The science of teaching adults. Adults differ from younger learners in their degree of MOTIVATION, level of cognitive maturity, LEARNING STYLES, and experience of the world. Hence the approach to teaching them differs[or, should differ]

Andragogy is described as the 'art and science of *helping* adults learn' (Knowles,1983) – not only just acquire knowledge, but to learn in order to achieve self-development and growth. Andragogy encourages AUTONOMY, SELF-DIRECTION, and EXPERIENTIAL LEARNING. It contrasts with PEDAGOGY and the traditional 'REPRODUCTIVE' MODELS of education.

anomie. 1. Feeling of ALIENATION and insecurity in SL learners when living in the TL community. The feeling arises from the consciousness that the learners have veered away from their own COMMUNITY and native culture and that they are amidst an alien community which has not accepted them as member.

Achievement of high proficiency in another language and the resultant change in one's views and attitudes may develop in one anomie. An associated feeling may be one of loss of self-worth caused by a sense of emptiness, and lack of alternatives **2.** The critical attitude of an individual to their own race/society/culture, and their role in it. Individuals with such an attitude are supposed to be favourably disposed to the learning of a SL because they are not considered to be ethnocentric, and have the desired flexibility and criticalness generated in them by anomie.

anomy. *See* anomie.

anthropology. The study of people, SOCIETY, and CULTURE. These and language use are closely related. The value-system of a people, their cultural norms, and social practices are reflected in their language and the choices it makes. The English kinship term *uncle* or *aunt(y)* and their approximation to multiple differentiated terms in Indian languages is an example of this.

anxiety. A mental state of vague or situation-specific fear. SL learners may suffer from it on account of their slow progress in learning (specially when compared with PEERS), inability to turn in ASSIGNMENTS, harsh attitude of parents, reprimand by teachers, tests/examinations and the prospect of poor performance in them. Often the feeling that one is being judged by teachers or peers may be a source of anxiety. Even the feeling of being ignored by teachers/peers may drive one to anxiety. A touchy apprehension of one's CASTE, colour, social origin may also be a source. Anxiety is sometimes a personality trait of some learners.

Anxiety can be debilitating or facilitating. The former has an adverse effect on learners' performance. It may make the learner indifferent to school work or disinclined to RISK-TAKING in learning. Debilitating anxiety may develop a general feeling of inferiority. On the contrary, facilitating (or, facilitative) anxiety helps learners to improve on their performance by making them put in more effort.

Anxiety could be an anticipatory reaction or it may follow the learner's apprehension that her performance on a particular occasion has been poor. *See also* STRESS.

aphasia. A disorder marked by partial or total loss of language abilities. The disorder follows some physical damage to the brain area. There are different varieties of aphasia-auditory, optic, syntactic, and so on.

a posteriori **syllabus.** A SYLLABUS that emerges from a course of study that has been taught. Usually syllabuses are adopted in advance, and teaching takes place in accordance with what has been specified in them. Such syllabuses are known as *a priori* syllabuses. *See also* HIDDEN CURRICULUM.

applied discourse analysis. Analysis of DISCOURSE to see how language use reflects discriminatory attitudes, prejudice, etc. *See also* CRITICAL DISCOURSE ANALYSIS. Discourse analysis itself has generally been concerned with linguistic aspects of discourse. *APPLIED*

DISCOURSE ANALYSES look at embedded attitudes in discourse.

applied linguistics. An inter-/multi-disciplinary field of study and knowledge dealing with language-based problems and finding their solutions. It came into prominence around the middle of the twentieth century, and has been defined in different ways. Broadly speaking, Applied Linguistics concerns itself with the application of linguistic theories & research in linguistics to LT and language education in general.

apprentice approach to reading. Learning to read by reading 'REAL BOOKS.'

apprentice model. *See also* CRAFT MODEL.

approach. [In the context of LE] **1.** A set of coherent classroom practices. Usually there is a theory of LL & LT from which the principles governing the classroom practices are derived. The phrase COMMUNICATIVE APPROACHES illustrates this. The approaches represent certain underlying principles grounded in theory 'approach' is often used interchangeably with the general expression 'METHOD' or 'METHODOLOGY.' **2.** Some writers [**Example**, Richards and Rodgers, 1986/2001] use *approach* to mean the theoretical CONSTRUCT itself i.e., the theory of the nature of language and of LL to which the classroom practices adhere.

appropriacy. *See* APPROPRIATENESS.

appropriate methodology. Home-developed METHODOLOGY of LT that suits, and is in consonance with the local 'cultures of the classroom,' the social context, and the CULTURAL background of the learners and the teacher. The concept of Appropriate Methodology contrasts with the expert-generated, imported methodologies tested elsewhere. Holliday, A. (1994) proposes adoption of Appropriate Methodology to rectify current biases in methodology [in ELT]. Appropriate Methodology is about making SL teaching 'more appropriate to the social requirements of students and educators in different environments...' (*ibid.*, p.1).

appropriateness. Suitability of speech or writing to the occasion. Appropriateness expects the fulfilment of the conditions of both ACCEPTABILITY and ACCURACY – one sociolinguistic and the other grammatical/stylistic. Appropriateness is judged with reference to the occasion or CONTEXT of a particular utterance and its communicative effect. **Example**, it is not appropriate to make critical remarks about a person in her presence at a meeting convened to bid her farewell.

Linguistic/stylistic appropriateness is judged with reference to the variety of language used. The choice of the right REGISTER and variety such as FORMAL/informal and SLANGY depends on the context – who speaks/writes to whom, when, and where, and so on. Appropriateness is also a matter of maintaining a consistent POINT OF VIEW and a proper TONE in one's speech or writing.

appropriation. Learning or internalisation of a concept, word, or rule of grammar. Vygotsky hypothesised that learners 'appropriated' i.e., acquired concepts, words and grammar rules through their participation in social interaction and input processing.

approximation. In COMMUNICATION,

9

producing utterance that is close to being correct (linguistically and/or communicatively) but not quite there. Approximation is a feature of SL use and indicates the user's effort to be correct and intelligible. **Example,** Inability to correctly produce the initial cluster/*sk/*in 'school' leads many users of ESL to say/iskul/ – an instance of phonological approximation. Approximation could also be lexical, syntactic, and PRAGMATIC, and is an INTERLINGUAL strategy. *See also* COMMUNICATION STRATEGIES.

approximative systems. Learners' developing competence in a SL, also known as TRANSITIONAL COMPETENCE or INTERLANGUAGE. The developing competence of the learner at any given point of time is considered to be a system in itself. It may include GENERALIZATIONS about the TL grammar that many would judge erroneous. But, with most learners, they are passing features. With the assimilation of more INPUT, the system, it is hypothesised, would shed the untenable rule-formulations. *See also* LEARNER LANGUAGE.

a priori **syllabus.** *See* A *posteriori* syllabus.

aptitude. [in the context of language learning]. An individual's potential for achieving some skill, or being able to perform it well. Aptitude indicates an individual's special inclination or natural ability to perform an activity such as learning a new language successfully (in future, if given facilities and training). Aptitude is judged on the basis of an individual's present ability. *See* APTITUDE TEST. Aptitude is considered to be different from

general cognitive abilities of learning and acquiring skills, and is constitutive of INDIVIDUAL LEARNER DIFFERENCES. Some of the characteristics of learners with LL aptitude are: ability to infer grammatical and morphological rules from language input; to perceive sound distinctions and remember them.

aptitude tests. PROGNOSTIC (language) TESTS designed to predict the likelihood of the test-taker being able to learn well a new language formally. Such tests are based on the premise that some learners are better disposed to learning a SL than others. The design of a language aptitude test reflects the test designer(s)' concept of what SL learning consists of, and this understanding usually accords with a theory of language and of SL learning. The two well-known language learning aptitude tests are *Modern language aptitude test* (MLAT) and *Language aptitude battery* (LAB).

argot. SLANG, esp. the variety used by the members of a particular professional group. In earlier times, *argot* referred to the jargon used by criminals.

army method. *See* the ARMY SPECIALISED TRAINING PROGRAMME (ASTP).

the army specialised training programme (ASTP). An FL teaching programme set up by the US government in 1942. The purpose of the programme was to impart government personnel (esp. in the army) conversational fluency in FLs to enable them to perform certain language-related functions during World War II. For this purpose, US universities were asked to develop training programmes. Though the programme lasted only a couple of years between 1942–45, the programme is considered to be a significant event in the history of FL teaching. There emerged from it a way of teaching known as the *Army Method*, a characteristic of which was intensive oral drilling. In this feature the method was a precursor to the American approach to SL teaching, the AUDIOLINGUAL METHOD.

articulacy. Ability to communicate one's thoughts, views, feelings, etc. effectively. Articulacy, though generally synonymous with COMMUNICATIVE COMPETENCE, additionally suggests forcefulness.

Halliday et al. (1964) make a distinction between 'literacy' and 'articulacy' and define the latter as 'the measure of a person's total control of his native language.'

articulation exercises. Practice work in producing SL speech-sounds correctly, intelligibly and distinctly. The oral production of sounds can be of single sounds as of/*f*/, or of sounds occurring in SYLLABLES and WORDS initially (*fine),* medially (*perfect*), or finally (*rough*), and sometimes in phrases. The teacher may have to use devices to demonstrate the shape and position taken by the organs of speech when producing the difficult sounds. Demonstration helps the understanding of friction, rounding, voicing, aspiration, etc.

artificial language. A language invented to serve as an auxiliary medium of universal communication. Such a language is marked by simplicity and logicality. A well-known example is that of Esperanto, devised in 1887 by Ludwich Zamenhof (1859–1917), a Polish physician.

assessment. Generally and in academic settings, the process of making a careful judgement of the knowledge and achievement of a learner or a group of learners in a particular subject based on their performance in it.

Assessment, in the context of language education, is evaluation of a person's language performance or, her ability to use language for communication. It is usually done by judges who use for this purpose carefully evolved instruments, and leads to evaluative statements about the progress made or levels of knowledge achieved. *See also* SELF-ASSESSMENT. *Cf.* Evaluation, and Measurement.

assignment. A task students are asked to do as part of instructional programmes. In the school teaching context in India, pupils are set 'homework,' generally in the nature of reinforcement and practice activity.

An assignment can be a task relating to tutor- specified reading, writing work, a PROJECT or whatever the tutor deems necessary for consolidating learning and making it more effective.

assimilation. The process of learning something by absorbing it mentally and thus making it part of one's knowledge system.

In Piaget's theory of cognitive development, assimilation is the application of a SCHEMA to a new perception of a person, event, or thing. In this process the incoming information undergoes modification in the light of the existing cognitive structure. A complementary process, according to Piaget, is that of ACCOMMODATION. The two processes together aid the learning process of ADAPTATION.

association. Mental operation of establishing connection between people and/or things. Mental associations are impressionistic.

In language teaching, the mental ability to associate may be exploited as memory-aid. It may also serve learners to recall associated ideas and vocabulary for a variety of language-/communication-related activities. *See also* ASSOCIATIVE LEARNING.

associative learning. Learning by establishing association, **Example**, between words and meanings. The process of associating works in different ways. Dog may be associated with loyalty and tiger, ferocity; a pen with a pencil; a kitchen with food, or fire.

ASTP. *See* the ARMY SPECIALISED TRAINING PROGRAMME.

attainment. What one succeeds in learning. In the educational context, attainment or achievement is generally seen in relation to academic programmes, to courses of study undertaken. It is seen as resulting from learning and teaching. Hence tests and exams that evaluate attainment are known as attainment tests. They contrast with PROFICIENCY TESTS.

attainment tests. *See* ACHIEVEMENT TESTS.

attention. The faculty of focusing one's mind on one thing: mental activity directed towards cognition of its object. Learner attention is considered to be an important contributory factor to learning, and is necessary for explicit learning and noticing.

Attention being selective, subject to partial voluntary control, and its span being limited, teachers may need to use strategies to train learner-attention.

attention span. The duration of a learner's mind remaining actively engaged in a learning task. As young learners have shorter attention-span, good teachers, in order to sustain their attention, periodically switch classroom activities.

attitude. A person's belief, or opinion on a subject. These are often tied up with AFFECTIVE FACTORS **1.** In the context of LE, attitude often correlates with the characteristic way in which one tends to react to a language or its speakers. A positive attitude and its related attribute, MOTIVATION, are considered to be important predictors of success in learning a SL. **2.** In the context of writing. Writers' attitude towards their subject communicates to the reader their feeling – critical, friendly, etc. The attitude marks the TONE(1) and STYLE(1) of the writing.

attitude scale. A device for measuring what someone feels [about something], and the degree of the intensity of feeling. Often used in questionnaires, the scales are calibrated. They may offer 3 to 5 or 6 choices. An example of a scale with 4 values:

Much history taught in schools is ideologically distorted

1	2	3	4
strongly agree	agree	disagree	strongly disagree

An advantage of using an attitude

scale is that opinions and their shades receive numerical value. However, a particular number on the scale, **Example**, 4 = strongly disagree, may not always indicate the same 'value' of the response [by different individuals] since there are individual variations among the respondents leading to varying weighting of the chosen response. A well-known scale for measuring attitude is the Likert Scale. *See also* THURSTON-TYPE SCALES.

attitude tests. Scales designed to find out personality traits relating to the test-taker's beliefs and opinions. The commonly used format is that of a questionnaire in which the test-takers are asked to respond whether they agree or disagree with each of a set or sets of statements, and indicate the extent to which they agree or disagree. [*See* ATTITUDE SCALE] The statements relate to the object of the attitude. As the data for attitude tests comes from self-reports, there might often exist a gap between people's assessment of their attitudes and their actual behaviour/beliefs.

attrition. Language loss. Exclusive use or dominance of another language may gradually lead to the decline and loss of an individual's knowledge of, and skill in, a language previously learnt. When communities come under the influence of another DIALECT/language or when they move to an area where another language is spoken, they may gradually lose their own language. The phenomenon is also known as language death or language obsolescence.

audience awareness. The writer's appreciation of who she is writing for, and who will be her likely readers. Audience awareness, an important consideration in writing for communication, helps the writer situate her writing, i.e., give it a social context. Contextualising the writing in this way constrains linguistic choices – choices of vocabulary, form and style – to contextually appropriate form and style giving it proper orientation and effect. Considerations of the kind mentioned above contrast with the excessive emphasis in much SL writing on achieving linguistic accuracy.

audiolingualism. A theory of SL learning. The method that it proposes incorporates AURAL-ORAL techniques. Popular in SL teaching in USA between 1945 and 1965, Audiolingualism reflects in its practice the tenets of structural linguistics and the BEHAVIOURIST LEARNING THEORY. Audiolingualism follows such principles as the primacy of speech and of oral work in the classroom, and correct second language habit formation through drills and practice. Learning a language is mastering its structure and form. The teaching of 'meaning' does not have an important place in it: nor does an explicit teaching of grammar rules. Use of the learner's MT and practice in TRANSLATION are not allowed in audiolingual teaching. In oral practice the target is native speaker-like speech.

Audiolingualism is associated with such claims as the predictive power of CONTRASTIVE ANALYSES, close correspondence between what the teacher teaches and the learners would learn, and the infallibility of native speaker intuition. Making errors in language use by learners is considered stigmatic. Teachers must not let learners be exposed to language errors.

audiolingual method (ALM). An aural-oral-practice-based method of SL instruction. *See also* AUDIOLINGUALISM.

audio-visual aids. Mechanical and non-mechanical supports to teaching used with the intention of making it more effective. The aids serve as illustrations, examples and models [of pronunciation and speech], and help make teacher explanation clear, and learner perception precise. The aids include blackboard work, audio recordings, pictures, maps and charts, illustrated magazines, clippings from newspapers, slides, films and television programmes. Resourceful teachers use them in a variety of ways.

audio-visual 'methods.' Language teaching techniques employing appropriate uses of listening and visual materials. Here the term 'method' is used rather loosely, though Rivers (1968) and Girard (1974) have suggested pedagogical approaches to using AV aids. Rivers terms the approach 'real' AV methods, and Girard 'integrated.' Since then, the media – film, video, music have come to be incorporated in (language)teaching. Further, the assistance of computers has given language teaching. new methodological orientations. Stern (1983) describes a specific method of language teaching developed in 1950s in France with the name 'The audiovisual method.' Its 'principal feature' is: 'A visually presented scenario provides the chief means of involving the learner in meaningful utterances

and contexts.'

auditory comprehension. Comprehension of what one listens to. The choice of the modifier auditory in the phrase is to contrast it with visual comprehension of the kind reading involves. *See* LISTENING, and LISTENING COMPREHENSION.

aural comprehension. *See* LISTENING

aural-oral approaches. *See* ORAL-SITUATIONAL APPROACHES.

authenticity. A measure of how close a language sample (written or spoken) is to its use in real contexts – how natural it looks. A sample is authentic if it has actually been used for real communication by the speakers(native or non-native) of the language, or is typical of the way they use it. What is authentic is real and convincing, and therefore reliable data.

Authenticity is a widely used concept and criterion in SL teaching and other areas of Applied linguistics. The recognition of authenticity as a desirable criterion came as a reaction to practices in linguistic description and LT that based themselves on contrived data.

In SL pedagogy, it is considered advisable to follow the principle in SYLLABUS DESIGN, construction of TEACHING MATERIALS, learning TASKS, LANGUAGE TESTS, and in TEACHER TALK. In CLT, the principle of teaching and learning language for genuine communicative purposes occupies a central place. However, the principle of authenticity in SL education is not an absolute one: it is pliable. It has to accommodate itself to the requirements of pedagogy and feasibility. **2.** 'Learner authenticity' refers to materials that are readable, interesting, evoke appropriate response and, while being generally authentic, are also in harmony with the aims of teaching.

Likewise, authenticity also refers to the learner's response to a learning task.

Theories of reading that emphasise the centrality of the reader in the reading process, consider that meaning of a text authentic which the readers construct for themselves.

authentic language-tests. Language tests that require test-takers to present samples of performance that match language performance [in the TL] in real-life contexts outside the school setting. An authentic language-test is thus a test based on tasks that closely resemble those usually performed in real use of language. *See* AUTHENTIC TASK.

authentic task. A language learning task that corresponds to real world use of language. Drafting a fax message is an authentic task; converting active voice sentences into passive is not – it is a PEDAGOGIC TASK.

authentic text. TEXT produced for genuine communication, not adapted, controlled or simplified for pedagogical use. A short story is an authentic text but not when written specifically for learners within the constraint of a vocabulary or list of structures.

authentic writing. Writing done for a real audience. A teacher-assigned writing task for the sake of making learners practice language patterns is not authentic. In such writing, often done mechanically, the writer's main concern is not to communicate but to avoid making errors. Such writing

carries no personal voice – beliefs, feelings, emotions – that diary- and story-writing may do.

authoritarian. Relating to a hierarchical order in which the decision-making power vests in one person or a few persons. Others obey them. AUTHORITARIANISM is a system based on inequality, control, and obedience to authority. *See also* POWER.

automaticity. The state/quality of linguistic ability that enables one to perform spontaneously and produce error-free language. Automaticity is acquired progressively through a period of language use in a variety of contexts. Its acquisition is aided by memory and cognitive application.

In some pedagogical models, **Example**, the AUDIOLINGUAL, automaticity in learners is sought to be achieved through PRACTICE, DRILL, MEMORISATION and HABIT FORMATION.

automatization. The process of SL learners using spontaneously their knowledge of the TL. *See also* AUTOMATICITY.

autonomy. Freedom from dependence in study. Autonomy has to do with the [SL] learners' willingness and ability to take responsibility for their learning, which may consist of deciding what they want/need to learn, how they can achieve it (learning style, approach, content material, etc.), and how they are going to organise or manage their study. Autonomy may also consist of having an understanding of how to monitor one's progress in learning.

'Autonomy' refers both to a learner's capacity/competence to be autonomous, and to its actual practice and

15

application. Young learners are usually not mature enough to be autonomous, but adult learners and learners in the distance/open mode of learning need to be so. Autonomous learning does not mean banishment of the teacher: the teacher has an important role to play in it.

auxiliary language. *See also* LINGUA FRANCA.

availability. The criterion of the usefulness of a lexical item in certain contexts. This contrasts with other criteria for selecting items for teaching such as the criterion of the FREQUENCY of their occurrence. An item may not occur frequently yet it may be indispensable, **Example**, BLACKBOARD, cited by Mackey (1965). *See also* DISPONIBILITE.'

avoidance behaviour. *See* AVOIDANCE STRATEGY.

avoidance strategy. STRATEGY in SL production of not using a TL structure or word the learner is not sure of using correctly. SL learners have been observed avoiding specific TL features under-represented in their knowledge of the language. Avoidance behaviour may be unconscious or motivated by the fear of being caught making a mistake. Related to avoidance is the learners' adoption of an indirect route to expression: periphrasis or CIRCUMLOCUTION. *See also* REDUCTION, and COMMUNICATION STRATEGIES.

awareness. The state of an individual's ability to understand (consciously) what is happening around her. The meaning of the concept varies from context to context. One may be aware of how one interacts with one's environment, or how one uses language – of how context determines the choice of form and utterance, and so on. *See also* LANGUAGE AWARENESS.

awareness raising. The process of making learners notice and become aware of how the TL rules operate. Meaning more or less the same are the expressions CONSCIOUSNESS RAISING (CR), grammatical CR, and language. To heighten learners' awareness, tasks and activities are designed for them to discover how [the TL] language works, what its regularities and surface inconsistencies are and how the TL and L1 SYSTEMS contrast. For more on this, *see* CRITICAL LANGUAGE AWARENESS, GENDER AND LANGUAGE, POLITENESS, AND TABOO.

B

baboo variety. Language [use] or a style of writing marked by elaborately drawn out sentences, floweriness, embellishments and ready-made expressions. *See also* CLICHÉ.

baby talk. 1. Speech typical of adults addressing very young children. Such speech is marked by extreme simplification, slow delivery, exaggerated intonation, etc. *See* CARETAKER SPEECH **2.** Speech of very young children. Such speech consists of single word utterances. Most of these words are often 'nonsense' words.

backsliding. The phenomenon of SL learners (under ANXIETY or pressure to communicate) reverting to a rule belonging to an earlier stage of their SL development. Backsliding is considered to be one of the causes of variability in INTER-LANGUAGE production.

backwash effect. Impact of an event or activity on something that precedes it, **Example**, of ATTAINMENT examinations on the instructional procedures or of PROFICIENCY TESTS on the candidates' preparation. Backwash is the backward movement of water or air. It refers to the waves that a moving boat creates behind it on either side. In its extended sense, it refers to the indirect effects following an action.

In LT contexts, examinations may cause healthy or unhealthy effect back on teaching and learning. **Example**, if the examination attaches importance to testing formal accuracy through multiplechoice/objective type questions, teachers and students would spend a lot of time on them preparing for the examination.

balanced bilingualism. A form of bilingualism in which an individual's competence in the MT does not suffer loss on account of learning and using a SL. The languages have COORDINATE status resulting from ADDITIVE BILINGUALISM.

balkanisation. Creating divisions in school life on the basis of specialisation, departmental hierarchy and territorial boundaries. Hargreaves (1994) feels that such divisions are hegemonistic and power-oriented. Further, they obstruct mutual co-operation and exchange of ideas across and among the community of teachers and hamper the solution of common problems. COLLABORATIVE approaches and a 'whole school approach' counter Balkanising division.

band. Rank indicating a particular level on a scale. Scale here refers to a proficiency scale developed for measuring language performance. *See also* DESCRIPTIVE ASSESSMENT, and DESCRIPTORS.

the Bangalore Project. *See* COMMUNICATIONAL TEACHING PROJECT (CTP).

banking concept of education. The concept that the teacher is a repository of knowledge, and the learners draw from her. Different from this is the concept that knowledge is jointly created by learners and teachers in the process of their interaction. *See also* CONSTRUCTIVISM.

barbarism. *See* SOLECISM.

Basic English. The 'British American Scientific Industrial Commercial'

(BASIC) developed between 1925 and 1932 by Charles Ogden and I A Richards. It has a limited vocabulary of 850 basic words – 600 nouns, 150 adjectives and the rest 'operative words' which include verbs, adverbs, prepositions, and conjunctions. Basic English was intended to be used as an international second language. But it did not catch on.

basic interpersonal communication skills. (BICS). The basic competence, the fluency, that even the most retarded children acquire in their first language. BICS according to Jim Cummins (1979) to whose writings the term belongs is the basic oral communicative competence in a language as different from the ability to use it for academic purposes which requires a level of literacy and cognitive ability, or CALP (COGNITIVE-ACADEMIC LANGUAGE PROFICIENCY). Cummins has drawn a distinction between the two.

behaviour. Generally, mental and physical responses, reactions, activities and operations of an individual. The term has been used differently by different writers.

In the classical behaviourist tradition, 'behaviour' includes only those responses which are overt and objectively observable and measurable. However, many writers are of the view that behaviour includes covert mental processes and constructs as well. We can draw inferences about mental processes of an individual by studying their overtly observable behaviour. It may be noted in this context that the currently dominant theory of ACQUISITION OF LANGUAGE sees it as largely a mental process – a process of innate knowledge of the principles of grammar unfolding itself in an individual's use of language.

behavioural. Pertaining to BEHAVIOUR. Something, for **example** a learning objective, is behavioural if it relates to what the learner must do in order to learn something. 'Behavioural' often stands in contrast to 'cognitive,' which is related to mental abilities and to *knowing* rather than *doing*. The two are of course related in that a knowledge of how to *do* leads to specific behavioural outcomes, i.e. action, and correct action needs knowledge to perform it. Together, in most cases, they result in a particular skill.

behavioural objective. An educational objective described in terms of behaviour that can be observed [seen and/or heard].

behavioural sciences. Disciplines that study the BEHAVIOUR of human beings. Major among them are psychology, sociology and social anthropology

behaviourism. 1. A scientific orientation towards psychology that emphasises the importance of empirical evidence and of an objective study of observable events. In its extremity, it excludes mental phenomena **2.** M West (1958) in his article on 'Factual English,' has used 'Behaviourisms,' a component of a spoken language, to mean 'delay words, polite clichés, gesture wordless noises.' **Examples** of delay words could be *Just a minute,* of polite CLICHÉS, *How do you do,* and of wordless noises, *Hi.* For West these form 'frills' are not necessary in[teaching] FACTUAL LANGUAGE (English).

behaviourist learning theory. A theory of learning including language learning. It views learning as the formation of habits. Habits are formed by administering learners specific stimuli to elicit responses from them. When the responses are correct, the learners are rewarded. Incorrect responses, symptomatic of incorrect learning, are put to corrective treatment. Applied to SL learning, the theory has developed procedures for administering stimuli, eliciting response, providing corrective feedback, etc.

In this learning theory, environmental factors have an important role [as different from internal/mental factors in mentalist theories of learning].

benchmark. A standard, a reference point. Benchmarking is a means of comparing one [set of] performance/ achievement etc. with another. Benchmarking practices are common in language pedagogy. For example, teachers in training may be shown benchmark performance, a real demonstration or a videographed one, to make them aware of the expected level of teaching performance.

bias. Element of prejudice or error. **1.** Textual materials may carry bias inherent in the writer's treatment of GENDER, colour, caste, customs, profession, age, CULTURE, religion, etc. and it may influence negatively the ATTITUDES of the learners. Similarly, language practice matrials (**Example**, comprehension questions) may consciously or unconsciously be so designed as to generate bias **2.** In language tests some of the sources of bias leading to inaccurate judgement of some candidates' ability may be: i) their unfamiliarity with the culture-related SCHEMA embedding the test-tasks. Candidates having familiarity with it will have advantage; ii.) Similarly, the test-taker's unfamiliarity with the test format; iii) examiners' strict evaluation of the performance of particular group(s) of candidates, or their preference for certain types of answers – considerations not having to do with the candidates' language proficiency. **3.** Influence of subjective response on one's judgement. Good handwriting and a tidy layout of the pages in as exam. answer-book may hide the linguistic blemishes and make the examiner award more marks/a better grade than the answer deserves. Known as 'HALO EFFECT,' such subjectivity may distort judgement in evaluation. **4.** Discriminatory attitude such as teacher bias.

bilingual education. In the school curricular context, the use of two languages (one of them being the learner's MT) as media of instruction. Bilingual education is also imparting literacy and proficiency in two(or more) languages. As a rule the fact of the native speaker(s) of a language being taught a SL makes the process bilingual.

There are different patterns of bilingual education. The two languages may not be used as media simultaneously, or all along the curriculum. There may at some stage be a transition from the MT to a SL as the medium of instruction.

One may be taught a SL bilingually, i.e., through the medium of one's MT. Provision for bilingual education has to be made in special sociolinguistic contexts to suit learner or COMMUNITY needs. One of them could be to make learners proficient in the two languages because it is perceived by the community that a good knowledge of both the languages would be useful. An example is the Indian context where English is now introduced early in the school curriculum. As a result, almost every child becomes a bilingual within a few years of school, with varying degrees of proficiency in the SL.

Bilingual education may be needed by the speaker of a minority language in a community in order to learn the majority language. Migrant communities may need bilingual education to preserve their own languages. Need for learning an INTERNATIONAL LANGUAGE (as English in India) is another motivation, esp. in the present-day globalised world.

The term 'bilingual education' is used differently in different countries. (Bialystok (2001:235) quoting Brisk (1998)) says 'In the United States, bilingual education refers to the education of children whose home language is not English; elsewhere it refers to education in two valued languages. It is common for European countries to offer bilingual education [in] schools where children are instructed in two languages, some subjects being taught in each. Normally one of the languages will be the national language and the other will be another high prestige language.'

bilingualism. The practice of using two languages regularly or alternatively by an individual or a speech community. There are various types of individual bilingualism. *See* **example**, Additive bilingualism, Balanced bilingualism, Consecutive bilingualism, and Simultaneous bilingualism.

People have different notions about bilingualism many of which sociolinguists dismiss. One of them is that a bilingual uses the two languages with equal fluency.

The other, until recently, was to view bilingualism as disadvantage. Today, well-developed bilingualism is considered to be supportive of cognitive development. *See also* BILINGUALISM and COGNITIVE DEVELOPMENT.

bilingualism and cognitive development. The question whether the learning of two or more languages affects the general INTELLIGENCE of the learner. There have been changing views on the subject ranging from that of BILINGUALISM causing a negative effect, to a neutral one, and from neutral to an additive effect. In the beginning decades of the twentieth century the view was held that maintaining two languages caused cognitive confusion, and retarded intellectual development. Since the 1960s there has developed a positive attitude towards bilingualism. The works of some Canadian scholars show that bilingualism does not lead to cognitive disadvantage as long as learners achieve at least THRESHOLD levels of linguistic competence in their first and second languages. *See also* ADDITIVE BILINGUALISM.

bilingual method. METHOD of teaching a SL in which the teacher uses the learners' MT as aid. The method was devised by C.J. Dodson in Wales and is described in his book published

1967. It was an innovation within the framework of the SOS (Situational-oral-structural) approach. Its innovativeness lay in its restitution of the learners' MT as an aid to associating meaning with form in the SL. The use of the MT was restricted to the teacher. The basic format of teaching was teacher-guided PATTERN DRILL, and all the four skills of the language were taken up simultaneously.

Although the attitude to the role of the MT in SL pedagogy has softened since then considerably, the Method itself did not prosper. One of the reasons for this was the behaviourist paradigm in which it was cast.

the bilingual method research project (1965–66). An experimental research project undertaken by the Central Institute of English, Hyderabad. The subjects were Kannada speaking 39 [19+20] school children of class IV, average age 8. The experiment lasted one academic year. A BILINGUAL METHOD was used for teaching English to the experimental group. And with the control group, the DIRECT METHOD was used. The Project led the researcher, Dr H.N.L. Sastri, to the finding that the Bilingual method was superior to the Direct method.

bilingual processes. The process of mixing elements of two languages in communication. In (social) settings where speakers of two or more languages or language varieties/dialects come in contact, or where a SL has a dominant presence, quite often in the communication of the speakers there results a mixture of two languages The process of language alternation in bilingual contexts is variously termed: CODE-MIXING, code-switching, DIGLOSSIA. The choice of language in mixing and switching has been noticed to be formally, distributionally, and functionally principled: not chaotic. Instead of being considered bad, CODE-mixing/SWITCHING is regarded by some linguists as enrichment of the users' communication repertoire, and widening of their language choices.

bilingual syntax measure. A TEST to measure a learner's knowledge of SL syntax.

black list. A list of those niceties not considered necessary in teaching a language for specific purpose(s). During the mid-twentieth century, language teachers were very enthusiastic about selecting, grading, counting and controlling the language content to be taught at different levels of SL instruction. This was done believing that there was a direct correlation between teaching and learning. M West (1958) recommended that Factual language should be so economical as to attain the 'precision' of algebra and get rid of the 'stylistic bogey of non-repetition, of synonyms', and of a number of structural items like, '*Little did I know*'...where, '*I did not know*' ... would do. He puts such items in a 'Black list'. Such lists are forgotten things today. But what is interesting is that injunctions of this kind are indicative of the certainty that LT experts had about what LT was.

blunderbuss. A convenient, broad spectrum i.e., imprecise but rather impressive-sounding word or phrase. Use of blunderbusses saves the user the labour of finding a simpler and more precise expression. Gowers (1954) has decried the use of blunderbusses, a marker of officialese. Among the examples given by him are such phrases as in relation to, in regard to, in connexion with and in case of, which find ready use in preference to 'simpler prepositions'.

book language. Language formally 'learnt' in the educational setting from books rather than 'acquired' from use in informal, interactive situations. This kind of language results from grammar-rules-aided learning sustained by TEXTBOOK-reading and frequent use of dictionaries. It generally has a formal, pedantic TENOR. It contrasts with the colloquial variety which is usually acquired through an (oral) interactive use of the language where much meaning is retrieved from the context. However, it is possible for 'book' language to become in due course a living, colloquial variety through a process of sustained interaction in authentic, natural settings.

bottom-up. (Process) beginning at the lower rungs, and moving upwards. In a bottom-up model of teaching, it is the learner who is the key mover: the teacher is a facilitator. In other words, a bottom-up approach to teaching is a LEARNER-CENTRED approach. *See also* BOTTOM-UP PROCESSING.

bottom-up processing. A mode of information processing. In COGNITIVE PSYCHOLOGY, bottom-up is the process of a person beginning with raw data or information which is already present (words, sentences, etc.) and then moving upwards to more abstract levels of operation. **Example**, in reading, the processing would move systematically from letters to word, words to phrase, phrases to clause, clauses to sentence, and finally, from sentences to the overall meaning. Thus the meaning of a text is obtained by putting together all the meanings of smaller units contained in it. In this model, reading/decoding problems are seen as linguistic, and the meaning is seen as lying there in the language of the text, and the reader's own contribution in the act of interpretation is considered insignificant. In contrast to this, top-down approaches to the interpretation of a text focus on its meaning and follow a holistic method. *See also* TOP-DOWN.

brain. An organ of the central nervous system situated in the skull. The brain controls thought, memory, feelings and other intellectual activities

brainstorming. A group idea-generating and problem-solving activity. In it, a group (**example**, of students and the teacher) meet together for the purpose of collectively generating ideas to work towards a solution to the problem at hand. Ideas are offered spontaneously, whether in the first instance they appear to be relevant or not. They are not shot down or criticised when put forward. They are all taken down first and then the most practical decision emerges collectively through consultation among the group. Because the atmosphere in brainstorming is positive, the group feels uninhibited in proposing ideas howsoever remote or silly they may appear in the beginning.

Brainstorming, devised as a language-class activity, has many pedagogic uses. In it learners are communicatively and cognitively engaged. They perform a variety of speech acts needed in consulting, reasoning, persuading, etc. Being uninhibited, they interact freely without worrying too much about accuracy. They are focused on meaning, – conditions that foster language acquisition. *See also* SYNECTICS.

bridge courses. Intensive REMEDIAL or revision courses. They aim at making good the shortfall in learning that creates a gap between the partially achieved TERMINAL BEHAVIOUR at the previous stage and the expected ENTRY BEHAVIOUR at the next stage of language education. Bridge courses try to teach what has remained unlearnt, or to remedy what has been wrongly learnt. This is done in the hope that by undergoing the intensive course the learners will come up to the required level for the next stage. Irrespective of learning deficiencies, bridge courses may aim at building for the learner a smooth transition from one stage to the next higher if indeed there exists a gap.

Bridge courses are based on an analysis/DIAGNOSIS of the learning deficiencies, areas of weakness of those who are going on to a new course or a new educational programme. Thus the courses have a specific focus. They may be general-proficiency-oriented or may target specific skill areas[such as that of listening]. The course instructors are generally given an orientation to teaching.

The model of teaching and practice in the courses depends on the course designer's/writer's theory of REMEDIAL TEACHING.

Broca's area. The area in the left hemisphere of the BRAIN from where, it is widely held, language ability is controlled – named after Paul Broca, a French surgeon of the nineteenth century. *See also* WERNICKE'S AREA

burn-out. The feeling of boredom, dissatisfaction and exhaustion caused by prolonged stress of teaching. It may occur when the teacher feels that she is not up to it, or her learners' achievements do not match her endeavour. It is suggested, **example** by Penny Ur (1996:318), that 'constant teacher development and progress can forestall or solve problems' caused by burnout. Further, burnout may act as a motivator to self-improvement, and spur professional development.

business language. The variety of a language used for trade and commerce. Though business language shares in common the language used in the other domains, it is the use of the language for business purposes that lends it its specific features.

The concept and pedagogy of business language is an off-shoot of a larger development: learning and teaching of a LANGUAGE FOR SPECIFIC (or special) PURPOSES. Business language courses [the most common are Business English courses]deal with the language and communication needs of business professionals.

C

CALP. *See* COGNITIVE ACADEMIC LANGUAGE PROFICIENCY.

canon. Criteria that set the STANDARD(1). For example, many consider what they call the Queen's English as the standard for English usage, and the British RECEIVED PRONUNCIATION as the model of pronunciation.

Some theorists have been critical of such canonisation because it privileges certain social classes, and VARIETIES of language over others. *See also* OWNERSHIP.

careful style. A monitored STYLE of speech and writing that avoids COLLOQUIAL forms and uses 'sanskritic' expressions – expressions used on formal occasions by educated and higher-status persons. SLANGY expressions and carelessly formed sentences are taboos in this style.

caretaker speech. Language (also known as 'motherese') deliberately simplified when addressing young children. Parents, babysitters, and other adults often use this kind of language when they talk to children. Caretaker speech is also the speech addressed to elementary-level users specially of a SL. Such speech is characterised by features like slow rate of delivery, short sentences, simple words, repetition and high pitch.

case knowledge. Knowledge of particular pedagogical 'cases' as a source and component of TEACHER KNOWLEDGE and experience. Case knowledge belongs to a teacher's personal practical knowledge. *See also* NARRATIVE FORMS OF KNOWLEDGE.

case study. A mode of EMPIRICAL research in which a single instance, for example an individual learner, a classroom or an [innovative] programme is studied. The study is primarily observation-based, and usually longitudinal in nature, i.e., it is carried out over a period of time. In case studies, multiple sources of evidence/data and multiple view points are taken into account.

catenation. [From Latin *catena* meaning *chain*.] Linking of related words. If in a lesson [in a classroom or in a book], the word spade (as a tool) occurs then the verb dig also should occur and be taught, as the two words are related. In teaching-materials and in teaching a SL controlled by a wordlist based on frequency count, it is quite likely that the word spade occurs but not the word dig. In such a case, the classroom teacher/writer of the textbook usually ensures that this link in the chain is also taught. *See also* CATENIZING.

catenizing. Memorising and learning chunks of language holistically in order that they can be produced spontaneously, and the learner acquires FLUENCY. H. Palmer(1917/1968:68) and N.S. Prabhu (1997:353) have discussed catenizing as a process in LA. *See also* SEMANTICISING.

the CBSE-ELT project (1988–1997). A curriculum renewal project at the secondary level in India undertaken by the Central Board of Secondary Education (CBSE), New Delhi with the help of some other agencies. The significance of the Project for LE in

India lies in its attempt to introduce on a large scale the teaching of English as a SL on *communicative* lines in the formal education system at the Intermediate level.

An important feature of the project was the involvement of the secondary teachers in curriculum implementation – designing the syllabus, preparing teaching and testing materials, and trialling them.'

chaining. A sentence-construction and pronunciation-practice-based language learning activity. In it a sentence with several tone groups and phrases difficult for learners to produce correctly, is set up as a model. **Example:** *It is impossible/for me to lift* this box of books

One of the learners produces

It is impossible...

The next one extends it a little

It is impossible for me to lift ...

This kind of chaining is forward chaining. Backward chaining would begin with

books and be extended to

box of books

and so on

The teacher monitors the learner-performance supplying necessary feedback. *Cf.* word chain.

chalk and Talk method. [of language teaching] The practice of teaching that depends primarily on oral instruction and blackboard work [by the teacher]. It is this practice that generally prevails in most schools. Besides the textbook and possibly a book of grammar and composition, the teacher is almost the only other source of access to the language, and the sole model of its pronunciation.

The method consists of verbal presentation by the teacher reinforced with her writing and drawing on the board. In the practice & consolidation work too, teacher-talk and blackboard work are the major sources of support. Corrective feedback too is given to the learners orally and visually.

challenge. A cognitively demanding task in learning. A situation that makes the learner apply mind and discover is a challenge. One of the current persuasions in language teaching is that to promote learning, teachers should create/make available to learners opportunities that offer challenge. This is to be viewed in light of the criticism of the incapacitating instructional practices that offer learners readymade solutions, and do not take them much beyond imitating, repeating, and memorising.

channel capacity. Learners' capacity to process utterances in comprehension or production. The capacity involves effortless deployment by language learners of their linguistic resources, which is limited in the beginning but gradually expands with increase in the learner's knowledge of the language.

chaos and complexity theory. The theory that there is no Newtonian cause-effect relationship among the factors involved in SLT and SLL. This lack of one-to-one correspondence between teaching and learning, between goals set up and results achieved, is also known as non-linearity or lack of symmetry. Larsen-Freeman (1997), using the metaphorical expression chaos and complexity has pointed to the unpredictability of the processes of classroom teaching and language acquisition. Despite our linear syllabuses, and clearly defined lesson aims, as Mellows (2002) comments, echoing Larsen-Freeman, '...progress and BACKSLIDING and unpredictable measures are the norm ... learners do not master one item and then move on to another.'

This observation has implications for language teaching, teacher training, and syllabus design.

checklist. An inventory-like INSTRUMENT used in evaluating textbooks and other materials for teaching and language-testing. Checklists may also be used to evaluate the performance of teachers in the classroom. A number of checklists have been developed for observing CLASSROOM INTERACTION. The desired/desirable features are first listed and then systematically organised to form the instrument. The selected features usually have theoretic and pedagogic justification for their inclusion. The application of a checklist shows whether the evaluated material/performance has all the required features.

chorus method. A way of giving beginning level learners of a SL practice in 'speaking.' In it the whole class repeats in unison and after the teacher the model utterance produced by her. The 'method' carries a strong influence of the principles and practices of ROTE LEARNING, monitoring and CONTROL, IMITATION, and HABIT-FORMATION. It is considered to suit learning in a large class. Gurrey (1955) warns against the misuse and harmful effects of chorus. It 'often encourages incorrect English ...' and mispronunciation. Under cer-

tain conditions, **Example**, small groups and quiet speaking, Gurrey asserts, the 'method' can bring good results. It may be noted that as in many phrases with the word "method" in them, the so-called 'chorus method' is only a procedure and NOT a METHOD in the sense of a set of structured procedures.

chronological age. The number of years one has lived since one's birth. As different from it is one's MENTAL AGE. In L1 acquisition there is a fair degree of correspondence between one's chronological and mental ages. Some anomaly arises when beginning learners of a SL are made to read materials that are written for lower mental age learners.

chunk. 1. A large piece of something. In the context of language, one of the referents of 'chunk' is a LEXICAL PHRASE or a multiword lexical unit **2.** A READING SPAN, a sequence of words grammatically and semantically so related as to form a group that a reader can take in at *one* glance. A chunk must be a meaningful unit grammatically complete though its optimum size varies from reader to reader. *See also* SACCADE, and SENSE-GROUP.

chunking. 1. In language acquisition. Acquiring and using CHUNKS of language holistically. It has been observed that learners in the beginning use chunks of language or prefabricated phrases before they can see them analytically. Analytic insight develops later. Also, much language use is in the form of chains of chunks or prefabricated language. **Example**, *this is a...; as a matter of fact...; I'd much rather...*.**2.** In language teaching. Breaking down language stretches into manageable chunks or parts for ease in comprehension and learning *See also* 'chunking' under Reading skills. **3.** Skill in FAST READING. Glancing in a succession of moves at CHUNKS[b] of text. *See also* SACCADE, and SENSE-GROUP.

circumlocution. A roundabout way of expressing an idea resulting in the use of more words than necessary. 'A long brush for cleaning the floor without sitting' is a roundabout way of expressing the meaning of 'broom'. Considered to be a negative feature in language use, it is one of the COMMUNICATION STRATEGIES, and a feature in the language of less proficient language-users.

class. *See* SOCIAL CLASS.

classical conditioning. Reinforcing several times the bond between stimuli and the response they generate so that the response occurs involuntarily when the stimuli are administered. *See also* CONDITIONING. Behaviourists see conditioning as a means of effecting change in behaviour, and of causing learning. For the difference between CLASSICAL conditioning and OPERANT conditioning, *see also* OPERANT CONDITIONING BEHAVIOURIST LEARNING THEORY and STIMULUS-RESPONSE THEORY.

classroom. 1. The place where the learners and teacher come together for the purpose of learning and teaching. **2.** Classroom or class also signifies the learners and the teacher as a group or COMMUNITY, and the transaction among them.

A classroom is usually a formal setting in an enclosed space, but there can be classrooms without walls. A classroom may be a bare space or one equipped with teaching aids. Classrooms in the educational, curricular framework involve some studial activity on the part of the learners. The participants in a classroom – learners and teachers – have defined ROLES and power relationships.

In an extended sense, and with reference to informal/naturalistic contexts, the street, the open world may be a classroom for a language learner. *See also* VIRTUAL CLASSROOMS.

classroom-centred research. Research on the processes of language learning and teaching in the classroom, also known as 'classroom research.' It encompasses a whole range of subjects from TEACHER TALK to learner-behaviour in the classroom. These include teacher INPUT and other input available to the learners, their response to the input; the FEEDBACK provided to them; CLASSROOM INTERACTION, and classroom teaching & learning experience.

classroom interaction. 'Talk' by teachers and learners in the language classroom. In a broad sense, classroom interaction consists of the INPUT and FEEDBACK provided by the teacher together with the learner output & response in the negotiated process/act of learning and teaching. These are considered to be of significance for language acquisition by learners. *See also* INTERACTION, and INTERACTION ANALYSIS.

Classroom interaction can take place at different levels, in a number of ways such as TEACHER-WHOLE-CLASS interaction, learner-learner interaction in groups or pairs. Some of the activities designed to promote interaction in the classroom are: INFORMATION GAP and other TASKS, ROLE PLAY, SIMULATION. Asking questions, seeking clarifications, and answering are some modes of interaction occurring in almost all classrooms.

classroom language. or the language of the CLASSROOM. The language forms and patterns teachers [should] use during the course of classroom teaching for social, personal, organisational, and instructional functions. J. Willis (1981) has used the expression in the context of presenting a model for the TL use in a SL classroom esp. by the non-native teachers. The intention is that the appropriate TL forms used by the teacher will not only serve as model but also reinforce learners' acquisition of idiomatic forms during the process of learning the TL.

Classroom language has been conceptualised by Willis differently from the language of 'CLASSROOM INTERACTION'. Studies of the latter are analytical and descriptive in nature with focus on acquisitional INPUT whereas *classroom language* is recommendatory of context-specific idiomatic language to be used by the teachers of [English] as a SL. Using a structural approach, Willis has organised the model patterns in the form of structural or SUBSTITUTION TABLES. *See also* PEDAGOGICAL DISCOURSE.

classroom management. The process of conducting learning-oriented activities in the formal instructional setting of the classroom. This requires deployment of a complex of skills and abilities

The principles and procedures of management can be grouped under two heads: 1. General and 2., Relating to language education, though in many cases they are not clearly distinguishable.

General managerial skills ensures that:

• learners have clarity about the goals of teaching, and objective(s) of the lesson;

• the lesson has a balanced structuring of MOVES, with appropriate time-allocation for each step – presentation, tasks and questions, and their monitoring and finally, giving feedback;

• the teacher is sensitive to (a) learner needs and interest, and (b) individual variation;

• the classroom setting is AFFECTIVELY relaxing;

• there is an atmosphere of co-operativeness among the class, not competitiveness;

• order, decorum and discipline are maintained;

• classroom activities are varied, and audio-visual aids are used to keep learner attention sustained;

• learner-participation is maintained, and there is a high level of learner involvement

In addition to these, the management of a SL classroom makes it desirable that the teacher

• chooses learning tasks that engage learners to focus on meaning;

• encourages learners to work in groups, and participate in peer-interaction;

• creates in the class an interactive atmosphere;

• manages interaction (nominates who will speak, allots turns, etc.) with a view to maximising LEARNING OPPOR-

TUNITIES;
- makes an appropriate choice of questions to be put – referential, display, etc.
- both CONTROL (2) and flexibility are used to promote in the classroom an atmosphere of creativity, spontaneity, RISK-TAKING, and discovering. That is, there should always be a certain degree of open-endedness (in the lesson) to allow for the alert teacher to utilise learning opportunities whenever they spring up during the course of classroom transaction.

classroom observation. A procedure of studying learning and teaching in the language CLASSROOM by systematically observing what actually happens there during instruction.[*See* Observation.] Observation is used as an instrument of research on classroom language learning and teaching in order to know how these happen and using this knowledge as base, to attempt improvement.

Classrooms drew scholarly attention during the 1960s when it was realised that prescription of teaching Methods was no solution the problems of SL teaching: nor were the attempts to study their comparative efficacy conclusive. The key to these was sought in CLASSROOM-CENTRED RESEARCH through observation.

classroom-process research. *See also* CLASSROOM-CENTRED RESEARCH.

classroom research. *See* CLASSROOM-CENTRED RESEARCH.

cliché. An expression or idea which has been used so much that it has lost its freshness and effect: **Example**, 'better half' for one's wife.

close reading. A model of reading and interpreting literary texts which considers them as self-contained, objective, and intricately woven entities. It considers [the] text as authority and meaning, unchanging and determinate, is assumed to reside only in the text. The reader has no *creative* role to play in interpreting it. *Cf.* READER THEORY. **2.** Close reading in the language-educational context denotes INTENSIVE READING.

closed question. A question with only one acceptable answer, **Example**, 'What is the first month of the year?' Asked by the teacher in the classroom, such questions do not allow much space for INTERACTION and LEARNING OPPORTUNITIES for the learner(s). *See also* TEACHER QUESTIONS.

closure-oriented style of learning. A style marked by preference for clearly stated rules, directions, etc., given by the teacher. Learners with such preference are FIELD INDEPENDENT They have poor TOLERANCE OF AMBIGUITY. *See also* LEARNING STYLE AND RISK-TAKING.

cloze. 'Closure' or the subjective closing of gaps. Closure is the mental/psychological tendency to see as complete even those forms that are slightly incomplete. In GESTALT psychology, closure is a process of perceiving. In reading we often perceive the correct word where actually an incorrect form of the word is printed. [This tendency often deceives proof readers].

cloze procedure. A technique for finding out the difficulty of reading pieces. For this, pieces of 250 words or so are selected, and every fifth word in them is deleted. The text with the deletions is administered in the form of a test. The test-takers are asked to supply the missing words. Each correct answer carries a mark. By comparing the average mark for each piece, the relative difficulty of the piece can be determined. The difficulty is judged in relation to a particular level represented by the group to whom the test is administered. The technique was first used by Wilson Taylor in the 1950s to assess the readability of newspapers.

cloze tests. Reading-based procedures for testing language PROFICIENCY. To prepare a cloze test, a reading passage is selected. From it, leaving the opening and the closing parts intact, every nth (usually V or VI or VII word) is deleted. Sometimes, instead of this, only SELECTED words are deleted, a method known as RATIONAL cloze deletion. Candidate have to supply the deleted word by filling in the gaps. They may either be asked to supply exact words as they appeared in the original text, or words appropriate to the context. Accordingly, the scoring is either verbatim or acceptable word scoring.

What exactly cloze tests measure is not known, but they are considered to be reliable tests of language proficiency as their scores correlate highly with the scores of other proficiency tests. Cloze is also used as a test of reading comprehension. Originally, in 1950s cloze procedure was used to measure the readability of a piece of writing. *See also* CLOZE AND CLOZE PROCEDURE.

clue. Something that suggests a solution/provides hint. Linguistic and semantic clues to meaning are woven into most texts. Hints to their meaning can be found in the text itself. In the sentence 'John does not take alcoholic drinks – he is a teetotaller.' The first part contains a clear hint to the meaning of the word 'teetotaller'. Good learners, instead of panicking at the sight of unfamiliar words, try to use their cognitive resource to discover meaning with the help of available clues.

code. A system of symbols, a set of rules. In the context of SL pedagogy, the term *code* has often been used to represent the linguistic forms and the set of FORMAL (2) rules of the TL GRAMMAR (1) in contrast to MEANING and FUNCTION. In the wake of the realization that an EXPLICIT KNOWLEDGE of the code, assiduously imparted in the classrooms, did not lead to FLUENCY, often acquired INDUCTIVELY and COMMUNICATIVELY, there arose during 1965–1975 a debate termed the 'Code-communication dilemma'.

Code and communication. *See* CODE.

code-mixing. The phenomenon of bi/multi-linguals using two or more languages or language varieties in the same conversation/piece of writing. The switch is motivated by situational or purely personal factors. Studies show that such mixing is rule-governed and patterned, not arbitrary. Also, resourcing two or more languages accounts for the richness of the speakers' communicative repertoire. *See also* BILINGUAL PROCESSES.

code switching. *See* CODE MIXING.

cognition. Mental processes and activities such as thinking and learning: the various modes of knowing – perceiving, remembering, imagining, conceiving, judging, reasoning, and problem-solving.

cognitive. Pertaining to COGNITION, to knowing, learning, perceiving, understanding, etc.

cognitive/academic language proficiency (CALP). Those aspects of SL proficiency (such as reading, writing, vocabulary, awareness of rules of grammar) that are strongly related to cognitive and ACADEMIC SKILLS. CALP can function in cognitively demanding situations and in context-reduced situations (where gestures, facial expressions, and immediate feedback are not available).The CALP in one language is transferable to another. Propounded by Cummins (1979), the notions of CALP and Basic Interpersonal Communication Skills' (BICS) are mutually contrasting.

cognitive approaches to language teaching. Approaches that consider learner's mind the prime mover in LL. In the twentieth century, cognitive approaches came as a reaction to the BEHAVIOURIST approaches that dominated the SL teaching scene roughly from 1930s to the end of 1960s. These approaches considered LL a matter of HABIT FORMATION. In 1957, Chomsky opposed this position by claiming convincingly that LL was essentially a matter internal to the learner's mind. Since then learning has increasingly been seen as mental activity, and language teaching has been addressing itself to the learner's mind. A major paradigm shift, this has brought important changes in classroom teaching methodology.

cognitive-code learning. An ap-

proach to teaching SLs advocated in the 1960s. It proposes that a systematic explanation of the grammar rules should precede practice in a given language-form. Formal practice, intended to cause INDUCTIVE LEARNING, occupies an important place in AUDIOLINGUAL approaches. Cognitive-code learning has been advocated as a complement to this. A conscious awareness of rules makes the manipulation of form/structure meaningful. *Cf.* MONITOR THEORY, and CONSCIOUSNESS-RAISING. *See also* COGNITIVE-CODE THEORY.

cognitive-code theory. The theory that the role of COGNITION and a conscious focus on grammar is important in LL/teaching.

cognitive learning strategies. Approaches (conscious or unconscious) to processing and manipulating information in LL in order to enhance learning. Some such strategies are: INFERENCING, DEDUCTION, rehearsal and summarisation.

cognitive perspectives on learning. Views that hold mental activity as basic to learning. Thinking, understanding, interpreting, and constructing knowledge are some of the mental processes. The human mind has the capacity to organise and reorganise information, to solve problems, to construct knowledge through applying various STRATEGIES creatively and through interaction with the environment. Cognitive perspectives have in recent years had a reorienting effect on [language] teaching. Consequently some of the new elements in teaching are to encourage learners to try to discover for themselves; to come to grips with learning CHALLENGES; to try to solve problems in learning.

cognitive psychology. A discipline that studies the processes of the human mind. They relate to LEARNING and the acquisition of knowledge, to thinking, reasoning, perceiving and similar other mental activities.

cognitive strategies. *See* COGNITIVE LEARNING STRATEGIES.

cognitive styles. Characteristic ways of perceiving phenomenon, conceptualising, and recalling information. Two well-known styles are FIELD DEPENDENCE/INDEPENDENCE. *See also,* LEARNING STYLE.

coherence. The quality of the sentences in a paragraph or the units of a longer DISCOURSE sticking together in a logical and CONSISTENT manner. Coherence is considered to be one of the essential qualities of good language use – spoken and written.

Coherence in discourse, according to some, is achieved through COHESIVE TIES or relations in linguistic features that make a TEXT a 'unified whole.' However, the view that relations of coherence are just linguistic relations does not have wide acceptance. A more satisfactory approach considers coherence in text 'a matter of content which happens to have linguistic consequence'.

Thus, coherence in a text is achieved through linguistic/cohesive devices in consonance with its meaning links. To achieve coherence, the communicative content of the text has to be systematically structured and integrated. Cohesive devices help achieve this.

cohesion. A quality of DISCOURSE achieved by syntactic and semantic links between sentences and their parts. As Rutherford (1987) says, cohesion is the quality 'that ties sentences together such that we perceive them as a single text'. *See* COHERENCE, and COHESIVE TIES.

cohesive ties. Devices of linking that bring in COHESION in discourse and account for the COHERENCE in it. A pronoun typically links elements of a discourse by referring back to a noun phrase, or forward. A similar role is played by words and phrases like SIMILARLY, NEVERTHELESS, CONSEQUENTLY. These words are cohesive ties.

collaborative dialogue. Dialogue (in L1 or the TL) learners are engaged in when performing a learning task, solving a problem, or building knowledge. The DIALOGUE mediates joint PROBLEM-SOLVING. The process is supposed to heighten the potential for learning and for exploring appropriate (context-relevant) verbal responses. *See also* COLLABORATIVE DISCOURSE.

collaborative discourse. Discourse that beginning learners produce in the process of conversation by using input in the form of words and phrases received from each other. This process of jointly constructing DISCOURSE is supposed to promote acquisition of SYNTAX.

collaborative learning. Learners working together in groups to achieve a common learning goal. They work collaboratively on LL TASKS, helping each other to find appropriate forms and constructions with which to build the answer. The instructional strategy of collaborative learning helps learners develop their social skills as well as the mental ones.

collaborative problem-solving. (In the context of LE and teacher-research.) A mode of looking for answers to professional problems with the cooperation of colleagues. The process could have the following stages – a teacher faces a problem, she tries to understand it, discusses it with colleagues, attempts a solution, colleagues join in to analyse the feedback, they reflect on it and find a solution. If necessary, the attempt is repeated.

This is an approach in the direction of co-operative self-reliance onwards to TEACHER RESEARCH AND SELF-DEVELOPMENT. Earlier, teachers used to depend on 'experts' whose prescriptions were general in nature and rarely matched the unique requirements of individual teaching-learning contexts.

collaborative research. Research [on language-education-related matters] in which internal and external researchers collaborate. The internal researcher is usually the teacher and the external the theorist. See also TEACHER AS RESEARCHER.

colloquial speech. Informal speech. Speech that avoids learned expressions and prefers everyday-use style. Contractions like *can't, won't* are typically used in colloquial speech.

colloquialisms. An expression (word, phrase or sentence) or pronunciation characteristic of informal language esp. of conversation. Colloquialisms are avoided in FORMAL(1) speech and writing. The *Cambridge International Dictionary of English*(1995) cites 'he is off his head' as an example of col-

loquialism meaning 'his behaviour is not reasonable.' See also COLLOQUIAL SPEECH.

the Colorado study. A study carried out at the university level to find out the relative superiority of the AUDIO-LINGUAL and the traditional methods of SL/FL teaching. It was carried out by Scherer and Wertheimer, and its report was published in 1964. It was inconclusive in the sense that its findings failed to establish the relative superiority of any METHOD.

command cards. Cards with commands printed/written on them. They are used with young learners to help them learn single words, phrases, and sentences printed on the cards. Learners are allowed to look at them for a few seconds and then they act in response to the command. The teacher does not speak during this process. Compare the technique with TOTAL PHYSICAL RESPONSE.

commercialese. Old-fashioned language of communication in commerce marked by dead FORMULAIC expressions. **Example**, *Yours to hand of twenty-fifth ultimo.* In plain language, which is preferred now, it means *I/we have received your letter of July 25* [July being the previous month. *Ultimo* in Latin means *last.*]

common core. The basics; the essentials. In SL teaching. Irrespective of their special needs in future, beginning and intermediate level learners are first taught the common core – essential vocabulary, sentence structures, etc. that form the foundation and are needed by all. At these levels, the courses are GENERAL PURPOSE COURSES.

communication. The process of conveying and receiving ideas and information. It takes place through a mutually shared and understood system of symbols, i.e. a language, and is embedded in a context and situation.

The message communicated is appropriate to the occasion, the addresser-addressee relationship and the subject of communication.

The act of communication follows linguistic rules, discourse rules, and social conventions. The process being interactive, the act of communication may go beyond simple receiving, and include understanding and conveying implications and overtones. In addition to spoken and written messages, communication may also include messages conveyed by gestures, signals, body language, and non-verbal sounds. Success of communication depends on its outcome, and not necessarily on the CORRECTNESS of the language used. *See also* COMMUNICATION PROCESS.

communication accommodation theory. *See* ACCOMMODATION 2, and SPEECH ACCOMMODATION.

The Communicational teaching Project. A research project undertaken by a team headed by NS Prabhu; also known as the Bangalore Project (1979–1984). The project was an experiment in SLT, and had a 'communicational' orientation in the sense that, in teaching, it focused on the learners' attention on MEANING (through engaging them in PROBLEM-SOLVING) and not on linguistic, i.e., grammatical, form. The project adopted a course different from the syllabus and methodology of the prevailing STRUCTURAL APPROACH in India and the then innovative CLT approach. It departed from the structural in not following a pre-planned or controlled progression, and it avoided some of the CLT principles as that of encouraging learner-learner interaction. The Project followed a classroom procedure which was, rather strictly, controlled by the teacher.

A guiding premise of the Project was that 'form is best learnt when the learner's attention is on meaning', language ability develops in direct relation to communicational effort, and that language structure as CONTENT (1) is unhelpful in LT. The Project was based on the assumption that in performing meaning-focused tasks, the learners unconsciously acquired the structural forms/grammar-rules. Thus the teaching on the Project consisted of a series of problem-solving TASKS, in which the learners were cognitively engaged. The tasks were not grammar-tasks but tasks relating to such fields as arithmetic, geography, logic, reference-skills. They were mostly reasoning tasks, and not information tasks. The assignment of the task was preceded by a pre-task in the nature of an ADVANCE ORGANIZER. Another assumption in the Project was that in the process of arriving at the right answer, learners would make mistakes in using the language which should be considered as a naturally occurring thing. Correction of the mistakes should be done incidentally, not in a pointed manner. The teaching on the Project was done on learners who were not beginners, i.e., they had already learnt some English.

communication process. A process

of transmitting and receiving messages. Transmission involves the communicator's need to communicate her selection of meaning and content as also the MODE, channel, and form of the message. The transmission is followed by the reception, comprehension, and interpretation of the message by the recipient and her response. For the cycle of the communication to complete, the process reverts from the receiver to the sender.

communication strategies. Communication-problem-management mechanism [also known as interlanguage communcation strategies] used by non-fluent SL learners during L2 interaction. The learners resort to these STRATEGIES, consciously or unconsciously, when facing a problem in expressing themselves in a SL. The strategies may lead to inappropriate lexical choices, unidiomatic usage or the production of incorrectly formed sentences, and/or imprecisely expressed meaning. These have received much attention in the literature on the subject though equally important are the strategies of AVOIDANCE and message abandonment. They comprise the giving up of a part of intended message in order to avoid using incorrect and uncertain forms.

Different from the strategies of avoiding, suppressing, altering, and of giving up the intended message is ACHIEVEMENT BEHAVIOUR. In it the learner tries to overcome the difficulty of communication by expanding her communicative resources. Achievement strategies are compensatory in nature as learners try to compensate for their limited linguistic repertoire by taking recourse to strategies like the following: INTERLINGUAL TRANSFER, OVERGENERALIZATION of the TL rules, CODE SWITCHING, literal translation, paraphrase, APPROXIMATION, and RESTRUCTURING (2). Mime and use of gestures may be some other such strategies.

The use of some achievement strategies like that of overgeneralization may also be considered to be part of interlanguage development/SLA process as they involve HYPOTHESIS (2)-formation and HYPOTHESIS-TESTING. Similarly, some other strategies may be seen as tools in NEGOTIATION OF MEANING to achieve communicative goals.

Focusing on the (learners')cognitive processes of resource deployment for communication has made some scholars to shift their attention from the linguistic output to the PROCESS of meaning-making in interlingual communication. *Cf.* LEARNING STRATEGIES.

A classification that distinguishes between the cognitive processes and the resulting product postulates two categories: CONCEPTUAL and LINGUISTIC. In conceptual strategy use, the concept to be communicated is formulated analytically. For example, to convey the meaning of an 'anorak' – a word that the user does not yet know or cannot recall – she may say something like, '…a coat with a zip to close it, and a cap'. This kind of strategy may also be classified, rather negatively, as circumlocution.

Just as linguistic strategies manifest themselves in various forms, conceptual strategies may result in hypernyms or superordinate terms for more specific ones, **Example**, animal for lion. Such lexical simplifications resulting from the language user(s)' deficient semantic performance are common instances of strategy deployment.

The strategies operate both in the learners' expression and comprehension of meaning.

communicative. Relating to COMMUNICATION. In phrases beginning with the adjective 'communicative', the accent is on meaning/message and its effective expression. Often the implicit contrast is with the LINGUISTIC or the grammatical aspect of the utterance. *See also* CODE.

communicative approaches to language teaching. Procedures in LT that focus on FLUENCY in language use – using language to communicate meaning – rather than on linguistic form and grammatical accuracy. Certain instructional principles and practices are associated with communicative approaches. For details, *see* COMMUNICATIVE LANGUAGE TEACHING.

communicative competence. The knowledge the users of a language acquire & possess that enables them to perform in the language fully proficiently both in production and comprehension of messages. *See also* COMPETENCE

To be communicatively competent is to be able to put oneself across appropriately and with naturalness & ease in various social and cultural situations. For this, one needs to possess GRAMMATICAL, DISCOURSE, SOCIOLINGUISTIC and PRAGMATIC competence. In addition, one should be able to use VERBAL and NONVERBAL strategies of communication

[STRATEGIC COMPETENCE] so that one is able to tackle complex communicative situations.

This definition does not assume that a communicatively competent person must possess the abilities of reading and writing. However, in the present-day context, literacy is almost universal though not everyone who can read & write is communicatively competent either in their MT or in a SL. *Cf.* ACADEMIC SKILLS.

communicative efficiency. A measure of speech INTELLIGIBILITY. Speakers try to accommodate their speech to their INTERLOCUTOR(s) in order to achieve a high degree of comprehensibility. Communicative efficiency ensures sustained INTERACTION, and involves adjusting, among other things, one's speech style, ACCENT, and vocabulary to the listener's. *See also* ACCOMMODATION (2).

communicative function. See FUNCTION.

communicative language learning. Participating in learning activities aimed at promoting the acquisition of COMMUNICATIVE COMPETENCE. Such activities are interactive in nature, and are generally related to NEGOTIATIATION OF MEANING.

To facilitate communicative LL, teachers set learners PROBLEM-SOLVING tasks that require mental application. Learners are led to use HEURISTIC procedures to find answers and learn. Classroom activities like GROUP and PAIR WORK, ROLE PLAY, and SIMULATION are considered to help in building the competence. Towards this end, learners write for real purposes, and do extensive TL reading for pleasure & information. *See also* COMMUNICATIVE LANGUAGE TEEACHING.

communicative language teaching (CLT). Teaching language for communicative proficiency: teaching a SL to enable learners to communicate meaning in it nearly as naturally and easily as they would in their MT. A term for such proficiency and facility is fluency.' *See also* COMMUNICATIVE COMPETENCE, and FLUENCY.

CLT became popular in 1970–80s as a reaction to the SL teaching practices that put too much emphasis on the mastery of language forms and structure to the near exclusion of meaning as was the case in the AUDIO-LINGUAL and the ORAL-SITUATIONAL approaches to teaching SLs.

CLT brought with it a package of principles and ideologies. They include:

– Achievement of COMMUNICATIVE COMPETENCE as the primary goal of language learning;

– Superiority of the AUTHENTIC;

– The paramount role of COGNITION in learning–HUMANISTIC principles that include those of co-operation and collaboration;

– LEARNER-CENTREDness;

– Tolerance of language ERRORS and SL learners' ACCENT(2)s;

– Minimisation of authority and CONTROL in the classroom;

– The TEACHER AS FACILITATOR role, and,

– The learner's MT as resource.

Although most of these principles are implicit in CLT approaches and they influence methodological choices, CLT is not a Method in the sense of a set of regimented procedures. *See also* COMMUNICATIVE LANGUAGE LEARNING.

communicative language testing. LANGUAGE TESTING (1) procedures that base judgement of the test takers' language proficiency on samples of language use elicited from them. The test items are so designed that they would be close to communication tasks performed in real-life situations, and these tasks relate to speaking, listening, reading, and writing in their various facets. *See* DIRECT TEST and INDIRECT TEST.

The principle of semblance to 'real-life language-use' has come as a corrective to language testing practices of an earlier era (roughly pre-1970) that based judgment on test-takers' performance in tasks that required them to do such things as fill in the blanks in sentences, pick the grammatically correct sentence from among incorrect ones. – hallmarks of the psychometric tradition of language testing.

New procedures for RATING performance are practised in CL testing to meet the requirements of RELIABILITY and VALIDITY.

communicative orientation of language teaching (COLT). An instrument for observing SL classrooms to judge how far the classroom transaction is 'communicative' in nature. In their initial phase CLASSROOM INTERACTION studies were motivated by the concern at teacher domination in the classroom. However, with the arrival of COMMUNICATIVE LANGUAGE TEACHING in 1970s, the focus of interest moved to the observation of communicative activities in the classroom. In 1980s,

Frohlich, Spada, and Allen developed the schedule COLT. It has two parts. The first 'describes classroom events at the level of episode and activity.' The other part 'analyzes the communicative features of verbal exchanges between teachers and students or among students themselves as they occur within each activity.'

communicative orthodoxy. [in the SLT context] The position that the INTERACTION in the communicative classroom should consist of genuine or natural COMMUNICATION. The orthodox position disapproves of the LOCK STEP modes of teaching as they permit little interaction. Even in many classrooms that may be called interactive, the orthodox say, communication follows a stereotypical pattern (**Example**, the IRF CYCLE) with DISPLAY QUESTIONS and artificial and controlled conversation.

Experienced teachers, however, do not agree with this position. They find it extremely difficult, if not impossible, to replicate in the classroom sustained 'genuine' communication.

communicative stress. Feeling of unease caused by the fear that one may not be up to the mark in one's oral communication. Learners in the SL classroom undergo such STRESS when faced with a task or a question the teacher has asked them. The stress may also set in at the daunting prospect of having to write answers in the examination-room. One may suffer from such stress even when using one's MT with members outside one's immediate community. This may be caused by the speakers' consciousness of their poor (formal) education, SOCIAL CLASS, and status, young age, etc.

community. A group of people who share a common language, CULTURE, etc and may live in the same geographical area. The notion of 'community' is a flexible one: philatelists [those who collect postage stamps] across the world may form a community, so may the followers of a Guru. A language community consists of the speakers of a language, or one of its dialects.

community college. An alternative system of education aimed at COMMUNITY development. The target group consists of the disadvantaged sections of society. The stress in the courses is on skills development for gainful employment.

community language learning (CLL). A method of SL teaching in which the teacher acts as a counsellor to client-learners. Learning activities are of a COMMUNICATIVE kind, and are primarily aimed at promoting oral skills. The learner is encouraged to gradually move from an initial dependence on the teacher to more and more AUTONOMY. The method was developed by a Professor of Psychology, Charles A. Curran and his associates around 1970, the same period when some other HUMANISTIC APPROACHES such as the SILENT WAY, and SUGGESTOPEDIA were developed.

The method is an adaptation of the COUNSELLING-LEARNING approach. Curran claims that CLL is HOLISTIC learning: it treats learners as 'whole' persons. That is, persons as the integration of their physical, affective, psychological, and cognitive aspects, each of which needs to be recognised and addressed. The learners are treated as a COMMUNITY with a supportive attitude for the other learners and trusting relationship among them.

Use of the learners' MT, which has an important role in the TL class, is intended both to facilitate learning, and develop a feeling of security among the learners. *See also* COUNSELLING LEARNING.

comparative method studies. Studies carried out to measure comparative efficacy of two (or more) METHODS of teaching a SL in terms of learning outcomes. A classic example of such a study is the one by Scherer and Wertheimer (1964) also known as the Colorado research. The studies have not been conclusive in the sense that they have not been able to establish comparative superiority of any one Method. It was found that learning outcome resulted from variables other than just a labelled Method purportedly used by the instructor. Hence comparative Method studies are no longer popular, and the present phase of SL teaching studies is known as the era of 'post-method pedagogy'.

compensatory competence. Ability to use verbal strategies of communication. It includes such strategies as of making up for one's constrained linguistic resources, intelligent guessing, and paraphrasing. *See also* ACHIEVEMENT BEHAVIOUR, and STRATEGIC COMPETENCE.

compensatory education. Special education programmes for the disadvantaged. *See also* INCLUSIVE SCHOOLING, SHELTERED INSTRUCTION, SPECIAL EDUCATION, and TEACHING LANGUAGE TO THE DISADVANTAGED.

compensatory strategies [of communication]. *See also* ACHIEVEMENT BEHAVIOUR, and COMMUNICATION STRATEGIES.

competence. 1. The knowledge & ability underlying one's [communicative] performance in a language. Knowledge and ability include sentence-creation ability, or GRAMMATICAL COMPETENCE, phonological competence, lexical repertoire and a mastery of these that enables one to use language skilfully. **2.** In the contrasted pair of terms competence and performance, Chomsky[in the1960s]used *competence* to denote the implicit 'knowledge' of grammar & syntax that an idealised, educated, native speaker of a language is presumed to have. Performance is an externalization of this knowledge in language use. Competence is IMPLICIT, PERFORMANCE overt. Chomsky's distinction is analogous to that of Saussure's between LANGUE and PAROLE.

The 'complete method'. Expression used by H. Palmer (1921) for what he calls 'the multiple line of approach' to teaching a SL. The cardinal principle in this is ECLECTICISM. Palmer's 'complete method' is the 'antithesis' of 'patent or proprietary methods.' In justification of the term Palmer says, 'Many...who practise eclecticism call it the philosophy of the complete life;' Palmer's eclecticism is a protest against the faddism of branded methods in language teaching. His eclecticism 'implies the deliberate choice of all things which are good, ...and ... may constitute a complete and homogeneous system'.

completion-type items. *See* ELLIPTICAL EXERCISES, and SUPPLY TYPE ITEMS.

composition. A writing task. Composition is both the PROCESS of writing and its PRODUCT. In the context of SL pedagogy, it includes at the primary and lower secondary levels copying or transcription, DICTATION, ORAL COMPOSITION, guided and CONTROLLED COMPOSITION, and only later, FREE COMPOSITION. In addition, composition-teaching includes the teaching of the mechanics such as handwriting, punctuation, and spelling. Composition is indeed a very broad term for a variety of writing work ranging from composing sentences [through such tasks as completing, converting, and combining them] to composing paragraphs. Billows (1961) goes as far as to say that composition is 'implicit even in all oral work, group work [chorus] and teaching of prose and poetry.' Chapman (1958) says, every sentence a learner makes or completes, in speech or writing, is an exercise in composition [in a SL].

In the Billows and Chapman kind of approach to teaching composition, the primary goal is for learners to achieve sentence-level accuracy as an end in itself. The purpose of composition writing, in such an approach, is to achieve ACCURACY through PRACTICE. The learner does not write to convey message to the reader. The only reader is the teacher, who in all probability will look at it to correct any language errors in it. Post-1970 approaches to composition and writing in SLT encourage expression of ideas and FLUENCY also, and treat writing as a means to communication. They attach importance to both content and form.

compound bilingualism. A form of BILINGUALISM in which an individual uses two languages concurrently. Compound bilinguals normally learn the two languages usually during their childhood, and simultaneously. Such bilinguals keep switching back and forth from one language to another according to the needs of the communicative situation.

comprehensible input. Language that learners are exposed to and can understand so that its processing leads to acquisition of language. It is one of the hypotheses in Stephen Krashen's model of SLA (1981) that 'comprehensible input' – input that is just at a slightly higher level of difficulty than the learners' current level of language proficiency/comprehension – will cognitively engage them in MEANING-MAKING, a process that leads to language acquisition.

Some scholars do not go as far as Krashen does in putting premium on the comprehensiblity of the input. They feel that comprehensibility alone is not a sufficient condition for acquisition.

comprehensible output. Language OUTPUT tailored by the learner so it becomes clear to the listener/reader. It is hypothesised that the learners' mulling over the message to make it comprehensible – their engagement with meaning – fosters language acquisition.

comprehension. The cognitive act of understanding spoken or written discourse [It is also the product of the act.] In the act of comprehending, an individual processes incoming data in the light of her knowledge of the language and the world.

Comprehension results from a negotiation of meaning which involves the TEXT/DISCOURSE and the reader/listener. In negotiating, the reader/listener uses strategies of comprehension. *See also* LISTENING, COMPREHENSION STRATEGIES, and READING STRATEGIES.

Comprehension can be literal in which only the surface meaning is received. When the implications of the text/discourse are plumbed to draw inference(s), reading/listening becomes inferential. (*See also* INFERENCING) Reading/listening requires both, literal, as well as inferential comprehension.

comprehension approach to language teaching. The approach to SL teaching that advocates that a period of training in listening and comprehension should precede oral production. The approach derives support from the observation of the process of L1 acquisition, where the learning begins with a long period of pre-speech listening and comprehension with no formal instruction. It is to be noted in this context that the teaching of SLs in the dominant mid twentieth century approaches began with oral practice. Alternative approaches include James Asher's Total Physical Response. *See also* TPR.

compulsory miseducation. Stance taken notably by the radical American thinker Paul Goodman (1964) against formal schooling. It is to be noted that formal schooling is compulsory for children in most countries. Goodman argues that our 'schooling fails to educate.' The school atmosphere inhibits spontaneity, practises coercion, regimentation and brainwashing, and encourages conformity and competitiveness. 'Institutionalised learning runs counter to the natural intellectual development of the young people,' the 'natural learning patterns of family and community.' *Cf.* DESCHOOLING.

computer-adaptive testing. *See* ADAPTIVE TESTING.

computer-assisted instruction (CAI) *See* COMPUTER ASSISTED LANGUAGE LEARNING.

computer-assisted language learning (CALL). Learning language with the help of computer programmes that present content and practice material, ask questions and record responses, provide correct answers and feedback. CALL is a LEARNER-CENTRED approach to LL/LT. It is considered to enhance the learner's AUTONOMY without constraining her access to resources. One can choose an activity or task of one's interest and do it at one's own pace and place.

The 'authoring system.' in CALL or computer assisted instruction (CAI) enables teachers to create lessons with tests, hints and aids specific to the needs of their students. With computer lessons, the task of learning becomes INDIVIDUALISED and convenient.

computer assisted language testing (CALT). Use of computers in developing and administering language tests. *See also* PHONEPASS TEST.

concept. An internal, mental representation of an object or objects with a complex of shared attributes. That is, a concept is an image or idea, which has a number of distinguishing features.

A concept is realised in language. A function of LA is the formation of concepts.

concept map. A SCHEMA: a graphic representation of an idea or a list of ideas (on a topic or subject) and its sub-topics/components. The map shows how the idea has been organised and how it is related to the sub-topics. In concept mapping, the listed ideas may be connected with arrows to explore how they fit together. Drawing a concept map may help one to clarify one's ideas for oneself and develop awareness. Such maps help in improving reading comprehension, making presentations, and in guiding the structure of written production. Concept maps are also known as semantic maps. They can be generated either individually or in a group. *See also* MIND MAP.

conceptual strategies (contrasted with the linguistic). *See* STRATEGIES OF COMMUNICATION.

concordances. A list of utterances/passages in which a particular word or item of usage occurs. The list is based on a book, the writings of an author, or CORPUS collected from real use of language in different contexts.

concreteness. A quality of STYLE; of TEACHER TALK. It is achieved by using appropriate vocabulary[adjectives, etc.], apt expressions, and examples.

For Harold Palmer (1921) an attribute of concreteness in teacher talk is 'lucidity' achieved through exemplification, explanation, etc. He recommends teachers four ways of concretising , or of 'SEMANTICISING', i.e., of 'furnishing a student with the meaning of given foreign units:' These are:

By immediate association [basically, through demonstration]; by translation; by definition; and, by context.

concurrent validity. A kind of test VALIDITY established for a newly developed TEST. To see whether it is a valid test or not, results on it are compared with the results on a well-established, standardised Test. [The population taking the tests is the same in both the two. It is also a precondition that they measure the same ability.] A high degree of concurrence/correlation between the two sets of test-scores indicates concurrent validity for the new test.

conditioned reflex. *See* CONDITIONED RESPONSE.

conditioned response. Response learned through conditioning. In BEHAVIOURIST APPROACHES, a response is a reaction caused by a stimulus, and learnt through conditioning procedures. *See also* CONDITIONING AND BEHAVIOURISM (1).

conditioned substitution tables. SUBSTITUTION TABLES from which sentences cannot be derived mechanically. *See* SUBSTITUTION DRILLS. The consideration of meaning constrains the learner to think and make an appropriate choice. An **example** from Michael West (1947): the skeletal structure is 'I (1) with the help of a (2)'. A sentence derived from it is 'I eat with a knife and fork'.

The choices given under (1) are (in a random order)*wash, eat, draw a straight line, learn* and under (2) *ruler, teacher, sponge, knife and fork, textbook, nailbrush.*

conditioning. A process of eliciting a

desired response from an organism by administering stimuli. The process is intended to change the organism's earlier (the pre-conditioning) behaviour. The organism learns to respond in a new way by associating the stimulus with the response The process is used in laboratory experiments. Psychologists Pavlov, Thorndike, and Skinner are the major names associated with conditioning experiments. For a time around the middle of the twentieth century, conditioning, one of the tenets in BEHAVIOURISM, was seen to be instrumental in learning, language learning included. DECONDITIONING is the process of psychologically preparing a person to give up previously formed habits, notions, prejudices, inhibitions, etc. and RECONDITIONING is the process usually following deconditioning. *See also* CLASSICAL CONDITIONING and OPERANT CONDITIONING.

conferencing. A process of consultation between teacher and learner specially on the learner's written assignment. It is a process of guiding the learner, and of discussing the points of difficulty.

confluent design for language teaching. An approach that merges traditional goals of language teaching with 'humanistic goals of intrapersonal awareness'. Proposed by Beverly Galyean in 1970s, the design gives importance in language teaching to self-reflection and to close relationship among class members.

consciousness-raising (CR) or, grammatical CR (in the context of language teaching, esp. of grammar teaching). Focusing learner's attention on the FORMAL aspects of language, its difficult or/and peculiar features, the similarity or contrasted feature of a form in L2 [or the TL] with one in the learner's L1, etc. CR does not involve practice in producing the TL features; it involves drawing upon the learners' knowledge. CR activities are aimed at developing the learners' metacommunicative and METACOGNITIVE awareness, and helping them discover and notice the rule(s) thereby adding them to their own (interim) grammars of the language.

consecutive bilingualism. A form of BILINGUALISM in which an individual has learnt the two languages successively, and not simultaneously. *Cf.* CO-ORDINATE BILINGUALISM.

conservatism in language use. Insistence on maintaining a standard of (linguistic) correctness and on observing the held tradition of USAGE. Language pundits and writers of books of grammar and usage are known for their conservative attitude Textbook writers and classroom teachers too insist on conformity to the CANON, which usu. is the formal, educated variety and follows the 'native speaker' norm. Educational tests and exams. have also by and large been conservative in matters of CORRECTNESS. There is perhaps a justification for this policy in language education.

Teachers have generally been conservative, and have discouraged students from using colloquial and regional varieties esp. in writing. However, variation in language use being common, there is greater tolerance and accommodation in evidence

43

now. Absolutes seem to be tempered with the considerations of contexts of language use.

consistency. 1. A quality of style in DISCOURSE, written and spoken. It consists in maintaining a uniform TONE and POINT OF VIEW. Tone has to do, among other things, with formal-informal and serious-humorous TENOR. Mixing the two in the same discourse such as a paragraph would be a mark of inconsistency. Maintaining a consistent point of view is avoiding unnecessary shift in number, person, tense, and avoiding contradictions. **2.** Consistency is also a desirable quality of individual items or groups of items on a TEST, and can be judged through standardised devices in language testing.

consolidation. 1. In behaviourist psychology. The process of making learnt behaviour long-lasting. (How this process operates internally in the learner's mind is not known.) **2.** Taking from the above, the pedagogical principle and the procedures that follow it, of making learners practice the item of learning presented to them until they achieve AUTOMATICITY. The main procedure that can lead to consolidation is considered to be PRACTICE 1.

consonant. *See* VOWEL AND CONSONANT.

consonant cluster. A sequence of two or more consonants occurring within a SYLLABLE as in slip, restraint, condensed. Speakers of one language often find certain clusters of another language difficult to pronounce.

construct. In a general sense, CONCEPT: something constructed by the mind, **Example** a THEORY. *See* CONCEPT and

HYPOTHESIS.

In LANGUAGE TESTING, 'construct' is the TRAIT or ability a test, or part of it, aims to measure. The test-score indicates, or is supposed to indicate, whether the test-taker possesses, and to what degree, the trait/ability being tested. *See also* CONSTRUCT VALIDITY.

constructed-response items. Test-items or tasks in which the test-takers have to produce answers they compose themselves rather than select from the choices given. Fill in the blanks type, short-answer type, and free-response type questions are examples. Different from the constructed-response items are SELECTED-RESPONSE ITEMS.

constructivism. A COGNITIVE view of learning. It holds that the learner's mind creates knowledge for itself in interaction with the environment around it. [The environment includes, among other things, peers, teachers, parents, and media resources.] The mind is regarded as an active agent rather than just a recipient. Learners do not just reproduce information: they construct knowledge by interpreting and reconstructing input and experience in the light of their own knowledge, understanding and perception. They transform input and experience to make them personally meaningful.

This view contrasts with the BEHAVIOURIST LEARNING THEORY, and contradicts the deeply-rooted faith in transmission models. *Cf.* RECONSTRUCTIONISM.

construct validity (of a language test). A measure of whether a Test conforms to a theory of language/language learning. By implication, the THEORY should be one that is currently upheld. A TEST conforms to a theory of language learning if it tests those TRAITS/ABILITIES that the theory holds as constitutive of knowledge of language. **Example**, currently upheld theories of language knowledge maintain that it consists of the ability to use the language fluently, correctly, appropriately, etc. in different situations. A test, part of a test, or a procedure would be considered construct-valid if it aims at testing this competence. Of course not everything that comes under language competence can be tested in one span. And the testing activity has to follow appropriate testing-norms and procedures.

contact session. (in DE). Face-to-face meeting between the learners and their tutor/COUNSELLOR. Universities follow different patterns of contact session organization.

content. Generally, what is taught or gets taught, what is learnt, what is tested, what one knows, what a book deals with – all in relation to a subject, **Example**, Physics. In the contexts of LANGUAGE EDUCATION, content may refer to **1.** [teaching materials] what they contain – lessons, topics, themes, but generally words and structures – thematic and linguistic content. **2.** [tests or test items] what a particular test or test item is measuring – abilities/skills/traits. **3.** [content teaching] teaching of content as distinct from the teaching of language forms. *See* Content-based language instruction and Sustained-content language teaching. **4.** [learner language] As in 3 above, a distinction is made between what the learner utters/writes [i.e., its content] and the language it is couched in from the angle of its formal/grammatical/stylistic correctness & appropriateness. **5.** [a language teachers' knowledge] Content-knowledge is their knowledge of the subject matter, of the language they teach: its grammar, phonology, morphology, semantics, and sometimes even the literary works in it. *See also* SUBJECT KNOWLEDGE.

content analysis. 1. Procedure/process of examining and analysing the content (*See* Content.1.) of textual materials to see what kind of lexical and structural items it contains and how frequently of they occur. The analysis may also involve examining the themes and topics dealt with, cultural references, BIASES, etc. **2.** Analysis of the content of TEST-ITEMS to see what the TEST is measuring.

content-based language instruction (CBI). SL teaching that integrates specialist content in it. CBI is an instructional format based on the premise that language-skills are acquired better when their learning is integrated with purposeful learning of content or subject-matter. In such teaching the instructional procedure focuses primarily on meaning and message and not on form or structure as is conventionally done in much SL teaching.

Thus in CBI, the subject-matter becomes the content of learning, and the process of learning is collaborative and focused on solving problems. It is through the process of learning a content subject such as biology or philosophy that the learners develop

their language skills. *See also* SUS-
TAINED-CONTENT LANGUAGE TEACHING.
cf. SKILLS-BASED TEACHING.

content-based language-teaching.
See CONTENT-BASED LANGUAGE INSTRUC-
TION. *Also,* LANGUAGE ACROSS THE CUR-
RICULUM.

content knowledge. *See* SUBJECT
KNOWLEDGE, PEDAGOGICAL KNOWLEDGE,
and TEACHER KNOWLEDGE.

content subject. A subject of study
consisting mainly of facts and ideas,
as different from subjects that require
mastery of SKILLS. 'History' is cited
as an example of the former and car-
driving of the latter. The BEHAVIOURIST
THEORY considers language learning as
skills learning. Models of teaching
based on this theory therefore emphasise the importance of PRACTICE
activities in learning. Based on this, a
distinction is made between knowledge
pedagogy and skills pedagogy.

content Syllabus. *See* CONTENT (1),
and PROCESS SYLLABUS.

content validity. [Of language tests].
A measure of the extent to which the
test content represents the knowledge
area which the TEST has been developed to test or professes to test. *See
also* CONTENT (2), and CONTENT ANALYSIS
2.' For **example**, in ACHIEVEMENT TESTS
the content of the test would be valid
(given the other conditions being satisfactory) if it covers all major areas of
the syllabus or the course of study on
which it is based.

content word. A word that has lexical
meaning. Adjectives, adverbs, nouns
and verbs in a language have lexical
meaning, and are also known as full
words. They are contrasted with FUNC-
TION WORDS – articles, conjunctions,
prepositions.

context. 1. The situation [the non-
linguistic environment] in which an
UTTERANCE/TEXT is produced. Context
in this sense could be the historical,
the geographical, or the social. In its
historical context the meaning of the
word 'chap' in the sixteenth century
was 'purchaser' or 'customer.' The
geographical context is the context of
the provenance of the INTERLOCUTORS
and the language(s) spoken in the
area where the communicative event
is taking place.

The social context relates to the participants in the communicative event
– the speaker-listener, or the writer-
reader, their MT, AGE, sex, occupa-
tion, etc.; the place where the event
takes place; its purpose, and time. As
communicative events are context-
embedded, they cannot be properly
understood in isolation. Smooth communication becomes easy because of
the shared context and presupposition
pool. **2.** The linguistic environment
in which a word, phrase or a longer
UTTERANCE/TEXT occurs. The particular
meaning of an utterance/text or a part
of it depends on, and can be understood
clearly by taking into account the parts
preceding and following it. For example, the meaning of the word host in
the following phrase is determined by
what follows it: a host of possibilities.
See also Contextual factors. **3.** With
reference to the teaching of language
items. SL teaching expects teachers to
frame illustratively in a context – situational and/or linguistic – the items of
language (words, sentences, rules, etc.)

to be taught. **4.** Parts of a literary work that come before an extract from it and follow it in the context of which the meaning of the extract can be understood. In many exam-question-papers on courses in language and literature, candidates are asked to 'explain with reference to the context...' This is done to find out whether they have read the text or not.

contextual factors/constraints in language teaching. Factors relating to when, where, and who with i.e., the time, location, and participants of an activity that limit its effectiveness or success. These factors have been observed to exercise great influence, often constraining, on the implementation of an APPROACH to language teaching or method. The constraints may arise from the non-availability of resources, lack of ENVIRONMENTAL support, lack of understanding or a lack of willingness on the part of the personnel. A solution, a method, or TECHNIQUE may succeed with one set of people in a particular environment but it may not do so in another. There may be nothing wrong with the method of teaching itself. Yet the assumptions and the beliefs of those participating in its implementation at a particular time and location may give it a different interpretation leading to its distortion or failure

contextualisation in language teaching. *See* CONTEXT 3.

contextual meaning. The meaning of an UTTERANCE/TEXT or a part of it in a particular CONTEXT (1). Contextual meaning is different from the literal meaning of an utterance/text. **Example**, *I like apples* may in a particular context

mean – *Please serve me apples.*

contextual syllabus. A SYLLABUS graded 'from the point of view of the situations which the pupils are to be taught to respond to.' (LA Hill, 1967). Hill proposed contextual syllabuses as an improvement on the STRUCTURAL SYLLABUSES then widely in use. He suggested that vocabulary and structure should be selected for the [graded] situations teachers would like their pupils to function in. 'It is much easier to learn a word or structure if it grows naturally out of a context than if it is taught without such a context, ...(*ibid.*: 118). *Cf.* SITUATIONAL SYLLABUSES.

contiguity learning. Learning resulting from the ASSOCIATION of events that occur together in time or place. DRILL and MEMORISATION work on this principle. It is to be noted that much vocabulary is learnt through association or pairing. **Example**, one may learn the words knife and cut by pairing them. *See also* PAIRED ASSOCIATE LEARNING.

contrastive analysis (CA). The discipline or the procedure of systematically describing and comparing two or more languages or their sub-domains to find out structural similarities and differences between them. Articles, infinitives are examples of sub-systems of a language, as are the phonological and semantic systems. Quite often aspects of culture as reflected in the languages are also contrasted.

CA has many applications outside language pedagogy, but it was first acclaimed for its supposed contribution to SL teaching. However, in recent decades, its claims have been subdued. From making claims of predictive certainty, CA has come down to a diagnostic and explanatory role. The two versions of CA are sometimes referred to as STRONG and WEAK.

However, in recent years there has been a revival of interest in contrastive studies. There is a reappraisal of the role of L1 in the learning of an L2. Also, CA is seen to be relevant to the study of DISCOURSE, PRAGMATICS, and CONTRASTIVE RHETORIC.

contrastive rhetoric (CR). A newly-developed, inter-disciplinary field that studies the organisation of DISCOURSE in different cultures. CR is based on the principle that cultures are different and so are languages. Accordingly, TEXTS are/may be organised differently in different cultures, and models of good writing vary from culture to culture. Concerned with this difference, CR studies the ways in which texts are organised in the learners' source and target languages. The study involves analyses of discourse, GENRE, and the relationship between the writes/ speakers and their education, cultural orientation, etc.

Though a widely acceptable theoretical MODEL for contrasting RHETORIC is yet to develop, contrastive rhetoric is of pedagogical significance in the teaching of writing [and speech] in a SL.

contrastive pragmatics. A contrastive study of the ways in which communicative functions (**Example,** persuading someone) are performed in different languages. The term 'contrastive PRAGMATICS' is analogical to contrastive linguistics, which is concerned with comparing the formal features in two or more languages.

control. 1. In behaviourist approaches. Systematic manipulation and modification of human behaviour by using appropriate REINFORCEMENTS and punishments. **2.** In SL pedagogy. The principle of facilitating SL learning by exposing the learners to, or introducing to them, language and/or content in a controlled, graded manner, i.e., in stages. The principle of control (of structure, vocabulary, subject matter) has been followed in many models of SL teaching. For its validity, the principle depends on norms for judging difficulty levels of the items for learning. For a time the practice of determining difficulty was based on 'linguistic' considerations grounded in the linguistics of the period. With the coming in of new theories, the linguistic-based norms have been questioned. Also, the principle of control derives from a theory of language learning which does not have many supporters today, although, in general, the principle of control in language teaching is a useful one. **3.** (In producing teaching materials) One of the modes in which this principle is followed is to simplify and shorten authentic texts, or deliberately write texts in simple language. *See also* SIMPLIFICATION, and SIMPLIFIED TEXTS.

controlled composition. Writing-task so designed as to control the possibility of the occurrence of language errors. Such tasks are based on a common pedagogical experience, and an assumption. The experience, an irritating one for many teachers, is of the frequently occurring language errors in the writing produced by learners who have not yet acquired dependable mastery of the language. And the assumption that errors are blemishes: their incidence can be forestalled and therefore should be forestalled.

To achieve this, controlled or guided composition tasks are devised. They are 'close-ended' (Alexander, 1971) in the sense that learners produce completed sentences or sentence sequences along 'predictable' lines.

The complexity of the controlled composition tasks ranges over a continuum beginning with very simple ones, requiring the production of PATTERNS from SUBSTITUTION DRILLS, going on to combining sentences so produced. Further on, there may be tasks like those that require rearranging jumbled sentences in a coherent order. Still further there might be tasks requiring meaningful choices to be made.

Controlled/guided composition has relevance in the context of LARGE CLASSES and the load of massive correction-work on the teacher. In its approach it is influenced by CORRECTNESS as the predominant goal of SL teaching, and a distrust of the learner's MT, the mother tongue as a negative factor. It pre-dates new conceptualisations specially PROCESS WRITING.

Though the theoretical underpinnings of controlled composition are in the construct underlying the STRUCTURAL APPROACHES to SL teaching, as a pedagogical tool it can be useful in building learner-confidence, and gradually helping her on to the way to free writing.

controlled vocabulary. List of words deliberately restricted for pedagogical purposes. The purposes include SL teaching, writing textbooks & other learning materials, and making dictionaries for learners. The rationale given for control is SL-learner-ease, interest and purpose.

In order to arrive at a controlled list of words, procedures for selection are adopted. See VOCABULARY SELECTION.

In *An International Reader's Dictionary,* M West used a vocabulary of fewer than 1500 words to explain the meaning of over 24,000 items. West considered these words [1490 to be precise] 'to be the commonest words in English or the words first learnt by foreigners(p. vii).'

A.S. Hornby's *The Oxford Advanced learner's Dictionary (ALD),* uses a defining vocabulary of 'just under three thousand words'(sixth edition, 2000).

controlled writing. SL-writing-tasks so designed that beginning and intermediate level learners are not hindered in their effort to write by difficult sentence-structure and vocabulary. *See* CONTROLLED COMPOSITION.

convergent validity. VALIDITY established by comparing the scores obtained on two or more tests measuring the same ABILITY. The procedure, often adopted for judging the validity of a newly developed language-test, is as follows – an established test with the same measurement objective (**Example**, the ability to communicate orally at a specified level/in specific contexts) is identified. The two tests are administered to a single group of candidates. If high correlation is found among the scores on the two tests, they may be said to measure the same ability and possess convergent validity. The procedure is also adopted for establishing the convergent validity of any two tests, and for judging the traits they measure.

conversion. Manipulation of linguistic forms that involves changing them from one into another: affirmative into negative sentences, questions into statements, and vice versa, transforming tenses, and so on. H. Palmer (1921a) includes under conversion exercises in translation, reading aloud, transcription, spelling drills and dictation. *See* STUDIAL METHOD. Conversion exercises may be done mechanically, or they may have built-in meaning-constraint.

cooperative development. An approach to TEACHER DEVELOPMENT based on co-operation between the MENTOR and the teacher trainee or between a senior and a junior colleague. The junior teacher or the novice finds in the mentor a helpful listener to her problems. The co-operative development approach contrasts with the approach AUTHORITARIAN supervisors adopt(ed).

co-operative group-learning. Extended phrase for 'COOPERATIVE LEARNING.'

co-operative learning. A mode of organising learning through solving problems collaboratively. [*See* COLLABORATIVE learning.] It refers to those CLASSROOM practices in which learners work together in small groups and help each other in doing academic tasks and solving problems. Cooperative group activities are considered to be a better alternative to teacher-fronted classes, and whole-class instruction.

Cooperative learning, i.e. working in a team, requires social skills of collaboration, of sharing responsibility, of allowing time and space to others and not monopolising, of soliciting PEER support and making such support available to others, and above all, of working for the group, rather than individual goals. These skills of cooperation do not come to one easily. Learners need training in appreciating the advantages of cooperative learning and in practising it. The training should precede participation in cooperative learning if it is to succeed. Cooperative learning classrooms need suitable physical and spatial arrangement. Cooperative learning is an affectively positive procedure. There is no competitiveness. On the contrary the learners' self-confidence and SELF-ESTEEM get a boost.

the cooperative principle. Rules for co-operation in conversation. Also known as Gricean Maxims after Paul Grice (1967/1975) who postulated four principles of co-operation in conversation: **1.** The principle of quantity requires that the speaker provide necessary information. **2.** The principle of quality requires that the information be true to the best of the speaker's knowledge. **3.** The principle of relation requires that the speech be relevant to the topic of conversation, and **4.** The principle of manner requires that the speaker speak comprehensively, unambiguously, concisely, and CONSISTENTLY.

This model of conversation has been found to be inadequate as it presupposes that the conversation will be between gentlemen who are willing to cooperate and be polite. What about conversation between persons of unequal power and position? It has been noted that in much conversation there is a kind of [unconscious] 'competitive use of language,' which runs counter to the principles of cooperation.

However, the maxims have applications in language pedagogy.

cooperative task. A learning TASK in completing which either a pair or a group of learners work together following the principles of COOPERATIVE LEARNING. The umbrella of such a task makes many learners feel affectively secure since they do not feel daunted by the prospect of individual evaluation. Such security and absence of STRESS is believed to bring out better performance, and foster positive qualities of cooperativeness.

coordinate bilingualism. A form of BILINGUALISM in which an individual learns a SL in instructed contexts, after having acquired a level of competence in L1 or the MT. *Cf.*, COMPOUND BILINGUALISM. In co-ordinate bilingualism the bilinguals' L2 is considered to be subordinate to their L1.

corpus. A body of 'naturally occurring' language data. Such data are a collection of TEXTS stored in a computer, which can be accessed. The data are carefully collected from language used in a particular domain(s). Study of actual samples of language-use helps in many ways. Dictionaries can incorporate current USAGES and meanings. The corpus offers a vast range of information on such subjects as the pattern lexical items occur in and how collocation [association between words that frequently occur together] works. The grammar and LEXIS of a language can be described on the basis of sta-tistics relating to real language-use. Such studies have shown that actual usage does not often support the impressionistic statements made by grammar-book writers or compilers of dictionaries.

corpus-based grammar. Description of the GRAMMAR [of a language] based on the data representing the language used by its speakers in writing and speech. The data, huge in quantity, is drawn from a great variety of authentic language use in different walks of life, regions, and REGISTERS. Computer technology is used for collecting and analysing the data.

In such a grammar, the description of the PATTERNS of the language and how they are used represent actual USAGE and not someone's impression or personal preference.

correction. Negative FEEDBACK on learner performance: telling learners how and where they have gone wrong in using the language and how they can remedy the MISTAKE. Correcting learner mistakes is a pedagogical responsibility, and in most cultures, learners welcome it. *See also* ERROR TREATMENT.

correctness. 1. A measure of the ACCEPTABILITY of language used in a particular context. Generally, the correctness of a particular usage is its conformity with the contemporary conventions of language use: conventions that govern the USAGE at the time, and sanction it. Often what is considered correct in one VARIETY of a language may not be acceptable in another. Usage changes; language changes, and so do standards and notions of correctness. *See also* Correctness and language teaching. **2.** Correctness in contrast to FLUENCY. *See* ACCURACY.

correctness and language teaching. Discernment and discrimination in pedagogy of what forms should be recommended for learning as widely acceptable and as good language usage. Making such judgement has not always been easy. Teachers' normative attitudes have got in the way of legitimatising many instances of current idiom and usage. Further confusion arises in evaluation where different examiners uphold different standards

correspondence journals. Near authentic letters written by SL learners in the PRACTICE-TEACHING class taught by teacher-trainees. This technique for promoting almost real-purpose writing can be used in many ways. An **example**, first the learners write a brief letter of self-introduction to an as-yet-unknown correspondent. They put the letter in a folder with their names on the outside. These folders are distributed among the teacher trainees. Each trainee writes a reply to the letter received in the folder. The letter in reply is also put in the folder. For ease of identification, the trainees write their name on the folders. They are instructed not to make any corrections in the learner letters. They write a reply as they would do in the natural course of correspondence. The folders are given back to respective learners. This chain continues from week to week as long as the practice teaching course lasts. About 15 minutes are set aside every week for journal writing as it has to be done only in

the class. The advantages of writing correspondence journals are twofold. By participating in the generation of a running discourse, learners acquire the skill of communicative writing, and the trainees on their part an understanding of an individual learner and insight into how she writes and what her problems are.

co-trainer. *See* MENTOR.

counselling. Helping students with their problems. Secondary and post-secondary level institutions usually provide for students guidance and counselling services pertaining to such matters as personal and psychological problems, self-understanding and SELF-DEVELOPMENT, personality and human resource development, choice of educational courses, career and vocation.

Counselling and guidance are often used as co-expressions. But guidance is a more general kind of activity whereas counselling means establishing a personal face to face relationship between the student and the counsellor. *See also* VOCATIONAL COUNSELLING.

counselling-learning. A method of teaching in which the teacher acts as a psychological counsellor rather than an AUTHORITARIAN person. A counsellor is someone who tries to understand empathetically learners' feelings, emotions, needs, and problems and tries to help them get over the problems (of learning). *See* COMMUNITY LANGUAGE LEARNING.

counsellor. (in DE). Also known as the academic counsellor, the counsellor or the tutor is part of the academic support system – the human element in DE – for the learners. They can access her for such assistance as help with studies, guidance, removal of their academic difficulties. DE organizations usually make provision for periodic face-to-face contact between the learners and the assigned counsellor/tutor.

coursebook. The prescribed TEXTBOOK – the mainstay of the average language teaching class. The teacher in the class bases her teaching of the language on this book, and questions in the examination are usually drawn from it. Units of the book contain a reading text round which learning activities are built. In addition to the textbook, the course material may have a SUPPLEMENTARY READER and a WORKBOOK. Sometimes a book of grammar and composition and a literature text are also included.

Craft model. The method of professional TRAINING through apprenticeship. The learner learns by observing the expert 'master' and gaining experience and understanding of the craft through working with him and practising. Indigenous trades are traditionally acquired this way. The apprentices in due course gain enough expertise to become master craftsmen themselves. The craft model comes very close to the CO-OPERATIVE DEVELOPMENT and the MENTORING models.

creative-construction hypothesis. The hypothesis that learners subconsciously derive rules from the language they hear/read to construct their own language system(s), which makes them create and understand sentences. Many researchers are of the view that this creative competence to acquire language-rules is innate to

human beings.

It is hypothesised that the process of creative-construction operates in a similar way in the acquisition of both L1 and L2. In SLA, the learners' INTERLANGUAGE system gradually evolves in a consistent, rule governed manner, although the system manifests itself in a great deal of VARIABILITY in learner-language performance.

creative reading. Responding to (literary) texts insightfully. According to Morris (1972), creative reading contrasts with literal reading and with CRITICAL READING. Whereas critical reading 'is a strenuously active reasoning process,' reading 'insightfully' is 'probing beneath the surface' – 'to see the whole, to appreciate the form, [It] is part of the required response [quote from Pattison].' Creative reading is integrational in nature and requires a degree of emotional involvement.

The usefulness of this concept, not a very precise one, lies in reminding us of the painfully slow and literal reading to which many SL learners subject literary texts in a SL. *See also* READING.

creative thinking. *See* LATERAL THINKING, and PARALLEL THINKING.

creative writing. 1. Works of imagination such as poetry, drama, fiction. Such writing uses literary devices not ordinarily used in everyday language. Literary studies, an enormous field, deal with creative writing – its purpose, value, interpretation, and so on. **2.** An academic programme in writing – writing as different from COMPOSITION and ESSAY writing. In it the participants are taught such things as principles of writing, ways of beginning and concluding a piece of [creative] writing, narrating, describing, dramatising, building suspense. WORKSHOP is usu. the instructional mode.

creativity. In the context of language learning: the ability to generalise and to create/generate ever new sentences on the basis of the rule the learner has internalised. *See* Creative-construction hypothesis. In the context of 'literature,' creativity is the imaginative ability of producing works of literary value, such as poems and stories. The concept of creativity also applies to the generation of ideas in general. *See also* SYNECTICS.

credit. Weight/points assigned to an academic course-unit according to its content-load and duration in terms of hours of teaching and student work involved. The duration is worked out on the basis of the numbers of lectures, TUTORIALS, WORKSHOPS, and such other activities participated in. The practice of credits is used in the semester system of education. Students have the choice of core and elective courses. Each course/course unit, also called MODULE, has its assigned weighting. For each semester's work, a student has to earn a specified minimum number of credits. In such a system, EVALUATION is based on periodic test results, appraisal of performance in tutorials, discussions, etc. and the semester-end examination.

criterion. A STANDARD (1) applied to judge something, **Example**, learner performance on a test. Selection of criteria requires their VALIDATION so that their application is not arbitrary and does not lead to unfair judgement

criterion-referenced tests. Language tests aimed at judging the examinees' competence in relation to the specified criteria. Such tests measure how well an examinee can perform a given [communicative] task, which is the CRITERION for ASSESSMENT. The criterion may be laid down in terms of performance/ability-level or specific content domain. **Example**, in the domain of oral skills, content could be specified as topics, text types, and operations/functions such as thanking, persuading. Similarly, the ability-level may be specified HOLISTICALLY or analytically.

criterion-related validity. VALIDITY of a new test established on the basis of its closeness to other tests using similar CRITERION. A new language test needs to be validated against some established NORM, usually an existing test dealing with the same TRAIT(s)/ability(-ies) as the new one. This procedure employs statistical measures to arrive at correlation, and is aimed at determining CONCURRENT VALIDITY. Such validity will depend on the closeness of correlation between the two sets of scores.

Sets of scores on two parallel forms of a test may be compared with one another to measure the test's RELIABILITY, a precondition of its validity.

In some cases, the criterion may be the future performance (on a test). This criterion-related validity, known as PREDICTIVE VALIDITY, is judged by the degree to which a test accurately predicts future performance.

critical discourse analysis (CDA). The analysis of TEXTS [spoken or written] in terms of IDEOLOGY and POWER. CDA believes that texts are imbued with ideology and power. **Example,** the unequal capacity of participants in DISCOURSE events to control texts is a matter of power (Norman Fairclough, 1995). Fairclough, an important exponent of CDA, says, 'A range of properties of texts are regarded as potentially ideological, including features of vocabulary, and metaphor, grammar, presuppositions and implicatures, politeness conventions, speech-exchange (turn-taking) systems, generic structures and style" (1995:2). He cites the example 'The Soviet threat cost the West dear,' which carries the implication that 'there is/[was] a *Soviet threat*'. The use of the article *the* before *Soviet threat* 'triggers' the presupposition. CDA and critical language *awareness* are interrelated. *See also* APPLIED DISCOURSE ANALYSIS.

critical incident. A significant event in a teacher's professional practice. The event may be a routine one but is considered significant by the teacher as it triggers professional REFLECTION with implications for the TEACHER'S BELIEFS, and it may mark a turning point. The notion derives from Tripp (1993).

critical language testing. Language testing that questions the negative effects of tests, and asserts that LANGUAGE TESTING as it is practised is not neutral and unbiased. It is felt by many that tests the way they are used have a harmful effect on test-takers. Language tests are often used for discriminatory purposes. Their controlling power and GATEKEEPING role make them liable to misuse.

critical linguistics. Linguistic study that takes the stance that language use – spoken or written – is imbued with IDEOLOGY and POWER and subtly carries in it the users' ideological persuasions, prejudices, etc. Language forms offer choices that can be made use of [sometimes deliberately] to obscure/conceal, and to mislead. The passive voice may be employed to suppress the identity of the agents. The free indirect speech may be used to blur and merge POINTS OF VIEW. Critical linguistics argues for using linguistic analyses to bring out the covert biases, distortions, and ideological loading in texts.

critical literacy. More than a functional ability to read and write. Critical LITERACY involves political and cultural AWARENESS and the ability to see and question the ideological position held by the writer/speaker in a TEXT.

critical moment in classroom practice. A turning point in teaching, a point when things change as a result of a critical perception. *See also* CRITICAL INCIDENT.

critical pedagogy (CP). View of education that challenges it as an institution of knowledge- transfer. CP questions the uncritical reproduction in public education of the established VALUES, IDEOLOGY, and power structure. It argues that education, instead of being reproductive, should enable students to question the prevailing CURRICULUM structure, and power structure.

CP advocates that learning should derive and emerge from the learners' own experience and understanding. For it, there is no pre-defined body of knowledge to be transferred to the learners. CP, in relation to language, sees an interelationship between experience, language, and POWER. Paulo Freiré and Ivan Illich are some exponents of this view.

critical period hypothesis (CPH). The HYPOTHESIS that there is a period of optimum efficiency – the period from early infancy to mid-teens – during which acquisition of language(s) takes place naturally provided exposure to the language(s) and opportunities of meaningful INTERACTION are available to the acquirer. With advancing age, the plasticity of the brain is supposed to decrease making it difficult to process INPUT for acquisition, esp. in the area of PHONOLOGY and pronunciation.

The neurosurgeon Penfield advanced in 1950s the view that after the age of 11, language learning becomes 'unphysiological', and this view led to the development of the hypothesis.

critical reading (CR). Reading with one's eye on any hidden meaning (s), BIAS (es), etc. in the text. A critical reader does not necessarily accept meaning as objective, obvious or self-evident, and questions the writer(s)' assumptions. The reader evaluates the worth of the text before accepting or rejecting its message. CR examines the manner in which specific texts reinforce or challenge relations of power, eg., through the patterning of linguistic choices. With the reader trying to access the 'hidden', unvocalised socio-cultural and political assumptions, reading becomes a subversive activity challenging the dominant meanings as commonly accepted meanings – 'meaning' is seen a power play. *See also* READING WITH RESPONSE (2).

cross-linguistic influence. Influence of the grammatical, morphological and/or semantic system(s) of one language, usually the learner's MT, on another, usually the TL. (It may also operate in the reverse direction.)

In the behaviourist paradigm of SL learning/teaching, such influence was viewed as negative, as causing hindrance in learning. Contrastive studies were taken up in 1950s and 1960s primarily to predict possible areas of cross-linguistic influence and forestall it. However, INTERLANGUAGE and subsequent theories take a positive view of such influence and consider its manifestations as instances of STRATEGY deployment by the learner. *See also* LANGUAGE TRANSFER and TRANSFER OF SKILLS.

c-tests. A variant of CLOZE TESTS. They consist of several (5 to 7) short, authentic, texts instead of one as in the cloze tests. Another point of difference between them is that, in C-tests, the second half of every second word is deleted. (In cloze tests whole words are deleted.) C-tests, though tougher, are considered to be a good HOLISTIC measure of competence.

cue. A stimulus to understanding something. In LT, cues may be used as prompts to help learners to find words, discover meanings and so on. In PATTERN DRILLS, verbal or visual cues are given for learners to produce the target pattern or the target transformation. *See also* MISCUE.

cultural discontinuity. [In the context of SL education]. The gap between the culture of home and that of school. SL learners, when they enter school, may have to acquire a different way of talking, communicating, and interacting consistent with the new language. The school environment may necessitate acquiring new socialisation patterns. This change accounts for the discontinuity. Discontinuity may also result from the difference between the home dialect and the variety of the MT used in school and the NORMS of APPROPRIATENESS they adopt.

cultural relativism. The view that the CULTURE/cultural and ethical norms and practices of one COMMUNITY is/are neither superior nor inferior to that/those of another. They are only different. And to understand a community one should study their culture and cultural/ethical beliefs and practices.

culture. The traditional and organised ways in which a COMMUNITY or group of people think and behave in family and in different domains outside it. Culture usually includes customs, beliefs, social and religious practices, moral values, legal system, music, art, values cherished in individual and social life, and even superstitions. Individuals, through interaction acquire their culture in the SOCIETY they are born and live in. Thus culture is socially acquired, and cultural knowledge is shared in common by the members of a community.

Language is part of one's culture and also a potent source of in-group dissemination and transmission of culture.

The CONCEPT has encompassed varying areas of meaning depending on how the user defines the term. In an extended sense, it can be said that the members of an educational institution, or of a class in it, form a distinct community, and each such community has a culture and profile of its own. We talk of 'youth culture', 'large-class culture', etc. in the sense of patterned behaviour.

culture conflict. The mental clash an individual or a group/community experiences when confronted with a choice between two opposing cultures or sets of cultural practices, each sounding attractive and appealing. As languages are culture-embedded, earning a SL may create such a conflict.

culture-free tests. Language tests so designed that they carry no BIAS and do not permit advantage to any particular social, cultural, regional, or ethnic group or class.

culture(s) of learning. *See* LEARNER BELIEFS; TEACHER BELIEFS and CULTURES OF THE CLASSROOM.

cultures of the classroom. Patterns of behaviour, norms and conventions that develop in a CLASSROOM over a period of time. Each classroom constitutes a domain and has its own unique CULTURE. It may be governed by factors like power-sharing among the teacher and the learners, LEARNER BELIEFS, TEACHER BELIEFS, [local]social values, traditional learning and teaching practices such as MEMORISATION.

culture shock. ANXIETY felt by learners of a SL manifesting itself in such feelings as that of isolation, frustration, resentment and even hostility. The anxiety/shock results from the alienness of the new language and the CULTURE it represents, and is felt more when learning the language in its cultural context, i.e. it the country where it is spoken as the first language. Culture shock is considered to be an initial stage in ACCULTURATION.

culture-specific pedagogies. Ways and contents of teaching sensitive to specific cultural contexts. The concept derives from the observation that what may be appropriate in one cultural context (such as in the monolingual English-speaking countries) may not be so in a multi-lingual, multicultural, or multireligious country. Language pedagogy has to be sensitive to the learners' CULTURE(s), value system(s) and LEARNING STYLES. The learners' knowledge of language(s) other than the TL offers a potential resource that can be gainfully exploited. *Cf.* RECEIVED METHODOLOGY.

curricular constraints. Limitations that get in the way of attempts to change [also termed *reform* and *renewal*] a curriculum. *See* CONTEXTUAL FACTORS/CONSTRAINTS and CURRICULAR INNOVATION.

curricular innovation. Introduction of a radically new approach to the instructional process. [*See* Approach 1.] An example of this is N.S. Prabhu's COMMUNICATIONAL TEACHING PROJECT. Numa Markee (1997:46) defines curricular innovation thus : it 'is a managed process of development whose principal products are teaching (and/or testing) materials, methodological skills, and pedagogical values that are perceived as new by potential adopters'. He warns us, however, that not all innovation turns out to be beneficial.

curriculum. Academic programme(s): in its rather literal and conservative sense, a course of study. Curriculum is often loosely used synonymously with SYLLABUS, which essentially is the specification of the content of teaching. But curriculum is a more inclusive concept than syllabus. Going beyond the scope of 'syllabus,' curriculum refers to the entire learning situation/ academic programme, and includes the details of the plan of instruction, its objectives, ways of implementing it, list of readings and other resources, methodology of teaching, learning experiences, and evaluation procedure. Though comprehensive, some teachers find this concept, based on Ralph Tyler (1949), unsatisfactory as it does not accommodate such things as individual needs and differences, and changing teaching and LEARNING STYLES.

curriculum development/renewal. A principled process of introducing and implementing changes in CURRICULUM. Changes may be introduced in order to fine-tune the curriculum to its various aspects such as learner-NEEDS, processes of learning and teaching, EVALUATION procedures, TEACHER DEVELOPMENT, and the overall educational goals. Approaches to curriculum development may differ according to the belief systems, commitments and ideologies of those who motivate the process TOP-DOWN OR BOTTOM-UP.

There is a notional distinction between curriculum development and curriculum renewal. Whereas curriculum development suggests that the process begins from the beginning, curriculum renewal is a recasting and refinement of an existing curriculum. In this respect curriculum development is curricular innovation. *See also* CUR-RICULAR INNOVATION.

Another general expression is curriculum change, which means the same as renewal.

curriculum goals. The OBJECTIVES that the CURRICULUM/education should achieve. Different thinkers on education have prioritised different goals from the transmission of knowledge and cultural values to the bringing out of the learners' potential and facilitating their development, to education as an instrument of social change.

D

data-driven processing. Cognitive PROCESSING that is guided by the input or the data. *See also* BOTTOM-UP PROCESSING.

decision-making. The process of choosing or finding a solution. The concept has come to be used frequently in the context of TEACHER EDUCATION. Teacher education aims, among other things, at enabling teachers to take their own decisions in the day-to-day teaching according to the requirements of the context (which is ever variable), rather than expect guidance from above/outside.

declamation. (The art of delivering) an impassioned speech. One of the language- related activities in schools is declamation, in which pupils learn how to deliver speech that expresses effectively feelings and emotions. *See also* ELOCUTION, and RECITATION (1).

declarative knowledge. Factual knowledge: knowledge of facts, concepts, principles. In the context of (S)LE, declarative knowledge, in contrast to PROCEDURAL KNOWLEDGE, implies knowledge of the formal rules of grammar that has not been internalised by the learner, i.e., knowledge without the concomitant ability to use it in language performance.

deconditioning. *See* CONDITIONING

deductive learning. Learning with the help of EXPLICIT rules. The rules are codifications of what learners adopting INDUCTIVE approaches would arrive at from their observation. In deductive learning, learners begin with rules. In inductive learning they arrive at them. *See also* INDUCTIVE LEARNING.

deductive methods. Methods of teaching in which the general law, the rule, is explained at the beginning of the learning process. In the converse mode, the INDUCTIVE, learners arrive at the rule through such procedures as INFERENCING and DISCOVERY. A good example of the deductive approach in SL teaching is the GRAMMAR-TRANSLATION METHOD. *See also* DEDUCTIVE LEARNING, and INDUCTIVE LEARNING.

deep learning. *See* STUDY APPROACHES.

deep structure. The underlying STRUCTURE of a sentence. TRANSFORMATIONAL GENERATIVE GRAMMARS make a distinction between the surface and the deep structure of a SENTENCE. The oft-quoted **examples** are the following two sentences which have identical surface structure –

sub.+ v.(be)+adj.+ *to*-inf

1. John is easy to please
2. John is eager to please

At the deep structure, the first sentence means:

'it is easy for someone to please John' whereas the second : 'it is John who is eager to please someone.'

deficit hypothesis. A hypothesis about, or a theory of, educational failure. It relates linguistic failure to educational failure and says that learners from socially and economically deprived backgrounds may not achieve high enough competence in the [standard variety of the] language to be able to make a mark academically. Therefore failure at school is attributed to lack of 'enough language.' (M. Halliday 1978:

102). This theory does not have many supporters. Halliday is of the view that such theories are 'nonsense'.

deficit model of education. A compensatory model of education for learners from minority groups and disadvantaged sections. *See also* TEACHING LANGUAGE TO THE DISADVANTAGED.

deficit theory. *See* DEFICIT HYPOTHESIS.

defining vocabulary. The words used to explain the meaning of a word [or, phrase] as in a DICTIONARY. For their definitions, LEARNER'S DICTIONARIES use a limited set of words. The set usually consists of around 2500–3000 words. Michael West (1935) used a defining vocabulary of fewer than 1500 words [a list of 1455 'common and important' words].

The VOCABULARY is selected according to pedagogical criteria, and the list is usually appended in such dictionaries. The idea is that if the learners know the limited number of words in the set, they will have little problem in understanding the definitions. However, dictionary-makers have faced the problem of avoiding difficult words in the definitions. Trying to do so has often resulted in the definition becoming long and tortuous.

definition. A statement of the features that characterise a category or a CONCEPT. These features distinguish the category or concept from other categories and concepts. In general terms, a definition is a statement of the meaning of a word or phrase, such as appears in dictionaries following the headword.

demonstration. A TECHNIQUE in presenting a learning item. The item could be a grammatical form [**Example**, the present perfect continuous tense] or a difficult pronunciation, intonation, or some other point. Demonstration by the teacher is intended to show the learners the correct form/way so that they may understand, imitate, and practice. In demonstrating, the teacher may use actions and objects: he/she may use gestures, write/draw on the blackboard or take the help of mechanical devices such as projectors.

demonstration lesson. A lesson taught by a MENTOR or a supervisor on a teacher-training programme to illustrate teaching for the benefit of the teachers in training Demonstration lessons have traditionally been an essential component of language-teacher training programmes. Jean Forrester (1974) says, 'The obvious purpose [of such lessons] is to show how the principles enunciated in the lecture room... work out in practice. An ounce of demonstration is worth a pound of theory...' It has been pointed out that what an expert teacher can achieve in the favourable conditions of a specially set up demonstration is hardly within the means of an average teacher teaching in unfavourable circumstances [as most teachers of a SL have to]. But a more cogent reservation about the demo is the assumption underlying it that teaching in one setting is replicable in any other. Even if the lesson is intended to be the demo of the application of a particular technique, it can not be assumed that all teachers should or will use it the same way, given the uniqueness of each teaching event

density. The proportion of difficult

items in a sample or text. The density of difficult items is measured in terms of the number of their occurrences per, let us say, 1,000 words. The items could be unfamiliar words, or words from specialised vocabularies/technical jargon. They could be sentences with a specified number of subordinate clauses/embeddings. High density is generally a measure of difficulty.

deprivation. Disadvantage, dispossession, deficiency, and disorder relating to language acquisition opportunities owing to interrelated factors of exploitation and suppression, low class/caste and economic status, and COGNITIVE deficiency.

deschooling. 'Deemphasising the influence of school-system in education' particularly classroom-based, teacher-fronted instruction. In this sense, the term derives from the Austria-born American educationist Ivan Illich (1926-2002) and his book *Deschooling Society.* Illich finds the traditional school-system oppressive [for children]. He advocates free and independent learning at home and in the community. *Cf.* 'COMPULSORY MISEDUCATION.'

descriptive assessment. Assessment of performance in a language test reported descriptively. Generally assessment of language performance is reported in the form of a letter grade or numerical score. In CRITERION-REFERENCED/communicative tests this might also be done in the form of a PROFILE or of BAND-scales, which essentially is an evaluative description of the levels of the test-taker's performance in different skills areas such as speaking and writing. The levels of performance in different skills areas may be labelled poor, satisfactory, good, etc. *See also* DESCRIPTORS AND PROFILE.

descriptive approach. An approach to language usage that believes in describing the language as it is used by its speakers, without making value judgements about any particular form or variety. As different from descriptive are normative approaches in which prescriptions are made about appropriate usage.

descriptors. Brief descriptions of test-taker performance at different levels of proficiency. They are typically used in communicative language tests, often in combination with a RATING GRID. Following is an example of a descriptor: <u>pronunciation</u> frequently unintelligible.

development. Progressive change in the lives of individuals leading to their growth.

In the context of teachers, development is a reconceptualization of teacher training TRAINING is considered to be an exercise in conditioning the trainees to deal with a limited set of problems according to the instructions or 'ready-made answers' given to them. 'Development' on the other hand is an open-ended process preparing the teacher-students to eventually take control of their career and professional growth. In contrast to the emphasis in 'training' on conforming to the expert-instructor and following her uncritically, 'development' stresses thinking, initiating, discovering, and innovating.

developmental interdependence hypothesis. The hypothesis that achievement of high levels of competence by learners in L2 depends on similar competence in L1. It has been noted that there is a high degree of transferability of skills across languages.

developmental errors. Language ERRORS occurring during a learner's normal process of language learning and development. 'Sitted' used as past tense of the verb – sit, is an example of a developmental error. Such errors do not result from interference or negative TRANSFER from a language already known but are natural to the process of acquisition, in which learners test the hypotheses they have developed about the grammar of the language. When the HYPOTHESIS formed happens to be incorrect, they go wrong, committing an error which may be an instance of developmental error. Such errors nevertheless are instances of learners' creative efforts. Development errors are passing phases in the ACQUISITION OF LANGUAGE.

developmental psychology. The branch of PSYCHOLOGY that studies the process, sequence, and mechanism of change during the life span of human beings esp. during their childhood.

developmental sequence. The sequence in which SL learners acquire specific grammatical structures such as negatives and interrogatives. Research shows that these features occur in the learners' INTERLANGUAGE in a given sequence unaffected by their L1. *See also* the MORPHEME STUDIES, and the NATURAL ORDER HYPOTHESIS.

devolution technique. Technique used for multiplier effect in teaching language to very large groups. A model lesson is given to a number of group leaders who in turn give the same lesson to smaller groups of learners.

diagnosis. In the context of language education. The process of identifying or the determination of the nature and cause(s) of such negative factors as learner weaknesses, learning deficiencies, learning disorders.

diagnostic assessment. *See* ASSESSMENT, and DIAGNOSTIC TESTS.

diagnostic tests. Language tests that aim at finding out what the examinees know and can do and what they do not know and cannot do. Diagnostic tests are used for judging the levels of achievement of the examinees so that they may be placed in appropriate groups/classes for instruction. Such tests are also given in order to decide whether further teaching and remediation are necessary in particular areas, and if so which and what kind of teaching and remediation are needed. The purpose of DIAGNOSIS could also be achieved by using PROFICIENCY TESTS or ACHIEVEMENT TESTS.

dialect. A VARIETY OF LANGUAGE associated with a group of people usually living in a particular geographical area. A dialect could also belong to the members of a particular SOCIAL CLASS. Usually, a language has many dialects distinguished according to such features as the variation in pronunciation, items of vocabulary and rules of grammar. 'Cockney' is a dialect of English as Awadhi is of Hindi.

The standard variety of a language is also one of its dialects.

dialogic teaching. An interactive model of teaching. Dialogic teaching

63

challenges and questions the traditional 'monologic,' or 'teacher-monopolised teaching' in the transfer-of-knowledge approach. *Cf.* BANKING CONCEPT OF EDUCATION.

dialogue. Literally, a verbal interchange between two or more people. But the term is also used in many extended senses. One of them is a particular mode of asking students questions, the mode Socrates used. Known as Socratic dialogue, it consists of a series of questions and answers. In this mode, each successive question is a little more fine-tuned, and takes students up on their answers just preceding. Socratic questions make students think hard, and critically constrain them to make their answers explicit.

In LT contexts, dialogue-centred pedagogy contrasts with the 'banking model' [the BANKING CONCEPT OF EDUCATION].

Current notions of dialogue see in it elements of 'voice'. [VOICE (2b)]. Dialogue involves a critical reflection of the givens, and is supposed to have the power to transform knowledge and reality.

dialogue journals. A written mode of interaction between an individual learner and the teacher on an instructional programme. The interaction is in the form of written conversation, which could take place through e-mail also. It is an ongoing dialogue usually extending over a term or semester. The learner writes regularly in a journal (register/diary/file) and the teacher responds. The learner's conversation is an uninhibited expression and evaluation of what and how she has learnt.

[Uninhibited in the sense that the learner feels free to voice her views, and also when doing so, she does not feel overly hindered by considerations of linguistic correctness.] The teacher in her turn writes positive comments avoiding criticism and correction. The benefit from this open but private and regular exchange of ideas is dual: the learner reflects on and monitors her learning and the teacher gets feedback and an opportunity to elucidate. Also, the learner gets individualised attention.

The conversations need not be long stretches but they should be revelatory. A better understanding of teaching, and of the learner and teacher by each other as well as better communication between them should flow from dialogue journal writing. *See also* JOURNAL WRITING.

diary. A written account of significant events happening in one's life and one's personal response to, and retrospection on them. A diary is usually maintained on a daily basis, and chronologically. It is personal, and private.

diary-keeping. The practice of writing a DIARY by teachers/by learners. The diary is used to record the user's private reflection – feelings, needs, problems, etc. – on the teaching done or received

The diary-content may be used as data in research on teaching. When so used, it is TRIANGULAED with CLASSROOM OBSERVATION and learner ASSESSMENT. *Cf.* JOURNAL WRITING.

diary studies. Research investigation into teaching based on DIARY records. A diary is a systematic record of significant events during one's teaching over a period of time. The purpose is to reflect on one's own teaching, self-review and draw conclusions about what works well and what does not, and observe the patterns of failure and success, their nature and causes. Along with recording the details such as the questions asked, the instruction pattern, the diarists also record honestly their feelings and experiences during the process of teaching. The diary might reveal surprises and discoveries – all of significance in teaching.

dictation. A traditional language-classroom activity in which the learners write down the sentences/passage read aloud/spoken by the teacher. Groups of words in a passage are read out two times distinctly and with short pauses between them (the word-groups).

Dictation is an INTEGRATIVE language exercise, which gives learners practice in applying simultaneously more than one skill – LISTENING, comprehending, phonological sensitivity, GUESSING and INFERENCING, writing (including SPELLING and punctuation).

Dictation can also be used as an IN-DIRECT TEST measure (like CLOZE TEST) in testing language proficiency. The scoring is usually done on an exact word, exact spelling basis, though many teachers do not attach much importance to accuracy of spelling. For them, the learners'/examinees' grasp of the overall STRUCTURE is more important.

The choice of the passage to be used for dictation is a principled one. It is carefully weighed for its LEVEL, content, nature and other aspects of suitability.

Dictation need not lead to a (written) transcription. In an oral form of dictation the learner/testee repeats the spoken word, phrase or sentence.

dictionary. A reference tool. It contains words (and phrases) arranged alphabetically, and followed by explanations of their meanings. Additional information relating to grammar, pronunciation, and etymology may also be given.

Dictionaries are of many types. Some of these are: MONOLINGUAL, bilingual, trilingual, pronouncing, REVERSE, etymological. There may also be subject specific dictionaries. LEARNER'S DICTIONARIES, designed specially for the learners of a language as a SL, have a PEDAGOGICAL orientation. They include information likely to be useful for learners. Many present-day dictionaries are CORPUS-based.

dicto-comp. An INTEGRATIVE language learning task that combines LISTENING comprehension with the task of re-constructing the TEXT in written form. Learners listen to a short, dense text. When doing so, they take down brief notes and then try to develop the notes to reconstruct the passage listened to into a coherent and linguistically correct text. Then they compare their texts with the original one. The process stimulates into action such cognitive skills as noticing nodes of meaning, thinking, judging and taking down notes. The task is integrative in nature because it involves listening, interpreting, and negotiating meaning to give it a faithful and coherent expression in writing.

dictogloss. *See* DICTO-COMP.

didactic functions. Functions and forms typically used by teachers during classroom instruction. Keeping order and discipline is a well-known one, so is asking questions. These have their linguistic correlates which have been studied under TEACHER TALK. *See also* TEACHER QUESTIONS.

difference hypothesis. A version of DEFICIT HYPOTHESIS: theory of educational failure. It claims that educational failure is partly caused by the fact that pupils speak a dialect and not the STANDARD VARIETY of the language. The hypothesis does not have many subscribers. *See also* STEREOTYPE HYPOTHESIS.

differentiation. Treating learners according to their individual needs. In INSTRUCTION, differentiation implies taking into account learners' LEVEL of proficiency and other variables. *See* STREAMING.

difficulty. A measure of whether the majority of learners/the target group can do a task correctly within reasonable time. The task may relate to LISTENING, READING, SPEAKING, WRITING, or be metalinguistic in nature [*See also* METALANGUAGE.] The task may be a classroom activity, it may occur in textual materials, or in a test.

difficulty level. A measure of how easy or difficult a task is. For example, the DIFFICULTY level of a TEXT for reading can be ascertained by judging the following: **1.** (a) the RANGE of VOCABULARY used. The vocabulary is matched against an appropriate WORD LIST; and (b) the FREQUENCY and DENSITY of new words outside the list. According to one estimate, more than 25 new words [words not known to the reader] per thousand running words makes a text difficult. Another measure of the difficulty of a text worked out on the basis of the words used in it is known as LEXICAL DENSITY. *See also* TYPE-TOKEN RATIO **2.** the complexity of the SENTENCE STRUCTURES used – length, number of phrases and embedded clauses. **3.** (a) the number and nature of allusions, figures of speech, and unfamiliar/foreign expressions. (b) phrasal verbs and idioms. **4.** the CONTENT matter – the GENRE, field and TENOR of discourse, and its conceptual and cultural content.

Difficulty is judged in relation to the learner(s)' perceived levels of COMPETENCE (1) in language skills. Competence levels are usually estimated on the basis of test scores.

diglossia. The phenomenon of there co-existing in a speech community two varieties of a language, each with its specific roles/functions/domains. Sociolinguists term them High (H) and Low (L). Broadly, H is the standard, formal variety and L is used in everyday conversation in family, with friends and in other informal contexts. Usually the members of the community exercise choice of the variety according to the specific purpose of use.

diglot-weave method. *See* MIXED-CODE READING METHOD and SANDWICH STORY METHOD.

diphthongs. Vocal glides within the same SYLLABLE. In the articulation of a diphthong, the tongue glides from the position of one VOWEL and in the direction of another, as in 'fine.'

directed-response items. Test ITEMS

that restrict the choice of responses. An example is an item that has blanks to be filled in. In such items, the choice of the correct response is restricted by grammatical, contextual and semantic(meaning) constraints.

direct method. An approach to SL teaching in which only the TL is used for its instruction, and a direct association between form and meaning is sought to be created.

Inspired by NATURALISTIC LANGUAGE LEARNING principles, the direct method evolved in Europe during the concluding decades of the 19th century as a reaction to the GRAMMAR-TRANSLATION METHOD. The new method was hailed as reform in teaching languages.[*See* the Reform movement.] In it, instead of approaching a language through practice in translation and a study of the rules of grammar, a direct bond is sought to be established between a concept/ meaning and its representation in the TL. Some of the techniques used by the teachers are: intensive oral interaction in the TL, using the TL for questions and answers and all other activities in the classroom. Training in good pronunciation and CONVERSATION occupies a central place. The vocabulary to be taught is restricted to those that occur in everyday conversation. Use of the learners' MT is to be totally avoided (although some non-native teachers have found it difficult to do so).

direct tests. Language tests that base their judgement of the test-takers' abilities on their actual performance in the language. It may be mentioned here that in many formats of language testing, such as multiple-choice tests, judgements are based on indirect sources of information.

In the direct tests, the test-takers are made to speak/write as people would do in real life situations. Also know as face-to-face tests, direct tests are INTEGRATIVE in nature and are considered to be AUTHENTIC LANGUAGE TESTS.

disadvantage. *See* DEPRIVATION, and TEACHING LANGUAGE TO THE DISADVANTAGED.

disciplinary knowledge. *See* SUBJECT KNOWLEDGE.

discourse. 1. Language in *use* in speech and writing. Discourse implies a stretch of coherent/connected speech or writing usually longer than a clause or sentence. The constituent units of discourse are formally and meaningfully related which makes it COHEREN(CE)t. A discourse is coherent not only internally. It should be coherent externally also, i.e., it should relate to the contexts of the addresser and the addressee and their communicative purpose. 2. One of the several other related meanings: 'the special way of using language' within an institutionalised framework. Such use has its distinct features – conventions, content, theme, structure, etc. For example, the language characteristic of lawyers in the professional contexts may be called 'legal discourse.' It has its linguistic properties – lexical and structural. One can even talk of gender-marked discourse, such as 'male discourse.' Domain-specific discourse functions with its own conventions for describing, interpreting and evaluating it.

The meaning of the term 'discourse' is often sensitive to the theoretical context it is used in.

discourse analysis. Analysing the way sentences are linked to each other in a DISCOURSE to produce COHERENT stretches of language. As different from the tradition of analysing discourse in 'linguistic' terms with focus on the formal structural properties & on coherence and cohesion devices, is the recent trend to 'critically' study it against its sociological background. *See* APPLIED DISCOURSE ANALYSIS and CRITICAL DISCOURSE ANALYSIS.

discourse competence. The ability to produce coherent DISCOURSE (1). This ability, regarded as an essential component of COMMUNICATIVE COMPETENCE, is of great importance in SL learning and teaching. It has been noted with concern that many SL learners fail to go beyond sentence-level competence. Language-STRUCTURE-based teaching and DISCRETE-POINT TESTING may partly be responsible for this.

discourse management. Monitoring language (simplifying language and message complexity) addressed to a less proficient user. This is done to ensure comprehension and avoid possible hindrances to COMMUNICATION. *See also* DISCOURSE REPAIR.

discourse repair. Handling communication breakdown by using such devices [in speech] as rephrasing, restating, breaking a multi-embedded sentence into more than one, or just asking the INTERLOCUTOR to clarify.

discovery. The process and the product of cognitively active learning: of learners noticing inductively [and independently] and coming to perceive a rule about language and language

use. DISCOVERY APPROACHES to learning contrast with DEDUCTIVE approaches, and are considered to be better learning procedures.

DISCOVERY APPROACHES. *See* HEURISTIC APPROACHES.

discrete-point testing. Language testing procedure in which competence is sought to be tested through a series of 'paper-and-pencil' type of test-items each focusing on a particular component of the competence being tested.

In the psychometric tradition of language testing (to which this procedure belongs), a series of test items (relating to one skill area) constitute a test or a section of it. Each item is developed and selected through a process of rigorous analysis. A merit of such testing is the RELIABILITY of scoring that it ensures and its suitability to machine-scoring. However, as discrete-point tests are RECOGNITION TESTS and do not entail language production/use, their VALIDITY is questionable.

discrimination. Perception/judgement of differences relating to individual abilities. In language-education-related DISCOURSE (2), the term is used in several contexts: In LANGUAGE TESTING, one of the features of a good test is its discriminability, i.e., its capacity to differentiate among candidates possessing different levels of proficiency.

One of the components in the teaching of pronunciation deals with EAR-TRAINING to give learners PRACTICE in discriminating between sounds and between patterns of intonation. *See* SOUND DISCRIMINATION TEST. In the STIMULUS-RESPONSE THEORY, discrimination is learning to distinguish between different kinds of stimuli.

disorders of language. *See* LEARNING DISABILITIES.

display questions. 'Known-answer' questions. Questions asked by SL teachers to elicit correct language forms – questions that ask learners to display their linguistic knowledge, or are aimed at testing such knowledge. 'Known-answer' questions have no INFORMATION GAP.

Lacking in AUTHENTICITY, display questions do not exist outside classrooms. On the contrary, information-gap questions have an element of cognitive challenge, are OPEN-ENDED and engage learners in communicating meaning. *See also* TEACHER QUESTIONS.

disponibilite'. The criterion of AVAILABILITY applied in selecting vocabulary for pedagogical purposes, **Example**, in the preparation of word lists. *Disponibilite'* is a French expression. Words more likely to occur in a given context are more *disponible*. In the context of 'house,' the words *door* and *window* are more *disponible*.

distance education. The OPEN LEARNING SYSTEM of education. *See* DISTANCE LEARNING. With the emergence of new modes of instruction-delivery aided by electronic tools, distance education has become a generic term for the various non face-to-face modes of instruction and learning.

distance learning. A mode of learning in an institutional framework, which is largely SELF-(MANAGED) LEARNING. It is different from the conventional face-to-face mode of learning in that the learners mostly learn on their own, often with the help of print materials supplied to them. Media support (**Example**, radio and TV programmes) may also be made available. Distance education courses provide for periodic CONTACT SESSIONS for learners to meet their tutors and sort out their learning problems. Usually, distance learners are adults.

distractor. An incorrect response in a set composed of the key or the correct answer and some incorrect ones known as distractors. Multiple-choice (language) test items typically use distractors. Distractors are carefully framed and chosen to minimise the chance of candidates' guessing the correct answer.

distributed learning. Learning through online courses whether on campus or off campus. Learners may take advantage of these courses as supplementary input. Some universities in the West such as Harvard have made their course materials available online. Anyone can use them without having to pay. Distributed learning has all the advantages of DISTANCE LEARNING, and may be treated as an improved variant of it.

Dogme teaching. A movement in ELT in reaction to the traditional, mainstream SLT and its emphases. Dogme-style teaching is an adaptive one, progressing and developing as learner-teacher interaction in the classroom proceeds. There is little barrier between learner and teacher and individual differences are respected. Set course-books are dispensed with though a dictionary and a book of grammar are indispensable.

According to the IATEFL Global

issues SIG News, November 2003, Dogme teaching was developed at International House, Barcelona on the analogy of a 1995 film 'Dogme 95' by Danish film-makers – a group who want 'to rid cinema of an obsessive concern for technique...' and 'superficiality and trickery of mainstream film-making'.

It has been pointed out that the Dogme mode is a bit too unconventional, and suited only to a minority of teachers, esp. the native-speaking ones.

domain-referenced tests. Tests that evaluate the test takers' language ability and performance in a particular field of discourse or profession. Such tests are essentially CRITERION-REFERENCED tests as the criteria of performance are domain-specific. Test results indicate whether the test takers can perform satisfactorily using the TL in a professional domain, **Example**, information technology, medicine, aviation.

double-translation. A pedagogical device used esp. in teaching classical languages. In it a learner translates a TL text into her MT and then translates this back into the TL. It was practised in England in the sixteenth and the later centuries to teach Latin and Greek. Many teachers in modern times have used it in teaching a modern language. Commenting on the practice of 'double-translation', Howatt (1984: 34) says, 'The particular advantage of "double-translation", in the hands of a skilful teacher, is that it gives equal status to both the foreign language text and the equivalent text in the mother tongue. The method is intended to make the learner equally conscious of the structure and resources of his own language. Content is held constant while the resources of both languages are manipulated to express, as far as possible, a common array of meanings'.

drama techniques in language teaching. *See* DRAMATIC METHOD

dramatic method. Approach to SLT that uses drama techniques. The popular ones are play-acting, mimicking, ROLE-PLAY and SIMULATION. In the post-1975 era, writers on the subject have defined drama techniques more specifically. **Example**, Maley & duff (1978, 1982:6) underscore in drama techniques imaginative acts of self-expression. For them 'putting on plays in front of passive audience' are not real drama activities because words in them are 'mechanically memorised'. *See also* Simulation.

In the terminology of the past, drama techniques included classroom play-acting, action & speech, dialogues, and use of gestures and mime by teachers. [Gurrey: 1955:50–61.] Performance of plays by pupils in schools is often called 'Dramatic work'. Such activities are included in classroom work to introduce oral work, bring in a semblance of the authentic, giving learners opportunity to apply their minds to access meaning through the context, and of course to create interest. 'Dramatic method,' however, is not a method in the sense of a set of structured procedures.

dramatisation. *See* DRAMATIC METHOD.

drill. A technique in LT. *See* PATTERN DRILL. A drill-based exercise in the target items of learning does not usually involve practice in meaningful contexts: there is no PROBLEM SOLVING involved. Nor is drill-work pleasurable except perhaps for young learners.

Drills are mostly oral but they can also be written. *See also* SUBSTITUTION DRILLS.

dual medium education. Curriculum that uses two languages concurrently as medium of education. *See also* BILINGUAL EDUCATION. The Central Schools Organization in India provides for the use of two languages: English for teaching science and maths, and Hindi for social-cultural subjects like history. The Canadian immersion education is similar to this.

It has been claimed that dual medium education brings cognitive gains to learners and facilitates concept formation. It also improves their linguistic ACCURACY and FLUENCY in the two languages.

dual language education. *See* BILINGUAL EDUCATION.

dual immersion. Foreign language education programmes in which two groups of learners each learn a second language: the other group's MT. Usually 'immersion' is one-way learning: French-speaking learners learning English or the other way round. In double immersion programmes, speakers of Spanish learn English, and English-speakers Spanish, as is done in some schools in southern USA. In this approach, two groups of learners learn each other's language as a FL. *See* IMMERSION EDUCATION.

dysgraphia. Problem in writing. It may arise from brain injury or illness, and may range from poor handwriting to difficulty in expressing thought in writing. Dysgraphic problems, or written language difficulties, are considered to be related to problems of processing: auditory, perceptual, visuals.

dyslexia. A learning disorder (also known as alexia or word blindness). Dyslexics face problems in reading. This developmental problem is supposed to be caused by abnormalities in those parts of the brain that participate in language-related functions. There are several types of dyslexia. One of the problems dyslexic children face is the inability to see the letters of a word in the sequence they are written/printed.

dysphasia. A variant of aphasia. *See* APHASIA.

ear training. A drill in listening and perceiving correctly [SL] sounds and speech. This is generally done through DICTATION-practice and listening to recorded speech, dialogues, tapes and broadcasts. Teachers in the classroom may produce utterances, often with contrasted features, for learners to recognise and discriminate PHONEMES, ACCENT(1)s, tones and other segmental and SUPRASEGMENTAL features. To sharpen learners' phonetic sensitivity, exotic or 'nonsense' sounds may be used deliberately. *See also* SOUND DISCRIMINATION TEST.

easification. Making a complex text easy to understand. This may be done by breaking a long sentence with many embedded clauses into simple sentences; or by using a descriptive phrase in place of a difficult word; or by adding an amplificatory phrase/clause in juxtaposition to a difficult expression. A text can be made easy to understand with the help of a diagram or a flowchart representing its content as accurately as possible.

Learners can easify for themselves learning tasks by resorting to MNEMONIC DEVICES, associative devices, TRANSLITERATION, coding, and so on.

eclectic. (Approach, practice, etc.) that does not follow any one system or METHOD but judiciously chooses from different systems what is considered to be best, practical, or useful. *See also* ECLECTICISM.

eclecticism. The principle of choosing, according to one's need, elements from different APPROACHES/schools of thought and practising them as parts of one congruent METHOD. H. Palmer (1921) called it 'the multiple line of approach...'

ECLECTIC-ism avoids the dogmatism of the labelled methods of language teaching. A teacher's eclectic practice may draw from her knowledge and experience, and her perception of what good teaching should be.

ecological perspective on language education. The view that the approach to understanding the complexities of the language classroom should not be through the prescriptions of the experts and the generalizations of the theorists but through a study of the specificities and of the 'reality of teaching as it is lived out in classrooms' (Tudor: 2001:2). Tudor (*ibid*) asserts that the 'perspective offers an alternative to a positivistic and hierarchically based approach to the conceptualisation and planning of teaching programmes'.

education. The process of imparting and acquiring knowledge. Education is also the outcome of these processes as indicated in the utterance ' She has received good education'.

For most thinkers, the aim of education is bringing out the potential of the individual, an idea close to the etymological meaning of the word.

Education can also be acquired through self-study and from one's analysis and reflection on one's experience. Here the scope of education gets extended from knowledge, which is generally stressed in formal education, to understanding. *See also* FORMAL

INSTRUCTION, and TEACHER EDUCATION.

educational culture. Community-specific practices, beliefs, and expectations relating to formal EDUCATION. For example, in the oriental contexts, learning practices of MEMORIZATION, LEARNER BELIEF that knowing FORMAL GRAMMAR-rules ensures proficiency in language use; learner expectation that their language errors should be pointed out to them, cultural norms of learner modesty (subservience, etc.)and of teacher behaviour and the assumption that the teacher is above questioning, are all parts of the educational culture of the East – the *guru-shishya* tradition. Many of these are being questioned though.

educational linguistics. Study of language relevant to formal and informal EDUCATION at all levels. A term modelled on 'EDUCATIONAL PSYCHOLOGY' and 'educational sociology,' educational linguistics deals with those areas where language and education intersect. Thus educational linguistics would include languages in education – first, second and foreign: approaches to teaching, learning, and language use; language policies and programmes; BILINGUALISM, MULTILINGUALISM; LITERACY, inequity, marginalization, etc. The list is open-ended and expanding. The inter-disciplinary area of educational linguistics has arisen in response to the growing interest in the role of language in education.

educational psychology. The branch of PSYCHOLOGY that studies it in relation to teaching and learning particularly of young learners. Educational psychology is an essential component of teacher education programmes as it tells them about learner psychology and the problems of CLASSROOM MANAGEMENT and how to get over them. A knowledge of educational psychology can help teachers understand the processes of learning and teaching.

educational setting. The formal, classroom context of learning. Mostly, people learn SLs in educational settings. The INSTRUCTED LEARNING of this context contrasts with the learning in NATURAL SETTINGS. *See also* NATURALISTIC LEARNING.

educational technology. Mechanical Systems such as language laboratories used as support in education/language teaching. During 1960s and 1970s, there was a great enthusiasm for using technology, esp. in connection with PROGRAMMED LEARNING. These days computer-based technologies are being widely used in (language) teaching. *See* COMPUTER-ASSISTED LANGUAGE LEARNING.

'efferent' reading. Reading for information. It is contrasted with 'aesthetic reading,' – 'efferent' from the Latin meaning to 'carry away." S McKay(1982) has cited Rosenblatt (1978), who has drawn the distinction

efficient reading. *See* FAST READING.

elaborated code. Expression used by the British sociologist Bernstein (1971), in relation to MT learning & use, to refer to a variety of language use (by educated classes in Britain) marked by accurate grammar, regular syntax, some abstraction and complexity as when discussing a problem in a formal context. He distinguishes 'elaborated code' from RESTRICTED/

public code used by the masses. Bern-stein's claim in 1971–1973 that there was a systematic relationship between SOCIAL CLASS and language use has not been found tenable.

elicitation. Drawing oral/written responses from learners. Elicitation is one of the classroom techniques for helping learners to produce a target response, and thus help them learn it. There are various techniques for eliciting.

elliptical exercises. Language practice tasks of 'fill-in-the-blanks' or of SUPPLY-TYPE ITEMS. Such exercises have a variety of format. Exercises with ellipses that occur in continuous stretches of language longer than a sentence are considered to be pedagogically better than those that occur in isolated sentences though the latter kind may be more efficacious in focusing the learners' attention on a particular item for learning. [*cf.* Cloze test.] Elliptical items are also used in language testing.

elocution. The art of speaking in public. Some features of elocution are correct pronunciation/articulation, RHETORICal delivery expressive of feelings and emotions. The latter requires appropriate modulation of voice and use of gestures (hands, eyebrows, etc.). *See also* DECLAMATION, ORATORY and Recitation.

emotion. A strong, subjectively experienced or behaviourally displayed, feeling. Examples of emotional feelings are love, hate, anger, fear, terror. Emotions and AFFECTIVE FACTORS are interrelated. Feelings of emotion contrast with reason, COGNITION, knowledge. Emotion, esp. the negative ones, often finds vent

through the adjectives one uses.

emotional intelligence (also, emotional literacy). EMOTIONal and social skills: ability to maintain a positive attitude, to empathise, and to control anger, aggression, interpersonal conflicts, etc. The emotionally intelligent have an awareness of their own feelings and those of the others. It has been observed that much educational process has dwelt on learners' cognitive development to the neglect of the emotional aspects of their PERSONALITY causing a kind of 'emotional illiteracy.' In current approaches to language education, co-operative and collaborative techniques are being increasingly preferred. [*See* COLLABORATIVE LEARNING and CO-OPERATIVE LEARNING.] Emotional intelligence is considered to contribute to academic success.

empiricism. The theory that asserts that experience and observation are the source of all knowledge. Empiricists do not attach significance to such things as mental processes, that cannot be observed directly. Empirical methods of study rely on scientific methods of investigation, experimentation, and evidence.

The linguist Leonard Bloomfield (1887–1949) was an exponent of empiricism in linguistic study, and considered language as basically behaviour governed by the STIMULUS-RESPONSE principle, and something external to the mind. N. Chomsky rejected this premise and asserted that language is intrinsic to the mind, an innate faculty.

empowerment. Giving somebody freedom and authority to do something. Generally, all education is empowering: it imparts learners knowledge and skill and this is a well-established way of empowering. In other contexts, teacher empowerment means, among other things, giving power to the teacher to decide what will be taught, and how. Similarly, learner empowerment could, for example, mean allowing learners to have a say in how their performance will be evaluated.

enculturation. *See* ACCULTURATION and SOCIALISATION.

engaged pedagogy. Pedagogy with ideological commitment. *See also* CRITICAL PEDAGOGY.

ENGLISH FOR ACADEMIC PURPOSES. *See* LANGUAGE FOR ACADEMIC PURPOSES.

ENGLISH FOR GENERAL PURPOSES. *See* GENERAL PURPOSES LANGUAGE COURSES.

ENGLISH FOR SPECIFIC PURPOSES (ESP). Specific learner-NEEDS oriented curriculum in English. *See also* LANGUAGE FOR SPECIFIC PURPOSES. ESP or LSP being relevant to the restricted needs and limited time of particular groups of learners, emerged during 1970s as an alternative to the comprehensive, general purpose teaching of SLs/English. *See also* BUSINESS LANGUAGE.

English Language Teaching (ELT). A body of pragmatic approaches to the teaching of English as a S/F L. The approaches were initially developed by British teachers teaching the language in the former British 'colonies.' They gave currency to the term, which carries a contrast to the teaching of English as literature, or as MT. The approaches, influenced by the DIRECT METHOD, have basically been ORAL-SITUATIONAL During the post-1950 era, ELT adopted STRUCTURAL APPROACHES

as a result of the Mid-twentieth century developments. ELT has been constantly evolving and accommodating in it new insights in SL pedagogy. Currently, a preferred expression for ELT is ESOL (English to speakers of other languages). Parallel to it there developed in North America more or less a similar pedagogic APPROACH(1), termed teaching of English to speakers of other languages (TESOL), and in that parlance ESL is the most frequently used referent for English [second] language pedagogy.

enrichment. Developing enabling skills among learners rather than using the pedagogy of telling and the TRANSMISSION APPROACH. In the enrichment pedagogy, care is taken to create an ACQUISITION-RICH(classroom) ENVIRONMENT and make available to the learners plenty of language experience. Recognising the learners' role as major contributors to their own learning, teachers build the SL learners' competence on the knowledge and experience they already possess. An important resource learners bring with them is their cognitive ability and the knowledge of their MT. This knowledge is not considered a negative factor interfering in SL learning but an enrichment-resource

Principles encouraged in enrichment classes include LEARNER-CENTEREDNESS, enriching learner background; INDIVIDUALISED INSTRUCTION; CO-OPERATIVE LEARNING, REFLECTIVE LEARNING, DISCOVERY LEARNING, interactive learning and PROBLEM SOLVING. Need for any remediation is pre-empted by making available rich input through multiple sources – reading, participation in interactive tasks, educational video, media-support and such other things. The media is used as a resource for learning. **2.** 'Enrichment' has also been used in a general sense of enriching the form and structure-based input with an AWARENESS of how these are used in various cultural contexts, with illustrations from literary texts.

enrichment programme. An educational programme aimed at enriching the environment of learners from the disadvantaged sections of the society.

entrance tests. Tests designed and given to select candidates (eligible in other respects) for entrance to courses of study, generally professional courses. Such tests may also be used to recruit candidates to jobs or to permit them to enter professions. Being CRITERION-REFERENCED, entrance tests are (or, should be) designed to judge the candidates' potential for performing well on the programmes/jobs they would be inducted into. Entrance tests are also known as selection or GATE-KEEPING tests.

entry/entrance behaviour. [also, Initial behaviour] The ability, knowledge or proficiency in an area that a learner already possesses when she enters an instructional programme. Entry behaviour may be measured through a test. Such a MEASUREMENT helps i) the teacher/instructor to decide the level at which to pitch the programme and the instructional methodology to be adopted; ii) the writers of teaching materials to prepare books and other instructional materials at appropriate levels of difficulty; and iii) to identify

learner needs, and the goals of the programme. For evaluation, learning outcomes may be matched against the entry behaviour. *Cf.* EXIT BEHAVIOUR.

episodic knowledge/memory. Knowledge or memory of personally *significant*, autobiographical, and emotionally-charged events and things. They are related to specific time and place. If personal-experience-related events and things are likely to be remembered for long, episodic knowledge has implications for learning and teaching. *Cf.* CRITICAL INCIDENT, and SEMANTIC KNOWLEDGE.

EQUAL-APPEARING INTERVALS METHOD. *See* THURSTON-TYPE SCALES.

equilibrium. Balance between a learner's existing knowledge and the new experience. The balance results from a creative process [in learning] of mutually adjusting what the learner already knows and what she is encountering. New experiences and knowledge modify the mental SCHEMATA and in turn get modified. The conceptualisation of such a process of cognitive development contrasts with the older notion of learning moving along a simple arithmetic process of addition. Knowledge received from teachers and books were additions to the learners' quantum of knowledge and their[the learners'] role was simply that of recipients. The notion of 'equilibrium' forms part of Piaget's DEVELOPMENTAL PSYCHOLOGY and the larger cognitivist, CONSTRUCTIVIST views of learning.

equity. Fairness and equal treatment to everyone: not letting one section or group have unfair advantage of such things as educational opportunities. In the context of Education, one of the pre-occupations has been with *quality*. Another with *numbers*. Equally important is the concern for social justice, for providing equal opportunity to all, and doing away with the gulf between the privileged and the underprivileged.

error. *See* LANGUAGE ERROR.

error analysis. A systematic study of errors committed by learners in their use of a SL. It is carried out in several steps. First the CORPUS is selected from which the data are drawn. They could be drawn from written or spoken samples. This step is followed by the identification of errors, which are then classified and described. Explanation of the errors in terms of their likely causes/sources follows. Frequencies are worked out, which may be followed by suggestions for remediation. It is to be noted that not all errors can be explained satisfactorily.

Error analyses and their findings have uses in language pedagogy and its planning. Language errors being products of psycholinguistic processes, their study can help in understanding LANGUAGE ACQUISITION.

error correction. *See* CORRECTION, and FEEDBACK (1a).

error gravity. The seriousness or severity of a LANGUAGE ERROR. An error may be LOCAL (**Example**, concerning the use of a less important word in a sentence) or GLOBAL causing miscomprehension of a serious nature. The gravity of an error may not relate only to INTELLIGIBILITY. It may also concern ACCEPTABILITY. Experienced teachers know that some errors disappear in course of time while some others tend to fossilize. ERROR TREATMENT in instructional programmes needs to be prioritized according to such considerations as the gravity and the time available.

error treatment. Dealing with LANGUAGE ERRORS made by [SL] learners: providing them FEEDBACK. Teachers have generally had a condemnatory attitude to learner errors. The BEHAVIOURIST LEARNING THEORY believed in forestalling the occurrence of language errors. The model of language teaching following the theory took great care to prevent learner exposure to language errors. Attitudes have now become more tolerant in the light of new research in [SL] learning. Tolerant, because errors are considered to be inevitable in the process of language learning. And most of them are transient, features of TRANSITIONAL COMPETENCE. Not all errors need EXPLICIT correction. With more input and exposure to the language, learners shed many of them. Those that persist and are recurrent need corrective intervention. An exhaustive correction of *all* the mistakes major and minor being counter-productive, teachers are advised to be selective, to focus on the serious ones. From this point, it may be useful to distinguish between types and classes of mistakes. Grammatical errors, for example, as different from the infelicities of STYLE and IDIOM. Errors of CONTENT are secondary to language errors.

It is not considered advisable to interrupt learners for correction when they are focused on meaning as when speaking. The teacher may note the errors of pronunciation etc. and discuss them in the class later.

ESPERANTO. *See* ARTIFICIAL LANGUAGE.

essay. A long COMPOSITION in prose on a given topic, in which the writer expresses her thoughts, feelings, experiences, and views relevant to the subject, following such principles of good writing as COHERENCE, clarity, UNITY, and CONSISTENCY and a well-structured framework for the PRESENTATION of the subject matter.

Essay writing, in addition to being a course requirement, also forms part of sit-in exams. On language courses, essays may have to be written as test of WRITING skill.

essay exams. EXAMINATIONS in which the examinees have to write full answers. The exam. requires them to have some skill in ACADEMIC WRITING. Essay exams contrast with DISCRETE-POINT TESTING and SUPPLY-TYPE ITEMS. *See* ESSAY TESTS.

essay tests/essay-type items. Language tests or language test items that require the examinees to produce the answers in writing. Contrasted with the so called OBJECTIVE type items, essay-type items (also known as free response items) suit the testing of the examinees' language production ability. For a time essay type questions went out of fashion as it was said that the SUBJECTIVE scoring that went with them led to a lack of reliability in evaluation. And it is axiomatic in language testing that what is not reliable cannot be valid. However, evaluation of communicative cometence necessitates that the examinees 'produce' language as one does in real communication (written or spoken). COMMUNICATIVE LANGUAGE TESTING has since developed procedures to ensure reliability.

establishment. Another expression for the process of CONSOLIDAT(ION)ing through PRACTICE what has been presented/taught. It refers to the process of making the teacher's teaching part of the learners' long-term memory. This process is [sought to be] achieved by engaging learners in using/practising/repeating in context the item(s) taught.

esteem. High regard, respect. *See* SELF-ESTEEM

ethical. That which is deemed to be proper and right. Consideration of norms of ethicality are both internal to an individual and socially determined. *See also* ETHICALITY.

ethicality. Fairness in decision-making in matters related to language education. Ethicality expects decisions to be equitable. Some of the domains where EQUITY is expected are in choosing TEXTBOOKS/textual CONTENT for prescription. Similarly, in choosing the content of the tests, **Example**, of a passage used in a test of reading comprehension. IDEOLOGY, cultural presuppositions, and belief systems imbue all texts. These may prejudicially influence the readers' views, cultural norms and VALUES and develop in them ANOMIE. Since language tests often play a decisive role in such vital matters as selections for jobs and admissions to courses of study, it is only proper that the selection of their content, their administration and evaluation procedures be fair.

ethics. Philosophy or set of rules that

distinguish between what is deemed to be 'good' or acceptable and what is deemed to be unacceptable in human behaviour. What is acceptable or unacceptable is judged by the community consensually. Human behaviour in the context of this book includes teaching and professional conduct, and community includes the professional COMMUNITY.

ethnocentrism. Feeling that the ethnic group one belongs to is unique and different from other groups. There are two mutually contrasting ATTITUDES that SL learners may have towards the TL-community vis-à-vis their own COMMUNITY/ethnic group. They may feel that by mastering a SL they may lose their cultural identity. Such learners have a high estimate of their own language and CULTURE, and consider the SL/TL culture a threat to it. On the contrary, some learners may have a positive attitude towards the target community and be motivated to interact and integrate with that community. It has been asserted that such learners acquire a SL comparatively easily. Learners who have a high sense of in-group loyalty, i.e. ethnocentrism, may face difficulties in learning.

ethnographic approaches to the study of CLASSROOM INTERACTION. Approaches that view the CLASSROOM as a community with its own NORMS of behaviour. To study the interaction in the classroom and its discourse, the approaches apply ethnographic techniques. Some of the basics of these are that the class is treated as a social and cultural setting. The study consists of an observation of the activities, in-teraction and behaviour patterns of the members of the community. The observer is also a participant in the classroom community, and a significant part of the data for study consists of what the members themselves feel and think. It is claimed that an ethnographic study of the language classroom can give a better understanding of the classroom dynamics. *See also* CLASSROOM-CENTRED RESEARCH.

ethnography. *In situ* study and description of the life and CULTURE of a SOCIETY or ethnic group. The procedures used in the study include detailed observation, INTERVIEWS [3], and QUESTIONNAIRE. Observation may include participant observation, non-participant observation, diaries and journals. These sources of information provide multiple perspectives on the phenomenon being studied, such as the use of languages in a multilingual society.

evaluation. A systematic collection of information about the performance of an individual, a group of individuals, or of a teaching-course or any other programme to judge its merits and weaknesses in order to take decisions for further action. Evaluation may use multiple sources of data – CASE STUDY, INTERVIEW, OBSERVATION, QUESTIONNAIRE and test results. Evaluation procedures could be applied to the appraisal of language tests, classroom teaching, and TEACHING MATERIALS. Evaluation goes beyond testing, which is concerned only with judgement of the test-takers' ability. *See also* ASSESSMENT.

evaluation of teaching materials. Judging the quality and value, and the suitability of materials to their objectives and for their users. There are systematic procedures for carrying out the EVALUATION. These procedures could be applied before the materials are finally readied for use, while they are being used or when they have been used by learners. At the pre-use stage, the materials are trialled on an experimental group. Shortcomings may surface at this stage. What is observed in the during-use-in-actual-classrooms evaluation is what learners actually do with the materials – how they use them. At the post-use stage, a cautious attempt is made to see possible relationships between learning outcomes and the materials used. Of course there are other variables that influence learning outcomes. Yet a move towards some objectivity in evaluation is preferable to impressionistic judgements.

evaluative categories. The constituent areas of language performance that a test evaluates. **Example**, in testing the writing ability of a candidate, the following evaluative categories, among others, may be used: grammatical correctness; IDIOMATICITY and STYLE; and DISCOURSE organisation

examination. A formal, ASSESSMENT procedure in the educational context. It is usually conducted at the end of a course of study or a part of it, annually or half-yearly. Being ACHIEVEMENT TESTS, exams. are based on prescribed courses of study. Exam results lead to the award of degrees and certificates recognised for employment and other GATEKEEPING (access control) purposes.

examination-oriented teaching.

Teaching of language done with the primary goal of making the learners get through the EXAMINATION(s) or score high marks. In such teaching, developing the learners' competence is subordinated to teaching them techniques of scoring marks. Some features that mark such teaching are a selective teaching of topics likely to figure in the exam. and memorisation of ready-made answers. In the process, critical skills of solving problems, of thinking, analysing, seeing relationships, contradictions, etc. and of evaluating get neglected.

exchange. 1. Units of communicative INTERACTION between INTERLOCUTORS. An exchange is a unit of spoken language interchange consisting of at least an utterance [**Example**, a question] and the answer to it. The question and the answer may be accompanied with the speaker's remarks, observations and comments. **2.** One of the 'ranks' in the [L1] classroom discourse i.e., teacher-pupil talk in the classroom. Sinclair and Coulthard (1975) developed a model of describing classroom interaction, based on Halliday's (1961) rank scale approach. It postulates a hierarchy of 5 ranks: lesson, transaction, exchange, move, act, in the same order. A teaching exchange typically has the IRF structure. *See also* IRF CYCLE.

exchange journals. DIALOGUE JOURNALS written by PEERS. *See* PEER JOURNAL WORK. The difference between the two is that an exchange journal is a written medium of exchange between peers, i.e., two students, not between teacher and student. In the exchange, the partners may be in different SL classes [maybe, located at different places] or in the same class/school. The writings for exchange are usually on an assigned topic. One of the gains, besides the pedagogical, of such an exchange is the understanding and appreciation of the other's views and way of looking at things that should develop during the course of the exchanges. Arranged e-mailing is becoming a popular medium for the exchanges.

exit behaviour. The ability, knowledge or proficiency in an area that a learner has gained [purportedly] as a result of a course of study/instruction undertaken. Exit behaviour is judged on the basis of the result of an exit test. Typically, exit behaviour is compared with the ENTRY BEHAVIOUR to assess the gains made by the learner as also to judge the efficacy of instruction/the course given. *See also* TERMINAL BEHAVIOUR.

exit tests. Examinations given to learners at the end of instructional programmes. The purpose of exit tests is to measure the progress made by the learners during the programme of instruction. Exit tests are in effect ACHIEVEMENT TESTS given at the end of courses of study. All EXAMINATIONS are forms of exit tests.

Exit test-results are usually compared with the entry test-scores to measure learners' achievement but may also be used to measure the success of the instructional programme.

expansion. 1. As a writing task. Elaboration/AMPLIFICATION of an idea, a pithy/epigrammatic expression, or an outline. Expansion is a language learning and language testing task. It involves possession of a good vocabulary, appropriate use of words and a higher level writing ability besides ideas, knowledge and experience. Though PRECIS writing and expansion are opposites, the principles of writing governing them are the same. **2.** As an exercise in SENTENCE building. It involves addition of appropriate modifiers and other subordinate units to enlarge the given skeletal SENTENCE STRUCTURE. **3.** In language acquisition. The process of adding deleted elements in learner talk. A learner in the beginning may say, *milk hot.* Later, as her experience of the language increases, she may learn to expand it to a full sentence: *The milk is/was hot.*

expectancy theory. The theory that if one knows a language one would be able to anticipate what is likely to follow in a given context. **Example**, The incomplete sentence *He flogged the horse....* is likely to end with *mercilessly/to death.*

experiential learning. The process of (usually) adults using their experience and knowledge of the world as resource for learning. In experiential learning personal experience is at the centre of learning. The learners consciously process their experiences (of their actions) by REFLECTING on them and their significance in order to derive CONCEPTS and generalizations. This may involve asking questions, analyzing, relating, and arriving at deductions. In this mode of learning, the learners' experience works as investment in learning, the mediation of which is facilitated by the learners' cognitive maturity.

Experiential learning contrasts with

learning in the traditional pedagogical contexts, where knowledge is imparted and received from external sources, usually the teacher and books. In those contexts, learners, being young, require external help.

experiential learning approach. An approach to learning [a SL] which does not depend on a set SYLLABUS and set textbooks. There is little face-to-face teacher control or teacher dependence in it. Learners work on their own and also COLLABORATIVEly in groups. The approach suits advanced level adult learners who have already acquired some competence in the language and can assume charge of their own learning. The approach can also be applied to teacher(SELF-) DEVELOPMENT. *See* EXPERIENTIAL LEARNING.

experimental learning. The process of putting an idea/theory/HYPOTHESIS to practical test in order to arrive at some finding/discovery and learn from it. *See also* EXPERIMENTAL TEACHING.

experimental teaching. Teaching done in order to test a HYPOTHESIS. In some teacher- education institutions one could do experimental teaching as a PROJECT and part of course work. The teacher-pupil, in consultation with the MENTOR, designs an experiment, conducts it on real students, maintains a systematic record, and writes a report at the end of the experiment. The report is evaluated for CREDIT. There may be more than one examiner.

Experimental teaching as part of an academic programme is an experiment-oriented individualised course of instruction and is more concerned with the PROCESS of experimenting.

expert. One who possesses knowledge and experience in a particular domain and can not only present exemplary performance in it but also theorize. Expert performance in certain domains such as teaching, may be more challenging than in certain others.

explicit. Directly, clearly or overtly stated. 'Explicit learning' refers to the process of learning in which the learner is aware of how he is learning. In language learning, 'explicit' refers to the overt and intentional acquisition of knowledge of language. *See* EXPLICIT KNOWLEDGE.

'Explicit teaching', **Example**, of grammar, involves formal treatment of the rules of grammar.

'Explicit correction' of learner error is directly pointing out the mistake, and making the learner correct it.

explicit knowledge. (In the context of the knowledge of L2 grammar.) A conscious analytic awareness of the formal rules of the TL. This concept is contrasted with that of 'implicit knowledge,' which means 'an intuitive feeling of what is correct and acceptable' in language use.

Children acquire their MT and develop their competence in it implicitly, whereas adults learning a SLoften insist on getting explicit knowledge.

exploitation. Making use [by teacher] of a LEARNING OPPORTUNITY [for learners] that springs up during the course of teaching. The advantage is that there is a ready and an authentic context for the item of teaching. **Example**, On a cold morning the teacher asks one of the pupils in the class to shut the window to stop the draught coming in. The pupil remarks, 'Sir, the window is *break* [or *breaked.*]' The teacher exploits the opportunity to teach in context the forms *broke* and *broken*.

exposition. Giving a systematic explanation of a phenomenon along with information and commentary on it. One can do so orally or in writing. Prose writings are traditionally classified into four major types: those dealing with – exposition of ideas; description of a process, place, person or thing; narration of events; and ARGUMENTATION. Exposition is achieved mainly through analysing, enumerating; showing cause and effect, comparing, contrasting, and defining.

expository mode of teaching. A MODE in which the teacher is the main performer: the learners are passive listeners to the teacher's EXPOSITION. This mode stands in contrast with the HYPOTHETICAL MODE of teaching. The concepts are contributed by J. Bruner, 1966.

expository writing. *See* EXPOSITION.

extensive reading. Reading for pleasure and reading fast. Extensive READING is reading in quantity with general COMPREHENSION, without the reader bothering too much about the meanings of individual words.

It is widely held that extensive reading leads to gains in reading ability and improves the reader's overall LINGUISTIC COMPETENCE. A precondition for this of course is that the reading material be interesting to the reader, absorbing and AUTHENTIC. *See also* NON-DETAILED READING, and SUPPLEMENTARY READERS.

extralinguistic. Features that do not form part of the VERBAL language but add to the message nevertheless. The speaker's provenance and BODY LANGUAGE are two of these. *See also* KINESICS, and NONVERBAL COMMUNICATION.

extroversion/introversion. Personality TRAITS – characteristic of the extent to which an individual is more interested in the outside world or her own thoughts and feelings. Extrovert and introvert are not mutually exclusives but the two ends of a continuum. Ambiverts may be said to be the people near the middle point.

It has been claimed by some teachers that extroverts being sociable and RISK-TAK(ING)ERS, make LEARNERS: 'GOOD LANGUAGE LEARNERS.'

eye-mouth reading. *See* ORAL READING.

F

face-to-face communication. INTER-ACTION between people in which the INTERLOCUTORS are physically present. Such COMMUNICATION may to some extent rely on the immediate CONTEXT, and use EXTRALINGUISTIC features. The language use will vary according to whether the interaction is FORMAL or informal in nature.

face-to-face test. *See* DIRECT TEST.

face validity. A measure of confidence a (language) test evokes about it. A test evokes confidence in it if its appearance gives the impression that it will measure what it is meant to measure. Face VALIDITY is a concern mainly of non-specialists such as the test-takers, their teachers, parents, and test-administrators. A test should not only be valid: it should look valid. A task in translation purported to be a test of proficiency in speaking evokes little confidence in its validity, though hypothetically there might be a positive correlation between the scores on a translation test and a test of oral proficiency.

facilitating anxiety. *See* ANXIETY.

factual language. Language free of emotive content and literary embellishment. The language used in science and technology is considered to be factual. The need for factual in language pedagogy arose when it was realised around 1950s that a literary-texts-oriented teaching of a SL did not adequately prepare learners to study science and technology through the medium of a SL (English). This thinking may have been the beginning of LSP.

fast reading. Speed reading: READING for information, in one's MT or one's most active language, at about four hundred words a minute with a high degree of comprehension. A high degree of comprehension would be seventy per cent or above. In relation to its speed, reading may be categorised slow, medium, and fast. According to E. Fry (1963), a slow reader reads about 150 words per minute, a 'fair' reader 250, and a 'good' reader 350 words. As the speed goes up, the extent of comprehension goes down. Practised readers can easily switch from one to another speed. But most readers, esp. SL readers, lack this flexibility. Their lack of training makes them read at one speed – all texts irrespective of their nature.

Fast reading is no doubt a measure of 'good' reading. But reading speed is also determined by the nature of the text, the reader's proficiency in the language, and familiarity with the content of the text. Irrespective of these, certain texts require close reading, and the reader may decide to read them slowly for accuracy and a very high degree of comprehension. Conversely, certain texts require only a cursory glance. Mere speed without comprehension is of little value. One needs to be an EFFICIENT READER. Efficient reading means reading fast with a high percentage of comprehension. Speed and comprehension should go together.

Fast reading involves application of certain techniques, which need to be learnt. *See also* READING, READING STRATEGIES, and STRATEGIC READING.

feedback. 1a. In the context of teaching: the corrective or confirmatory information coming from the teacher to the learner(s) on their performance.

Feedback could be available in various forms including verbal response, comments on the learner's performance, or even in the form of teacher-gestures.

There are types of feedback and ways of administering it:

Confirmatory or affirmative information is positive feedback. It confirms learner HYPOTHESES that are at the back of learner-performance. Negative feedback/evidence indicates the incorrectness of the hypothesis.

Feedback can be evaluative (**Example**, in terms of 'good,' 'bad') or non-judgemental. Evaluative feedback is in the nature of the teacher's pronouncements on the correctness or incorrectness of learner utterances. It is considered to be more tactful in pedagogical contexts to administer negative feedback non-judgementally. *See also* F-MOVE.

Another mode of feedback is discoursal. In DISCOURSAL feedback, as Mercer (1995:26) says, the teacher makes use of learner responses/contributions by picking them up to 'incorporate them into the flow of classroom discourse in order to sustain and develop a dialogue between the teacher and the class'. For this purpose, the teacher makes use of the content of learner contributions rather than drawing their attention to such aspects as of form or erroneous usage. Hence explicit correction of

form is kept in abeyance. IMPLICIT correction, when made, takes an indirect route such as one of reformulating the uttered response. The teacher reformulates it in an IDIOMATICally and linguistically acceptable version.

Discoursal follow-up avoids DISPLAY QUESTIONS. It is with the help of REFERENTIAL QUESTIONS that the flow of classroom DISCOURSE (2) is maintained. *See also* CORRECTION.

1b. Feedback received from learner response. Though there is no exact correspondence between teaching and learning, students' response and performance both in the classroom and at the exams should be a source of feedback to the teacher, albeit indirect. **2.** On TEACHER EDUCATION programmes, prospective teachers receive feedback from their MENTORS/supervisors on their trial teaching performance. Techniques for balancing negative feedback with positive ones are usually recommended to the mentors so that their role becomes a supportive one and the teacher in training is AFFECTIVELY relaxed. **3.** Seeking and providing feedback is an integral part of conversation and NEGOTIATION OF MEANING.

field dependence/independence. COGNITIVE styles representing contrasted modes of PERCEPTION. A person with a high degree of field dependence would approach a subject in a global manner, in relation to the context whereas a person with a high degree of field independence would be analytical in her perception. She would be able to see the thing as isolated from the field in which it is embedded. **Example**, Some analyse truancy as an act of indiscipline unrelated to other factors. Some others see it in the context of its causes and the general atmosphere of indiscipline. There are psychological tests to measure these characteristics, which have bearing on an individual's LEARNING STYLE. However, the VALIDITY AND RELIABILITY of these tests have been questioned as they are based on tests of visual perception, which may not be a dependable indicator of learning styles.

filtration theory. A theory about how education should be spread in society or a community. It assumes that once the [upper] classes are [formally] educated, education will filter down to the masses in due course.

first language. The native language. The language learnt first. *See* LANGUAGE ONE, Home language, and Mother tongue. Sometimes the expression first language is also used to refer to the language used for communication outside home and family.

first language acquisition. The process or result of children creating a mental CONSTRUCT of language [and learning to use it]. This abstract construct, as the innatists [see below] claim, is not language specific. It consists of rules that are universal to all languages. In the innatist theory, the universal rules are termed as PRINCIPLES. Rules that are specific to particular languages are 'parametric' rules. Languages share the principles in common but vary parametrically. Children first acquire the principles and then parameters and learn to apply them in use as they come in active contact of language(s).

In the case of the first language, this process of rule-application in the beginning is limited to listening and speaking.

The BEHAVIOURIST THEORIES attribute learning to IMITATION and PRACTICE. Innatist theories claim that the acquisition of language happens because the humans are born with an innate capacity for it. Development of language in them is biologically pre-determined. This second position enjoys wide acceptance.

Observation of children acquiring first language shows that there is considerable uniformity in the process across languages. The young learners pass through similar stages and acquire PHONEMES and STRUCTURES in more or less the same order. They derive parametric [*see* PRINCIPLES AND PARAMETERS] rules of grammar from the INPUT they receive, and apply them in forming their own OUTPUT. Simple in the beginning, the grammar gains in complexity as evidenced by the ever-growing language repertoire of the learner.

fixation. In reading, the reader's eye stopping rather long at every word or every group of words. It makes reading slow. Good readers successively take in chunk after chunk of reading materials at a fast pace. Fixation is considered to be a faulty habit.

fixation pause. The brief moment when the eye takes in the visual input i.e., when the eye rests for the transient moment on one segment or chunk of reading before it moves on to the next. *see also* CHUNK (b), CHUNKING 3, and READING SPAN.

fixed choice item. A language-test item/language-learning task that supplies the responses and requires the test-taker/learner to choose the correct one. *See also* FORCED-CHOICE ITEMS.

flannel board. A flannel-framed board hung on the wall, as large framed painting are. FLASH CARDS with pieces of sandpaper pasted behind them can be stuck on the flannel for the pupils to see.

flash cards. Cards to help beginners recognise and read letters and words. A letter or a word is written black and bold on a card large enough to be clearly seen by all the learners in the class. The card is usually of the A4 size (21 × 30 cm.) [can be smaller] with pictures, letters, words on them, used for teaching purposes. The cards are briefly held up by the teacher for pupils to see, and then withdrawn. A variety of instructional procedures involve learners in such activities as reading, pronouncing correctly, combining words to form sentences, and even to write short compositions. Teachers may use simple dialogues and questions.

A flash card may also have a picture on it, in which case learners may be asked to name the object in the TL, and/or say a sentence about it.

fluency. The quality of ease and naturalness with which one expresses oneself in speaking and writing. One is naturally fluent in one's MT. But in using a SL, fluency may be affected because of a lack of confidence in one's LINGUISTIC COMPETENCE, inhibitions and other psychological constraints.

The term 'fluency' is used in two senses: i) hesitation-free smoothness or rapidity of speech delivery. This concept of smoothness and speed also applied to reading and writing. ii) Following Brumfit (1981 a), 'fluency' has come to mean, the ability to put oneself across comfortably in speech and/or writing. Brumfit's concept of fluency contrasts with what he calls ACCURACY, which relates to LINGUISTIC COMPETENCE. As he cautions, however, one is incomplete without the other. It will be noted that in both the conceptualisations of fluency there is the saliency of the element of smoothness.

Despite the contrast noted above, in an evaluation of ORAL skills, fluency may be defined particularly in terms of articulation and qualities of speech production, such as rapidity. Some associated qualities are a lack of hesitation and of repetition; clarity of enunciation, and correctness of ACCENTUATION and INTONATION.

f-move. The FOLLOW- UP or the feedback MOVE in support to the learner. One of the pedagogical functions of the classroom teacher is to provide learners FEEDBACK (1a) on their attempts to use the language.

focus. Prominence, emphasis. In DISCOURSE, spoken or written, it is usual for particular units of message/ information to be highlighted. The highlighting is done for emphasising or contrasting. In writing, focusing is achieved by placing the units of information in a particular sequence. This entails choosing syntactic arrangements that lend prominence to the unit of information to be focused on. An example of this is the choice of the passive form in English, in which the focus shifts from the subject to the object. Punctuation marks also play a role in focusing.

Though the syntactic arrangements apply equally well to spoken discourse, there are devices of focusing that are realised only in speech through ACCENTUATION and INTONATION. These include the placing of contrastive stress, nucleus, pitch movement, loudness and lengthening.

focus on form. Drawing learners' attention to grammatical usage. The teaching of the rules of GRAMMAR and USAGE has traditionally been the centrepiece of SL teaching, focusing mainly on grammatical ACCURACY. This practice in language pedagogy is contrasted with 'focus on meaning.' The two are not mutually exclusive though.

folktale. A prose narrative transmitted through a culture by word of mouth from one generation to the next. Told and retold and in the process modified and altered, many of the folktales pass into written literature. Aesop's fables and the Panchantra stories are two well-known examples.

Folktales – they usually have a moral to convey – have been used by elementary textbook writers. Pupils' familiarity with them have aided reading and remembering through anticipating and guessing. Folktales can be used for oral work and listening in SL teaching. *See also* the STORY METHOD.

follow-up. Further pedagogical action in order to consolidate the teaching already done: REMEDIAL TEACHING. The action is usually taken on the basis of the FEEDBACK (2) received. Follow-up measures need to keep in view a number of things – the nature and gravity of the deficiency needing follow-up

treatment, a pedagogically appropriate method of follow-up treatment, and the LEARNER CHARACTERISTICS.

forced-choice items. FIXED-CHOICE ITEMS: test items that offer fixed alternatives to choose the answer from. Multiple-choice items are typically forced-choice items. Although they suit the testing of reading-COMPREHENSION, LISTENING ability and VOCABULARY, they are not considered to be valid measures of the communicative abilities of speaking and writing. Forced-choice test-items provide little information on the test-takers' DISCOURSE-ability, an important constituent of COMMUNICATIVE COMPETENCE. However, the advantages of such items are that they are easy to score, and when they are valid measures, the rating-RELIABILITY they ensure contributes to item-VALIDITY.

foreign language. A language other than one's mother tongue learnt for cultural, academic or some special purpose. It is normally not spoken outside the classroom but may be used in occupational contexts, and for communication with foreigners. *Cf.* SECOND LANGUAGE.

foreigner talk. Speech deliberately simplified to help a SL learner/user understand the speaker's message. The adjustments in the speech are made by the speaker according to a rough and ready assessment of the SL learners' proficiency in the language.

forgetting. Inability to recall something (correctly) or failure to perform an action previously learnt. Forgetting is a learning problem and can be caused by a number of factors. Some of these are: the learner has not properly understood something and therefore forgets it. Forgetting is less likely when the learner takes interest in learning, or finds it interesting. LEARNING can become interesting if the learner pays attention. There is some circularity here.

When the learner can personally relate to something being taught or read, it becomes meaningful to her and she is not likely to forget it.

The learner's purpose is also a factor. Something learnt only for passing the exam is likely to be forgotten soon. Such learning is surface learning. Deep learning generally leads to lasting memory. *See also* STUDY APPROACHES.

form. *See* CODE.

formal. 1. Of language and style. Speech or writing using a standard variety, appropriate to formal occasions. Such language avoids features of COLLOQUIALISMS and SLANGY expressions as well as incomplete and lazily constructed sentences. **2.** Relating to forms that make up the pattern of a WORD, PHRASE or SENTENCE. Boy/boys and has been going are examples of form. Form-oriented study of language focuses more on their STRUCTURE (1) and less on meaning or FUNCTION. **3.** [Of learning] *See* Formal instruction.

formal code. *See* ELABORATED CODE.

formal instruction. Teaching in the CLASSROOM setting/educational context. Such teaching is usually done, among other things, with the help of prescribed text materials. Tests and exams are part of the instructional procedure. Instruction thus received is generally known as formal education. Its successful completion leads to the award of a degree, diploma or certificate.

formative assessment/evaluation. EVALUATION carried out when a programme/project is in progress in order to judge its strengths and weaknesses and thus to monitor and to improve it for optimum results. A development-oriented ongoing exercise, formative evaluation is carried out through reviewing such factors as the (suitability of) objectives, subject-content, learning methods, the role of the personnel, the utilisation of resources, the adherence to the schedule, and expenses.

Such evaluation also applies to regular teaching programmes and their participants.

An essential aspect of formative evaluation is the participation of the insiders (those who conduct the programme).

form-function dilemma. The question in SL education of the relative importance of EXPLICIT grammar-instruction and teaching for COMMUNICATIVE ability/FLUENCY. Today, both are considered to be important.

form-meaning dichotomy. *See* Form-function dilemma.

formulaic language. 1. Rubber-stamp language: language consisting of ready-made expressions and CLICHÉS. It makes dull reading. **2.** Conventionally established set language as used in ceremonies and legal documents. It is advisable to stick to it.

formulaic speech. Fixed-form expressions/sentences. Beginning SL learners who have not yet acquired the ability to create new sentences on their own, often use readymade or set expressions. **Example**, *I'm sorry I don't know*.

The speech of all language users, native or non-native, young or adult consists to a considerable degree of formulaic speech or prefabricated chunks of language such as *thank you very much.*

fossilisation. Cessation of learning. Larry Selinker (1972) concluded that at some stage in their development prior to attaining full competence in the SL, some learners stop acquiring correct forms to replace faulty ones established in their INTERLANGUAGE. This may happen in spite of continued availability of INPUT and INSTRUCTION. Fossilization sets in usually when learners have achieved a level of communicative sufficiency and there is no further motivation to outgrow ungrammatical features.

foundation courses. Introductory courses that serve as base for more advanced courses of study. In many DISTANCE EDUCATION/OPEN LEARNING programmes, foundation courses are compulsory courses in language skills for undergraduate students. These courses are intended to develop in them foundation-level linguistic competence and give them necessary theoretical inputs so that they are able to cope on their own with the courses they have opted to study.

frame. 1. Supporting structure. An **example** of a sentence frame: *He is a ...* this frame can be completed by supplying an appropriate noun to fill the blank space. Such frames are used as language exercises for practice in sentence-making. **2.** SCHEMATIC struc-

ture: knowledge structure. **3.** A programmed remedial unit in PROGRAMMED INSTRUCTION.

free composition. Writing task without using any external support in the form of relevant words, ideas, a structured frame or an outline. These items of support are normally made available in CONTROLLED COMPOSITION. Essays, stories and descriptions are products of free composition. Writing freely or writing on one's own needs an intermediate to advanced level proficiency in the language.

frequency. The number of times an item **Example**, word, grammatical structure occurs in a given corpus. The more frequently it occurs, the better it becomes a candidate to be selected for teaching. Relative frequency though is not the only consideration. Usefulness determined by need is an equally important consideration. *See also* SELECTION and VOCABULARY SELECTION.

frequency count. Statistical count of how frequently an ITEM occurs in a specific corpus.

In the past, a number of projects were undertaken to count, for pedagogical purposes, the frequency of vocabulary items, and items of structure, **Example** verb forms. The idea was to restrict the content of teaching to those items only that were most frequently-occurring, i.e., most useful for SL learners.

Today, computers help us to generate CORPUS-based data. The information thus gathered can help us take pedagogical decisions based on how the TL is actually used by its speakers.

frequency hypothesis. The HYPOTHESIS that the order in which SL learners acquire linguistic items depends on the FREQUENCY of the occurrence of those items in the INPUT they receive.

function. The purpose for which an UTTERANCE or unit of language is used. For **example**, utterances may be used for apologising, denying, praising, thanking, and so on. It may be noted that the form of a sentence does not necessarily indicate its function. The sentence – *who doesn't know Gandhi?* though interrogative in form, performs the function of asserting that everyone knows Gandhi. Thus there is no one-to-one correspondence between form and function. The same form may be used for different functions in different contexts. Similarly, more than one form may be used for the same function. **Examples**:

Will you sit down, please?

Please take your seat

Please be seated

Would you like to take your seat

[Though the basic function of these utterances is more or less the same, each of them carries a varying tone of formality and politeness.]

function(al) approach to language. An approach that looks at language in the context of its use in social situations – how it is used, what purposes it serves for its users, etc. In LT based on this approach, the main concern is to impart learners FUNCTIONAL ability in using the language, rather than teaching them the grammatical structure and the METALANUAGE that goes with it.

functional categories. Categories of words that perform grammatical functions. They include, among others, determiners, prepositions, tense-marking MORPHEMES. Being grammatical-function-performing words & morphemes, they are different from CONTENT WORDS. Functional categories belong to a closed system whereas content words to the open set. *See also* FUNCTION WORD.

functional grammar/linguistics. An approach to grammar/linguistics in which the notion of FUNCTION is central. It views language as an instrument of social interaction, and concentrates on the SEMANTIC and PRAGMATIC aspects of language.

functionalist model (of SL acquisition). The HYPOTHESIS that learners acquire language by discovering the relationship between forms and their communicative functions. Whether the hypothesis is tenable or not, it is generally accepted that engaging in communication helps speed up the process of language acquisition.

functional syllabuses. SYLLABUSES in which the language content is organised in terms of language FUNCTIONS. Since functions do not exist in isolation, language items (words and structures) needed for them are also specified. *See also* NOTIONAL-FUNCTIONAL SYLLABUSES. Identification in early 1970s (notably by D.A. Wilkins) of notions and functions as central to SL education is considered to be influential in developing functional syllabuses. *See also* NOTIONAL-FUNCTIONAL SYLLABUSES.

functional variety (of a language). The VARIETY used for everyday function or transactional communication. This variety is contrasted with the literary, scientific and other high varieties. Since people mostly use the functional variety, there may be a case for this variety of the TL to be taught where it suits learner needs and purpose.

functions of language. The purposes for which language is used. Language is used for a variety of purposes, and there are various ways and terminologies in which language function is classified. One classification is presented below:

giving information;
making requests and giving commands; expressing feelings (poetic); lubricating social relations;
playing on words creatively; and, talking about language (METALANGUAGE)

According to Halliday (1978), language has three main functions:

Ideational – the function of organising the language user's 'experience of the real or imaginary world.'

Interpersonal – the function of establishing and maintaining relationship between people

Textual – the function of creating written or spoken texts

Each of these reflects a different, though related, social function of language.

Elsewhere, in the context of L1 acquisition, Halliday (1975) has drawn a basic difference between the pragmatic and the MATHETIC functions of language. The PRAGMATIC has to do with using language for everyday transaction, whereas the MATHETIC has to do with language as a means of learning, thinking and reflection. In addition, the aesthetic function, the third category, has to do with imaginative use of language – language as creation.

function word. A word which shows a grammatical relationship in a SENTENCE or between sentences. Which, in and and in this preceding sentence are function words. Such words do not carry much meaning on their own but perform the important function of indicating relationships that structure meaning. They are also known as 'form words,' 'grammatical words,' 'structure/structural words' and are contrasted with CONTENT WORDS.

G

gatekeeping. Controlling and deciding as to who qualifies for something and who does not. Job interviews are typically gatekeeping exercises. Language tests do the same.

gender. A way of classifying according to sex or grammatical category. There is a distinction between 'grammatical' gender and 'social' gender. Languages have different ways of assigning gender [masculine, feminine, neuter] to words. For example, in Hindi the word for the moon is masculine, but in German and French it is feminine.

Social gender relates to biological sex: male, female. Gender-studies in this context focus on issues such as gender-linked differences and BIASES in language and language use. Interactional sociolinguistic studies of gender and language enquire into issues like power, dominance, and subordination in various domains of language use. *See also* GENDER and LANGUAGE.

gender and language. The interaction between GENDER and language. It has been noted that some USAGES and STYLES in language use are gender-specific. Thus, men and women tend to prefer certain language forms over others. Also, in some languages certain forms are used exclusively by either men or women.

Language use by men carries tones of POWER and domination, and language has been seen as a force to maintain power relations.

In conversation, which is considered to be an equal opportunity activity, power relationship is often unequal: men tend to control and dominate. Gendered speech styles have also been noted. *See also* GENDER BIAS, and SEXISM.

gender bias. Expression of prejudice against members of a particular gender. BIAS comes through references to women in textual materials and other domains of language use, such as TEACHER TALK. The references are usually derogatory showing girls and women in subordinate and STEREOTYPI-CAL images – cooking, washing clothes, etc. Awareness of this has made many curriculum-framing bodies to screen materials for gender bias and to eliminate it. *See also* GENDER AND LANGUAGE, and SEXISM.

general ability. General intelligence. It is hypothesised by some that underlying all special cognitive abilities there is a general factor or general ABILITY.

general English. A GENERAL PURPOSE course in English as a SL. It is a subject of study in school and college curriculam in many countries including India. It is usually a required subject for study. It includes textbook-based reading, composition/essay writing, grammar and usage. The textual materials consist of the main coursebook and SUPPLEMENTARY READER(s). they may include selections from literary works. Many courses also include PRECIS-writing and translation work.

generalisation. A process of inductively arriving at a HYPOTHESIS about a class or category of objects, events, etc. The hypothesis is formed on the basis of the observation of occurrences of a feature with some regularity in a given context. The hypothesis is extended (generalised) to other similar contexts. By observing, for **example**, the almost regular application of the *suffixed* to verbs to indicate past action, the learner derives the relevant hypothesis and applies it .to produce the form *sitted*. This particular application is an instance of OVERGENERALISATION.

In learning, generalization is an unconscious process. Incorrect generalizations usually get modified and reformulated in the light of further INPUT.

general purpose language courses. Courses designed for developing the overall proficiency of the learners in the four skills. They are generally labelled beginner, intermediate and advanced, according to the proficiency level they address Such courses contrast with specific-purpose courses. *See also* LANGUAGE FOR SPECIFIC PURPOSES.

general service list (GSL). A list of 2,000 English words occurring most frequently in speech and writing. The list was compiled in mid 1930s by Dr L.W. Faucett, Dr H.E. Palmer, and Dr M. West. The list was first published in 1936 as Part V of the Interim report on vocabulary selection. *See* AN INTERIM REPORT. Subsequently, in 1953 was published a revised and enlarged edition of the list. Compiled and edited by Michael West, the volume was titled *A general service list of English words*.

For nearly four decades, between 1925 and 1975, with the World War II intervening, there was a scholarly preoccupation with the counting of the most frequently used words. The idea was that since all of a language cannot be taught, nor was it necessary, the most frequent and hence the most useful words should be selected for teaching the learners learning the language as their SL or a FL. Similar attempts were made in India also during 1950s and 1960s.

The GSL has been highly influential particularly in ELT circles, and widely used in writing/editing textual materials – simplified readers, simplified[and often abridged] classics.

generative grammar. A model of grammar propounded by N. Chomsky that postulated that SYNTAX is the organising principle of human languages. Generative grammar is the set of FORMAL (2) rules that can generate 'all and only the grammatical sentences of a language.'

generative model of learning. A pedagogical model in which the learners are encouraged to derive meaning for themselves without depending on the teachers. They are encouraged to construct & generate meanings by applying DISCOVERY procedures, forming HYPOTHESES, making GENERALISATIONS based on the language-data they have encountered, and by asking themselves questions.

genre. TEXT type: a distinguishable VARIETY of literary, artistic, or language creation. Essay, poetry, drama, *madhubani* [painting], *aalha* [recital], business letters, and obituaries are examples of genres identified by their distinct STYLE, rhetorical structure, function and purpose. A distinction is drawn between literary and non-literary genres. Epics and tragedies are examples of the former, and a wedding invitation or a birthday card of the latter. In most cases such as the just- mentioned ones, generic conventions are culture-specific.Also, there may be sub-genres within a generic variety.

Genres follow patterned organization and distinct conventions of form and style, though there is always scope for innovation.

In language education, awareness of genre helps in recognising the structure and purpose of a TEXT. It makes it easy for one to comprehend a text and also to compose. Familiarity with generic conventions and constraints may help learners of a SL for academic purposes to tackle academic discourse.

There is a risk, however, in overusing generic conventions. It can turn the product into an assemblage of CLICHÉS.

genre analysis. Study of the structure, patterns and conventions of various TEXT types: the distinctive ways in which texts are organised. GENRE analysis is pertinent to LT as the learners need to know how texts are conventionally patterned and how their organization is related to their communicative purpose(s).

generic competence. Ability to use appropriately particular GENRES in professional settings. Generic competence is contrasted with LINGUISTIC competence and general COMMUNICATIVE competence.

gerogogy. The education of the aged as different from that of the children and of adults, although not many writers draw a distinction between the education of the adult and the education of the elderly.

gestalt. A German word meaning roughly 'an integrated whole', not just a putting together of the parts. *See also* GESTALT LEARNING.

gestalt learning. Learning something as an integrated whole rather than a sum of its units or parts. The expression derives from gestalt psychology which contends that mental processes and behaviour being organised wholes, cannot be analysed (without leaving something out) into elementary units. Gestalt psychology (a school of psychology founded in Germany in 1910s) rejects atomistic approaches to the study of human PERCEPTION and experience. It also rejects BEHAVIOURISM.

global assessment or global rating. A HOLISTIC rating of PERFORMANCE in which scores are awarded on the basis of the rater/examiner's overall impression of the candidates' performance. This mode of ASSESSMENT contrasts with the scoring procedure in DISCRETE-POINT tests where each test-item relates to a distinct and specific point of learning/assessment, and the test score is a cumulative of a series of scores the interpretation of which is NORM-REFERENCED.

Holistic assessment may be done using ANALYTIC categories of performance and BAND descriptors.

global education. Learning and teaching language(s) not only for communication and academic purposes but also for solving the problems of the world. Also known as 'world studies', global education addresses problems like poverty, disease, human rights, violence, international conflicts and environment degradation. In this perspective, the language teacher is not just a teacher of language: she is also an educator.

global errors. Errors that affect overall sentence organization. A distinction is made in language pedagogy between major and minor errors learners make in language-use. Major or global errors relate to faulty constructions that obstruct communication. Local errors, on the other hand, may be LEXICAL or MORPHOLOGICAL in nature and relate to single elements such as the plural or the past tense form. Generally, local errors do not hinder communication significantly.

global language. A language that develops a special role recognised in every country (Crystal, 1997). The global status of a language is associated with power – economic, political, etc. – of its speakers. A global status has been asserted for the English language

global learning. *See* GESTALT LEARNING.

global question. A comprehension question based on the text as a whole, and not on a particular unit of it.

glossary. A list of words and phrases alphabetically arranged, with their meanings. Textbooks for language learners usually contain glosses on difficult words & phrases often with hints on how to use them in writing and speech. H.G. Widdowson (1978) has drawn a distinction between what he terms 'priming glossaries' and 'prompting glossaries.' Priming glossaries supply the linguistic meanings of words and phrases, and prompting glossaries their meanings in the context

of their use in particular TEXTS. In the reading comprehension of a text both types of glossaries are pedagogically useful. The procedure recommended in this regard for helping learners with glossaries, is: Initial acquaintance with the general meanings of the items followed by the reading of the text, and then by their meanings as inferred from the context.

glossodynamic [GDM] **model** of language learning and teaching. A flexible and INTEGRATED approach to language learning and teaching proposed by Titone (1973), and Titone and Danesi (1985). It basically proposes blending of, and interaction among, the various methods and approaches to language pedagogy – intelligent ECLECTICISM. *See also* LANGUAGE TEACHING METHODS.

gobbledygook. Jargon used by civil servants. Deliberate AMBIGUITY is a feature of such language. *See also* JARGON, and OFFICIALESE.

good English. Internationally intelligible *and* acceptable formal or COLLOQUIAL variety of English. The notion of good English (in speech and writing), as that of good language, goes much beyond the considerations of grammatical CORRECTNESS. A grammatically correct sentence may have involved structure, and lack in conciseness. It may contain JARGON and obscurity and lack precision. Good English is generally considered: i) to conform to standard or widely acceptable modern usage; ii) to possess clarity and directness; iii) to have proper correspondence between meaning and its expression; and iv) be appropriate to the occasion. Good English is free of CLICHÉ, wordiness, and CIRCUMLOCUTION. Also, there is no intentional distortion in order to lie, conceal, or mislead.

good language. *See* GOOD ENGLISH.

good language learner. The learner who manages to learn a SL successfully. It is a truism that MT learning hardly ever fails. But success in SL learning is not evenly achieved. Researchers (one of them, Rubin:1975) have attempted to identify the factors that account for success. Some of these relate to APTITUDE, PERSONALITY factors and LEARNING STRATEGIES.

gradability.(In grammar and semantics). A measure of variability in degree. Gradable words allow for comparison of degree, **Example**, weak, weaker, weakest. An example of an ungradable word is express. Another concept in grammar relating to 'grading' is that of vowel gradation wherein a change of vowel makes a word to assume another grammatical function. An example is the verb write. By changing the vowel 'i' to 'o', we get the past tense form. *Cf.* GRADATION.

gradation. Ordering in a sequence items(for teaching). Gradation or grading of teaching ITEMS is a cardinal principle in the BEHAVIOURIST, STRUCTURAL-APPROACH-based plans for SL teaching. The items – phonological, lexical, structural, semantic – are first selected (*See also* SELECTION) according to such considerations as learner LEVEL and the time available for teaching, and then arranged in the order they would be introduced and taught. The principle underpinning gradation is that SL learning should be made less difficult by taking learners along in graded steps from easy to difficult, from what they have already learnt to what they are going to learn. However, it (the principle) is based on the questionable theoretical premise that learning can be externally controlled, ordered and sequenced.

graded materials. Contents of the MATERIAL FOR TEACHING LANGUAGE arranged in order of increasing difficulty and complexity. In such materials, new learning items are progressively introduced. Test-materials, whether part of instructional materials or independent, may also be graded according to their difficulty level. *See also* GRADED READERS.

grade readers. Reading books or READERS specially designed and controlled, or just designated as LEVEL-specific, to match the level of linguistic competence the learners have already achieved. Grade readers are a kind of PLATEAU READERS. The difference between *grade* and GRADED READERS, a thin one though, is that a *grade reader* is grade-specific and *graded readers* are a set or series of reading books arranged in order of difficulty.

graded readers. Books specially written or adapted for learners. Graded readers are a series of books in which the vocabulary, the grammatical structure, the length of the text(s), and often the subject matter are controlled with the intention to make them suitable for specific levels of language proficiency and cognitive maturity. The new vocabulary items and grammatical structures to be introduced at each level are pre-selected, and arranged in an ascending order of difficulty. The linguistic content (words, idiomatic expressions, grammatical structure) to go into the books are selected according to their suitability, and where it is felt necessary, they are simplified or suitably edited. Cognitive grading is done in psychological terms – what is less or more easy/difficult to learn, and in terms of the density of the occurrence of new words, unfamiliar concepts and cultural references.

There is usually a continuity of characters from one book to another. Because of this, the learners develop a familiarity with them.

The primary aim of the graded readers is to promote language ACQUISITION in SL learners through READING.

A criticism of the graded readers is that they contain made-to-order language, language that has been controlled to make way for pre-specified items of vocabulary and grammatical structure. The assumptions (underlying the construction of the Readers)that see close correspondence between what is taught and what will be learnt, appear to be questionable in the light of later research on the dynamics of classroom learning.

grading. *See* GRADATION.

grading system. A system of evaluating students' ACADEMIC performance in which grades (A, B+, B, etc.) are awarded instead of numerical marks as done traditionally . The GPA, the average of the grades earned for various performance samples in different courses, represents the rating of the overall performance on an instructional programme.

grammar. 1. The rules of SYNTAX and MORPHOLOGY the speakers of a language follow in using it. The rules govern the grammatical structure(s) of the language. Correctness/incorrectness of usage is judged with reference to these rules. Competent/native users of a language possess an IMPLICIT knowledge of the grammar of their language. (PHONOLOGY and SEMANTICS are treated outside 'grammar'.) **2.** The term 'grammar' is often used to refer to EXPLICIT descriptions of the underlying rules although they are so numerous, complex, and varying that an exhaustive description is well-nigh impossible. **3.** In the context of SLE, the term 'grammar' is sometimes used to refer to the learner's INTERLANGUAGE or interim grammar. A distinction is drawn between SCIENTIFIC and PEDAGOGICAL grammars. [*See also* PEDAGOGIC GRAMMARS.] Scientific or linguists' grammars aim at an accurate and objective description. Grammar deals with rules at the SENTENCE level. **4.** The term 'grammar' is sometimes used with the general meaning of regulatory principles. **Example**, in the phrase 'the grammar of discourse', it means 'organising principles.'

grammar teaching. 1. The teaching of the rules of GRAMMAR (1) as part of language education. Teaching of formal grammar is part both of L1 and L2 curriculum though their aims may be different. In the context of SL instruction, the teaching of grammar is generally aimed at imparting learners the knowledge and ability to use the language (grammatically) correctly.

Dissatisfaction with grammar-rules-based and TRANSLATION-based practices (in SL teaching), which depended on DEDUCTIVE modes, led to the development of a number of METHODS & approaches in which prominence is given to oral practice and to the acquisition of grammar inductively. Modern approaches to SL teaching present the rules of grammar in context and build its learning into language use – listening, speaking, reading and writing. A variety of techniques are used which engage learners in working on tasks, solving problems, focusing on meaning, and NOTICING. The choice of explicit teaching is related to LEARNER CHARACTERISTICS. **2.** The formal teaching of the rules of MT- grammar as part of the curriculum. Where the prestige/high variety of the learners' MOTHER TONGUE happens to be different from their HOME LANGUAGE, MT-grammar-teaching heightens their METACOGNITIVE awareness and facilitates the transition to the high variety.

grammar tests. Tests of language proficiency through grammar-and STRUCTURE (1)-related tasks. Such tests are contrasted with COMMUNICATIVE LANGUAGE TESTS. Some points of contrast/difference relate to whether the test: is a DIRECT TEST or an indirect one; whether it consists of DISCRETE-POINT (TESTING) items or DISCOURSE-based tasks; and whether it consists of AUTHENTIC(ITY) tasks. *See also* Authentic language-tests.

grammar-translation method. An approach to the learning & teaching of a foreign, classical, or a second language through the means of a FORMAL(2) study of the rules of grammar, and practice in TRANSLATION. It is perhaps the oldest bilingual method of language teaching. Reading and writing occupy important places in it, and aural-oral skills, a back seat. Explication of grammar rules and their application in translating from and into the TL are favourite learning-activities.

Despite numerous methodological innovations, the GT method survives partly because many learners, specially, adults, prefer being taught analytically with the help of explicit and formal grammar-rules. The process of coming to grips with abstract rules, and of engaging in translation affords some learners the satisfaction of occupying themselves with cognitively challenging tasks. The study of classical languages [**Example**, Sanskrit] has traditionally preferred the method.

grammatical competence. LINGUISTIC COMPETENCE as different from COMMUNICATIVE COMPETENCE. Grammatical competence is basically competence in producing utterances that are grammatically correct. Correctness here implies conformity to the rules of SYNTAX and MORPHOLOGY, and in speech, to those of PRONUNCIATION and PHONOLOGY also. It is axiomatic that grammatical competence underlies communicative competence, but is not enough in itself.

grammatical consciousness-raising. See CONSCIOUSNESS-RAISING.

grammaticality of an utterance – written or spoken. The degree of its conformity to the rules of GRAMMAR (1) irrespective of its social/contextual appropriateness.

grammaticality judgements. Judging whether a given sentence is grammatically correct or not. Performance on judgement-tasks administered to learners reveals whether they have acquired a rule or not.

grammatical syllabuses. SYLLABUSES in which the content for teaching is specified in terms of grammatical items and structures. Nouns, verbs, tenses, and conditionals are examples of grammatical items. STRUCTURAL SYLLABUSES are a form of grammatical syllabuses as the content in them is specified in terms of items of grammatical STRUCTURE (1).

'grandmaster' school of thought. [A GM is a person with the highest level of skill in chess.] A deterministic viewpoint/assumption underlying much language education – classroom teaching, textbook construction, lesson planning, etc. Robert O' Neill(1982) says, 'According to this view the teacher must know exactly what will happen in the lesson… . Anything that occurs in the lesson does so because it is part of the teacher's plan… . Objectives are clearly stated and adhered to' the teacher's "plans" are 'foreseen conclusions' There are concepts of teacher training which begin with an idealised model of the "good teacher" and then attempt to mould all trainees to this model…'.

Many teachers and textbooks writers also assume, or expect, perfect symmetry between the input provided [by them] and the learner output.

O Neill suggests that instead of expecting pre-determined and uniform results to follow as a matter of course, teachers, teacher educators, and instructional material writers should try to 'build on' the cognitive and HEURISTIC resources of the learners, their potentials and 'individual and differing strengths'.

grapheme. In a writing system, the minimal unit that can cause a difference of meaning. The difference between the meanings of sit and sat [apart from the difference of pronunciation] is caused by the units 'i' and 'a', which are different graphemes in the Roman alphabet.

graphics. (The study of) the art relating to the writing of the letters of the alphabet. [There are languages such as Chinese that use non-alphabetic scripts.] It involves perception of letter shapes and their production. In the production of writing, some important things are the circles, curves, and lines in the small and capital letters[where the distinction applies], the blank space between words, and between lines, writing words in a straight line, linking the letters in a word, and proper consonance between the sizes of the letters in a word. Graphics involves the study of different styles of handwriting and stylised writing, **Example**, the written as if it is printed.

In a wider sense graphics relates to visual images, including those generated by computers.

graphology. The study of the written system of a language (sometimes, of handwriting also).

gravity of errors. *See* ERROR GRAVITY.

GRICEAN MAXIMS. *See* THE CO-OPERATIVE PRINCIPLE.

group assessment. Assessment of the performance of a group of learners on an assigned task. A group or groups work on a joint PROJECT. The ASSESSMENT of the product leads to a single grade. The modalities of the task and the assessment of its product may vary from context to context.

Group methods that include COLLABORATIVE LEARNING and GROUP WORK are considered to reduce competitiveness and foster the qualities of co-operations considered to be conducive to learning as it puts learners affectively at ease.

grouping. 1. Putting associated/similar items in one group – items that fit together. For example, words for teaching may be grouped semantically or according to the parts of speech they belong to. Similarly clauses/sentences having the same pattern would be grouped together. **2.** *See* STREAMING and ABILITY GROUPING.

group-work (GW). A mode of instruction which departs from the traditional whole-class teacher-fronted mode. In GW, learners work on their own in PEER groups under the supervision of a perambulating teacher. GW is considered to be specially suited to TASK-BASED classroom procedures.

Peer interaction, – which is less intimidating than the conventional teacher-learner interaction – is supposed to encourage active participation [in learning], and learner NEGOTIATION OF MEANINC. GW also provides opportunities to learners to use STRATEGIES OF COMMUNICATION when working on a common task applying themselves cognitively to negotiate solutions. It has been argued that participation in the learning process through meaningful interaction, negotiation of meaning, and frequent strategy deployment – they are all cognitive activities – facilitate language acquisition. *See also* the second paragraph under GROUP ASSESSMENT.

guessing. A COGNITIVE process of RISK-TAKING in solving a problem by intelligently drawing INFERENCES from the contextual CLUES. Studies of GOOD LANGUAGE LEARNERS show that one of the LEARNING STRATEGIES they use is guessing.

Guessing is however viewed negatively in language testing as TEST-ITEMS that permit random guessing of the key may defeat the very purpose of testing.

guidance. *See* COUNSELLING.

guided composition. *See* CONTROLLED COMPOSITION.

habit formation. Inculcation of correct language through PRACTICE and DRILL in the target item of STRUCTURE (1) or language usage. The practice is carried out until the item is considered to have become part of the learner's habit.

To forestall faulty habit-formation care is taken i) not to let learners make language ERRORS, and ii) not to let them be exposed to them.

Habit-formation is a tenet in the BEHAVIOURIST model of language teaching.

halo effect. A kind of BIAS that influences judgement. For example, in evaluating the language performance, the judgement of the RATER may be biased because of the influence on her of such factors as her previous impression of the candidate's ability' or the candidate's performance on an earlier task.

Similarly, in research the judgement of an attribute may be biased because of another attribute which is not being tested. For example, in judging the phonological accuracy in the speech of a subject, one's judgement may be influenced by his/her voice quality.

heritage language. 1. [Of migrant communities moving from their national group or culture to other areas.] The language spoken by the parent COMMUNITY and associated with its identity. An interesting feature of the quest for it is that many second generation immigrants are choosing the INSTRUCTED LEARNING mode to acquire literacy skills in the heritage language – the way one learns a FL/SL. **2.** A classical language becoming extinct: a language no more spoken but forming part of a community's cultural inheritance.

heuristic. Encouraging/involving problem-solving through DISCOVERY procedures. They relate to creative methods of finding answers by adopting the process of testing the possibilities oneself, and discovering the principle, the rule, that relates to the problem and leads to its solution. In learning, the heuristic procedure is considered to be a superior way of obtaining knowledge, and is contrasted with the procedures of obtaining it second-hand. *See* HEURISTIC APPROACHES, DEDUCTIVE LEARNING, DISCOVERY.

heuristic approaches in language teaching. Approaches that encourage the learners to unravel such complexities as the working of the (sub) systems of a language by applying their cognitive abilities. These may be the abilities of deriving rules and generalising, of HYPOTHESIS-formation and hypothesis-testing, comparing, relating, and systematising. Heuristic approaches in teaching assist and train learners to apply their inherent ability to discover and learn for themselves. *See also* HEURISTIC.

hidden curriculum. The tenor and content of what actually gets taught rather than what is prescribed and intended. In following a given SYLLABUS, different institutions and teachers adopt different practices: certain items get more emphasis and importance and a lot of unintended and incidental teaching comes in. Also teaching comes laced with teacher-ATTITUDES, IDEOLOGY and PREJUDICES. These also become part of CURRICULUM and impact learners in invisible ways.

A syllabus drawn on GRAMMAR-TRANSLATION lines may have been implemented COMMUNICATIVELY. In some places the teaching might be AUTHORITARIAN while in others it could follow LEARNER-CENTRED principles. In this way, what get actually included and taught and the way they are taught (though often unrecognised) form the hidden curriculum.

hierarchy. The order in which sets/categories of factors/features/rules are arranged on a scale. The scale has quantified levels, ascending and descending. The ordering is based on the perceived levels of complexity of the items. They may also be ordered according to their usefulness. Usefulness is worked out on the basis of the relative frequency of an ITEM in a given CORPUS.

Items for teaching during a semester or in a particular class may be arranged hierarchically. (ii) Teachers may prioritise the skills and abilities they would treat differentially on a course of study. Instructional materials may be developed following a hierarchical structure. (iii) Since all language ERRORS committed by learners are not of equal gravity, a hierarchy of ERROR GRAVITY is often set up for their treatment. **2.** In semantics: meaning relationship according to inclusion. For **example** *flower* is a superordinate term or hypernym. Rose, daisy, tulip are its hyponyms. *See also* HIERARCHY OF NEEDS.

hierarchy of needs. The seven levels of human needs postulated by Maslow (1968, 1970). The most basic are physiological, survival and security needs. Once these are fulfilled, men look for the fulfilment of social needs of belonging and self-esteem. These are followed by intellectual needs. At the highest level is the need for SELF-ACTUALISATION.

The hierarchy has implications for education. Learners struggling with basic needs may not be sufficiently motivated to attend to intellectual needs. All learners need social acceptance and ESTEEM. Educational environment denying these may not be conducive to learner achievement.

holistic. Integrated. In the context of language teaching, it means treating the various skills of language as integrated rather than discrete. *See also* HOLISTIC APPROACHES TO LANGUAGE LEARNING/TEACHING.

holistic approaches to language learning/teaching. Approaches that treat language and learning in their totality. *See* HOLISTIC. These approaches address the psychomotor, AFFECTIVE and COGNITIVE aspects of the learner and of learning as interconnected and interdependent. So do they treat the various skills of language.

holistic assessment. *See* GLOBAL ASSESSMENT.

holistic scoring of language performance. An impressionistic ASSESSMENT leading to a single score. The score, usually a letter GRADE, is (or, is supposed to be) a comprehensive evaluation arrived at globally. Holistic scoring is applied to DISCOURSE-level language output and is often used in COMMUNICATIVE LANGUAGE TESTING. To avoid BIAS and subjectivity, measures are taken to ensure RATER- and rating-RELIABILITY.

Different from holistic scoring is ANALYTIC SCORING in which the constituent TRAITS of the ability being assessed are assigned scores separately. Later, these scores may be put to form an overall score/grade. The constituent traits are identified carefully and rationally.

home language. The language one is born into. It may be a DIALECT [of the MOTHER TONGUE] spoken in the family, and first acquired by the child. In many cases the home language is very dissimilar to the STANDARD VARIETY. Yet beginning-instruction in schools is imparted through the latter, treating it and the home language as almost the same. This may add to the difficulties faced by the mono-dialectal learner beginning formal education.

homework. *See* ASSIGNMENT.

homogeneous. 1. In language testing. Internally consistent. It is considered desirable that the components of a test be homogeneous, and focus on the skill being measured. **2.** In relation to a group of learners: a class. A class is homogeneous if it consists of members who are of a uniform kind. Such a class is considered to make for smooth teaching.

humanism. Broadly, a belief system, philosophy, or network of ideas that considers individual self and experience as of central importance. It emphasises the need for an individual's growth and fulfilment through SELF-ACTUALISATION and search for meaning in life, and believes in the development of the whole person. It holds important the role of human emotions, thoughts and feelings in shaping human learning. Two of the prominent names associated with humanism are Carl Rogers and A.H. Maslow.

humanistic approaches to language teaching. APPROACHes that attach equal importance to both the intellectual and the emotional development of the learner. In such approaches, the learners are treated as individuals with their own PERSONALITY, feelings, views, and creativity – all of which are to be respected. AUTHORITARIAN practices have no place in these approaches, and a sense of responsibility is to be developed in the learner. Learning is a co-operative venture between the learner and the teacher. HUMANISM is considered to be one of the elements of COMMUNICATIVE LANGUAGE TEACHING. New methodological proposals for teaching like TOTAL PHYSICAL RESPONSE, THE SILENT WAY, COMMUNITY LANGUAGE LEARNING, and SUGGESTOPEDIA are recognised as humanistic.

humanistic psychology. An approach to psychology concerned with the needs, well- being and personal growth of the individual. It addresses itself to the study of human beings as individuals, their capacities/potential such as creativity and love, and fulfilment of such needs as AUTONOMY, identity, SELF-ACTUALISATION, and self-knowledge.

hypercorrection. 1. The tendency to overdo a linguistic feature to sound very correct. Some users of ESL, for example, produce exaggerated diphthongs sounding thereby rather artificial. **2.** *See* Overgeneralisation.

hypothesis. 1. (In research). A supposition made (on the basis of initial observation) for further testing and confirmation. A hypothesis is proposed in a way that it can be empirically proved or falsified. (*See* Empiricism.) However, the term is not always used in a strict sense. There are many hypothetical CONSTRUCTS that cannot be empirically tested. And, many THEORIES exist in the form of hypotheses. **2.** In language acquisition. Language learners form hypotheses about language. They are derived from the data learners come across. With exposure to more data learners may have to either reject or modify some of the hypotheses formed initially. This cognitive process is considered central to language acquisition, and symptomatic of learning.

hypothesis testing. The cognitive – conscious or unconscious – process of the language learners putting to test in their use of language the hypotheses they have tentatively formed. The testing may bring forth feedback in the light of which or in the light of further, divergent data, the learner may have to reject the tested HYPOTHESIS(2), or modify it to be tested again for confirmation. Language ERRORS in learner output are considered to be the products of hypothesis-testing. Hypothesis testing is part of the language acquisition process.

hypothetical mode of teaching. Bruner's term for an interactive mode with much greater initiative for learners than is allowed in a teacher-dominated mode. Learners are encouraged to apply their minds, form HYPOTHESES(2), think, DISCOVER, and learn, rather than depend on their teachers. *See also* EXPOSITORY MODE.

I

ideation. A mental activity leading to CONCEPT formation. Prabhu (2002) defines ideation as 'the process of developing ideas or concepts by which we can gain an understanding of the nature of the world we live in'. It is through ideation that we get at knowledge. Further, according to Prabhu (*ibid.*) ideation leads to the development of language competence.

ideational function. *See* the reference to Halliday under Functions of language.

ideational scaffolding. *See* ADVANCE ORGANISER and SCAFFOLDED INSTRUCTION.

ideology. System of ideas. Different individuals, social and political groups, social, political, educational movements, institutions, castes, sects and classes possess their own doctrines, convictions, beliefs, myths and worldview to which they are committed and by which they are guided. These are collectively known as ideology, and language is one of the major mediums through which ideology finds articulation. Study of the language used by a SOCIETY reveals, among other things, ideologies at work in that society.

idiomatic. Style of speech or writing that sounds natural and grammatically correct to the [educated] users of the language. It is not easy to define/ describe features that account for naturalness but one would say that idiomatic prose has a COLLOQUIAL ring, and does not sound contrived, artificial,

affected, or pedantic. It is certainly *not* a collection of set expressions as embellishment.

An idiomatic expression is a set phrase: its meaning is different from the literal meanings of the words in it put together. *There you go* is such an expression.

idiosyncratic dialect. *See* LEARNER LANGUAGE.

image. [In language teaching] A word-picture.(*See also* the last paragraph under METAPHOR.) Images are mental pictures/impressions with the help of which complex things are often communicated holistically. An example: M. West (1960) refers to the image of 'the teacher as an obstacle.' Such a teacher is more interested in her teaching, her 'own performance as Protagonist' than in her learners' learning, the efforts they make to learn.

imitatio. A composition task in learning classical languages. It consists of producing composition in the TL carefully imitating the stylistic and rhetorical devices of a model author.

imitation. In language learning: copying SPEECH or sentence PATTERN. Imitation is the way children acquire elements of language such as ACCENT and INTONATION. Classroom teachers as models encourage imitation. Theories differ on the role of imitation in language learning. The BEHAVIOURIST THEORY believes that imitation is central to the process of learning. Mentalists, however, think that imitation applies only to the learning of such 'superficial' aspects as ACCENT and INTONATION. Acquisition of things such as meaning and rules of SENTENCE STRUCTURES belong to 'deeper' mental processes.

immersion education. A model of BILINGUAL EDUCATION in which students learn through two languages. One of them is their MT. In this model, students sharing a common MT are taught CONTENT SUBJECTS through a SL but there is little formal teaching of this SL as language. Students are expected to become proficient in the SL through the content instruction in it. Immersion education has been practised in Canada, where there are two major population groups – English-speaking, and French-speaking.

The Central Schools in India using DUAL-MEDIUM teaching, represent a similar albeit an older system.

In a dual-immersion bilingual programme, speakers of Language A learn Language B, and the speakers of Language B learn Language A. *See also* DUAL IMMERSION.

implicit. Things such as mental processes not directly observable. They are not only not observable directly, they operate outside the awareness of the individual. *See also* EXPLICIT.

incidental learning/teaching. Learning or teaching that occurs in the context of some other activity, and not as part of a planned course. Also known as 'peripheral learning,' incidental learning can be involuntary learning from the stimuli present in the environment.

Incidental teaching could be a by-product of the main teaching or a result of the teacher making a digression from it.

inclusive schooling/education. Education that accommodates difference and diversity and addresses special needs of the learners. Special-needs-learners are learners with disabilities. The mainstream education, teachers and learners have generally adopted a segregationist rather than an integrative attitude towards the learner population that falls outside the majority group, often socially advantaged and intellectually clever. It has tried to impose homogeneity and adopt a NORMATIVE attitude. Inclusive education seeks to make provision in education for the minorities. For example, in the language curriculum, it would include an introduction to, or a study of, SIGN LANGUAGE used by the hearing impaired. *See also* SPECIAL EDUCATION, and TEACHING LANGUAGE TO THE DISADVANTAGED.

incorporation strategy. Forming an utterance by incorporating in it chunks from the previous UTTERANCE. SL learners often construct utterances by borrowing portions of the preceding utterance and adding a word or two at its beginning or end. **Example,**
Question: *Do you like ice-cream?*
Answer: *I no like ice-cream.*

indigenisation. The process of an outside language like English in India being increasingly used by indigenous people, and getting subjected to local influences including those of grammar, phonology, and vocabulary. By being used in the new social and cultural milieu, the indigenised language develops new features and a new identity which qualifies it to be called a variety in its own right. Kachru (1983), among others, has claimed this status for English in India.

indigenous approaches. Locally

developed approaches to teaching as different from imported packages. Much theorizing and prescription on SL teaching until recently have been expert-driven and often products of laboratory conditions. Not surprising that they have not worked when practised in a different context and milieu. Instead of relying on experts and external sources, need has been felt for exploring alternatives that use local expertise and resources better suited to local conditions. The local here may include indigenous traditions of learning, TEACHER BELIEFS, learner ATTITUDES, and institutional resources.

Some educationists suggest that if these factors are reckoned, approaches that work in specific contexts may be developed.

indirect method. The DEDUCTIVE mode of teaching SLs with the help of the rules of GRAMMAR & vocabulary and some support from the MT. In other words 'the indirect method' is the GRAMMAR-TRANSLATION way of teaching, and the term appears to be a kind of back formation from the DIRECT METHOD.

C.J. Dodson (1967: pp37-8) has this to say about the Indirect Method. 'In its extreme form the Indirect Method implies that the learner is initially presented with a set of grammatical rules and a certain amount of foreign language vocabulary together with a printed text incorporating the new rules and words.' In his comments on the Method, Dodson 'deplores' the neglect in it of oral skills.

indirect tests. Tests of language knowledge that do not involve pro-

duction of DISCOURSE by the test-taker. Indirect tests of language proficiency are designed to draw inferences about the test-takers' language competence on the basis of tasks such as multiple-choice test-items. Such items typically make test-takers either to recognise the correct answer amidst distractors, supply words to fill in vacant slots, transform sentences, spot errors, or correct them. But they do not require them to produce discourse representing their language- competence, as direct tests of speaking and writing do.

individualised instruction. INSTRUCTION suited to the specific level and needs of individual learners.

individualisation. Less teacher control and a lot of learner AUTONOMY in language learning. In it SELF-INSTRUCTIONAL MATERIALS and aids are made available, and the learners decide what they will learn. They take on the responsibility for their learning.

individualism. Principle that put the rights of the individual above social rights. Individualism believes in the autonomy of the individual which it seeks to hold up. It also justifies attitudes and behaviour that show personal independence and ability to take one's own decisions, and resist domination by others. *Cf.* INDIVIDUALITY.

Trends in LE in the direction of learner-AUTONOMY, OPEN LEARNING, and learning to learn may be said to accord with the principles of individualism.

individuality. Characteristics or uniqueness of an individual's PERSONALITY that distinguish her from other individuals. Each learner (in the class) is in a way unique since she has her own individual characteristics and differences. Hence she deserves to be treated as an individual. The practice, however, has generally been to treat learners as an undifferentiated mass. *See also* LEARNER CHARACTERISTICS.

individual learner differences. *See* LEARNER CHARACTERISTICS.

individuation. A psychological process of the development of the self. A concept derived from HUMANISTIC thinking, individuation relates to the development among learners of a sense of personal worth and identity, of their individuality, and their belonging to a group or community. A sense of self-worth is considered to make one a good learner. Similarly, a sense of belonging to a community/group contributes to making one a better participants in an interactive/communicative class.

induced errors. LANGUAGE ERRORS resulting from the nature of the formal instruction that learners receive. For example, many teachers when explicating the meaning of a text, use the structure *The writer says that...* so frequently that learners are led to use it in constructions where they are not appropriate, **Example**, *The writer says that why do people....* Such errors are also known as teacher/teaching induced errors.

induction. (In learning, the aprocess of) arriving at a conclusion/GENERALISATION from specific data, clues and examples. For the generalisation to be valid it is necessary that the data be large and representative.

inductive learning. Learning by observing and drawing GENERALISATIONS. Exposure to data/INPUT(1) is an impor-

tant condition. In learning by INDUCTION, learners are exposed to a lot of language data but are not given EXPLICIT rules. The DIRECT METHOD is based on learning by induction. A good example of inductive learning is the acquisition of language(s) by children. *See also* DEDUCTIVE LEARNING.

Inferencing. Inferring implied meaning(s): drawing conclusions by interpreting facts and applying one's reasoning and knowledge of the world.

In the context of LL, inferencing may be defined as the cognitive skill of quickly comprehending discourse [written/spoken] or units of it using one's knowledge of the language, the context – linguistic and situational – in which it occurs, and one's personal knowledge. In inferencing, some imagination and techniques of intelligent GUESSING are applied.

One of the traits attributed to the GOOD LANGUAGE LEARNER is a sharp inferencing ability. It is to be noted that implicit in the process of READING is constant inferencing and guessing (among such other things as anticipating). So is the case in conversation, where NEGOTIATION OF MEANING proceeds as the interlocutors judge the implications [value] of the UTTERANCES [rather than their signification].

information gap. Situation in which a person does not have, and needs, the information that her INTERLOCUTOR has. In authentic, real-life communication, the participants often say or write things aimed at supplying information so that the gap between what they have to say, or know and what the other participant(s) know(s) may be filled. This is an important purpose and function of COMMUNICATION.

Information-gap tasks are used in SL classes to bring in AUTHENTICITY. Such tasks engage pairs or groups of learners in (re)constructing information on the basis of verbal and visual prompts and cues provided.

information transfer. A learning task: a language-testing task. The performance of the task requires the learner/test-taker to (i) comprehend the prompt material presented in one mode, and (ii), to represent it through another. The MODES for presenting information could be verbal or graphic. The verbal include written/spoken texts such as dialogues, narrations, descriptions. The graphics include charts, diagrams, graphs, tables and such other objects.

The transfer-task of first comprehending information and then expressing/representing it in a different mode is an INTEGRATIVE task, and engaging in it involves effort after meaning: understanding & interpreting it and then communicating it verbally/graphically. This is considered to be supportive of language acquisition.

initial-reading methods. Approaches that introduce beginning learners to reading. There are different approaches and methods, and these have been treated here under the following: Alphabetic method, Apprentice approach, Look-and-say (method), Phonics, psycholinguistic method, the sentence method, Sight reading and Whole-word approach.

initial teaching. Introducing/presenting

to the learners teaching items (words, structures, etc.) for the first time. (*See also* PRESENTATION.) Initial teaching is contrasted with re-teaching of the item for the sake of practice or for REMEDIAL TEACHING.

initial teaching alphabet (ITA). Phonetically and 'rationally' modified system of ALPHABETS to help beginners to read. In such a system spelling inconsistencies are avoided by making one letter represent one sound.

The ITA experiment has not been very popular. *See also* INITIAL TEACHING METHODS.

innateness hypothesis. *See* LANGUAGE ACQUISITION DEVICE.

innovation. *See* CURRICULAR INNOVATION.

input. 1. Language data (written and spoken) a learner is exposed to. It is hypothesised that learners 'acquire' language by processing the input, which involves comprehending it and relating it to the context of its use. Mere exposure to the input is not enough. **2.** [In pedagogical contexts.] Input is what language learners receive from TEACHER TALK and interaction with the teacher and the peers. It is observed that the input a teacher provides the learners is not very effective unless they pay attention and make it INTAKE. **3.** [In language testing contexts.] The word, phrase, sentence, extended discourse (printed/recorded/spoken), or the graphic material used as stimulus to elicit response (oral or written) from the test-taker(s).

input hypothesis. Hypothesis put forth by S. Krashen (1982) that learners acquire language when they receive input that contains structure that is a little higher than their level of competence and comprehension at that time. *See also* COMPREHENSIBLE INPUT

inset. Training of in-service or practising teachers. A distinction is drawn between the education of those who are training to become teachers and have no prior experience of formal teaching, and the education of those who are already in the profession. The training of prospective teachers is sometimes referred to as initial training. In-service training is usually given in the form of REFRESHER COURSES.

institutional discourse. DISCOURSE (2) specific to the context of an institution. The context determines the nature of the discourse. For example, the interaction and discourse in a classroom follow a pedagogic orientation and are institution-specific.

instructed learning. Formal-teaching based learning of a language. There are two major contexts of language learning: (i) in a NATURAL SETTING (as happens in the case of the mother-tongue); (ii) in a formal way as in the CLASSROOM setting – the latter kind being 'instructed learning.' The two modes have their attendant characteristics.

Sometimes, to make learning effective, some approaches to SL INSTRUCTION try to create in the classroom the semblance of a natural setting. *Cf.* STREET LEARNING.

instruction. Teaching of a particular skill or subject. Generally it takes place in formal contexts, primarily in teacher-fronted classroom settings. There are, however, in use alternative modes for the delivery of instruction.

See also INSTRUCTION DELIVERY MODE/STRATEGIES.

instruction-delivery modes/strategies. Ways of reaching out instruction to learners. There are two basic modes: face-to-face and distance. Modern technology has made possible and available various combinations of these two.

Presentation of teaching or supervision of learning in the face-to-face mode employs a variety of TECHNIQUES and activities. Some of these are: LECTURING, talking & blackboard use, individual work, GROUP-WORK, drama, ROLE-PLAY, debate, demonstration, listening and responding to recorded material, video-based interaction, LANGUAGE-LAB practice, picture/cartoon-motivated oral or written work, computer-based work, and learning coupled with physical activity.

In the DISTANCE LEARNING mode, the major means of delivering instruction are self-instructional package and multi-media package.

instructional-design planning. A process for course development by the instructor(s) and planning team, with more attention to specific details and individual study. It is similar to CURRICULUM-planning, but more comprehensive in that it includes such additional factors as instructional problems, LEARNER CHARACTERISTICS, task-component analysis, INSTRUCTIONAL-DELIVERY plan, and support resources.

instructional media. The audio-visual media [new and/or old] when used for teaching. Some newspaper features, radio broadcasts, films, and TV programmes are produced with the express objective of providing instruction. They have generally been used as support in mainstream education, but they play a more significant role in distance education and open learning systems. There are for the learners in these systems regular radio and TV channels that broadcast instructional programmes. They may support, or be independent of, institutional face-to-face and distance mode programmes of education.

In an indirect way, media programmes (news, films, serials, etc.), though not designed for pedagogical purposes, offer a rich source of language experience and INPUT. They carry AUTHENTIC contexts of language use, and on the TV the visual support facilitates comprehensibility, and cognitive applications.

New technology has made it possible for the media to become more interactive with learners, making instant FEEDBACK possible.

instructional objectives. Learning outcomes that teaching in the instructional setting plans to achieve. It is useful to set up objectives and work for them though there may not always be symmetry between instructional endeavour and learning outcomes.

Taxonomies of objectives have been set up in the past as part of CURRICULUM planning and development. In this area, the work of the US educationist Benjamin Bloom is well known. He worked out mid-twentieth century a detailed taxonomy of educational objectives. They relate to three domains of human development: cognitive, affective, and psychomotor skills.

instrument. A tool designed and developed for the purpose of measuring and judging. A LANGUAGE TEST is an instrument. So is a CHECKLIST.

instrumental motivation. *See* MOTIVATION.

intake. That portion of INPUT that the learners notice, process, and make part of their memory & knowledge. The process of intake occurs in various ways, primarily through mental effort. This distinction between input and intake was made by S Pit Corder (1967).

integrated language teaching. An approach to language teaching in which the four skills of language – listening, speaking, reading and writing are taken up simultaneously rather than sequentially. Integrated approaches see the various skills of language as inter-related and mutually reinforcing. *See also* INTEGRATIVE.

integrative. Involving more than one language skill. A language task is integrative if it requires the learner, for example, not only to read & interpret a text but also to write the interpretation as a well-composed piece

integrative motivation. *See* MOTIVATION.

integrative reconciliation. A cognitive process in learning. In it the learner is supposed to meaningfully relate and synthesise newly-learnt things with the previously learnt ones. The process needs the instructor's guidance and the learner's co-operation. Reconciliation follows PROGRESSIVE DIFFERENTIATION. Learners are known to approach new knowledge in the light of what they know already. Instructional techniques cognizant of this help learners to integrate. *See also* ACCOMMODATION (1), and ASSIMILATION.

integrative test of language. Test of language (proficiency) through tasks that brings into play a combination of skills. For example, a writing TASK tests INTEGRATIVEly the test-takers' knowledge, among other things, of sentence construction, vocabulary, and discourse constraints. The notion of 'integration' (specially in language testing) is a back-formation concept from a reaction to tests that comprised a succession of DISCRETE-POINT (TESTING) items each of which focused on a single element of language. **Example**, the correct response to an item like *'He ... home yesterday.' (go)* requires the test-takers to display their knowledge of the appropriate verb form in the restricted and isolated context of the given sentence frame. Used in the PRACTICE-based, form-oriented, SL pedagogy and discrete-point LANGUAGE–TESTING, such atomistic treatment of language is now considered to be lacking in VALIDITY.

intelligence. In general terms, the capacity of the mind to learn, think and understand quickly, to make judgements and to reason logically. Intelligence is cognitive faculty, distinct from the factor of affect. [*See* EMOTIONAL INTELLIGENCE].

Intelligence consists of groups of sub-abilities specific to different mental functions. It is a factor considered facilitative of language learning.

Some psychologists hold a unitary view of intelligence, i.e., intelligence was one single, integrated TRAIT. The

view has been challenged in favour of multiple intelligence. The concept of 'multiple intelligence' relates to intelligence in more fields than only in the cognitive – appreciation of art and music, emotional stability, etc.

intelligence quotient (IQ). Ratio of MENTAL AGE to chronological AGE, expressed as a percentage. It is a figure arrived at by dividing the mental age (say 12)of a child by her actual age (say 10) and then multiplying the outcome by 100 (in this case $12 \div 10 = 1.2 \times 100 = 120$). An IQ of 100 is considered to be average. The mental age is arrived as a result of a standard test developed to measure the INTELLIGENCE of a child/person below the age of 18. What constitutes intelligence has been a matter of debate, and its measurement has not been free of cultural BIAS.

intelligence tests. TESTS to measure INTELLIGENCE. The French psychologist Alfred Binet (1857–1911) is considered the pioneer of modern intelligence testing. He and the psychiatrist Theodore Simon(1837–1961) developed Binet-Simon Tests. Along with their later adaptations, there are now available a number of intelligence tests. Generally, a test consists of sub-tests each aimed at measuring a particular ability such as the ability to read and comprehend or the ability to write, or to reason verbally. The measurement leads to a score, INTELLIGENCE QUOTIENT.

intelligent eclecticism. *See* GLOSSODYNAMIC MODEL, and ECLECTICISM.

intelligibility. A quality and a measure of how easily and how well someone's speech can be understood. The criterion of intelligibility is related mainly

113

to articulation and pronunciation. A related concept is that of 'comprehensibility', which is a measure of how well the meaning of a text – its language and subject content – can be understood by the learners at a given level of proficiency.

Intelligibility of speech and comprehensibility of texts are not absolute qualities. They are relative to the context and the listener/reader's background knowledge and ability to process spoken and written messages. A domain where intelligibility is of great importance is that of classroom pedagogy.

intelligibility and correctness. The question whether FORMAL(2) correctness is sufficient condition for the INTELLIGIBILITY of speech. It has been noted that ACCURACY and intelligibility do not always go together, and a perfect pronunciation is not a precondition for intelligibility (Abercrombie, 1949).

Also, LINGUISTIC intelligibility alone is not a sufficient condition for efficient communication. Catford (1950) has shown that despite intelligibility, an utterance may remain ineffective.

intensive reading. Reading a text in detail, and for its details. Such reading is usually (but not necessarily) applied to short, and richly- or intricately-woven texts. **Example**, poems and legal documents. The aim of intensive reading, necessarily slow, is to achieve a high degree of accuracy in COMPREHENSION.

In many contexts of LL&LT, textual materials have been subjected to one invariable style – the style and speed of intensive reading irrespective of the nature and purpose of the text. This makes reading a slow and laborious process and learners do not learn to vary speed to suit different reading needs such as those of SKIMMING and SCANNING. *See also* CLOSE READING and READING STRATEGIES.

interaction. The VERBAL communication-process of meaning-negotiation between two or more interactants. Interaction includes interpersonal language use and social interaction, though in the present context of LE, the reference is to the verbal exchanges between the teacher and the learner and among learners, also known as CLASSROOM INTERACTION. Learner participation in this is significant as it is considered to be conducive to LA. Hence, a variety of learning activities have been ingeniously devised to foster acquisition through interaction. New formats of classroom teaching encourage learner-learner interaction in PAIR WORK and GROUP WORK. *See also* INTERACTION ANALYSIS.

LISTENING and READING also become interactive processes when the listeners/readers are focused on meaning.

From an educational point of view, epecially in teacher education and in teacher research, analysis and study of interaction is of key importance to the understanding of learning and teaching.

In language testing, the oral COMMUNICATIVE COMPETENCE of the test-takers is judged on the basis of their performance in simulated interaction. *See also* NEGOTIATION OF MEANING.

interactional modification. Communication adjustment and repair resorted to by the participants in conversational interaction. These are done to ensure that there is no miscomprehension. Modification techniques in oral communication are used when there are glitches. Some of these techniques are comprehension checks, requests for clarification, and for confirmation.

interaction analysis. Analysis of CLASSROOM INTERACTION – of language use by the teacher and the learners in the classroom. The data for analysis is collected through coding systems, observation, and audio and video recording. The purpose of the analyses is to research into classroom procedures and learning and teaching.

interaction in the classroom. *See* CLASSROOM INTERACTION.

interactionist learning theory. The theory that acquisition of language results from an interaction between the learners' innate mental abilities and their linguistic environment. This position is an INTERFACE between the opposite claims that either extremely minimise the role (in language acquisition) of innate abilities or that of the linguistic environment.

Interactionist theory also corresponds with the position according to which language acquisition is seen a result of the learner's engagement in social interaction and communication.

interactive approaches to reading. Approaches to text-decoding which see it as an interplay between the BOTTOM-UP and TOP-DOWN approaches, and treat them as mutually compatible. It considers that both knowledge of form (CODE) and its discrete units, and a holistic approach to meaning are necessary in interpreting texts, to which the readers may bring their own meanings. There is a constant interaction between the reader and the text in the act of reading. *See also* READING PROCESS.

interactive language teaching. Language teaching, especially SLT, in which INTERACTION between the teacher and the learners and among learners themselves plays a central role.

interdependency hypothesis. The hypothesis that the development of a skill or TRAIT in one area will lead to the development of that trait in another area, given opportunities. *See also* INTERDEPENDENCY PRINCIPLE.

interdependency principle. The notion that COGNITIVE-ACADEMIC LANGUAGE PROFICIENCY (CALP) is common across languages and is transferable from L1 use to L2 use. The notion has implications for BILINGUAL EDUCATION. If true, it means that educators should ensure that learners have a good grounding in the MT before a SL is introduced to them. Jim Cummins (1979) is a strong exponent of the principle. It may have a message for those countries where a large number of people want the teaching of English as a SL to begin in the elementary classes where learners are still learning their mother tongue.

interface position. The position that mediates between two extreme views on an issue, and avoids the either/or choice.

interference. The negative influence of the rules in the grammatical, phonological, and semantic systems of the learner's MT over her learning of a new language-system. The

BEHAVIOURIST LEARNING THEORY held that those MT rules that were different from the corresponding rules in the SL were potential sources of interference, and caused learning difficulties. Interference or negative TRANSFER onto the SL being learnt may be caused not only by the MT influence; it may also result from the learner's contact with some other language. See also CROSS-LINGUISTIC INFLUENCE and LANGUAGE TRANSFER.

interim grammar. A limited set of rules of grammar learners form [in their minds] at different stages on their way to ever-growing knowledge of the language they are learning. Interim grammars are passing phases. Learners keep expanding them as they DISCOVER new and more complex rules.

interim report on vocabulary selection. Report of a conference held in 1934 under the auspices of the Carnegie Corporation. It was published in 1936 by P. S. King & Co. The purpose of the Conference was 'to study the FREQUENCY with which various words occur in spoken and written English'. The idea was to use the findings as the basis for selecting vocabulary for learning English as a foreign language. The Report included a GENERAL SERVICE LIST of two thousand most frequent English words.

interlanguage. (IL). A distinct linguistic SYSTEM different from a learner's native language and the target SL but related to both. The term was coined by Selinker (1972) to refer to the language system created by learners learning a SL. The system is an interim grammar of the TL the learner has created for

herself. It is a system that contains the rules of both, the learner's L1 and the TL. It is hypothesised that learners move towards a mastery of the language through successive 'interim grammars' that they construct in their minds by forming rules derived from the data they receive as input. At any given intermediate stage the 'grammar' is considered to be more or less 'systematic' [though it has a lot of VARIABILITY] in that it has its own rules, which may be at variance from an educated [native] speaker's grammar of the language. But since the rules, as evidenced in the learner's use of the language, are often consistent, linguists do not treat them as incorrect. They would rather like to call them systems that approximate the TL grammar. Since the learner's system is a developing one, it is treated as reflective of his/her transitional competence. And, instead of being indicative of failed learning, it is indicative of learner achievement.

Since its coinage, the term has come to be used in a number of slightly varying meanings. IL refers to both, the process of approximating, and the outcome/output of the transitional competence.

interlanguage/interlingual communication strategies. See COMMUNICATION STRATEGIES.

interlanguage grammar. Learners' developing SYSTEM of the SL GRAMMAR. The 'grammar' is a dynamic and ever expanding system. INTERANGUAGE grammar consists of the rules learners have formed and internalised at a given point of time during the process of the expansion of their interlanguage. VARIABILITY is a characteristic of such grammars.

interlanguage talk. Language used by SL learners. In non-native learning environments much input for it is derived from the peer-talk interlanguage.

interlingual transfer. Transfer of a rule in one language to the use of another, also known as 'INTERFERENCE'. **Example**, in English the word *news* is an uncountable noun and is used in singular number, though the word appears to be in plural number form. If in the learner's MT, the equivalent of the word news is a countable noun and can be pluralized, she is likely to apply this to English also creating expressions like – *many news are...*, an instance of transfer.

Interlingual transfer is also a COMMUNICATION STRATEGY SL learners may have to recourse to.

interlingual errors. Errors resulting from INTERLINGUAL TRANSFER.

interlocutor. A person taking part in a dialogue or conversation. In LT, interlocutory activities are built in to develop among the learners communicative abilities. An interlocutor in testing oral-communication-competence through oral INTERVIEWS (2) is an interviewer who may either act as a participant-judge or facilitator, or both. But usually the two roles are performed by separate persons, and they are trained to perform their roles in such a way that there is no distortion (or minimal distortion) in the evaluation caused by the interlocutor effect.

internal consistency. A quality of a language TEST. It is a measure of how well the scores on individual items of a test or on its divisions correlate with each other.

international language. A language that people (can) use to communicate with each other across national boundaries. An international language facilitates global communication and is used in a variety of contexts and for a variety of purposes such as aviation, business and commerce, education, information, and socio-cultural interaction. An international language may have more non-native speakers than native and may be a LINGUA FRANCA for the former.

International Phonetic Alphabet (IPA). An alphabet of about 95 characters/symbols or phones in which each symbol represents a speech sound. Also known as the phonemic alphabet, IPA is so devised that it can represent all the PHONEMES in the languages of the world. The alphabet has been devised with the aim of providing a universally agreed system of notation for the sounds of languages.

inter-rater reliability. A measure of consensus between or among raters judging independently the performance of candidates on a language test.

interteaching. The stage when a student-teacher (teacher-trainee) is learning to teach. The concept, derived from an analogy with INTERLANGUAGE, posits that a teacher in training comes to the job with an already conceived theory of teaching. This theory is based on her previous experience of being taught and of observing teaching. Interteaching passes through successive modifications and reconceptualisations as the student-teacher reflects on her own and others' teaching and gains deeper insight.

interview. 1. A formal meeting at which candidates seeking jobs are asked questions by the employers or their representatives. Sometimes in combination with the oral questions, the candidates are asked to perform certain tasks. The main purpose of the interview is to judge the candidates' suitability for the job they are being interviewed for. **2.** The interview mode is applied in COMMUNICATIVE LANGUAGE TESTING to judge the candidates' oral COMMUNICATIVE COMPETENCE. In addition to the interviewer, there are usually observers who rate the candidates' performance. This is done to bring in RELIABILITY in scoring. **3.** A tool for gathering information for research or evaluation purposes. Interviews may be structured or OPEN-ENDED. The latter may be held, unnoticed by the interviewee as part of some other activity, **Example**, teaching.

interview scale. An interview-schedule/a QUESTIONNAIRE in which questions in the form of statements are ranked according to the degree of agreement/disagreement to be indicated by the respondents. *See also* ATTITUDE SCALE.

intonation. Pattern of variation in the pitch of the voice – rising, falling, falling-rising. When we speak, our PITCH goes on changing; it is seldom that we speak on a monotone. Pitch variation forms d.fferent patterns over utterances. For most linguists, the term 'intonation' refers to the melody in speech, resulting from variation in pitch.

intralingual. Something that operates, belongs, or generates from within a language as different from something that exists outside it. An intralingual error is an ERROR based on analogy drawn from the rules of the language, **Example** He *sitted* on the chair.

introspection. Looking into one's mind, into one's experience of such things as learning and teaching. In REFLECTIVE practice – both learning and teaching – introspection has an important role.

introversion. *See* Extroversion.

IPA. *See* International Phonetic Alphabet.

IQ. *See* INTELLIGENCE QUOTIENT.

IRF cycle. The 'Initiation, Response, Feedback/follow up' cycle: the typical sequence of exchange between the teacher and the learner(s) in the classroom. It begins with the teacher asking a question or eliciting response. Learner answer/response thus elicited is followed by the teacher evaluating it and/or providing FEEDBACK.

It is noted that the IRF cycle repeats frequently in an interactive classroom. Instances of the IRF sequence may not be many in classes where the teacher adopts an information-transmitter role, or the LOCK-STEP styles of teaching, *See also* Triadic dialogue, and F-move.

island vocabulary. *See* Restricted vocabulary.

ITA. *See* Initial teaching alphabet.

item. 1. A discrete/distinct UNIT (1): a single thing in a group or list of things. In the LE context, the term is often used to refer to *linguistic items* such as a PHONEME, sound, WORD, or STRUCTURE. **2.** TEST ITEM. A constituent element in a language test, particularly a DISCRETE-POINT one.

item analysis. Evaluation of TEST ITEMS by applying statistical measures to see whether a test/test item possesses, and to what degree, the required attributes.

item bank A pool of pre-analysed TEST-ITEMS to be drawn from for such purposes as developing language tests, revising them, and creating parallel versions.

item difficulty. A measure of how difficult or easy it is to correctly answer a test item. Based on results of test-trials, item difficulty is judged by the frequency with which correct or incorrect responses to the item are given. Such judgment helps so moderate the difficulty level of a (language) test.

J

jargon. Technical terminology used by specialists in a profession. Since it is difficult for laymen to understand it, 'jargon' has come to mean language that is unintelligible or meaningless. Use of too many difficult words in one's speech or writing inflicting obscurity on the listener/reader is viewed unfavourably.

jigsaw task. A language learning task in which the learner has to fit together correctly parts of a sentence, and sentences in a paragraph. To create the task, sentence-parts and/or sentences are jumbled up. Care is taken to ensure that there is only one correct way of reassembling them.

A jigsaw task is a cognitive task. In trying to reassemble the pieces, the learner has to consider meaning and permissible syntactic-combinations.

The jigsaw language-task takes after a jigsaw puzzle – a picture so cut into irregular pieces that they can be put together to correctly form the complete picture.

journal. A written record of events. In the context of LT, it is a narrative of the writer's activities, comments on them, experiences and responses to situations, and even beliefs, etc. A journal is different from a DIARY. The writing of a journal, intended to pro-mote the writer's thinking and self-expression, has a pedagogic orientation, and can be shared with teachers, peers and others.

journal writing [JW]. A strategy for promoting REFLECTIVE LEARNING. It is a mode of reflective interaction between an individual student and teacher. Students on a particular instructional programme write in a journal (notebook) their REFLECTION(1) and observation on teaching. JW is also done by novice teachers in training undergoing the PRACTICUM component. In JW, the writers think reflectively about their own observations on, and experiences of teaching or learning and put down their reflections and observations.

The teacher reads through the journal once a week and writes her comments on the margin. The comments [may] lead to further reflection in the student and also in the teacher. Recorded oral discussion and interview may also follow.

The reflectiveness and the heightened awareness created by JW are supposed to help enrich experience, give clarity of thought and argument; develop mutual understanding and problem-solving-skills. JW can be instrumental in ACTION RESEARCH.

The reflective element of journal writing distinguishes it from diary keeping. It is also different from academic writing tasks in its purpose.

K

knowledge. The sum of information possessed by a person. This may be derived from experience, scholarship or understanding. Knowledge has been classified into types: ANALYTICAL, factual, PROCEDURAL, etc. Factual knowledge is also known as DECLARATIVE KNOWLEDGE. In LE-related contexts, one may also refer to METALINGUISTIC KNOWLEDGE.

knowledge about language (KAL). METALINGUISTIC AWARENESS about one's language. It contrasts with that implicit knowledge which is reflected in one's use of one's language. But KAL is not just a knowledge of the grammatical terminology. KAL consists of such awarenesses as of how accents and dialects of a language inevitably change across time and space. Such awareness is considered not only to sharpen one's understanding but also to develop perspective, and tolerance of differences. *See also* LANGUAGE AWARENESS.

knowledge-in-action. Knowledge that underlies action such as teaching. The knowledge derives from the practitioners' observation, REFLECTION (2), and insights and is externalised in their performance. Schon (1983) has used the concept in the context of teachers' professional practice.

knowledge structures. *See* SCHEMATA.

L

laddering. Providing the learner facilitative and enabling conditions – stimuli, cues, assistance – that make it possible for the learner to move on their own from their current level of understanding/competence to the next. *See also* SCAFFOLDED INSTRUCTION and ZONE OF PROXIMAL DEVELOPMENT.

language. A rule-governed SYSTEM for conveying and receiving meaning – a means of COMMUNICATION and social INTERACTION. Meaning here includes experiences, feelings and emotions, ideas, and thoughts. The system is a set of symbols – sounds or speech symbols and written symbols. [Signs and gestures may also be considered symbols as they perform the same function as spoken or written words.] Linguists consider speech as the primary form of language, and writing, that followed much later in history, is the way speech is conventionally represented

A language chooses arbitrarily the symbols it uses. Thus there is no logical connection, **Example**, between the meaning of the word 'book' and how the word is pronounced or written. Different languages use different symbols for the same meaning. However, the symbols are 'meaningfully discrete', i.e., changing the sequence and position of symbols or substituting them may change the meaning of a word (**Example**, GOD-DOG).

Languages men use are unique in many ways: Only human beings are gifted with this faculty. MENTALIST THEORIES claim that language is instinc-

tual to humans. Though animals use a rudimentary form of signalling, human language is very different from animal communication. Language can be used for talking about what happened in the past or somewhere else, but the signalling used by animals relates only to the immediate. Language being creative, one who knows a language can create ever new sentences in it.

A language is not a monolith: it consists of a number of DIALECTS and VARIETIES distinguished along the axes of time, place, user, purpose and the domain/context of use.

'Language' has been looked at from different perspectives. A linguist studies it as an abstract system, whereas the study of its use in communication, in society, is the domain of the sociolinguist.

Human languages are natural languages, but there are also ARTIFICIAL LANGUAGES such as Esparanto, and of course there are computer languages.

language acquisition. *See* ACQUISITION OF LANGUAGE.

language acquisition device (LAD). The innate, biologically programmed, mechanism instrumental in acquiring the GRAMMAR(1) of a language. The linguist N. Chomsky has hypothesised that LAD is pre-ordained in humans with the underlying rules of UNIVERSAL GRAMMAR. Operating on the language input received, it selects and activates rules appropriate to the language(s) the child is exposed to.

The MENTALIST THEORIES subscribe to the LAD hypothesis. It discounts the environmentalist position on LL. However, it is debatable whether LAD constitutes a unique 'mental structure' in the human brain or is part of the general cognitive faculty of skills-learning.

language across the curriculum (LAC). The centrality of language in learning (and teaching) the various subject-areas in the curriculum – biology, maths, history and so on. LAC is one of the language-related movements of the last quarter of the twentieth century that see language playing a key role in education.

In SL pedagogy, LAC is the integration of language learning with CONTENT (3) learning.

Traditionally, languages have been taught in the language classrooms for their own sake. However, some theorists hold that language is acquired better when the learner is focused on meaning, on learning something other than the language itself. *See* CONTENT-BASED LANGUAGE INSTRUCTION.

language alternation. A bilingual technique in SL teaching. It consists of restating the learners' utterances in the target language.

language and thought. The question whether thought is dependent on language for its expression, or can exist independently of it. It is a much debated question: the question of linguistic determinism; the question as to how language determines thought and to what extent. It seems reasonable to hold that though language may not totally control thought, it does influence thinking in many ways, and that language and thought are deeply related. *See* SAPIR-WHORF HYPOTHESIS.

language awareness. Knowledge about language (as different from pro-ficiency in using language). Awareness about language – its nature, its role in human life, etc. – comes from focusing attention on language in use.

Initiated by the works of E Hawkins in the early 1980s (and following the publication of the Report of the committee of inquiry into the teaching of English language 1988) by the British Department of Education and Science), the language awareness movement in Britain has gained momentum. The movement attaches significance, among other things, to the development of children's explicit understanding of language as a system. *See also* KNOWLEDGE ABOUT LANGUAGE.

language community. *See* COMMUNITY.

language contact. A situation in which two (or more) language COMMUNITIES come in contact. This leads to BILINGUALISM and influence of one language on the other. In such a contact situation, PIDGINS may also develop.

language death. *See* Attrition.

language didactics. Second/foreign language pedagogy. Borrowed from Mackey (1965), Girard (1972) uses the term language didactics for what was considered then a newly-emergent discipline of SL teaching. The salient features of this discipline were: subscription to the BEHAVIOURIST LEARNING THEORY, the STRUCTURAL-SITUATIONAL approaches to language teaching & syllabus designing, SELECTION and GRADING of the items of structure, and VOCABULARY CONTROL based on the counts of the frequency of their occurrence. The theory of language learning prescribed a teacher-controlled format of teaching measured in the three basic steps of PRESENTATION, PRACTICE, and REMEDIATION (or, further practice). Typical of this approach was a negative attitude to learner creativity and their cognitive initiatives.

language education. A cover term for the study and practice of LT and related areas. It includes the development of curriculum, writing of instructional materials, language learning and classroom teaching, and language testing.

language error. An unacceptable instances of language use – a deviation from the norms of correct usage The sentence, 'They is gone contains', an instance of language error. Learners may make errors in using a SL, or in using another dialect/a standard, formal variety of their MT.

language exchange. A social and informal language-learning arrangement between two persons called partners. Each of them is a native speaker of a language foreign to the other. This means that they do not share a language in common. They however share the need or desire to learn the other's language.

For this the partners mutually arrange to meet periodically. Learning is reciprocal. The primary mode is conversational exchange, and the focus in the exchange is on spoken language, and culture.

The learning situation in the exchange is, to a large extent, NATURALISTIC with plenty of INFORMATION GAP.

The partner, who lives in the same area/region, is found through the internet, advertisement or personal contact. Language schools too may arrange ex-

change. In that case, the practice may become structured benefiting from the guidance of the school-faculty.

language experience approach. An integrated approach to reading and writing. In it the learners are supposed to learn language HOLISTICally without separating reading from writing, etc.

language for academic purposes (LAP). Learning and teaching a (SL) to develop competencies such as reading esp. of expository texts and formal/ACADEMIC WRITING. Though ACADEMIC SKILLS are equally important for students pursuing higher education through their mother tongue, LAP learners are typically those who are going to receive post-secondary and tertiary level education through the medium of a SL.

In LAP courses, special attention is paid to the language problems of the students particularly the non-native ones. These problems relate to such skills as understanding lectures, writing ASSIGNMENTts, and participating in SEMINARS. It is arguable whether LAP is very different in nature from LANGUAGE FOR SPECIFIC PURPOSES.

language for business purposes. *See* CUSINESS LANGUAGE.

language for general purposes. *See* GENERAL PURPOSE LANGUAGE COURSES.

language for specific purposes (LSP). Learning and teaching of a language, esp. a SL for a purpose particularly identified as target. LSP contrasts teaching and learning targeted at the achievement of language proficiency of a general kind. School teaching of a language is usually of this kind. Designed to address specific language-needs of particular groups of learners, LSP syllabuses and teaching materials are tailored according to a prior analysis of the needs of the group, its level of proficiency, and the available time and other resources. Such courses are skills- and result- oriented. *See also* ENGLISH FOR SPECIFIC PURPOSES.

language functions. *See* FUNCTIONS OF LANGUAGE.

language games. Planned activities structured as games with the purpose, often hidden, of making the participants learn a pre-identified language-point. There is an element of CHALLENGE in them. They create for learners situations in which they enjoy using the language.

For practising 'yes/no' type questions in context, a simple game could be one of asking questions about an object:

What is it?

Is it a - - ?

Games are usually more complex and interesting than the above example. They may be 'played' by whole class, a group, or a pair. As in physical games so in language games there is scoring and there are referees. Language games lead to follow-up language-use activities, such as writing.

language laboratory. A location for learning & practice in a SL with the help of mechanical aids. Generally, recorded materials (tapes, CDs, DVDs are used. There are individual booths with tape-recorders/TVs and headphones for learners. Each of them is connected to the console from where the tutor can monitor the learners' performance and provide FEEDBACK. Language labs are particularly suited to practising speech sounds, accent, intonation, etc. They can also be used for teaching listening comprehension, and reading comprehension. The scope of mechanically-aided language instruction can be much enlarged with the addition to the language lab of video facilities and computers. But that would be going outside the original design of the labs as it was during the middle years of the twentieth century, when much store was set by PRACTICE, habit formation and other principles of the behaviourist theory, and by PROGRAMMED LEARNING.

language learning. *See* ACQUISITION OF LANGUAGE.

language learning aptitude. *See* APTITUDE.

language learning theories. Hypotheses about how languages are learnt or acquired. A number of theories on the subject have been proposed. They can be limited to three broad categories: behaviourist, cognitivist/NATIVIST, and *interactionist. See* THE BEHAVIOURIST LEARNING THEORY, COGNITIVE APPROACHES TO LANGUAGE TEACHING, THE COGNITIVIST PERSPECTIVES ON LEARNING, THE INTERACTIONIST LEARNING THEORIES, and THE SOCIAL LEARNING THEORY.

language loyalty. The phenomenon of an individual or a community retaining its own language. The question of retention and maintenance arises only when the individual or the COMMUNITY is faced with the domination of another language. In such a situation the individual/community may resist the domination and hold on to its language or gradually lose it. *See also* LANGUAGE SHIFT.

language of the classroom. *See* CLASSROOM LANGUAGE.

language one (L^1). The first acquired language, usu. one's MOTHER TONGUE, native language, or VERNACULAR. The expression is used in (applied) linguistics and in pedagogic contexts to contrast the first acquired language with the language(s) learnt later. To refer to them, short forms L1, L2 or L^1, L^2 are often used.

There is a basic difference between the two: L1 is acquired without any previous knowledge or experience of learning any language; it is the other way about with a second or another language. The implications of this are of significance in SL/FL teaching and learning.

L^1 = L^2 hypothesis. The hypothesis that the process of acquiring an L2 is either identical or not very different from that of acquiring L1. The hypothesis is based on a marked similarity between the kind of language produced at the early stages of learning L1 and a SL. However, the hypothesis is a controversial one.

language practice. *See* PATTERN DRILL.

language planning, Explicit, systematically planned and institutionally organised interventionist measures to guide and control the role of languages in a multilingual society/country. It is typically aimed at controlling the use of language(s) in the public domains, including education.

Apart from this kind of functional status- planning, language planning may aim at controlling the development of a language, or the changes in it. Such measures are usu. taken in order to apply some IDEOLOGY or principle, for example to maintain the purity and use of the standard form of a language. Thus the planning may relate either to the STATUS of a language or its CORPUS.

Language planning may be motivated by considerations like national pride, EQUITY, cultural identity, efficient communication, regional balance, social and educational development. Usually, the socio-cultural, political, and educational contexts are taken into account when doing the planning.

language policy. Political decisions resulting from LANGUAGE PLANNING. The underlying motivation for language policy is mostly political rather than linguistic.

language proficiency interview. Test of proficiency in speech/spoken language. Such tests are (oral) INTERVIEW(2)-based. A variety of RATING devices and levels DESCRIPTORS are used. LPI tests use delivery and scoring modes that are either human, or machine mediated, fully automatic, or combinations of these.

language shift. Move from the use of one language to another by an individual or a community as a result of gradually adopting the language of another group or place. The change is brought about by a number of factors some of which are migration, mobility to a (usually 'higher') socio-economic stratum, formal education, or the adoption of an 'empowered' dialect.

language skills. Traditionally, the four macro skills of language: listening, speaking, reading, and writing –

(LSRW). Each of these can be broken down in a hierarchy of sub-skills.

language teaching methods. Approaches to language teaching, generally in the context of S/F L Teaching. [*See also* LANGUAGE TEACHING STYLES, METHOD, and METHODOLOGY.] Different writers have classified the METHODS differently.

Methods may be distinguished according to the language SKILLS emphasised in them, **Example**, grammar-translation vs. oral-aural. They may be distinguished along the learning theory underlying their practices, **Example**, behaviourist vs. mentalist.

Titone and Danesi (1985) classify methods into 4 groups:

1. *Inductive* (**Example**, the SUGGESTO-PEDIA and the AUDIO-LINGUAL methods),
2. *Deductive* (**Example**, the GRAMMAR-TRANSLATION method),
3. *Functional* [they use the term 'approaches.'] (language-teaching based on a NOTIONAL-FUNCTIONAL syllabus.), and
4. *Affective-based[methods]*(**Example**, TPR or SUGGESTOPEDIA)

To this one may add a fifth category of methods that are ECLECTIC in nature. See, for **example**, THE COMPLETE METHOD.

language teaching styles. Sets of coherent teaching TECHNIQUES (in practice) consistent with a particular APPROACH(2) to SL learning and teaching. The expression style is preferred by some over method because the latter suggests a rigid set of prescribed procedures, which are hardly ever followed fully in actual classroom practice. It has been noticed that during classroom-teaching, teachers [have to] resort to a mix of elements from different methods. Therefore, terms like style or strategy seem to describe the mix more appropriately. 'Style' and 'method' are not incompatibles. A COMMUNICATIVE style may, for example, be used even with the GRAMMAR-TRANSLATION METHOD.

language testing. 1. The process of examining language abilities & performance of test takers. The test takers may be students undergoing a course of study or completing it, applicants for jobs, or for admission to educational institutions, or just anyone interested in getting done an ASSESSMENT of their language abilities/Aptitude. The assessment may have a variety of purposes, which determine the orientation of the test to be used. *See* LANGUAGE TESTS. The major concern in testing has been the achievement of VALIDITY and a high degree of RELIABILITY, integral to validity. Language testing inevitably leads to certification – test-scores treated as indices of ability level and performance quality. Some new formats of (second) language testing may record test outcome in the form of descriptive statements or PROFILE instead of percentages, percentile scores or, as in educational contexts, marks and grades. **2.** A field of study dealing with the theory and practice of the construction, development, and administration of LANGUAGE TESTS and the interpretation of the scores.

The test-purpose determines the test-type the most common of which are those concerned with the assessment of ACHIEVEMENT and of PROFICIENCY.

Tests are also developed to measure such language-related attributes as ATTITUDE and INTELLIGENCE, and may be used for predicting.

Performance on a test is interpreted in terms of some reference-point. It may be a NORM or certain CRITERION.

The theory and practice of language testing has generally followed the prevailing theory regarding what language is and what it means to know a language.

Though testing is not language-specific, the discipline owes its growth and development to its need in the twentieth century in the contexts of S/F L education. *Cf.* EVALUATION AND MEASUREMENT.

language tests. Instruments designed to measure language-related abilities and aptitude. Language tests are more commonly used in S/F L contexts.

A Test is usu. a battery of TEST ITEMS, each intended to test a particular skill/sub-skill or TRAIT. Alternatively, it may consist of tasks. Tests have a variety of formats, and vary in their focus according to their purpose.

Tests have a great variety ranging from simple, informally devised classroom tests to standardised tests such as the Test of English as a Foreign Language (TOEFL). Such tests follow rigorous procedures for selecting items, analysing them, making the Test consistent and reliable, and establishing its validity.

According to their design and nature, tests may be categorised as DIRECT, DISCRETE-POINT, INTEGRATIVE, and 'communicative', etc. They may elicit oral performance or written, and may also be machine administered, and scored.

language through actions. An action-based strategy in SL teaching. In this, language learning takes place is association with the performance of actions by the learners. Language learning coordinated with action forms an essential component of SL teaching at initial stages. *See also* TOTAL PHYSICAL RESPONSE.

language through literature. 1. An approach in SLT in which literary texts (or their translations) are used as base for language learning and for communicative activities. A discussion of such things as the characters in them, their actions, and the motivations that drive them can become a rich resource for meaning-focused interaction in the language classroom. Literary texts, authentic as they are, can lead to a variety of classroom learning tasks, including writing tasks, with scope in them for imagination and expression of feelings and experience. **2.** An approach to the selection and construction of TEACHING MATERIALS for reading-based SL instruction (at the secondary or the post-secondary level). The approach takes language teaching forward from the limited goals of the mastery of vocabulary and structures. Alongside doing this, it also aims at sensitising the learners to imaginative uses of language, STYLES of writing, GENRE, LANGUAGE VARIETIES, etc.

In devising language through literature materials, first the language areas to be taught are determined on the basis of a NEEDS ANALYSIS, ERROR ANALYSIS and other DIAGNOSTIC measures. Then suitable texts from AUTHENTIC writing, preferably literary, are selected. The suitability is judged according to the text's linguistic content, its comprehensibility and complexity – whether it will suit the age-group, proficiency level and interest of the learners. If necessary, the texts are modified, adapted. Modification also relates to vocabulary and sentence-structure specifications for the material. A structured set of exercises/practice material follows each reading text. Exercises involve practice in all the four skills. In India, the approach was developed at the Central Inst. of English in 1960s.

language transfer. 1. The process of using 'in some unspecified way' the knowledge of the MT or some other language in learning a SL or a new language. A quote from Rutherford (1987 :8)may help to understand the phenomenon of language transfer: 'Everyone who has acquired a native language, ... unconsciously "knows" something about how to acquire any other language. That being so, we might therefore expect that this prior "knowledge" will manifest itself in some way through what the learner attempts to produce (i.e., say and write) in his new language at the earliest of learning.'

In the context of SL acquisition, transfer refers to the carryover of rules of the MT syntax, phonology, or semantic system to the new language being learnt and used. When the rules of L1 or some other language known to the learner get in the way of the learning of correct rules in a new language, they are supposed to lead to ERRORS.

Such an interference is an instance of negative transfer. Positive transfer is not easy to identify. **2.** The notion of transfer also applies to the transfer of skills. For example, if one has learnt how to read and write in one's MT, one can transfer these abilities to reading or writing in a SL. *See also* CROSS-LINGUISTIC INFLUENCE, INTERFERENCE, TRANSFER and TRANSFER OF SKILLS.

language use. Using/use of language for COMMUNICATION. Speaking and writing (i.e., production of language with a purpose) as also listening and reading constitute language use. In communicative approaches to language teaching, the emphasis in learning activities is on using the TL for authentic purposes *Cf.* PATTERN DRILL.

language use – purposes. *See* FUNCTIONS OF LANGUAGE.

language varieties. Slightly varying 'forms' of a language. The variation may be in grammar, phonology and/or word-usage. The variation arises from the use of the language for different purposes, at different places, in different situations, and by people of different social CLASSES, professions, etc. Thus the language used by priests in sermons forms a distinct variety from others such as the one used in the market place. Despite the variations, the varieties of a language share a common core. The 'standard' form of a language is also one of its varieties. *See* STANDARD VARIETY, and VERNACULAR TONGUE.

language Vs literature controversy. 1. The controversy whether the teaching and interpretation of literary texts should use the tools of linguistic analysis or rely on the traditional modes of literary criticism. **2.** The controversy arising from the assertion made in 1960s by SL teachers that SL learners wishing to acquire language competence should not be forced to study works of LITERATURE. They should be taught 'language skills.'

langue and parole. The abstract language system, the GRAMMAR(1) of a language, and the language actually produced by its users following that system. The terms were used by the Swiss linguist Ferdinand de Saussure early in the twentieth century.

Langue is the abstract communication system that all speakers of a language share in common. *Parole* is the utterances of real people underlying which is the grammatical system *langue*.

Chomsky has made a similar distinction between COMETENCE and PERFORMANCE. A person's language competence is her knowledge of the GRAMMAR (1) of the language: the system internalised by its speakers that enables them to use the language in performance. Performance is her externalization of this knowledge in use, i.e., *parole*

LAPSE theory. A model of comprehensive teacher education in ESL. LAPSE is an acronym made by James A. Alatis (1973/1974) to represent the areas of study which according to him are 'crucial' in the preparation of teachers of English as a SL. Though Alatis was talking in the context of ESL teachers, what he said may apply to the education of SL teachers in general. The letters in the acronym stand for: L – Linguistics. A – Anthropology. P – Psychology [psychology of language acquisition]. S – Sociology of language or sociolinguistics. English:

(i) English
(ii) Education

(i) English includes 'courses in the history of English language and literature' as well as courses in English linguistics. Education 'includes all things pedagogical' specially methodology of SL teaching including supervised practice teaching, etc., and language testing.

Alatis is aware that the 'LAPSE theory' might sound 'whimsical,' but he quotes authority to justify it. What it recommends represents the thinking in early 1970s on the contents of a teacher education programme.

large class. A teacher-fronted, teacher-controlled, non-interactive language class. There is no agreed optimum number of students in a language class. Yet a class having more than thirty–thirty-five students is generally considered large. Apart from its number, a large class is identified by certain INSTRUCTIONal procedures such as teacher-centredness, LOCK-STEP style of teaching, LECTURE presentation, less attention to individual learning needs and LEARNING STYLES. Large classes have fixed seating arrangement and give an impression of crowdedness.

'Non-interactive' in the definition above is not intended to suggest that the learners in a large class have no mental participation or interaction. What is meant is that in a large class it is not possible to have much verbal INTERACTION between teacher and learners, and among learners themselves. *See also* 'PROBLEM' CLASSES.

lateral thinking. A multi-pronged way of looking at problems with a view to finding solutions. In this mode of thinking, imagination plays a part in establishing links between things not normally associated with each other. Non-lateral or linear thinking approaches a problem in a simple, direct, manner, seeing direct connections between things. Lateral thinking tries to discover links that would normally be given up as unlikely. It cuts across established brain patterns, and encourages divergent ideas. The concept of lateral thinking and the invention of the term is attributed to Dr Edward de Bono, who claims to have invented it. *See also* PARALLEL THINKING.

learner. A person who is learning a language. In the context of SL education, 'learner' usu. refers to somebody (irrespective of her age) who is not yet fully proficient in the TL. She may or may not be formally enrolled in an educational institution.

LEARNER AUTHENTICITY. *See* AUTHENTICITY.

learner beliefs (about language learning). Learners' notions of, and attitudes on, such things as their competence and how they learn, what they need to learn, what they should be taught, what learning techniques they should adopt, what role the teacher should play in teaching, and whether it would be good for them to be teacher-dependent, or self-dependent. The popularity of private tuitions young learners take is indicative of the belief, among other things, in the dependency role of the learner and in teacher-driven learning. Many learners believe that the way to

learn a language is through an explicit mastery of the formal rules of grammar. The belief-system of a learner influences her learning, esp. of a SL.

learner-centred. Approaches, materials and methods that primarily address, and respond to, learner needs. This implies that these [approaches, etc.] take due cognizance of such learner-related things as their preferred STYLES OF LEARNING, their individual characteristics, their special social, cultural, and educational contexts. In these [approaches, etc.] the learners are not passive, but active participants in the organisation of teaching. They participate in making decisions about what they will be taught, how and in which order and how they will be evaluated. Awareness is created in them for them to develop the ability to judge, and to wield responsibility. They are encouraged to articulate their views and preferences. However, learner-centred curricula do not relegate teachers to a minor position. In fact, they empower teachers to take initiatives, negotiate with learners, and take decisions jointly – decisions consonant with the particular instructional contexts.

learner-centred classroom. A classroom learning environment where LEARNER-CENTRED TEACHING is practised. In such a classroom, among other things, the accent is on learners working co-operatively in groups to achieve their goals in learning. Teacher help and guidance are available. *See also* LEARNER-CENTRED TEACHING.

learner-centred teaching. An innovative model of/approach to language pedagogy. It envisages a new culture of

learning and teaching. The distinctive features of which are:
- it is implicit from the beginning that the teacher's role is that of a facilitator: learning has to be done by the learner;
- learners are weaned off their dependent role;
- teaching aims at developing among learners i)cognitive structures to understand and solve problems; and ii) enabling skills so that the learners may move towards AUTONOMY in learning – to become autonomous;
- for this, the learners are encouraged to take responsibility for their learning;
- they are made available opportunities for interaction & individual work,
- they are treated as individuals – as cognitive and affective entities (individuals with self-esteem and confidence in their ability to learn)
- they are encouraged to learn at their pace, according to their preferred styles and needs of learning;
- there are no strictly set procedures for teaching;
- the mode of learning encouraged is the social, non-competitive mode. COLLABORATIVE LEARNING and GROUP WORK are part of this culture.

Some of the traditional practices not favoured are the dispenser role of the teacher, and the use of authority, control, and threat.

Learner-centred teaching is a relative concept. Learner-centeredness is a matter of degree, not an either-or situation. It does not mean relegation of the teacher. In fact, it is the teacher who is needed to guide the learners to autonomy and responsibility.

learner characteristics. Cognitive, affective, and social characteristics of individual learners. Learners as individuals may differ according to their AGE and maturity level, MOTIVATION for learning, ATTITUDE towards the subject, APTITUDE for learning the given language/subject, expectations from the course of study, cultural and socio-economic background, and learning disabilities, if any. These have a bearing on individual learning. With special reference to SLL, certain characteristics become more significant. They relate to learner-age, their aptitude and motivation for learning languages, their knowledge of another language, knowledge and experience of the world, and the affective factors such as ANXIETY.

learner diary. A personal and private notebook in which learners writes about their learning experience – their successes and failures in learning. Learners generally take these as a matter of course without stopping to think about them. Writing a diary inevitably sets in motion the process of thinking and reflection, and develops awareness of the cognitive and METACOGNITIVE STRATEGIES of learning. If this is the major objective then the diary can be written in the mother tongue, although the content may be the learner's experience of learning a SL.

A learner diary in this sense is not meant for writing schedules, class notes, etc. *See also* DIARY KEEPING, and DIARY STUDIES.

learner's dictionaries (LDs). LDs are dictionaries designed for SL learners addressing specifically their learning needs. Going beyond glossing and indicating the part of speech and pronunciation of words, which almost all dictionaries do, LDs help their users with such useful information as relate to the grammar and usage of a word, its style value, and PRAGMATICS. Most LDs use a restricted defining vocabulary, usu. of two to three thousand common words. They do not provide etymology or diachronic meanings.

learner differences. *See* LEARNER CHARACTERISTICS.

learner-instruction matching. Striking harmony between the teacher's teaching style and the learners' LEARNING STYLES. It has been observed that many teachers are so preoccupied with the content of their teaching that they ignore learner factors, cognitive and affective and personality factors.The teacher's awareness of these is supposed to bring instruction in line with learner styles and make it effective.

learner language. Language produced by a learner. A language LEARNER's developing competence in the language is reflected in the language she produces, which is different from that of a fully competent user of that language using the same dialect/variety. A learner's language is marked by simplifications and GENERALISATIONS and, in the case of SL learners, by language TRANSFER. Since the developing competence is dynamic in nature, there is constant VARIABILITY in the learner's language. Expressions like transitional competence, idiosyncratic dialects (Corder), approximative systems (Nemser), and interlanguage (Selinker) have been used to describe learner language.

learner strategies. *See* Learning strategies. It is possible however to differentiate between the two. Learner strategies are STRATEGIES learners adopt in general. Learning strategies are those that are applied to learning.

learner support. (in DE). Help made available to learners to enable them to study on their own. It includes learning materials (print and non-print), media support, and face-to-face counselling and other modes of tutor support, such as telephone tutoring, correspondence, and FEEDBACK on ASSIGNMENTS. Support and individual- or group-counselling could also be made available at summer schools, and CONTACT SESSIONS. It is implicit that the support should respond to learner needs and problems. *See also* SELF-INSTRUCTIONAL MATERIALS.

learner training. A process of enabling learners to understand how they learn (or how to learn) in order to make them learn on their own, and to enable them to achieve AUTONOMY in learning. The training includes an explicit focus on LEARNING STRATEGIES. Further, learners are made to develop awareness of their present level of knowledge and proficiency and of how they can improve it: awareness of what their problems are and how they can try to solve them.

The training may relate to specific skills such as reading. It may also be about learning in general.

learner typology. Classification of learners into types, **Example,** FIELD DEPENDENT/INDEPENDENT, extrovert/introvert/ambivert, having preference for INDUCTIVE or deductive mode of learning. *See* Learner characteristics and Learning style.

learning. In very general terms, the process of acquiring what may be called 'knowledge' – knowledge of something, or skill in doing something. Learning is behaviouristic, cognitive and social. It may be aided by or effected through study, practice, observation, interaction, experience, and/or instruction. Instruction could be self-instruction or teacher-controlled. Learning is reflected in the individual's behaviour or state of knowledge.

1. The CONSTRUCTIVIST position on learning holds that learning is not just acquisition but re-creation of meaning in interaction with one's knowledge, experience, and understanding, as well as interaction with others.

Although learning results from internal, mental processes, inferences about it are drawn from changes in observable behaviour, such as one's language OUTPUT. **2.** In the context of SLL, Krashen (1982) has drawn a distinction between acquisition and learning. Acquisition is the natural process – the way children pick up their MT. And learning is the rather painstaking process of becoming proficient in the language with the help of teachers and books. *See* also ACQUISITION OF LANGUAGE

learning approaches. *See* STUDY APPROACHES.

learning-centred. (Teaching) that focuses on the process of LEARNING. The concept learning-centred highlights its contrast with *learner-centred. See* LEARNER-CENTRED.

Some, however, prefer to use the expression learning-centred rather than learner-centred so as to, in the words of Tudor (1996; viii), 'emphasise the goal of teaching as that of "maximising learning". Thus *learning -centred* is expressive more of an emphasis rather than any radical difference.'

learning disabilities. Disorders of PERCEPTION, processing, MEMORY, and ATTENTION that some children may suffer from. They occur, purportedly, due to (mostly genetic) abnormalities in those parts of the brain that participate in language-related functions. Often they result from injury or damage to specific areas of brain concerned with particular language functions. The disorders manifest themselves in language learning problems relating to reading, writing, hearing, and oral expression. A person with such a disability may confuse between 'up' and 'down,' or write 'saw' for 'was.' Among such disorders DYSLEXIA has received most attention. Some other disabilities are dysgraphia – a disorder in the ability to write; dysfluency – difficulty in expressing oneself orally; auditory and verbal agnosia – difficulty in the recognition of speech sounds.

learning materials. Materials learners can use to gain proficiency in the TL. 'Material' here implies texts produced specifically for learners. The materials may focus on one particular skill, such as writing, or an integration of all the major skills. They can have a variety of format from an un-sequenced series of tasks to one of structured progression.

In a way all materials intended for learners are learning materials. But in some contexts they contrast with the prescribed, course-bound TEXTBOOKS intended to be done in the class under the supervision of the teacher.

Going outside the strict pedagogical confines and viewing from the learner's point, anything from newspapers to atlases and from TV programmes to the internet that a learner can learn from is learning material. *See also* MATERIALS FOR TEACHING LANGUAGE.

learning opportunities. Junctures in CLASSROOM INTERACTION where a learner expresses difficulty in comprehending the teacher's meaning or signals inadequate/divergent construction of it. It has been noted that learners in the classroom trying to access MEANING-MAKING through their individual cognitive approaches, come out with formulations that may be revelatory, unique, or just erroneous. Such junctures constitute potential opportunities for learning, and need to be exploited.

learning strategies. 'Specific steps, actions or behaviours (observable or not) taken by the learner to improve his or her own learning progress and ultimate language proficiency'. (R. Oxford, 1990). Thus taking down notes in the class is a learning strategy. A plan made by a learner for study/learning is a strategy, and so are the steps/actions taken to monitor its progress and evaluate the outcome.

A strategy can be related to MEMORY, or to cognition, such as reasoning deductively; it can be 'social' in nature such as seeking somebody's co-operation by asking her for help. Some strategies such as making mental associations are not observable and may be adopted unconsciously.

Learning strategies have been classified into such types as direct and indirect; METACOGNITIVE, cognitive, and AFFECTIVE; cognitive and behavioural.

Cognitive strategy deployment involves using specific, conscious ways of tackling learning tasks, and metacognitive strategies are used to manage and control the learning process.

Behavioural strategies are observable but the understanding of the cognitive ones is based on guessing and on one's own experience. For example, when a learner comes across a difficult word she may consults a dictionary, which is an observable behavioural strategy, but how exactly she internalises the meaning of the word and its usage, is a matter of subjective construction.

A criticism of work on learning strategy is that it is based largely on interviews of and reports by learners. What actually happens in the minds of the learners when they are learning is not directly accessible.

learning style. An individual's approach to learning and problem-solving. Some prefer to perceive information visually rather than through audition, and vice-versa. Information organisation may be inductive, or deductive, or a combination of the two. Memorisation, or writing out may be the preferred mode of learning by some. Perceiving information or approaching a problem analytically or globally is also a matter of learning style, so is adopting an introverted or extroverted mode. *See also* COGNITIVE STYLES, FIELD DEPENDENCE/INDEPENDENCE, and INDUCTIVE LEARNING.

learning theories. HYPOTHESES about

how behavioural changes of a relatively permanent kind are made. Two major sets of THEORIES that have been proposed are: the behaviourist theories of stimulus-response and reinforcement, and the mentalist theories of how human mind thinks and learns. *See also* LANGUAGE LEARNING THEORIES.

lecture. A formal, oral, PRESENTATION (3) in which the speaker follows closely notes written out in advance. The audience (consisting, in most cases, of students) does not generally interrupt the lecture for clarifications, etc., though questions may be asked at the end.

The present trend is to use mechanical aids like an OHP or a multi-media projector to support/illustrate the points in the lecture. Outside the pedagogical context, the expression *presentation* (3) is used in preference to lecture. Lectures vary in their level of formality and the space they allow for audience interruption.

lecture method. A mode of INSTRUCTION that consists of extended teacher presentation, in the TRANSMISSION mode, to a large group of students. Lectures, usually for adult learners but in many cases for teenagers also, are monologic in nature and may employ the 'CHALK AND TALK METHOD.'

The lecture treats a subject in detail. The students are expected to listen to the lecturer and take down notes. Lectures can, however, be made interactive with the members of the class participating and contributing.

lecturette. A mini discourse, a short LECTURE. Lecturettes are constructive interventions in the form of an explanatory, analytical, or clarifying DISCOURSE intended to help the learners during the course of their engagement in some (learning) task, esp. when they face some perceptual difficulty. Lecturettes may be used when learners are busy doing tasks in the classroom individually or in groups, in demonstrations, PRACTICE TEACHING, and LOOP INPUTS. When to intervene is a matter of the teacher's decision and it depends on her perception that the class needs help. A lecturette may also be occasioned by the learners' appeal for help.

lesson analysis. An analytical examination of a lesson. The analysis takes into account the objective(s), the plan and its execution, the procedures adopted and the techniques used, treatment of the skills, the handling of PRESENTATION, content, PRACTICE, evaluation, seating arrangement, time distribution, blackboard work, and other classroom management skills. Lesson analysis hinges on a theory or model of teaching.

Different theoretical approaches to teaching will apply different descriptive norms. Analyses can be made for the benefit of the lesson-teacher, but they are mostly used for research and study purposes.

Though the analysis is intended to be a descriptive one, it can indirectly become an evaluation pointing towards the lesson's successes and failures.

lesson observation. A component of TEACHER EDUCATION associated with TEACHING PRACTICE, aimed at developing among pupil-teachers a critical awareness of teaching process and procedure. When one of the pupil-teachers practice-teaches, her peers formally observe her do so. They have an observation proforma or CHECK-LIST given to them by their MENTOR or supervisor. It contains an ordered inventory of the steps in the lesson with graded evaluative categories [**Example**, poor, good, very good]. The teacher-pupils may also be given the plan of the lesson.

The lesson and its observation is followed by a review session in which the lesson-teacher and the observers analytically discuss the lesson. The exercise, in which the mentor also participates, is meant to be of educative value for the teachers in training.

lesson planning. Preparing a plan for teaching a classroom lesson. The plan is a blueprint for pedagogical action and takes into account such things as the aims and objectives of the lesson, the salient aspects of the topic or the skill to be focused on, how the topic will be introduced to the class, and how it will be developed through examples, activities, tasks, etc.

A detailed plan lists the aids, if any, to be used and the blackboard work to be done. Further, devices for checking comprehension/learning and receiving feedback; QUESTION-TECHNIQUES and ELICITATION of learner response are also listed.

In the pedagogical models related to the ORAL-SITUATIONAL and the STRUCTURAL APPROACHES, a lesson plan envisages a classroom lesson as embracing three major steps: PRESENTATION, PRACTICE & CONSOLIDATION, and EVALUATION & REMEDIATION. The pre-teaching planning has to do with SELECTION and GRADING.

The model assumes that once the specifications are pedagogically implemented, expected learning outcomes will follow. The assumption is questionable. So also is the belief that a plan can preordain a lesson given that interactive classroom language-teaching is in the nature of a negotiation and an open-ended activity.

Lesson planning is best seen as a teacher's preparation for teaching in which she has given thought in advance to the difficulties, possibilities, eventualities that may arise during the course of a lesson and how to tackle them.

In TEACHER EDUCATION programmes, lesson planning is an important part of the PRACTICE TEACHING component [which includes PEER TEACHING].

levels. 1. Stages. The stages of learning/education have traditionally had [a convenient] staging at three levels: elementary, secondary, and advanced. The educational system also has basically this 3-tier staging. Language courses and language tests are usually designed for these levels (ii). Levels also refer to learner achievement and performance. Adjectives like low, high define it. Some language tests categorise learner achievement/performance in terms of the levels on a scale. Each level has a corresponding descriptor of the expected performance at that level. *See also* DIFFICULTY, and DIFFICULTY LEVEL. **2.** Levels (of language). Major aspects of the complex system language. Traditionally grammar (SYNTAX), PHONOLOGY, and SEMANTICS (including MORPHOLOGY) have been considered to be the levels at which language is studied. Some scholars add to these DISCOURSE, LEXIS, and PRAGMATICS.

lexeme. The smallest distinctive unit in the meaning system of a language. A lexeme is a different category from a WORD. A lexeme may be a word or a phrase. The phrasal verb – *do away with* is a lexeme as is each individual word constituting the phrase.

lexical. Relating to words. *See* LEXIS.

lexical approaches to language teaching. Approaches that place LEXIS at the centre of (S)LT. Lexis is VOCABULARY(1) or what DICTIONARIES primarily deal with – words and phrases. Lexical approaches contrast with the traditional approaches that have considered the learning of GRAMMAR as most important. With the shift of emphasis in recent times on to learning and teaching of how to *use* the language, the acquisition of words and phrases has come to be seen as very important. Also, linguistic theories asserting the innateness of UNIVERSAL GRAMMAR, find that what learners need to concentrate on is the acquisition of lexis.

Lexical approaches have implications for SYLLABUS design. *See also* CHUNKING (1), and LEXICAL PHRASE.

lexical chunks. *See* CHUNK, CHUNKING and LEXICAL PHRASE.

lexical density. An index of different types of words used in a text. Also known as TYPE-TOKEN RATIO, lexical density is worked out to find out the difficulty level of a text. The number of different types of words in a text is divided by the total number of words or word tokens in it, and the qotient is multiplied by 100. The resulting figure is in per cent, an indicator of the DIFFICULTY LEVEL of the text. The assumption is that the more the number of different types of words, the greater the difficulty.

lexical-functional grammar (LFG). A theory of SYNTAX within the general framework of GENERATIVE GRAMMAR. The theory considers words as playing a significant role in syntactic structures and the grammatical functions of sentences. For example, case relations are as much a function of the lexicon as of syntax. 'Functional' refers to grammatical functions of the elements of syntax. The relationship between the verb and its subject and/or object is a grammatical-functional relationship.

lexical item. *See* LEXEME, and WORD.

lexical phrase. A phrase such as 'how about...' 'as soon as'. It is a prefabricated chunk of language, formulaic in nature, and occurs frequently in one's speech/writing. The chunk consists of more than one word and is used to perform a pragmatic function.

Lexical phrase – a lexico-grammatical unit – is distinguished from IDIOMS, CLICHES, and COLLOCATIONS on the criterion of specific pragmatic function.

It is claimed that language learners initially acquire and use lexical phrases holistically. Acquisition of such phrases forms the basis of creative rule-forming processes.

lexical word. *See* CONTENT WORD.

lexicogrammar. A unified approach to the study of lexis and grammar/ structure. SYNTAX and LEXIS have traditionally been studied as different categories. Lexicogrammar does not make any rigid compartmentalization of grammar and lexis.

lexicography. Dictionary-making. It basically consists of giving the meanings of the words in a language alphabetically arranged. In addition to the meanings, a DICTIONARY may also provide such information as etymology, syllable- division, pronunciation, and usage notes. *Cf.* LEXICOLOGY.

lexicology. A branch of linguistics. It is concerned with the study of the lexicon of a language, of word meanings and origins.

lexicon. All the words and phrases used in a language: the VOCABULARY(1) of a language as listed in a dictionary.

lexis. The VOCABULARY(1) of a language as different from its syntax. Lexis includes words and word combinations.

library language. A SL used primarily for the utilitarian purpose of reading the [advanced-level] texts available in it and of deriving information from them. The expression became popular in India following the Education Commission Report (1964–66) which recommended the retention of English in the country's educational system for accessing books and learned journals on such specialised subjects as engineering and technology – subjects on which not many books had been produced in Indian languages. The status of a library language stipulates the cultivation of reading comprehension as the most important skill.

linear programme. *See* PROGRAMMED LEARNING.

linearity. One-to-one correspondence; perfect symmetry. In the context of language education, this refers to such assumptions educational planners and teachers have had as what will be taught will also be learnt, and in the same order. Observation of language learning does not seem to support the assumption. *See also* CHAOS and COMPLEXITY THEORY.

linear sequencing. Arranging items of learning and teaching in lines rather than chunks or masses. In many SL curricula, items of structure and vocabulary for teaching are selected and organised in a sequence. [STRUCTURAL SYLLABUSes present a good example of this.] They are to be taught in the given order and learners are supposed to learn them in the same order. Such arrangement is based on the assumption that learning takes place in discrete units and follows an incremental process. This view of learning has been replaced by concepts that view learning as organic.

lingua franca. The language that links the various [language] groups in a COMMUNITY. In multilingual communities there usually is a language, either native to the place or of foreign origin that serves as a major means of communication among the groups speaking different MOTHER TONGUES. For intra-group communication people generally use their MT, which they mutually share, and depend on a lingua franca for inter-group communication. Lingua franca users are generally bilinguals, and their lingua franca carries influence of their MT.

The terms 'auxiliary language' and 'link language' are generally used synonymously with lingua franca.

linguicide. The death of a language. Language death may be caused by a number of factors. Languages may die because they are starved of support: They do not receive nourishment from the educational system and the cultural policies of the state, or their users gradually stop using them. They may wither due to competition from other, dominant languages, or they may be systematically killed.

linguicism. 'Discrimination by means of language'. It lies in treating 'some languages more developed and suited for modernization, technology, etc. and others, usu. of underdeveloped countries, as less developed.' [Skutnabb-Kangas, T. and J. Cummins (1988)].

Attitudes related to linguicism have implications for language teaching.

linguistic competence. GRAMMATICAL COMPETENCE in a SL as contrasted with the user's COMMUNICATIVE COMPETENCE.

linguistic context. See CONTEXT.

linguistic human right. The right to enjoy and develop one's language: the right to learn one's MT as part of formal education at school. The implication of this is that the state has to provide this facility to the children of linguistic minorities. Minorities should have the right to establish and maintain their own educational institutions and have the power to decide curricular matters relating to their languages.

linguistic item. See ITEM.

linguistic method in SL teaching. Teaching of a SL that is not literary-text-biased, and that concentrates on language skills (esp. oral skills) for communication. The expression 'linguistic' method was used in 1950s to highlight this contrast.

linguistic relativity. In anthropology and linguistics, the term refers to the HYPOTHESIS that postulates that language and culture are deeply related. So much so that a language limits its user's world-view: (as Wittgenstein has said, 'the limits of my language are the limits of my world.') as each language has its own way of categorising and organising concepts and experience. See also LANGUAGE AND THOUGHT, and SAPIR-WHORF HYPOTHESIS.

linguistic syllabuses. SYLLABUSES that specify curriculum in terms of grammatical/structural and vocabulary items for teaching & learning. Such syllabuses contrast with those that are designed in terms of notions, functions or tasks. See also GRAMMATICAL SYLLABUSES, and STRUCTURAL SYLLABUSES.

linguistics. A data-based, systematic study of language in accordance with a THEORY of language structure. Linguistics provides an efficient way of describing a language(s).

The study of language in relation to other areas of study has led to the emergence of interdisciplinary fields like SOCIOLINGUISTICS, PSYCHOLONGUISTICS, EDUCATIONAL LINGUISTICS. See also Applied linguistics.

linguistics and language teaching. The question whether a knowledge of linguistics is relevant to language teaching. Most people seem to agree that it is, though only to a limited extent. During the 1950s and the 1960s there was a great deal of enthusiasm for the newly emergent discipline of modern Linguistics. And it was claimed that linguistics could solve the problems of language teaching. See also METHODICS.

linguistic universals. See UNIVERSALS,

LINGUISTIC.

link language. *See* LINGUA FRANCA.

linkword method. A MEMORY-based technique for vocabulary teaching. Learners are given associative links – links they are familiar with – to learn a new word or item in the TL.

listen-and repeat. A pronunciation DRILL. Learners listen to sounds, words, phrases, or full sentences and then repeat them as closely/accurately as possible. The purpose of the drill is to make the learners acquire the target form accurately. The listening material may be pre-recorded and played in the class or orally produced by the teacher. The teacher usually provides immediate feedback on learner performance.

listening. The act of so hearing spoken language/oral communication as to understand what is said in it. Listening involves accurate reception of the auditory input and simultaneously interpreting its meaning, explicit and implicit. Listening is more a matter of paying attention to what is meant than to what is actually spoken. This involves a range of skills and abilities – the ability to hear precisely, or fill gaps with intelligent guesses when the background is noisy or distracting, comprehend the literal [and the intended] meaning of the spoken discourse interpreting it at the same time in relation to the context.

The context includes the occasion, speaker/listener's shared knowledge and assumptions, the TENOR of the discourse, and the speaker's intention. Thus going beyond literal comprehension, listening is a matter of deriving right inferences and activating relevant SCHEMA. It also involves accessing speech conventions, politeness principles, understatements, hedges, and mitigators.

Spoken language comes in a variety of forms and GENRES-from casual conversation to prepared discourse read out as if spoken spontaneously. The spoken discourse could occur in a face-to-face situation or be an audio/video recorded one. However, not all listening requires full attentiveness. On some social occasions conversation may be casual and PHATIC using FORMULAIC LANGUAGE and requiring routine responses.

listening comprehension. Also known as auditory comprehension. *See* LISTENING.

listening (the teaching of). Teaching how to receive oral communication in a SL and to participate in the communication as listener.

A variety of learning tasks based on conversations and other types of spoken DISCOURSE are used for developing listening comprehension. Teachers use pre-listening tasks to prepare ground for comprehension. During listening, illustrations and pictures may be used as aids. Post-listening activities are in the nature of comprehension check, feedback, and follow up. Learners' attention may be drawn to such features of speech as INTONATION, contrastive ACCENT (1), discourse markers, and TOPIC-signallers.

The listening material may include spontaneous speech, **Example**, face-to-face conversation, telephone conversations, debates and discussions, broadcasts, TV serials or excerpts from them, audio- or video-recorded materials, and materials derived from other modes of rehearsed speech delivering structured discourse such as a news-bulletin.

In line with the principle of AUTHENTICITY in CLT, the importance of learners' exposure to authentic listening materials is being stressed in language pedagogy these days. Controlled or cosmetically treated texts often used in academic discourse carry challenges of a different kind from those that listening situations in real, everyday, life present.

However, in teaching a SL there is a case for developing limited purpose listening ability. One may have to use the language only with fellow countrymen in limited contexts of use. In pedagogical settings where the intention in SL listening is to receive input for content knowledge and information, there is justification for using only carefully structured texts for listening. This usually is the case with SL learners for specific purposes (LSP and LAP).

The mechanical aspects of listening are also important. Some of these are proper hearing, recognising phonemic differences, features of speech such as contractions and other elisions, weak forms, and *sandhis*.

listening comprehension strategies. STRATEGies used by listeners in the communication process to comprehend message(s) by processing the information in the input received. In this process, the listener resources on her experience of the world, knowledge of the topic, familiarity with the context of the utterance, and knowledge of the language. Thus almost simultaneously with the speech being listened to, the listener is engaged in a process of interpretation. The process involves using such strategies as that of INFERENCING, elaboration, summarization, deduction, and translation.

literacy. The ability to read and write. This, however is the conventional, and now almost dated, definition of the term. Today, 'literacy' is used in much broader senses. It implies more than a functional command of reading and writing. Literacy includes not only satisfactory levels of communicative skills, but also a level of social and political awareness.

The stereotypical concept of literacy that discriminatingly divided communities into literate and illiterate has been challenged: a single-block concept of 'literacy' has made way for 'literacies.' To be literate today means to possess social and political awareness – awareness of one's rights and status in society, of exploitations, deprivations, empowerment, etc.

Contrasted varieties of literacy have been posited – lay literacy Vs critical or emancipatory literacy, literacy of oral cultures Vs literacy in 'modern' cultures.

Literacy types and practices vary – local literacy practices **example**, that of the *maktab, pathshalas* and *madarsas*, family literacy, domestic literacy, school literacy, functional literacy, survival literacy, textual literacy, L2 literacy, etc. Visual literacy has to do with critical reading of 'visual' 'texts' such as TV-commercials and broadcasts for their authenticity or lack of it, hidden biases, manipulation of values, and employment of the visual content through such cinematic techniques as juxtaposition and superimposition. Multiliteracies include proficiency in using electronic devices, specially computers.

literacy-based approach to language teaching. Approach to language teaching that goes beyond imparting linguistic competence and fluency in the TL. Alongside it also aims at creating among the learners awareness of why what is said is said, how it is related to the contexts – the context of occasion, of speaker–listener relationship; of the mode – written or spoken – how it is organised as coherent message, and how it is culturally determined. Thus 'literacy' here implies and subsumes the abilities of analysis, interpretation, and critical thinking – in short, metacommunicative awareness.

literature. In its common sense, creative works such as novels, poems, plays. They have certain characteristics. They are well-crafted works of imagination with emotional appeal.

Much language teaching has traditionally been based on literary texts. *See also* LANGUAGE THROUGH LITERATURE.

lock-step. A marching style in which each marcher follows as closely as possible the one in front of her. Applied to teaching, it refers to the teacher-led mode in which the class closely follows the teacher and there is little interaction between them, or among the students. Every student in the class 'is expected to do the same thing at the same time in the same way.' This allows little space for individual freedom – to follow one's own pace or speed of learning, choice of subject, interest, etc.

logical problem of language acquisition. The problem of explaining how learners are able to master in a short time the infinite intricacies of the system of a language. The problem arises in the face of the claim made by some that language learning results from the exposure and input received by the learner. The rules a language uses are so many and so complex that it does not appear humanly possible to learn them all the way we learn other things. There must be a knowledge structure innate to humans in terms of which children's ability to acquire linguistic competence can be explained and the problem resolved.

look-and-listen exercise. A language learning activity in which learners look at pictures [in a picture-book, on the wall, etc.] as they listen to recorded material or teacher-speech dealing with the pictures. The pictures may, for example, be of two persons talking, as in a comic strip. The listening material consists of conversation appropriate to the situation in the picture. The exercise is intended to help develop the learners' language ability including their LISTENING COMPREHENSION.

look-and-say method. An approach to the teaching of reading to beginning learners. In it, they are introduced to 'whole' words. The assumption is that by looking at whole words children will develop a sight vocabulary, and learn to associate the meaning of words with their shapes. From single words, learners can gradually move to longer stretches. In this approach that is influenced by GESTALT psychology, learners are trained to perceive the features and shapes of words as a whole rather than a series of discrete letters that constitute the word. The approach contrasts with the method of beginning teaching with individual letters of the alphabet, or of introducing children to sound-letter combinations. *See also* PHONICS.

look-and-say exercises. Speech-practice activities based on pictures and objects. Depending on such factors as the learner age, their proficiency level, and the aim(s) of the lesson, a variety of techniques can be used in these activities. The simplest is to ask learners to look at a picture or an object and orally produce a sentence about it. The picture may be in the book, the workbook, on a wall hanging, or drawn by the teacher on the blackboard. It could also be projected on a screen. The pictures could be single ones showing something simple, or some crowded scene. They may consist of a sequence illustrating a story.

Making effort to talk about the picture or narrate a story about it in a SL is supposed to develop the learner' competence to communicate. The exercises can be made more complex.

loop input. A teaching strategy. In it the teacher does not transmit to the learners the content of the input through lectures or other forms of direct presentation. Instead she makes learners acquire it through a process of experience built into the instructional process. In language-teacher-training, one of the ways of providing input

through the process of experience could be as given below: During a training session the trainees will act for a short while as students. The experience of performing learner-role, i.e., the experience of 'learning' as 'students', it is expected, will lead the trainees to grasp the trainer's message on how to teach/how to get over a pedagogical problem. The expression 'loop input' in this sense has been coined by Tessa Woodward (1991).

the Lorge-Thorndike list. A WORD LIST [for teaching English to Foreigners] based on FREQUENCY count in printed English covering a variety of GENRES. Irving Lorge and Edward L. Thorndike reported in 1938 the semantic count of the 2000 commonest words. The semantic count was a count of how frequently a particular meaning of a word occurred. It was based on the differentiation of the various meanings of a polysemic word in *The Oxford English Dictionary*. Later Dr M. West used the semantic count for his GENERAL SERVICE LIST.

loud reading. *See* READING ALOUD.

LSP. *See* LANGUAGE FOR SPECIFIC PURPOSES.

LSP course design. Specifications and structure of courses meant for learners who wish to learn a particular for their specific needs. A specific need, for example, could be to obtain an advanced level knowledge of medicine available through the TL.

Such courses are LEARNER-CENTERED. An analysis of NEEDS precedes the specification of course content. LSP courses are designed for a homogeneous group of learners whose language needs are the same or nearly the same.

Early versions of LSP courses were REGISTER-based and emphasised the mastery of specialist LEXIS and the frequently used syntactic patterns in a given register.

LSP instruction. Teaching a language for specific purposes. There is no particular methodology applicable to all LSP courses. The choice of the method and techniques to be used on such courses depends on the nature of the content and the learner-related factors such as their objectives, level, and the time available for study as well as the language skill(s) preferred for the purpose. Some of the techniques used in LSP instruction are: use of structured tasks, PROBLEM-SOLVING activities, CASE STUDIES, ROLE PLAY, and visits to sites.

M

Machiavellian motivation. Desire to learn a language with the intention of using it to subjugate or otherwise control and exploit the speakers of that language.

Machiavelli, a sixteenth century Italian courtier, is known for his counsel of deceit, guile and opportunism as motivations for power and control.

macroteaching. Teaching a language lesson in a class of normal duration as part of a teacher-training programme. The expression is a kind of backformation to MICROTEACHING.

the Madras ELT (MELT) campaign. A large-scale intensive in-service training programme in teaching English. Based in Madras, it was implemented in 1950s and early 1960s, with the help of the British Council. The model of teaching used in the programme was the STRUCTURAL APPROACH.

MAIN COURSEBOOK (MCB). *See* TEXT-BOOK.

manipravalam way of reading. *See* MIXED-CODE READING METHOD.

manipulative activities. Rigidly structured practice activities in language learning. These activities require learners to manipulate form mechanically – orally or in writing. SUBSTITUTION drills are an example of such activity. An **example** is the following in which learners are asked a) to produce sentences using the choices supplied, and b) to change them into past tense.

My uncle is a doctor/teacher/engineer/ mechanic/carpenter/surgeon.

manual method. A method of teaching communication to the deaf using SIGN LANGUAGE. Contrasted with this is the ORAL METHOD. In it the learners are taught communication with lip shapes – making appropriate shapes to express meaning, and reading the shapes to receive it. A combination of the two methods is considered to be a better procedure.

mapping. Organising information in a diagrammatic form for self-clarification, PRESENTATION (3), or developing into full-length writing. *See also* CONCEPT MAP.

mastery learning. An approach to organising INSTRUCTION. It assumes that given sufficient time, appropriate materials and instruction, all learners can learn successfully and attain mastery. The strategy here is to find out how much time, according to her APTITUDE and learning ability, etc. an individual learner will need, and then to allow this. The approach is attributed to John B. Carroll and Benjamin Bloom, both in Block (ed) 1971. A precondition to mastery learning is diversification of instruction to meet individual needs.

matching tables. A version of SUBSTITUTION DRILLS. Whereas sentences can be generated from a substitution drill mechanically, matching tables necessitate making appropriate choices by taking into account the factor of meaning as in the following. Items from different columns cannot be mechanically combined to form appropriate sentences.

Subject	Verb	Object	Prep. phrase
He	carried	a letter	in a bucket.
John	wrote	cricket	with me.
Mohan	played	the water	to me.

Matching tables are an improvement on substitution tables.

matching-type items. Test ITEMS in which the correct response has to be matched with the appropriate choice among a set of responses supplied.

materials development. Designing of teaching material according to its objectives and the needs of its users. Materials are usually developed by professionals. Teachers also develop materials for their students and now, in some places, learner participation in the process is welcomed. Apart from the general principles relating to DIFFICULTY LEVEL, learner interest, etc., materials should take into account insights into how learners acquire a (second) language. *See also* MATERIAL FOR TEACHING LANGUAGE.

materials evaluation. *See* EVALUATION OF MATERIALS.

materials for teaching language. Texts of different kinds and in different modes used in language instruction to aid learners develop their competence. These include TEXTBOOKS/READERS, SUPPLEMENTARY READERS, WORKBOOKS, and listening materials. *Cf.* LEARNING MATERIALS.

mathetic function. FUNCTION OF LANGUAGE as an instrument for COGNITION, as a 'means of learning about reality'. Language as a way to acquire knowledge, and not just proficiency.

Following the distinction made in Halliday (1975), N. S. Prabhu has made a plea for the mathetic role of English as a World Language. His argument is that much attention has been paid to English as a language of communication across regional and national boundaries. Equally importantly should English be treated as the 'medium of a knowledge paradigm'.

maxims of co-operation. *See* the COOPERATIVE PRINCIPLE.

meaning. The idea expressed or thing represented/signified by a word, phrase, or sentence. Meaning is also the MESSAGE conveyed in a longer discourse. Whereas the meanings of words, phrases, or even sentences in isolation are more or less finite as found in dictionaries, meanings of UTTERANCES often vary according to the context, the way the interaction proceeds, and what the speaker/writer intends to convey & how the listener/reader receives and interprets it. *See also* SENSE.

meaning-making. Trying **1.** to understand the message(s) in an UTTERANCE or TEXT, and **2.** to communicate message(s) through speech and writing. Meaning-making involves listening, speaking, reading, and writing. It is widely held that engaging in these activities for authentic purposes promotes the acquisition of language.

measurement. A process of quantifying the ability/knowledge of learners/test-takers. Measurement suggests a PSYCHOMETRIC approach, i.e., use of instruments(such as a STANDARDISED TEST), and arrival at precise values in terms of numerical quantity – scores, etc. Certain segments of language knowledge such as spelling and

147

articulation of individual PHONEMES do lend themselves more easily to measurement.

measurement-driven instruction. *See* EXAMINATION-ORIENTED TEACHING.

mechanistic approaches to reading (and its instruction). Approaches to developing speed reading, and measuring it. A typical activity in these is to project the text on screen with the help of a machine. The display of the text is timed. Within a short time-span, counted in minutes, the reader has to read a specified number of words.

The assumption in the mechanistic approaches appears to be that READING is a mechanical skill rather than primarily a cognitive one, and can be made more efficient when speeded up under pressure of time. The approaches are applied to training such personnel as busy executives ever short of time. *See also* FAST READING.

mediation. The process of facilitating one's own or others' learning. It is hypothesised that learners mediate learning & access or create new knowledge through mental processes not yet fully understood. These include processes of DISCOVERY, INDUCTION, deduction, GENERALISATION, TRANSFER, and applying to the new and the unknown what is already known.

Mediation is a cognitive STRATEGY aimed at enhancing one's learning: it consists of creating links [that would help remembering, learning] between things. Use of mediators is one of the many strategies that resourceful learners employ.

Mediation could also be causative – being instrumental to others' learning. It often happens when people interact.

One gains information and knowledge from the other(s)' – the mediator's – knowledge and experience.

In a direct way, the teacher in the classroom is the pivotal facilitator and mediator. *See* the MEDIATION THEORY.

The concept of mediation can also be used in its extended and general senses. For example, an overt knowledge of the rules of grammar mediates learning. Similarly, engaging in translation activities is to mediate meaning/comprehension.

mediation theory. The THEORY that teachers and other adults [should] help learners to move up from their current level of knowledge and understanding to the next higher. This mediated accretion – learning being a succession of such accretional moves of mediated learning experiences – is a cognitive process and presupposes, among other things, learners' willingness and co-operation. The theory is attributed to the Israeli psychologist, Reuven Feuerstein (1991).

medium of instruction. The language teachers use [or are supposed to use] in teaching different subjects in the curriculum. It is also the language in which the learners read their books, and write their exams.

When the medium is a SL, the learners' competence in the language improves as it would not to the same extent if the SL was learnt in isolation.

the MELT campaign. *See* MADRAS ELT CAMPAIGN.

memorisation. Learning by committing information to MEMORY. An age-old learning-practice, it is considered an inferior approach since when memorising, one's constructive and critical cognitive faculties are generally not active. The practice may, however, be viewed as a LEARNING STRATEGY in which the learner first commits the material to memory and then. subjects it to constructive processes later. For H. Palmer (1921), 'memorising' is a process of language acquisition and consists of CATENIZING and SEMANTICISING. He was of the view that memorizing of speech, which involves associating words with their meanings, is a way of acquiring language.

Memorisation may be a short cut to remembering and learning in the early years when the cognitive faculties are not well developed. One does not easily forget things learnt during the early years of one's education. Certain areas of learning, such as verb paradigms, lend themselves well to memorisation. *See also* ROTE LEARNING.

memory. The cognitive faculty of retaining and recalling information, ideas, past experiences, etc. Memory enables us to interpret new experience in the light of what we know already, and remember.

Information first received is stored in short-term memory and is likely to be forgotten if no attention is paid to it. When attention is paid to the new, incoming, information and it is mentally processed, it passes into long-term memory (LTM). There are intermediate stages also between the point when input is received and when it gets stored in LTM. LTM has infinite capacity and what is stored in it is not forgotten although one may not always be able to recall it.

Memory could be visual or auditory. It is also classified into types according to the nature of the thing(s) remembered. Factual things belong to declarative memory. It includes episodic memory and semantic memory. The latter has to do with ideas, principles, etc. (*See* Episodic knowledge.).

mental age. A measure of one's level of INTELLIGENCE. *See* Intelligence quotient.

mentalism. The principle that human behaviour cannot be explained without taking into account the mental phenomena.

mentalist theories of language acquisition. Theories that subscribe to the hypothesis that capacity to acquire language(s) is innate to human beings, and reject the position that languages are learnt through imitation and habit formation. *See also* COGNITIVE APPROACHES TO LANGUAGE TEACHING.

mentor. An experienced teacher who acts as counsellor and guide for novice teachers/teacher-students/teacher-interns undergoing pre-service TRAINING. Teacher training programmes, esp. the initial training programmes, consist of a major component of PRACTICE TEACHING or a hands-on experience of teaching wherein the would-be teachers get professional training. During these TEACHER EDUCATION internship programmes, mentors are assigned to the trainee teachers [mentees] to guide and support them in teaching-practice. Their co-operative intervention is intended to help the novice teachers reflect on their pedagogical problems, see the link between theory and practice, and learn the skills of teaching.

Mentors are drawn from the teaching staff of the institution where teaching practice takes place.

The interns have their assigned supervisor or tutor at the college of education where they are registered. The mentor is located at the spot, in the institution where practice teaching is organised.

In effect, mentors act, in association with the institutional Tutor, as co-trainers. But in the current DISCOURSE (2) of language education, expressions like 'trainer' and 'supervisor' are considered unsuitable for the supportive role of a mentor. One suggests fixity and closed-mindedness and the other authority. *See also* MENTORING.

mentoring. On-site counselling of teachers in training. *See also* Mentor. A mentor (as an experienced teacher) normally performs a collaborative role in planning for teaching, observes teaching, provides feedback, aids insight and reflection, and evaluates – evaluation often being a necessity in institutionalised programmes of teacher training. New approaches to TEACHER EDUCATION prefer a non-judgemental feedback and a non-directive mentoring. Working with the trainee [mentee], solving their immediate problems, providing feedback, and establishing a professional dialogue with them helps the mentees understand the art and craft of teaching. The mentoring approach to inducting teachers to the profession is considered to keep them affectively relaxed.

message. The 'information' conveyed in a COMMUNICATION, oral, written or non-verbal.

message adjustment. The reformulation of the meaning/message the teacher is trying to convey. The teacher may reformulate in order to remedy learner-incomprehension and/or to accommodate learner interpretation of the intended message. Adjustment comes about when the teacher is sensitive to the feedback from the learners and modifies accordingly what she is trying to communicate. Message adjustment is one of the principles in verbal communication and classroom interaction.

metacognition. Being aware of, or understanding how one thinks and learns. It includes awareness about such things as how we reason, solve problems, and remember. Metacognition involves the monitoring of one's learning by such activities as planning how to learn, and evaluating learning outcomes. In language teaching, metacognitive knowledge about reading and writing has led to research in STRATEGY-use and training. Besides its application in language learning, metacognition is also an instrument for teachers in their professional development. They apply metacognition when they reflect critically on their experience of teaching – what they taught, how and with what degree of success. Such metacognition, it is assumed, leads them to learn from their experience and to try to explore solutions to their pedagogical problems.

metacognitive strategies of learning. STRATEGIES used consciously to manage and conduct one's learning. The learner decides with full awareness what strategies to use, when and how. Metacognitive strategies include such managing skills as planning, MONITOR-ING, and evaluating learning activities. These are applied to exercise an active control over one's own cognition

metacommunicative awareness. *See* LITERACY-BASED APPROACH TO LANGUAGE TEACHING.

metadiscourse. Those verbal elements in a text/discourse that perform the function of guiding, controlling and giving direction to its message for the benefit of the reader/listener. A text/discourse may consist of two types of information: its message proper and the verbal devices used to present it. An **example** of the latter is: *to put it in different words...*

Learners of a language for academic purposes need to learn proper use of metadiscourse.

metalanguage. Language used for describing language. It usually consists of technical terminology. Linguistics, the study of natural language(s), uses metalanguage in its DISCOURSE (2).

metalinguistic input. Information given to learners regarding their linguistic production and language use, specially about the shortcomings in them. This information could be direct – in the form of correction of errors/ unacceptable forms/constructions, etc.

– often supported with relevant rules of grammar, and usage conventions. Indirect input is in the form of asking learners to confirm what they meant (confirmation checks) or clarify (clarification requests) often with the intention of making them understand where they had gone wrong (and learn).

metalinguistic awareness/ knowledge. Awareness of the nature of language and language learning. This involves an awareness/EXPLICIT KNOWLEDGE of grammar rules, usage conventions, and familiarity with technical terminology used in grammatical/linguistic description. CONSCIOUSNESS-RAISING techniques help create such awareness. Although metalinguistic awareness is awareness for its own sake, it is considered to be a means of reinforcing L2 knowledge, and accelerating the pace of learning.

metaphor. A way of expressing an abstract concept in a 'concrete' manner. A metaphor enforces a highlighted point of partial similarity between two things, persons, places, situations. The listener/reader is able to understand from the context the highlighted point. Thus a metaphor consists of giving somebody/something a name that belongs to some other, **Example**, *Rana is a tiger.*

Metaphors play a role in language teaching discourses too. They help to form CONCEPTS, and lead to new ideas. **Example**: M. West (1960: 36–7) says, 'Grammar is the bones of a language … in the ordinary class-room lesson … those bones rattle. The problem is to make those bones live.' Metaphorical expressions like AFFECTIVE FILTER and LOOP INPUT. aid understanding complex points of LL & LT.

metaphrasis. A composition task in learning classical languages. It consists of producing a transformation of a poem into prose, and of a prose piece into a verse.

method. (In the context of LT) A set of procedures systematically arranged in an overall plan for teaching. Thus, an AUDIOLINGUAL-method class would typically begin with a dialogue orally presented by the teacher, and followed by DRILLing in the projected ITEM of learning. A Method is implicitly or explicitly based on a THEORY of language and language learning.

The term 'method' is variously used often to mean METHODOLOGY. Whereas 'method' refers to labelled methods – some of which are: GRAMMAR-TRANSLATION, DIRECT, AUDIOLINGUAL, – 'methodology' generally means a set of procedures for doing something, **Example**, teaching. 'Method' is theory-driven and rigidly cast, methodology is not necessarily so.

Methods are formulated by experts and are by their very nature pre-determined, though, in practice, the dynamics of classroom teaching defies pre-determined plans. In the actual process of teaching they often have to be altered or abandoned. As Edmund Burke has said, 'Nothing in progression can rest on its original plan.' *See also* LANGUAGE TEACHING METHODS, METHODOLOGY, and POST-METHOD CONSTRUCTS.

method effect. [In language testing]. The effect on the test result of the test method used. It is postulated that different test methods, DIRECT/indirect, DISCRETE-POINT and so on, may elicit different facets of the test takers' language performance. This may affect the scores.

methodics. In plain words, language teaching METHODOLOGY deriving its justification from theoretical principles in LINGUISTICS. Halliday *et al.* 1964, say that Methodics is 'a framework of organization for language teaching which relates linguistic theory to pedagogical principles and techniques.' (Emphasis added.) Further, the term "has come into use" following the attention paid to linguistic theory and its influence on language teaching decisions. Noteworthy here is the addition of the suffixes to METHOD. Methodics thus becomes a science [as is Physics] purportedly following its adherence to *The Linguistic Sciences.*

The term does not seem to be in use anymore. It was the product of an age when it seemed that linguistics could solve the problems of language teaching by making it more 'scientific.' *See* LINGUISTICS AND LANGUAGE TEACHING.

methodology. Procedures systematically used in performing a job, **Example**, teaching. In the LT context, sometimes the distinction between 'METHOD' and 'methodology' is confused. Method (usually with a capital M) is used to refer to a labelled Method of language teaching such as the DIRECT METHOD. Methodology is used in a general sense for a set of procedures not necessarily based on any particular method or theory. It may combine some procedures derived from the DIRECT METHOD with some others from the GRAMMAR-TRANSLATION METHOD.

Methodology is the how of a lesson and accords with its what, the subject matter to be taken up in the class. Methodology is a matter of the teacher's choice, and it is contextually determined.

microteaching. A teacher-training technique. In it, different teaching skills are practised under carefully controlled conditions. It is based on the idea that teaching is a complex set of activities involving a complex set of skills which can be broken down into different micro-skills. These can be practised individually, and later combined with the others. The notion of skills in this context is not very precise. Some specific examples of skills that the trainees may practise in microteaching are: how to do the following in the language classroom:

Use the blackboard; treat a learner ERROR; pose a cognitively challenging question; make an initial PRESENTATION of a verb-tense form; conduct a learning task; act as facilitator to one of the groups engaged in performing a segment of a TASK.

Although most of these examples could belong to a 'COMMUNICATIVE' classroom, microteaching itself is a construct of the BEHAVIOURIST, TRAINING-oriented models of preparing teachers. So is the concept of teaching that underlies it – teacher-fronted classrooms; teacher-controlled learning. The principle of microteaching is based on the assumption that teaching a full-duration class [macro-teaching] is too complex [and daunting] a task for those preparing to take up teaching as their profession. They first need to be 'trained' to handle 'efficiently' and atomistically the discrete units that are considered to compose the global act of teaching. There is resemblance between this principle and those behind its contemporary, PROGRAMMED INSTRUCTION.

The steps in microteaching-training usually are:

1. demonstration of microteaching procedure by the instructor(s);
2. explanation of the rationale;
3. making the trainees teach different units, or the same one, in small PEER-GROUP;
4. retrospection by the trainee on her performance as she went along in teaching;
5. analysis, review, and evaluation of the performance by the group under the supervision of the instructor;
6. if considered necessary, giving another chance to the trainee to re-teach and improve on the earlier performance;
7. successful trainees doing microteaching on real learners;
8. if necessary, repetition of steps 4 and 5, above

The micro-lessons may be recorded on audio- or video-tape for analysis and discussion as part of the training programme.

After going through the preparatory steps, the trainee is expected to have acquired sufficient experience, understanding and confidence to undertake fuller teaching.

mind-map. A diagram that represents the network of associations and ideas in the mind when one thinks about a subject. **Example**, when thinking about a CLASSROOM, the associations that may appear in our mind include teacher, instruction-delivery, and student questions. Asking students to evoke associations to their mind-maps could be a suitable lead-in to learning and teaching, esp. as a pre-writing activity. BRAINSTORMING could be an aid to activating mind map. *See also*

CONCEPT MAP

minimum adequate behaviour. A set of FORMULAIC expressions in the TL. These include forms to express politeness, apology, and hedging. M. West (1960) was of the view that the school learners of a SL (English) needed, in addition to a vocabulary and intelligible speech, some knowledge of the forms of the kind referred to above.

minimum adequate grammar. 'The grammatical system of a language sufficient to meet fundamental and urgent communicative needs' (Wilkins, 1979). Wilkins suggests that the choice of what should go into the MAG in a SL should be a pragmatic decision taking into account the learner's COMMUNICATIVE needs and the time available with them for learning. It may include such items as 'semantic universals' and significant speech FUNCTIONS in the TL.

The idea is noteworthy as a plea for combining the teaching of grammatical form with that of meaning and function.

minimum adequate pronunciation. Ability in a SL to pronounce intelligibly the items in a minimum usable vocabulary for speech. M. West (1960), author of the construct, felt that Indian school-learners of English did not need so much the niceties of INTONATION etc. as a minimum holding of words, and an intelligible pronunciation speech to express themselves.

minimum adequate vocabulary. A vocabulary of 1200 headwords, in a SL (English) put together by M. West (1960) as a 'usable first stage' and as 'the aim of the school course' – a list of words 'to be taught and remembered.' It is intended to be a vocabulary both for reading and speech, and consists mainly of CONTENT WORDS. The items are listed alphabetically and also arranged and classified subject-wise. The MAV was claimed to be the smallest self-contained vocabulary of normal English.

minimum learning outcomes. *See* MINIMUM LEVELS OF LEARNING.

minimum levels of learning (MLLs). Minimum learning outcomes. Learning competencies expected to be mastered by every child by the end of a particular class or course of education. Some Boards of school education in India have prepared a suggestive (rather than prescriptive) inventory of minimal levels of skills and abilities that learners must possess at each successive stage to be able to cope with their studies. The inventory is intended to serve as a guideline for SYLLABUS framers and TEXTBOOK writers.

mining approach. A theoretical MODEL (1) in education in which the learner/student is seen as a rich mine. Teaching in this model, therefore, is supposed to aim at discovering the jewels a student has within her, and making her discover and bring out her own potential and hidden talents. The approach is based on the teachings of the Persian spiritual educator Bahaullah (1817–92), and finds echo in the observations made by many other spiritually- oriented teachers. It may have relevance to language teaching as well.

miscue. Deviation learners make in reading from a text. A term coined by Kenneth Goodman, 'miscue' contrasts with 'mistake.' Miscues represent a learner's (children reading in their

MT) attempt to make sense of the text. Miscues may relate to (i) sound/symbol relationship, (ii) grammatical expectation, or (iii) expectation of meaning. *See also* READING MISCUES.

miscue analysis. ANALYSIS of deviations learners make in reading a text out aloud. *See* Reading miscues. The data for the analysis are obtained by making children read a text out [aloud]. One or more than one person carefully mark the deviations on a copy of the text. Analysing the MISCUES has a DIAGNOSTIC purpose. If consistent, they indicate the reading and decoding STRATEGIES a learner is using. Avoiding the correct-incorrect judgement, the analysis sees miscues as meaning-making strategies: strategies revelatory of the cognitive processes of the reader in reading – complex processes (not just decoding a text word by word) conditioned by the reader's linguistic, pragmatic knowledge and experience. Analysis indicates that miscues are systematic. A technique in the analysis is that of 'retrospective miscue analysis' in which the readers are asked to comment on the miscues they made.

miseducation. The failure of schooling to educate. *See also* COMPULSORY MISEDUCATION.

mistake. Deviation from grammatically correct forms/constructions occurring in learner output of SL. Corder (1967) quoting Miller, drew a distinction between mistake and ERROR. Errors, he said, were SYSTEMATIC indicating the learner's competence in the language at a particular stage of learning. Mistakes were the product of chance circumstances, such as distraction, and therefore not significant.

mixed-code reading method. A BILINGUAL reading method of helping learners read in a SL with the support of their MT. In this method, the lexical and syntactic forms of L1 and L2 are so mixed that what results is a COHERENT text. The readers' knowledge of their MT helps them to understand the meanings of the L2 forms in the text. Such texts are carefully devised following the principles of linguistic contrast and gelling, and graded so that over a course of instruction the support is gradually reduced until the learners reach a point where they do not need it for reading an L2 text.

This technique, known as *Manipravalam* was used by Tamils in South India during the eleventh to fifteenth centuries to read texts in Sanskrit. The technique was used in Burma, during the fifteenth century to help Burmese speakers read Buddhist scriptures in Pali. *See also* SANDWICH STORY METHOD.

mnemonic devices. Cognitive STRATEGIES for recalling information, for 'memory jogging.' Contrived by the learner, the devices help her to commit material to memory, or improve it. For example, to remember the main points on a topic, she may arrange the first letters in the points to form a word, an acronym, or a nonsense word. The acronym VIBGYOR represents the colours of the rainbow.

In language teaching, 'mnemonic pictures' may be used. They are pictures of situations, such as a cricket match in progress, or a market scene. The pictures help learners recall associated words and sentences to construct a description/narrative. They become the focal points and thus help guide and control the language work.

mode. The particular way in which something is done, **Example**, the oral or the written mode of language use. A text/discourse is created keeping in view the mode it would be presented in. **Example**, some texts are written to be presented as if spoken extempore.

model. 1. A (proposed) system: a design, structure or pattern of relationships relating to ideas or (theoretical) CONSTRUCTS. **Example**, CONSTRUCTIVISM presents an entirely new model of learning. **2.** An example for emulation. *See also* MODELLING.

modelling. Displaying an example for pupils to imitate and follow. In language classes, teachers often have to model pronunciation or some other point of learning. In teacher training, supervisors display for the benefit of the trainees models of teaching. When teaching writing, teachers often set up products of writing as model for the learners.

SL learners need good models of correct pronunciation, but in other areas models may have a constraining effect often discouraging initiative and creativity.

modified input. *See* CARETAKER SPEECH, AND FOREIGNER TALK.

modularity view. The view that the human brain consists of a set of modules each with its own mechanism relevant to different types of language knowledge. *See* Module (3) This view is still at the level of hypothesis. The contrary view subscribes to a unitary model of the brain. It holds that the human brain has just one organism undifferentiated for first language acquisition, SL acquisition and different kinds of knowledge and skills. Be that as it may, recent views of language learning place it firmly inside the brain, and make it imperative for those in the field of language pedagogy to focus on the cognitive aspects.

module. An independent UNIT (1) of a larger SYSTEM. This concept of an independent unit is applied and extended to the following contexts: **1.** A self-contained course unit. The contents of the unit and other details such as the expected learning outcome are specified. **2.** A learnt unit of behaviour. In J Bruner's theory of cognitive development, a module is the outcome (in the form of organised learning) of the process of solving a problem. **3.** A distinctive language module in the human brain. It is hypothesised by the proponents of UG that the module embodies the mechanism for language acquisition. Some postulate the existence of more than one innate module in the mind [perhaps mutually complimentary mechanisms], while others like the psychologist Jean Piaget argue that language is manifestation of a more general faculty of cognitive skills. The concept of modularity has implications for understanding the nature of language acquisition.

monitor. To cognitively maintain a regular check or watch over oneself (or someone else). 'Monitor' as noun refers to any of the various devices for watching/checking an operation. *See also* MONITORING.

monitoring. Carefully watching how

something such as one's learning progresses over a period of time. Monitoring is applying EXPLICIT knowledge. One could monitor to correct one's spontaneous production of language. Speakers are noted to revise at points segments of utterances they produced. This kind of conscious editing/monitoring is more frequently, and often more assiduously, applied to one's written products.

monitor model/theory. A theory of SL learning developed by S Krashen during 1976-1982. The THEORY is based on a set of five HYPOTHESES.

The first deals with the acquisition-learning hypothesis. It considers the two as separate processes – one refers to the way children acquire their MT, and the other to the conscious process of INSTRUCTED LEARNING. *See* the NATURAL APPROACH. Though some of the claims relating to the distinction are controversial, the distinction itself has been highly influential in establishing the superiority of the meaning-focused as different from the form-focused modes of learning and instruction.

The second hypothesis is the claim that the acquisition of grammatical structures proceeds in a predictable order. 'Acquirers of a given language tend to acquire certain grammatical structures early, and others later'. (Krashen: 1982, p. 12).

The third, the monitor hypothesis, relates to the function of 'learning.' When a SL is formally learnt, the learner tends to consciously apply the rules of grammar to her language output in order to monitor or edit it. This process of monitoring is a slow

and halting process. *See* LEARNING (2). Superior to this is the fluent use of the acquired system.

The fourth, the INPUT HYPOTHESIS says that language acquisition is promoted by COMPREHENSIBLE INPUT given to and received by learners.

The last is the Affective filter hypothesis. *See* The AFFECTIVE FILTER.

The monitor theory created a lot of excitement among those concerned with language education when it was propounded around 1980. It was subjected to a lot of critical debate. The dust has settled now but certain contributions of the theory stand out as reminders to language teachers. They are, briefly, the superiority of 'acquisition; processes, the importance of INPUT, and of AFFECTIVE FACTORS in language education.

monoculturalism in language/literature teaching. The practice of using CONTENT that represents only one set of values, one culture, one predominant line of thinking, judging and only one social VARIETY of the language. The values and culture thus upheld are usually those of the dominant class(es) among the native speakers of the language. Implicit in such a practice is the assumption that the native speakers' values, attitudes and norms as reflected in a particular variety/group of texts are the only valid ones. Monoculturalism is contrasted with plurality of cultures, norms, dialects, etc.

monolingual. A person, COMMUNITY, DICTIONARY, etc. using only one language. Monolingualism contrasts with bilingual, BILINGUALISM, and MULTILINGUALISM.

monologic teaching. A pedagogical MODEL in which knowledge is seen as the creation of the teacher, and flows downwards from her to the learner. The mode of instruction in it is transmissive, and there is little scope for exchange of equivalent knowledge, or even for the 'experience' of the learners to be accommodated, respected. The unequal power distribution and the unidirectionality of monologic teaching, it has been pointed out, damage the self-concept and confidence of the individual learner.

morpheme. The smallest unit of meaning. A word may consist of one or more than one morpheme. The word 'act' has one morpheme in it, but 'rapidly' has two: rapid+ly. Of these, the first one is a free morpheme, i.e., it can stand on its own, but 'ly' (an adverbial suffix indicating 'manner') is a bound one. Some words may be composed of a string of morphemes.

morpheme studies. Studies based on the HYPOTHESIS that as a result of universal processing strategies, learners of an SL acquire grammatical functors, such as MORPHEMES, in the same order, and that this order is similar to that in L1 acquisition although it may vary in the case of adult learners.

There has been difference of opinion among researchers both about the procedures adopted in the studies and the findings drawn. However the findings indicate a strong possibility of there being a natural sequence in the development of SLA. *See also* NATURAL ORDER HYPOTHESIS, and DEVELOPMENTAL SEQUENCE.

morphology. Study of the relationship between the STRUCTURE/shapes of words and their meanings. Morphology studies WORDS formed by putting together constituent morphs – prefixes, suffixes, infixes. Processes of affixation, derivation, inflection lead to the formation of words.

morphophonemics. The study of interrelationship between PHONEMES and MORPHEMES. The two levels are interdependent.

motherese. *See* CARETAKER SPEECH.

mother tongue(MT). The first acquired language/DIALECT. It is acquired as part of one's developmental process beginning infancy through a process (not yet conclusively understood) of constructing meaning and rules from the input received and through effort to communicate. A number of expressions with slightly different connotations are used to refer to MT. The most common ones are FIRST LANGUAGE, NATIVE LANGUAGE and PRIMARY LANGUAGE.

In MULTILINGUAL contexts, children may simultaneously acquire more than one language/dialect as MT. In relation to such contexts expressions like HOME LANGUAGE; the dominant, or the stronger language may be used. Linguists use the shortened form, L^1 *Cf.* TAUGHT MOTHER TONGUE, and VERNACULAR TONGUE.

motivation. The mental phenomenon/ process considered to be the force that impels one, and directs one's behaviour, towards goal-achievement. A number of factors lead to the build up of the impelling force. They include the incentive value of the learner goal, the keenness of her desire to achieve it, her ATTITUDE and the effort she puts in.

According to Gardner (1985), motivation 'refers to the combination of effort plus desire to achieve the goal of learning plus favourable attitudes towards learning the language' and towards the COMMUNITY of the speakers of that language'.

Williams and Burden (1997) have approached motivation from what they term a CONSTRUCTIVIST viewpoint. 'A constructivist view of motivation centres around the premise that each individual is motivated differently (p.120).' They propose the following definition of motivation 'which is essentially cognitive, but fits within a social constructivist framework'

'Motivation may be construed as
• a state of cognitive and emotional arousal,
• which leads to a conscious decision to act,
• which gives rise to a period of sustained intellectual and/or physical effort,
• in order to attain a previously set goal (or goals).'

Motivation is not a permanent trait of an individual. It is dynamic in nature since attitude, PERSONALITY factors and AFFECTIVE variables are not permanent characteristics of an individual. They vary according to the context and the remaining two interacting factors mentioned above *viz.* effort and desire. The duration of motivation varies according to the contexts of a person's/learner's goal orientation.

There are two sets of contrasted terms in the literature on motivation:

instrumental and integrative orientation: Gardner and Lambert (1972), particularly Gardner, have made a distinction between two types of orientation in motivation. They relate to learner attitude, to why one wants to learn a second language. Instrumental-oriented motivation is caused by the considerations of the practical advantage of learning a language – promotion in job, financial gain, etc. whereas the integrative reflects 'a sincere and personal interest in the people and culture' with whom the target language is associated Further, that it is integrative motivation that presages better, successful learning of a SL. Lukmani's (1972) study in Bombay[among other studies], however, does not support the superiority of the integrative over the instrumental. The contexts of learning an INTERNATIONAL LANGUAGE as a SL or as a LINGUA FRANCA have led to raising questions about integrative orientation being a presage to successful learning of a SL.

intrinsic and extrinsic motivation: The learner with intrinsic motivation does not have the desire for any apparent reward. For her the experience of engaging in an activity and the satisfaction thus derived are their own reward. In the intrinsically motivated learners there is a willingness to face challenges. Such learners are usually 'deep' learners. [*See also* STUDY APPROACHES.]

On the other hand, extrinsically motivated behaviour is aimed at getting some reward outside the activity: examples – employment, success in examination, admission to a course of study. However, the two are not exclusives: both may be present in the case of some learners.

move. A unit of analysis of CLASSROOM INTERACTION. The pedagogical discourse in the classroom has been analysed as consisting of a succession of events or 'a sequence of moves.' *See* IRF MOVE/ TRIADIC DIALOGUE. One of the well-known systems, though an early one, for analysing classroom interaction was put forward by Bellack et al. (1966). It consists of four moves or pedagogical functions: structuring, soliciting' responding, and reacting.

multilingualism. Use of two, three or more languages by an individual or by the members of a speech community.

Whereas 'multilingualism' is used with ref. to a COMMUNITY/society, BILINGUALISM refers to individuals even to those who may know more than two languages.

multi-media approaches to instruc- **tion.** Technology-based alternatives to the teacher-fronted, face-to-face modes of teaching. In it, instruction is delivered through media-supported self-learning materials. Needless to add, the approach calls for much greater learner initiative and responsibility.

In the multi-media approach, facilities of face-to-face-, radio- & phone-in-COUNSELLING, and teleconferencing are made available to help learners sort out their difficulties.

multiliteracies. *See* LITERACY.

multiple-choice tests. *See* DISCRETE-POINT TESTING/FORCED-CHOICE ITEMS/ SELECTED-RESPONSE ITEMS.

multiple line of approach. *See* ECLECTICISM.

multi-skill approach in language teaching. *See* Integrated language teaching.

N

the Nagpur list. The recognition (English) vocabulary of class XI students in the Chhotanagpur area of what is now the state of Jharkhand in India. The list forms part of a study carried out in 1960–61 by Helen Barnard. Upwards of seven-fifty students of Ranchi University were tested for their reading vocabulary. The preliminary results showed that they knew about fifteen hundred words 'out of a possible total of twenty one' (Barnard: 1961).

Barnard's work belongs to the era of vocabulary count and VOCABULARY control but is significant in that it gives language teachers an idea of the vocabulary attainment of an average Indian learner after five years of learning a SL.

narrative. 1. A COHERENT, written or spoken account of an event or a series of connected events. Most stories are narratives. A narrative implies a NARRATOR (1). **2.** How one [**Example**, a teacher] thinks and feels and how one acts in one's professional life. 'A person's overall past record of experiences in private life as well as in personal life'. (Connelly and Clandinin, 1988: 20). 'Narrative is the study of how humans make meaning of experience by endlessly telling and retelling stories about themselves that both refigure the past and create purpose in the future'. (*ibid.* 24).

narrative forms of knowledge. [With reference to TEACHER KNOWLEDGE in relation to classroom practice.] The tacit knowledge of teachers as different from their 'theoretical' knowledge. [*See* the Paradigmatic forms of knowledge.] This knowledge is in the form of their personal experiences. It comes through their NARRATIVES (2), and is context-specific.

narrative inquiry. A method of research into teachers' PERSONAL PRACTICAL KNOWLEDGE. Narratives are also teachers' stories of their experience, or field text data for research. Analyses of the field text data by researchers, who call themselves 'narratologists,' lead to an understanding of teachers' knowledge – their practical principles, personal philosophy, and such other things.

narrative writing. Writing that deals primarily with events. Events are usually described chronologically or in the order of their happening. Chronological order is indicated with the help of adverbial expressions of time, such as after that, soon, in no time, immediately, later. Time signification is of importance in narrative writing.

However, skilled writers, such as novelists may take liberties with the chronological sequencing of events. They may begin a narrative not at the beginning, but somewhere later, **example,** in the middle and present the story up to the middle through flashback

narrator. 1. The teller of a story – one who recounts it. All narratives imply a narrator. The narrator may be an all-knowing (omniscient) author or a hidden one. Events may also be seen and narrated by one of the characters in the story, or by an outsider. Though a narrative is created by its author, the author and the narrator are different personae, and not to be mixed. **2.** The disembodied voice instructing/speaking to the test-takers in LANGUAGE TESTS administered telephonically or through audio-recorded tapes. **Example**, in a STANDARDISED, COMMUNICATIVE LANGUAGE TEST, the test-taker hears the following, which is one of the many such 'narratives' directed to the test-taker: *You will now be asked to give your opinion about a familiar topic.*

nation. A COMMUNITY of people sharing such common factors as history, language, CULTURE, and descent. They usually live in one geographical area.

national language. A language considered to be the main language of a NATION-state, **Example** French in France. It is also the country's OFFICIAL LANGUAGE. In case of India, all the eighteen languages listed in the Eighth Schedule of the Constitution of India are national languages, although only Hindi and English are the official languages of the Government of India.

national syllabuses. SYLLABUSes developed as reference models to be adopted or adapted by the educational institutions in a country.

native language. *See* MOTHER TONGUE.

native language support. The support one's knowledge of one's MT makes available in SL learning. It is now widely held that success in SL learning, and general academic achievement are related to one's MT literacy skills in the formal, educational context.

This contrasts with the view generally held until recently that one's MT was a barrier to learning a SL.

native speaker of a language. One who is born to a language (or, a DIALECT) as are, for example, Englishmen to English or one of its dialects. In FL teaching the VARIETY used by the educated native speaker is held to be the NORM (2).

nativisation. *See* INDIGENISATION.

nativist approaches. Theories and approaches that stress the genetic or inherited influence on human behaviour. Regarding language acquisition, nativists postulate that language is a biologically inherited faculty. *See also* Nature and nurture.

natural approach. An approach to classroom learning and teaching of SLs. In its new assertion, it is associated with Krashen and Terrell. Strongly influenced by Krashen's 'MONITOR' and 'INPUT' hypotheses, the approach emphasises the adoption of 'natural' learning processes – processes that characterise children acquiring their MT: processes in which the focus is on COMMUNICATION skills through meaning-focused INTERACTION in stress-free environment. In the natural approach, 'COMREHENSIBLE INPUT' is considered to play a vital role in the acquisition of language. Focus on grammatical form has no place in instruction, although a limited role is allowed to functional grammar as supportive and supplementary to acquisitive activities.

naturalistic language learning. Acquisition of language in the way most children acquire their MT or HOME LANGUAGE, unaided by FORMAL INSTRUCTION. Naturalistic learning is unconscious and informal. Language acquisition takes place through receiving INPUT, and through engaging in interactive processes of communicating meaning for real purposes in real time in situations where there is INFORMATION GAP between the interactants. Recent models of SL teaching seek to incorporate these features as principles.

naturalistic observation (of a SL classroom). Observation of an everyday lesson in its normal setting with usual participants.

Though in naturalistic observation recordings of the lessons are made and transcribed and field notes are taken, it is essentially a qualitative method, and subjectivity is accepted as natural.

natural method. An approach to SL teaching based on naturalistic principles of language learning, or the way children acquire their MT. The approach was advocated and practised during the second half of the ninteenth century. It is a precursor of the DIRECT METHOD.

The salient features of the METHOD are oral work, direct association of meanings with words, INDUCTIVE teaching of grammar, and avoidance of TRANSLATION practice.

naturalness criterion. 1. The CRITERION of AUTHENTICITY, the criterion that as much naturally occurring samples of the language should be used in its teaching as possible. Contrived examples and made-to-order materials violate the naturalness principle. **2.** The CRITERION that one's language should sound natural and IDIOMATIC. It should be free of JARGON, CLICHÉS, affectations, etc. and SL teaching should aim to achieve this.

natural order hypothesis. The claim that learners acquire the rules of language in a predictable order and not necessarily according to the order they are taught in or according to the simplicity/difficulty criterion of the form/rule. Although there appears to be some agreement on the MORPHEME acquisition order, any large-scale claims based on the hypothesis have been disputed. *See also* MORPHEME STUDIES, and DEVELOPMENTAL SEQUENCE.

natural setting (for SL learning). Environment infused with the SL or the learner's TL. In such an environment, the TL is used all around for various purposes in a variety of domains. This has implications for SL learning. Its ACQUISITION-RICHNESS provides learners ample INPUT, and interaction & LEARNING OPPORTUNITIES.

nature and nurture. The question whether the faculty of language is basically genetically determined, or a product of environmental influence. In language education there has been a controversy whether the faculty of language in the human beings is a result of nature or nurture. The question relates to two opposing positions: the innatist and the acquired behaviour positions. Theories of SL learning and *teaching* have been premised on the two differing positions. The BEHAVIOURIST school bases itself on the premise of 'nurture,' and the innatists on 'nature.' A third, a pragmatic-eclectic position, keeping the controversy aside, selects principles from both. *See* COMPLETE METHOD, EC-LECTICISM, and GLOSSODYNAMIC MODEL.

need. A situation in which something that is not available is necessary.

There are various types of needs such as biological, physiological, social, emotional. See Needs hierarchy, and Needs. Some needs are associated with drive, and act as motivating factors, **Example**, the need for achievement.

needs. (in the context of SL education, and of LSP). The language needs of SL learners in relation to their profile and goals. Profile here includes such things as learners' background, cognitive resources, ATTITUDES, age group, and the achieved proficiency in the TL. Goals refer to the objectives to attain which they wish to learn the language. In addition, needs relate to the situations of communication in which the learners will be expected to perform. Thus the specified needs may be described in terms of skills, language CONTENT (3), and communication situations. Needs need to be taken into account for developing curriculum that addresses itself to the specific learning-requirements of particular groups of learners, and can be accomplished within relatively short time.

needs analysis/assessment. The procedure of identifying/analysing problems, types of NEEDS, priorities of goals, and performance in a programme. The procedure may be carried out by administering DIAGNOSTIC TESTS, QUESTIONNAIRES, conducting INTERVIEWS, or observing the participants in target situations. The results of needs analysis are used in curriculum design.

needs hierarchy. See HIERARCHY OF NEEDS.

negative selection. See SELECTION.

negative transfer. See INTERFERENCE, and TRANSFER

negotiated syllabus. See PROCESS SYLLABUS.

negotiation of meaning. The interactive process of conveying and arriving at meaning. The process involves two parties – addresser and addressee – who could, for example, be speaker-listener, teacher-learner. Negotiation is an integral part of meaningful communication between them whether through oral discourse or written.

The concept 'negotiation of meaning' is used in three language-education-related contexts: conversation, teaching, and learning. Negotiation proceeds through several micro processes such as

• comprehension checks (Do you follow?) and confirmation checks (OK?),
• responding to these,
• seeking/giving clarification,
• adjusting (to feedback received) [MESSAGE ADJUSTMENT] in the form of clarification and other responses,
• using modification devices such as re-formulating the message or simplifying the language.

The feedback, **Example** response to confirmation checks, may be requested or provided verbally or non-verbally. Negotiation is necessary to bridge the possible or real gap between what the addresser intends and what the addressee interprets.

Gap of this kind is typical of many classroom-teaching situations where the teacher is the only or the dominant voice, and may remain beyond any feedback from the learners. They generally accept and memorise whatever the teacher gives them. 'Negotiation'. if any, is limited to their minds. Negotiation is also the process of engaging with texts/tasks – engagement in meaning -making activities when reading a text or doing a task.

neurolinguistics. An interdisciplinary area joining PSYCHOLINGUISTICS and neurology. It studies mainly the neurological brain-functions in relation to language acquisition and use.

neutral language/neutral English. A form of a language [English]with a minimum of cultural background, free from national biases, and that can be used for utilitarian purposes such as international communication by those who have learnt it as a SL. L.A. Hill (on 'Factual language': 1967) noted in 1950s that the third world countries needed to teach and learn neutral English.

new key approach. The AUDIOLINGUAL method. Nelson Brooks (1964), who popularised the term 'audiolingual' also used the term 'new key' to refer to the method. An important element in the teaching approach/method was the use of audio-visual aids and the language laboratory.

new method readers and new method teaching. An approach to teaching and preparing language teaching materials for the UNFAVOUR-ABLY CIRCUMASTANCED learners of a SL [English] advocated by M. West during 1920–1940. A salient feature of the approach is that it places very high the skill of reading in the learning of a SL [English]. The development of the reading skill is seen as an instrument of self-learning after school. The materials for reading are in CONTROLLED VOCABULARY. The teaching approach is oral- and drill-based.

newspeak. Language manipulated for political propaganda and for suppressing seditious ideas. It is deliberately controlled to mislead. Hence it is marked by such qualities as AMBIGUITY, euphemism, and obscurity. George Orwell was the first to use the word in this sense in his novel *Nineteen Eighty-four* published in 1949.

Non-detailed reading. Independent reading. School and junior college curricula have traditionally prescribed for reading two types of texts: one for 'detailed' reading or study, and the other for non-detailed reading. Champion (1937) opines that the former is meant for pupils to 'learn' reading, and the latter to 'practice the art of reading.' He considered the non-detailed more important since through it the learner experiences 'independent and continuous reading,' which is real reading. *See also* EXTENSIVE READING, RAPID READING, and SUPPLEMENTARY READERS.

non-linearity. *See* CHAOS AND COMPLEXITY THEORY, and LINEARITY.

norm. The point of reference for judging something. **Example**, for judging the correctness of an individual's production of language, oral or written, a standard VARIETY of the language may be used as norm.

norm-referenced tests. Language tests that judge an individual candidate's performance in relation to that of the whole group to which the candidate belongs. The performance of the whole group is used as the norm, and the performance-report is usually in the form of a PERCENTILE rank. Such

tests contrast with the CRITERION-REF-
ERENCED ones.

note-making. A study-related activity in which one gathers from more
than one source information on a
topic/subject.

note-making and note-taking.
ACADEMIC SKILLS of condensing information. NOTE-TAKING closely adheres to
the spoken/written text. But in NOTE-
MAKING, more than one source of information may be used and it may additionally include the note maker's own
reactions and evaluation of the original
discourse – written or spoken.

note-taking. The process of writing
the main ideas of what one reads
or listens to. It can take place either
simultaneously with reading/listening
or subsequently.

noticing. Paying attention. It is hypothesised that a SL learner's mere
exposure to the language is not
enough. Learners should understand
the language and notice how it is
used. Receptivity thus heightened,
paves the way for learners noticing
FORM(2)al aspects of the language and
how they interact with MEANING to create MESSAGE. Through such conscious
processing, INPUT becomes INTAKE.
Intake becomes UPTAKE when learners
are able to use the noticed rule/item
communicatively.

notional-functional syllabuses. Syllabuses in which language content is
arranged in terms of i)meanings learners would need to express in their use
of the language, and ii), FUNCTIONS that
go with these meanings. Notional syllabuses, mooted by D.A. Wilkins (1976),
mark a departure from those based on
grammatical forms & structures found
unsatisfactory for developing communicative competence. It has, however,
been noted that the inventory of notions [like time, quantity, and space]
and functions [like evaluation, sua-
sion, and argument] that forms such
syllabuses, turn out to be similar to
STRUCTURAL SYLLABUSES in that they
become a repertoire of learning units
to be presented one at a time. Also,
they deprive learners 'of the opportunity to exploit the generative potential
of grammar (i.e., the ability to use syntactic rules to create new sentences.)'
(Markee, 1997:46, referring to Brumfit
(1981b) and Paulston (1981). *See also*
FUNCTIONAL SYLLABUSES.

notional grammar. A grammar organised according to the meanings a
language is used to express rather than
according to grammatical forms.

nuclear english. *See* SIMPLIFIED MOD-
ELS.

nursery rhyme. *See* RHYME.

O

objective. **1.** In the context of language testing, used as an adjective to refer to tests that use DICRETE-POINT and ELLIPTICAL test-items. TRUE-FALSE TYPE ITEMS also qualify as test-items of the objective-type. **2.** In the context of curricula, objectives are what they plan to achieve. Syllabuses usually state their objectives in terms of skills and abilities learners would [be expected to] acquire. B. Bloom (1956) has classified educational objectives under three domains: cognitive, affective, and psychomotor.

Though AIMS and OBJECTIVES are used synonymously, and quite often together in a phrase, some writers distinguish between the two. Widdowson (1983), for example, thinks that OBJECTIVE refers to the immediate or short-term result to be achieved by a lesson, whereas AIM is the long-term, overall goal.

observation. A means of collecting data in EVALUATION. The evaluation could be of learner-performance or teacher-performance. CLASSROOM OBSERVATION techniques are applied to the study of CLASSROOM INTERACTION and the behaviour of learners and teachers. In LANGUAGE TESTING, observers may be engaged to rate the performance of the test-takers.

officialese. Language typically used in official documents. AMBIGUITY, avoidance, and CIRCUMLOCUTION are some of its features. *See also* BLUNDERBUSS and GOBBLEDYGOOK.

official language. The language officially adopted by the government of a country or State for use in its offices, and for use by the judiciary and legislative bodies. Some multilingual countries may recognise more than one language as their official language.

ontogeny model. A THEORY about MT influence on the acquisition of SL phonology. According to it, language errors resulting from the influence of the MT phonology are greater in the early stages. With time the number of the errors goes down. The explanation given is that in the beginning the learner has little else to fall back on than the MT. The MODEL derives from the work of R.C. Major (1987) as cited in J. Jenkins (2000:106–7).

open-ended. Admitting of not one but several possibilities. An open-ended question can be answered in many correct ways. Different from open-ended are questions or TEST ITEMS that admit fixed or restricted responses.

open learning. Off-campus learning, largely self-instructional; learning through non-conventional modes and characterised by freedom. 'Open' because there are no walls that cloister educational institutions, and learning is not bound by the restrictions that are normally there in the institutionalised set-up such as schools and colleges. *See also* OPEN LEARNING SYSTEM.

open learning system. A disjunctive yet a networked teaching-learning system. The system is composed of remotely placed learners and counsellors/instructors with a high degree of mutual accessibility, curricular structuring, and an efficient support mechanism that includes self-instructional learning materials. The system is characterised by freedom and flexibility. *See also* OPEN LEARNING. An alternative to the teacher-dependent, face-to-face mode, the system utilises the multi-media resources of information technology, and of technology in general. The support system for the learners consists of print, audio and video materials as also tutoring, COUNSELLING and feedback mechanisms. However, it is to be noted that openness is not an absolute: how much openness a system permits is a matter of degree.

open questions. *See* OPEN-ENDED.

operant conditioning. CONDITIONING in which stimulus control is applied to produce a behaviour response. Correct response is reinforced by providing reward to the organism. As a result, it begins associating reward with the behaviour-response to the stimulus. By repeating the process the connection between behaviour and response is strengthened leading to learning. Behaviourists have applied the stimulus-response-reward/reinforcement-learning chain model to draw principles for teaching including language teaching. Conditioned learning in the OPERANT mode is conceived differently from learning in the CLASSICAL mode. [*See also* CLASSICAL CONDITIONING] In operant conditioning, the subject does something to achieve the reward which is a source of pleasurable experience. In classical conditioning, the response to the stimulus becomes automatic through repeated administering. Applied to learning, the operant mode is held superior as it associates learning with effort-making resulting in agreeable experience.

Operant conditioning is also known as Skinnerian conditioning, after B.F. Skinner (1904–90), the American psychologist. *See also* The Behaviourist learning theory and the Stimulus-response theory.

opinionnaire. A QUESTIONNAIRE. *See* Attitude scale, and Scaled questions

optimal age. The best or most favourable age when to begin learning a SL. *See*, in this regard the critical period hypothesis. Some academics hold the view that SL learning should begin when the learner has achieved some cognitive maturity and academic skill in her L1. *See also* COGNITIVE/ACADEMIC LANGUAGE PROFICIENCY.

oracy. Competence in oral communication, both speaking and listening. Sociologists have noted that children from disadvantaged sections of society suffer from verbal deprivation, and are not communicatively very fluent in their MT. They have argued that language education at the school should compensate for this deficiency by developing oracy in the classroom.

oral. Concerned with language and speech.

oral-aural approaches. *See* ORAL-SITUATIONAL APPROACHES.

oral bilingualism. The BILINGUALISM of those who can speak two (or, more) languages but cannot read nor write. Migrant labour in urban areas and those living in places on either side of which different language communities inhabit, acquire such bilingualism.

oral composition. A teacher-directed, classroom activity in which learners orally compose a related sequence of sentences. The stimulus is usually provided by the illustrations in the book, or some picture elsewhere, or an object. The activities may range from controlled to free. A fully CONTROLLED one would present learners a set of jumbled sentences they have to rearrange correctly, and as they do this they speak out the sentences. A semi-controlled activity would provide bare points to be developed into sentences forming a coherent composition. FREE COMPOSITION would be a response to a topic suggested to a learner to speak on. Pedagogical management and feedback by the teacher, as in teacher-fronted classes, will monitor the activity. However, the COMPOSITION could also be a collaborative, PEER-managed, PAIR and GROUP WORK.

oral comprehension. *See* LISTENING.

oral drill tables. *See* SUBSTITUTION DRILLS.

oral interview. A mode of judging/ assessing language proficiency in speech. In it interviewers/judges engage in 'conversation' with the candidate. Or, the candidates may interact among themselves while the judges observe. The conversation/discussion is structured and the judges, who may be trained in the job, use RATING scales with defined/described levels of PERFORMANCE (1). The number of judges, the tasks, the criteria used in judging, the duration of the interview, and the procedure for candidate participation may vary according to the design of the interview/test. Oral interviews are DIRECT TESTS of speech proficiency and are considered better procedures than

tests based on OBJECTIVE(1) items.

oral method. 1. *See* Oral-situational approaches. **2.** A method of teaching language to the deaf through lip-reading and shaping of speech.

oral proficiency. The composite ability of expressing oneself effectively in oral communication. To be proficient in oral communication is not only [to be able] to use language intelligibly or just [grammatically and phonetically] correctly. It is also to use language that communicates the speaker's meaning effectively. Effectiveness, besides INTELLIGIBILITY and linguistic CORRECTNESS (grammatical and phonetic), is a feature of how the discourse is organised and structured. Effectiveness also includes APPROPRIATENESS of the speech to the situation in which the utterance is made.

oral reading. 1. Reading with lip movement or vocalisation and sub-vocalisation. In oral reading, the reader moves her lips and utters the words either audibly or internally. This mode of reading, if for comprehension, is faulty and tiring. *See also* READING. **2.** Reading aloud. *See* READING ALOUD. A distinction is, however, made between 'oral reading' and 'reading aloud' – between loud reading and reading aloud.

oral-situational approaches. Approaches to S/F L T. Developed during 1930–1960 mainly by British teachers and applied linguists, the APPROACHES(1) are a formalisation of the contents of the SL curriculum in terms of principled SELECTION and GRADING of vocabulary and grammatical items. There is a lot in common between the O S approaches and AUDIOLINGUALIM. In both, speech and oral practice occupy the most significant place although the two sets of approaches developed independently of each other.

An important feature of the OS approaches is that of teaching language items in meaningful relation to the situation of their use. New language items are introduced and practised situationally. *See also* SITUATIONAL TEACHING.

oratory. The art of speaking in public eloquently using RHETORIC and flourish (hand movement, gestures). *See also* ELOCUTION.

order of development. *See* DEVELOPMENTAL SEQUENCE AND NATURAL ORDER HYPOTHESIS.

orientations to study/learning. The purpose or MOTIVATION in undertaking a particular course of study or enquiry. These could be, among others, vocational, academic, personal, or social. *See also* STUDY APPROACHES.

output. (in SLL). Oral and written production by learners. It is postulated that speaking and writing in the TL to communicate meaning helps the learner to acquire it since the process involves HYPOTHESIS TESTING, using COMMUNICATION STRATEGIES, and PROBLEM-SOLVING approaches. The study of learner ERRORS as appearing in their output gives an indication of the cognitive processes that may have taken place during the learners' PROCESSING of the output. It has been posited that output followed by FEEDBACK raises the learners' CONSCIOUSNESS (CR) and control of language and of the grammatical forms in it.

In a way, INPUT and output are complementary processes in SLA as input leads to the formation of hypotheses and output to their testing.

overgeneralisation. Mistaken application of a GENERALIZATION (based on past learning) to a case or an area to which it is not applicable (**Example**: 'sitt*ed*'). INTRALINGUAL in nature, overgeneralization is considered to be an inevitable phenomenon in learning, both one's MT and a SL.

overlearning. The process of continuing to PRACTICE (1) and study something even after it has been learnt. In BEHAVIOURIST approaches, PATTERN DRILLS are aimed at overlearning. *See also* TIME-ON-TASK.

ownership. Sense of belonging, possession, involvement (the opposite of ALIENATION). The concept relates to the SL learner's/user's attitude towards the TL – how free or inhibited they feel in it: do they feel they can take RISKS, and have the liberty to be creative, or do they feel constrained. Does the language in some sense belong to them, or are they on the receiving end? The learner's ATTITUDE is significant to their learning.

It is axiomatic that learners feel unconstrained and at ease in using the MT and often take creative liberties in it. However, the NORMS of CORRECTNESS in SLL, specially FLL, vesting with the native speaker, learner creativity is often stigmatised. The consequent timidity and inhibitedness hinders learning, and may affect SELF-ESTEEM. All this relates to the larger question of ownership. *See also* CANON.

P

pace. Tempo in teaching: the speed at which the class is conducted. Good pacing is sensitive to the learners' needs and speeds, and takes them along. Varied pace keeps learner interest alive.

paired-associate learning. A variant of ASSOCIATIVE LEARNING. In the paired-associate learning-tasks, learners are presented items that consist of a pair, **Example**, pen – red. When the first word in the item is given to learners, they are expected to produce the associated word. This is a way of increasing learners' vocabulary. *See also* CONTIGUITY LEARNING.

pair practice. A controlled, classroom activity in which learners practice in pairs. They may take on the roles of speakers A and B in a dialogue. They read out their portions from the scripted dialogue. Pair practice is teacher-supervised, and can have a variety of format. The teacher may divide the whole class into pairs, and each pair practices separately but the whole class practices together. *See also* PAIR WORK.

pair work. Pupils working interactively in pairs on a learning task. The task may have a variety of forms one of them being the INFORMATION GAP type. SL learners' participation in the task-related interaction engages them in MEANING-MAKING, which is considered to promote SLA. Fear has, however, been expressed that instead of using the TL, the learners may be tempted to use their MT, or when using the TL they might reinforce erroneous forms in their INTERLANGUAGE. In MT-teaching contexts, pair-work may bring relief from teacher-fronted instruction as the former, planned suitably, can engage learners in PROBLEM-SOLVING.

paper-and-pencil tests. *See* RECOGNITION TESTS.

paradigm. A MODEL (1) representing a THEORY or viewpoint; a particular form in which knowledge is pursued. An accepted model of how things work.

The word 'paradigm' is derived from the Greek word *paradeigma* meaning 'pattern'.

paradigmatic forms of knowledge. [With reference to TEACHER KNOWLEDGE in relation to classroom practice.] Generalizable knowledge of the principles of learning and teaching – knowledge emanating from research generalizable across a wide variety of contexts. Based on Bruner (1986), such knowledge is contrasted with narrative ways of knowing. *See also* NARRATIVE FORMS OF KNOWLEDGE.

paragraph. A DISCOURSE (1) unit – a written group of related sentences – organised in a consistent manner, usually dealing with one main idea. The sentences are related, i.e., they have a certain UNITY and relate to each other coherently. A paragraph may stand on its own or form part of a larger discourse. CONSISTENCY (1) and COHERENCE are not only internal to the paragraph, but they generally extend across to the other paragraphs preceding and/or following it when it occurs as part of a larger discourse.

paralinguistic features. Non-verbal

features accompanying vocal COM-MUNICATION. *See also* KINESICS, and PROXEMICS.

parallel thinking. Thinking in which each thinker is 'in parallel with all the other thinkers.' (E.de Bono) The traditional mode of thinking in arguments, according to de Bono, is 'adversial' in which 'each seeks to prove that the other side is wrong.' A constructive and creative way of thinking, says de Bono, is parallel thinking. In it the way forward emerges from parallel thoughts moving in the same direction. Instead of conflict, there is co-operation and coordination in thinking. *See also* LATERAL THINKING.

paraphrase. Reformulation, often in simpler words, of the meaning of a discourse unit. In reformulating or re-stating, the writer/speaker may try to gain greater clarity, or to make the utterance easier to understand. Teachers frequently recourse to paraphrasing in their classroom teaching. Paraphrasing is also an INTEGRATIVE learning activity involving both comprehension and expression, oral or written. Paraphrasing may also be a test-task, and a COMMU-NICATION STRACTEGY.

parole. *See* LANGUE AND PAROLE.

parsing. A WORD-based grammar-learning- exercise that consists of describing the units of a sentence grammatically, identifying and naming the part of speech [and its sub-division] they belong to and indicating their syntactic function. A key activity in the GRAMMAR-TRANSLATION METHOD of language teaching, parsing belongs to the tradition of the study of classical languages.

participatory approaches. Approaches to conducting programmes with the involvement of the participants esp. the beneficiaries. Many programmes are conducted in a TOP-DOWN (2) manner with their beneficiaries remaining at the receiving end. Much teaching still takes place with the teacher assuming the dispenser role and the learner that of the recipient. In a participatory approach, learners are partners and actively participate in the process of their own education.

participatory education. A democratic MODEL of education. *See also* PARTICIPATORY APPROACHES. The concept [and practice of] participatory education is ideologically oriented.

participatory evaluation. An approach to the EVALUATION of an ongoing programme or project by its organizers, manager(s), and instructors in it, not by outsiders. Thus participatory evaluation is a kind of collaborative self-evaluation.

passive listening. LISTENING as to a broadcast, in which the listener only listens but does not speak as one does in a conversation. Such listening is generally considered non-interactive. However, it can be interactive if the listener's mind is critically engaged in [mentally] responding to what is listened. Most TESTS of listening are of the passive kind.

Passive listening-practice has its uses in DICTATION, in preparing learners to speak, and as a pre-writing activity.

passive vocabulary. Words one is familiar with but cannot readily recall. *See also* ACTIVE VOCABULARY. One's passive vocabulary enables one to recognise and retrieve from the context the meanings of a much larger number of words when reading or listening. THESAURUSES help one to access words in one's passive vocabulary. Depending on the experience of language and on increasing or decreasing exposure to it, words in an individual's lexicon may move from passive to active and vice-versa.

pattern. '... a sort of framework or mould into which may be fitted a considerable number of similar sentences (or portions of sentences)' (H.E. Palmer, 1947.) The example She/broke/the chair/[subject+verb+object] represents a sentence pattern. In this sense, a pattern is a sentence-prototype. Phrases too have their pattern. 'Under the tree' and 'in the garden' belong to the same pattern of prepositional phrases. Similarly, scholars have classified verb patterns. *See also* PATTERN DRILL, STRUCTURE (1), and SUBSTITUTION DRILL.

pattern drill/pattern-practice drill. A language-practice exercise in which learners make new sentences on the given PATTERN. In the basic form of the drill, they just repeat [orally]the model sentence. A SUBSTITUTION TABLE may be used for this. Often complexity is introduced necessitating morphological and/or syntactic changes. An **example** of a base sentence and the cue/call words:

John cleaned the house. (*wash/car*)

As help, learners may be given some sample target-responses. Pre-recorded tapes are also used.

Pattern DRILLS may involve addition, COMPLETION, contraction, CONVERSION/TRANSFORMATION (2), inclusion, in-

tegration, or replacement, and even restatement. These constrain learners to make suitable grammatical choices. Implicit therein may be the expectation that in the process of carrying out the operation, the learner inductively automatises her language skills.

Though semantic considerations underlie grammatical choices, no explicit teaching of grammar-rules is done. What is targeted in pattern drills is rapid production of grammatically correct, but mostly uncontextualised, sentences. The drill itself does not tell the learners things like when to use the sentences, and where. Resourceful teachers may, however, give pattern drills a communicative orientation.

pedagogic discourse. The language characteristic of classroom instruction. It is marked by features which are avoided in normal speech. In pedagogic DISCOURSE(2), teachers mould their talk to suit pedagogic goals. They may deliberately use particular sentence structures, and target vocabulary- items in order to introduce them to the class, and highlight correct pronunciation by adding emphasis. Some other features are: repetitions, use of DISPLAY QUESTIONS, nominating students to answer, and giving them corrective feedback. *See also* CLASSROOM LANGUAGE, TEACHER QUESTIONS, and TEACHER TALK.

pedagogic grammars. Grammars specially designed and described for students in the manner of a textbook. They are designed to suit the needs of specified groups of learners keeping in view their age, the time available for teaching, and the level of the course of study. Such grammars are thus use- and skill- oriented. They include explanations, examples, and exercises/tasks for learning through practice the rules of the language. *See also* GRAMMAR (3).

pedagogical knowledge. KNOWLEDGE [also known as professional knowledge] that consists of a teacher's awareness of the dynamics of TEACHING as reflected in such abilities as the ability to organize the class, plan the lesson, conduct classroom routines, employ appropriately audio-visual aids, and steer classroom communication. The awareness as reflected in teacher action also includes a knowledge of the learners and learning, which includes knowledge of the psychology of learning, principles of feedback and REINFORCEMENT(1). In the case of SL teaching, it specifically includes CONTENT (5)-knowledge and the ability to administer pedagogic tasks, provide input, and generate interactivity. In the context of language education, subject knowledge and pedagogical knowledge are complementary.

pedagogical linguistics. *See* EDUCATIONAL LINGUISTICS.

pedagogic task. A task designed to make a learner learn or improve language skills. Asking learners to complete a sentence so that in the process of completing it they pay attention to a point of grammar and notice the embedded rule so they may learn it, is an example of a pedagogic task. Such tasks are instructional necessity though they may lack in AUTHENTICITY.

pedagogy. Generally, formal TEACHING, its methodology, and other related aspects. Sometimes the meaning of 'pedagogy' is expanded to include other curricular things than just classroom teaching.

With the spread of OPEN LEARNING systems, in certain contexts the term 'pedagogy' has come to be contrasted with ANDRAGOGY, and rather restricted to teaching, esp. children and adolescents in the face-to-face mode.

peers. Individuals who are equals in some respect. Students in a class or school are peers.

peer group. Group of individuals who have similar characteristics or equality of status. Teachers in an institution form a peer group. So do the students. Peer co-operation [CO-OPERATIVE LEARNING] and collaboration in learning [COLLABORATIVE LEARNING] are considered to be affectively and cognitively beneficial. In SL education, peer interaction is considered to be a significant source of input.

peer journal work. Writing of JOURNALS by students for perusal by peers. Such exchange is intended to promote student-to-student interaction, and mutual understanding of each other's viewpoint. *See also* EXCHANGE JOURNALS AND JOURNAL WRITING.

peer observation of teaching. A mutual arrangement between two teachers to observe each other's teaching with focus on a particular aspect. The aspect could, for example, be 'QUESTIONING'.

Being in depth, the observation notes such significant things as how frequently learners (or a particular learner) respond, the type, nature & purpose of their response, and how it is handled by the teacher. Such observation and the REFLECTION (2) it prompts are supposed to contribute to the professional growth of both the observed and the observer. An awareness of the significant aspects of teaching, and collegiality, communication and mutual confidence between the participating teachers are a precondition for the success of peer observation.

POT is an integral part of PRACTICE TEACHING on teacher-education programmes where the PT done is evaluated for grading. It has been observed that PEER-REVIEW sessions sometimes turn acrimonious and negative. For this reason, in many places judgmental comments are avoided. *See also* PEER TEACHING.

peer review. Feedback from PEERS on learners' (own) composition/writing. Peer review is a process of learning through interaction with peers. For this, small groups of about four students each (of the post-intermediate level) are formed. Group-members meet when they have looked at the composition written by one of the members and offer their comments and suggestions. The tutor may quietly chip in when the review session is on. It is one of the rules of the review that the comments made should, as far as possible, be constructive After the session, the writer redrafts her composition. Interaction with peers is supposed to boost the students' confidence and criticality. The procedure is considered preferable to teacher-driven correction which may smack of the use of authority and generate negative feelings among the students. The success of peer review depends on the kind of interactive culture and discourse the members develop for negotiation during the review. It should give prominence to the writers' creative effort and purpose. Overmuch concern with linguistic accuracy in the composition will certainly dishearten the writer. *See also* PEER GROUP.

peer review of teaching. *See* PEER OBSERVATION OF TEACHING.

peer teaching. 1. A pre-planned, supervised, structured, focused, and EMPIRICAL activity in a teacher-training programme. In it a trainee is asked to practise-demonstrate to the fellow trainees in a mini lesson the handling of a particular TECHNIQUE or strategy, or a pedagogic handling of an item of teaching.

A peer teaching lesson is different from real teaching, and is preparatory to it. The trainee under the guidance of a MENTOR/supervisor, pre-specifies the aim of the lesson to be taught, the successive steps in it, and the expected learner activities. Then follows the Execution of the lesson thus planned. Peer teaching being a teacher-training activity, an analytical review by the trainees follows the performed lesson. For this purpose the peer teaching lesson may be audio/video taped.

Though useful as a training activity, the practice of peer teaching embedded in the concept of PRACTICE and TRAINING, does not allow much scope for open-endedness and thus may lacks in authenticity', there being no information gap between the performing teacher and her peers. **2.** In non-training contexts, student-peer-teaching is a pedagogical strategy for creating space for learner autonomy. In co-operation with the teacher, better able students help their peers with tasks and problems.

the Pennsylvania project. A large scale study project involving high school students that hypothesised the methodological superiority of the AUDIOLINGUAL approach over traditional methods of FL teaching. The Project went on for two years and its report was published in 1970. The results seemed to suggest that the traditional, COGNITIVE-CODE approach, produced better results. However, there were many question marks, esp. about the execution, and it was doubted whether the teachers strictly adhered to the method. The experiment failed to demonstrate anything conclusively. *See also* the COLORADO PROJECT.

perceived need. Something, **Example**, a knowledge of another language than one's own, felt to be necessary. Need-perception is a motivating factor in learning.

percentile. A value on a hundred-point scale. It indicates the number of cases/candidates in a particular reference group scoring equal or lower scores [and also by deduction, higher scores]. If a raw score of sixty corresponds to the percentile rank of seventy-five, it means that seventy-five per cent of the candidates obtained a score of sixty or below and (only) twenty-five per cent scored higher than sixty.

perception. The process of the mind acting on sensory impressions: the process of knowing. The process is an active one, and in it the mind unifies and organises into a coherent form the input it receives. The input consists of such things as sights, sounds, sensations, and experiences that men come across in their environment. Activities like reading and interacting with people also form the input. The significance of these factors lies in what the mind makes of them – the perception. Important in perception are also the individual's knowledge of the world, past experience, and present needs.

In organising the input to make it coherent and unified, the mind selectively notices events, stores in the impressions, classifies and categorises them, translates and transforms them, draws inferences from them and learns.

performance. Actual use of language in terms of overt, observable, exhibited language behaviour in COMMUNICATION. In the context of LE, one's performance is an externalisation and index of one's underlying language COMPETENCE (1).

performance errors. Language ERRORS caused not by an ignorance of rules but by such factors as stress, hurry, nervousness, distraction, memory lapse, and habit.

performance tests. Language tests designed to measure the test-takers' ability to perform tasks in real-life-situations, such as, at workplace. This might necessitate the test-taker performing in an actual situation as different from an exam-setting. The skills to be measured are not just verbal. Problem-solving is also involved.

personal enrichment (of the learner). Providing to the learners support and encouragement by creating in them such AFFECTIVE qualities as self-confidence, SELF-ESTEEM, respect for NATIVE LANGUAGE AND CULTURE.

The significance of the need for this is to be seen against the background of the overemphasis in LE on PROFICIENCY and COGNITIVE development. Underachievement and failure, it is now felt, may to some extent be related to the lack of the qualities mentioned above.

personality. 'The totality of somebody's attitudes, interests, behavioral patterns, emotional responses, social roles, and other individual traits that endure over long periods of time' (Microsoft Encarta Dictionary). There are different definitions of personality, and different approaches to dealing with the concept. In some approaches, personality has been defined in terms of five broad clusters of TRAITS: hostile vs. agreeable; introverted vs. extroverted; impulsive vs.conscientious; neurotic vs. emotionally stable; and intellectually narrow vs. intellectually open.

In the context of LE, one can say in a general way that personality represents the sum of an individual's cognitive, affective, and social traits and behaviour. And, as a complex of individual characteristics it plays an important role in language learning. *See also* LEARNER CHARACTERISTICS.

personal practical knowledge of teachers. Teachers' pedagogical beliefs and practices. The knowledge evolves from their personal understanding, experience, and beliefs and their cultural context. These shape the teachers' practice of teaching. The knowledge grows and changes with time, and goes beyond what is learnt during formal training in pedagogy. *See also* PEDAGOGICAL KNOWLEDGE, and TEACHER KNOWLEDGE.

phoneme. The minimal significant UNIT (1) of speech in a language. The sounds/b/and/t/in 'ball' and 'tall', make them different words, and are different phonemes.

phonePass test. A machine-administered oral test of language proficiency using one or more of the following: tape recorders, computers, and the internet. To take the test, the test-taker may have to go to a designated site. The test can be used for a variety of purposes such as to interview job-seekers, applicants for admission to college/university programmes, or even as ACHIEVEMENT TEST.

phonetic alphabet. *See* INTERNATIONAL PHONETIC ALPHABET.

phonetic method. *See* PHONICS.

phonetics and phonology. Study of speech sounds:disciplines that analyse and study different aspects of speech sounds. (*See also* PHONOLOGY.) In very broad terms, phonetics deals with the production and perception of speech and sounds generally whereas phonology is language specific.

phonics or, the phonetic method. An approach to the teaching of reading to beginning learners. It adopts the technique of introducing learners to sound-letter combinations. **Example**, in this method, learners are taught how in the word mat, the letters M-A-T give the sounds they represent. From individual sound-letter combinations the learners are taken to larger units (SYLLABLES, WORDS, and so on.). *See also* ALPHABETIC METHOD.

phonology. Study of the PATTERNING of the speech sounds used in a language. While the PHONETICS of a language studies the concrete characteristics of the sounds used in it, PHONOLOGY deals with how these sounds function in that language. The traditional approach to phonology is by way of phonemics. Phonemics breaks up the streams of speech into sequences of contrastive segments. Apart from analysing these contrastive sounds of a language, phonology studies their combinatorial possibilities and constraints. Furthermore, it describes how its PROSOD(Y)IC features, that is, pitch, loudness and length, function to produce ACCENT (1), RHYTHM and INTONATION.

phrase. A group of words and MOR-PHEMES arranged in grammatically correct order, and functioning as a unit within a sentence. The first six words in the sentence above form a phrase.

picture cards. Cards large enough to be clearly seen by all the learners in the class, with pictures of objects or activities on them. These cards are held up for the learners to see, and language learning activities centred on them follow. The activities can have a great variety. Their pedagogical focus may vary from vocabulary building to sentence formation to oral and/or written communication. Collaboratively building a story based on the activities pictured, and narrating it [orally]or writing it is just one example.

There can be several pictures in a sequence like the comic strip frames lending themselves to exploitation for language learning/teaching. *See also* PICTURE COMPOSITION.

picture composition. Picture-based COMPOSITION-writing/teaching-technique. The picture composition book, designed for the purpose, contains sequences of pictures, each set illustrat-

ing a story. The Teacher's Book may in addition contain hints, notes, questions, index, and suggested vocabulary to help the teacher make pedagogical use of the pictures.

To prepare the learners for the composition task, the teacher may first engage them in oral work asking questions aimed at making the points of the sequence of picture-frames clear, and providing linguistic help in the form of key vocabulary and sentence structures.

The TECHNIQUE of thus engaging learners in (semi-)CONTROLLED COMPOSITION is intended to pave the way for FREE COMOSITION.

picture vocabulary. Vocabulary expansion activity based on the principles and procedures adopted in PICTURE COMPOSITION. Pictures, representing items selected from the word lists prescribed for the particular class of learners (usually elementary), are used to make them learn new words. The pictures represent concrete objects – plants, animals, things, people. They can be used either to introduce new vocabulary items or to test knowledge of words. Along with the teaching of new words, the teacher may take up related grammar points. The learners may be asked to use in sentences the new word, a synonym, antonym, or a derivative of it.

pidgin. An extremely simplified form of 'language' used as a common medium of oral, verbal contact among a community whose members speak different native languages but do not share a language in common. In such contexts, a pidgin develops in order to fulfil the essential needs of communication.

pidginization model. *See* ACCULTURA-TION HYPOTHESIS.

pitch. The level of sound – the 'highness' or 'lowness' of voice. Variation in pitch has phonological significance. *See also* INTONATION.

placement tests. Language tests used to identify examinees/students who would be suitable for being placed at a particular stage in an instructional programme. A placement test is normally designed according to the requirements of the instructional programme. *Cf.* ACHIEVEMENT TESTS. *See also* ABILITY GROUPING.

plain words. Direct and simple language. [For what is not plain language, *see also* OFFICIALESE and VERBIAGE. According to Martin Cutts (1979) [co-founder Plain English Campaign], 'Plain English refers to the writing and setting out of essential information in a way that gives a co-operative, motivated person a good chance of understanding the document at first reading, and in the same sense that the writer meant it to be understood.'

The concept of 'plainness' does not relate only to English. It is applicable to all written [and spoken] languages that may be used in diverse domains.

planning for teaching. Preparing a detailed plan of work for a whole term's teaching. Prepared collaboratively by all the teachers in a Department, the Plan helps distribute teaching time over the entire term, allocating slots of time to the different items according to their relative importance and learner needs. The plan also gives learners a clear idea of what they are expected to do. Here is a fragment of a sample plan:

Term I	Syllabus Items	Textbook Lessons	other Materials& Activities
Week 1, July 9–14	1 & 2	1	Composition wrt-1, topic …
Week 2, July 16–21 [Holiday on 18]	3&4	1 to be completed]	
		TEST	

A plan for teaching is different from an individual teacher's plan for teaching a particular lesson. *See also* LESSON PLANNING.

plateau. 1. The posited stage, the stage of secondary education, when SL learners would be ready for 'free reading.' In the models of SL instruction [dominant around 1950 to1965] that believed in externally controlling learning, the plateau was supposed to arrive when the learners had acquired a vocabulary of 1500 to 2000 words through reading simplified materials. *See also* PLATEAU READERS. 2. Phase of little headway. Learners working hard in their study arrive after a period a phase of fatigue and little progress. It is advised that when this happen, learners instead of forcing themselves to go on, should turn to some other activity for a while.

plateau readers. Reading MATERIALS designed to revise, REINFORCE(1) and consolidate learners' existing knowledge of words and structures in a SL. Since there would be no new items to cause problems, assumedly the learner reading the plateau readers would feel a sense of achievement. Plateau Readers are at different levels: **Example**, level 1 based on a vocabulary of five hundred words, and so on. *See also*, SUPPLEMENTARY READERS, and GRADE READERS.

plausibility. *See* (The teacher's) SENSE OF PLAUSIBILITY.

point of view. The [characteristic] way in which the speaker/writer/narrator sees [and interprets] persons, places, and events. The point of view directs linguistic shifts in the narrative.

portfolio assessment. A mode of performance-evaluation which takes into account a body of work produced by the person whose achievements are being assessed. Achievements here does not necessarily mean only results: it may also include processes and the efforts made. Considered to be a mode of 'authentic testing' portfolio assessment stands in contrast with the evaluation based on a single sample, such as an ESSAY.

positivism. The position that all knowledge is contained within the boundaries of science: objective observation is the only basis for the formulation of laws. The BEHAVIOURIST LEARNING THEORY and its explanation of language behaviour in terms of STIMULI AND RESPONSE carry deep influence of positivist thinking. *See also* EMPIRICISM.

P P P model of teaching. 1. A MODEL of PATTERN-PRACTICE-based SL pedagogy. The three Ps (PRESENTATION, PRACTICE, PERFORMANCE/PRODUCTION) represent the plan of classroom instruction. The procedure of SL teaching captured in this model forms the core of struc-ture-teaching-centred pedagogy, and draws its rationale from assumptions, **Example**, relating to LINEARITY, efficacy of mechanical DRILL, and avoidability of language ERRORS. **2.** Triple 'P' standing for 'particularity, practicality and possibility' has been used by Kumaravadivelu (2001) as the 'pedagogic parameters' in a POSTMETHOD, second language pedagogy.

'postmethod condition.' Rejection of the concept of a predetermined METHOD for SL teaching, and adoption of alternatives to it. Kumaravadivelu (2001 and 2003) has used this expression to signify the assertion of the importance of the teacher's own experience, self-analysis and understanding and their 'SENSE OF PLAUSIBILITY' as sources of principles to guide pedagogy and liberate it from the confines of imposed method(s). *See also* POSTMETHOD CONSTRUCTS.

postmethod constructs. New thinking about SL teaching after the abandonment of the quest for a 'best method'. Branded methods of teaching SLs have generated from experts who have based them on THEORIES of language teaching. As a result, actual classroom practices and experiences have inevitably been at variance with the expectations of a given method. Because of this, the practitioners of language teaching have looked for alternatives to Methods, which have emerged in the form of certain principles or CONSTRUCTS. They emanate from mutually interacting theoretical, empirical, and pedagogical awarenesses, and are pragmatic in nature. Some of them are: TEACHER – AS-RESEARCHER role;

LEARNER-CENTRED curriculum; BOTTOM-UP search for solutions; SL learning through meaning-focused, TASK-BASED engagements; INTERACTIVE-classroom procedures; creating language AWARENESS through CONSCIOUSNESS-RAISING and DISCOVERY-oriented activities; cognisance of individual (LEARNER-) differences/preferences; the language lesson as a cascade of MEANING-MAKING activities providing LEARNING-OPPORTUNITIES; and sensitivity to CONTEXTUAL CONSTRAINTS and variables. *See also* POSTMETHOD PEDAGOGY.

Postmethod pedagogy A conceptualisation: a proposal to replace METHOD-based and TRANSMISSIONal modes of language-teaching- practices. Among others, an exponent of this is Kumaravadivelu (2001). Postmethod pedagogy rejects the concept of Method as the controlling principle for SL teaching. It asserts that instead of being governed by theoretical models/methods of SL teaching developed elsewhere in lab-conditions with a radically different set of learners, SL teachers and teacher educators should develop APPROACH (1)es that are in consonance with local ecology, and are practical and possible. The proposal is similar to Holliday's (1994) proposal. *See also* APPROPRIATE METHODOLOGY.

postmodern education. An IDEOLOGIcal position on education that opposes, among others, the AUTHORITARIANism of the traditional educational practices, and questions the role of direct teaching.

power. Domination and control – AUTHORITARIANISM in education, and PRESCRITIVISM in language use. Some manifestations of the former are: forcing wards to study courses they are not interested in; steamroller attitudes of the Headmasters and class-teachers; crushing independent ways of thinking; exercise of power in course- prescriptions; using exams as tools of control over careers.

And in SL use – inflicting arbitrary NORMS of correctness and the PRESCRIPTIVeness of grammar-rules; stigmatising pupils' MT and prohibiting its use during school hours; privileging DICTIONARY-attested usage.

power tests. Tests designed to measure the level of a candidate's ability. To enable the candidate to do her best, time constraint is lifted. But the questions in such tests are so difficult that not all of them can be solved correctly despite availability of time. *Cf.* SPEED TEST.

practicality. A measure of [language] TEST-USEFULNESS. It has to do with how convenient, cheaper and feasible it is to administer a test in a given context. A test of oral skills that depends on uninterrupted supply of electric power may not be a practical one to administer at a place where power breakdown is frequent.

practice. 1. As activity: REPETITION of an act or a series of acts for the purpose of improving one's ability to perform that/those act(s). Practice-work, in one form or another, forms the core and bulk of much language learning. Esp. in SL pedagogy, learners practice correct speaking and pronunciation, writing and spelling, word- and sentence-structure. They also practice interpreting longer discourses, and applying rules of grammar. The choice of practice techniques depends on learner factor and the activity-goal(s). *See also* DRILL. **2.** In contrast to THEORY. Often an antithesis is seen between the two, esp. when the practicality and implementability of theory is doubted. In this second sense, 'practice' means what actually happens rather than what should happen [if theory were to prevail.]. *see also* PRACTICUM.

practice effect. Effect of previous practice on later performance, which may lead to a better result. In language testing, familiarity with the test-format acquired from previous experience of taking a similar test may result in a higher score on the later test(s). This may happen without there being any improvement in the test-taker's proficiency. Practice effect may thus cause distorted evaluation.

In experimental work, practice effect needs to be controlled in order to arrive at undistorted results.

practice teaching (PT). (Or, teaching practice/training practice). The practical, the teaching experience, component of TEACHER EDUCATION (TE) programmes.

On the PT programmes, the participants (also known as teacher-pupils/ teacher students/teacher trainees/ novices) teach actual classes to gain experience of teaching, and learn its skills.. An essential academic requirement of TE courses, PT has justification in the fact that teaching being a pragmatic activity, a trainee needs, in addition to the theoretical knowledge, practical experience of doing teaching.

PT is a systematically organised activity conducted under the guidance of (experienced) MENTORS/supervisors. Programme-formats vary. On many TE programmes, the trainees are first taught the principles and then given DEMONSTRATION LESSONS by their supervisors. Insights and reflectiveness are sought to be developed in them by making them participate in analysing the lessons. Their own initial engagement with teaching may be through MICRO-(PEER-) TEACHING. The programme, extended over a period, concludes with a set of macro-teaching lessons for 'real' students. For this the trainees are taken to regular teaching institutions. Their performance on macro-teaching is rated, and this rating forms part of the overall evaluation.

In preparation for practice-teaching, the trainees have to design LESSON PLANS, which have to be approved by their supervisors.

The institution of PT is a product of the period when a direct correlation between teaching and learning was taken for granted. The lesson plans conformed to the tenets of the prescribed METHOD of teaching which proceed in tandem with the tenets. Changed theoretical understanding favours open-endedness against rigidly pre-cast lesson plan. *See also* MENTOR AND MENTORING.

practicum. Theory in action – the practical application of principles. Language education has two sides to it: the knowledge part and the skills part. The knowledge of theoretical principles come to test in the practicum part, the practice of teaching. The theory-PRACTICE (2) relationship applies equally well to such allied areas as language testing and materials for LT.

pragmatic competence. The competence to use language in accordance with social constraints and conventions. Pragmatic competence is normally distinguished from LINGUISTIC COMPETENCE, and is part of COMMUNICATIVE COMPETENCE. *See also* PRAGMATICS.

pragmatics. Branch of LINGUISTICS that studies language in use, as different from language as abstract system. An UTTERANCE is not only a linguistic entity: it has a social and communicative function. Pragmatics looks at this latter.

pragmatic tests. TESTS of language COMPETENCE(1) that test DISCOURSE(1)-level ability in the context of sociolinguistic APPROPRIATENESS and ACCEPTABILITY. *See also* SOCIOLINGUISTIC COMPETENCE.

précis-making. Shortening and summarising a longer text – making a concise and precise statement of its contents cutting out the flab. A précis is the outcome of a process of understanding, compressing and editing the original so as to produce a well-organised and coherent composition. is an An INTEGRATIVE task, précis-writing expects TEXTUAL COMPETENCE on the part of the writer. It follows set conventions. *Cf.* SUMMARISING.

predictive validity. A measure of the power of a language test to predict the test-taker's ability to perform tasks similar to the ones in the real world. *See also* CRITERION-RELATED VALIDITY.

presage. The preparatory and formative stage. Differently from the dictionary meaning of the word, Dunkin and

Biddle (1974) have used it in the expression presage variables in their model for the study of classroom teaching. Presage variables stand for the formative and the professional training experiences of the teacher. These, according to Dunkin and Biddle, influence the teacher's classroom teaching (PROCESS). What result from the PRESAGE, PROCESS, and the CONTEXT variables, are the PRODUCT variables.

prescriptivism. The principle or the practice of prescribing rules, language-usage and usage-standards. Linguistic prescriptivism is the attitude that holds a particular VARIETY of a language prestigious or superior to its other varieties, and favours the adoption of this variety for use by the speakers and learners of the language. RECEIVED PRONUNCIATION was considered by many, during the first half of the twentieth century, to be the NORM of correct and good speech.

Though prescriptivism as a principle is generally disapproved now, there may be a case for it in language pedagogy as learners may need to be told what is considered widely acceptable and STANDARD.

presentation. 1. The process of the teacher introducing to the learners in the classroom the item to be taught [and learnt]. It could be an item of vocabulary, a sentence structure, a new concept or new material introduced the first time. A classroom lesson usually begins with presentation. Presentation techniques use devices like ADVANCE ORGANISERS and contextualisation to motivate learners and to facilitate their acquisition of the new item being introduced. The teacher attempts to provide INPUT in such a way that it may become INTAKE. In a BEHAVIOURIST pedagogic cycle as in the ORAL-SITUATIONAL and the STRUCTURAL approaches to SL teaching, presentation is followed by PRACTICE, CONSOLIDATION, testing and REMEDIATION. (*See also* the PPP MODEL (1).) **2.** As different from its signification of 'PROCESS,' the concept of 'presentation' is also used to denote the technique of introducing the topic (or, the introduction itself) in a discourse, oral or written. Amplification and conclusion usually follow. **3.** Even more generally, a presentation is a prepared performance such as a LECTURE or a report presented (often in conjunction with mechanical/electronic aids) before an audience. *See also* SEMINAR STRATEGIES.

pre-sessional language courses. Short, intensive, need-based BRIDGE COURSES for students going to undertake technical or professional education specialy through the medium of a SL. The development of ACADEMIC SKILLS figures prominently in such courses.

pretence in language teaching. Deliberately acting in the a particular way/inventing & performing activities to serve the purpose of language teaching in the classroom. DRAMATIC METHOD, SIMULATION and ROLE PLAY require pretence on the part of the players. Bender (1964) lists, and recommends, teachers and students a set of six pretences the first and the last of which are: '…making believe that each situation imported into the classroom is real.' [No. 6] and, '…teacher and students have no language in common' [No. 1].

pre-test. A practice test or trial test. A pretest may be arranged to familiarise the students with the main test to follow on which the actual evaluation will be based. The pre-test may also serve the purpose of a forerunner with a view to finding out any defects in the design of the main test.

Scores on a pretest administered at the beginning of a programme serve as baseline with which to compare the progress made by the learner-participants. The comparison should also indicate the degree of the success of the programme.

principles and parameters. Highly abstract rules of GRAMMAR (1) that underlie the use of languages. PRINCIPLES governing languages, it is held, are universal in nature – they explain the covert similarity between them. PARAMETERS, on the other hand, account for overt differences between languages. Children, it has been hypothesised, are born with the innate, UNIVERSAL principles of language. The environmental input fixes the parameters for the specific language(s) they are acquiring. **Example**, English has a head initial parameter. Hence the SVO [subject-verb-object] word order. Most Indian languages have a head final parameter that accounts for the SOV [subject-object-verb] word order.

proactive inhibition. Hindering of the learning of new habits by the previously acquired ones. Someone who has learnt that the word *work* as noun being an uncountable is used in singular number [and is not aware of the usage as in *the works of Shakespeare*] may be proactively inhibited in using the plural number form *frameworks*. Retroactive inhibition is the converse process.

problematization. Rethinking something [usually complex] that has/had been taken for granted; something whose solution is not simple. Problematizing may be teasing out a problem to make it visible, a problem that may have contradictions underneath which have not been seen as problems. Theoretical innovations [**Example**, in language pedagogy], attractive at the ideational level, often have a problematic aspect to their practicality and implementation.

problem-based learning. Learning in which the focus is not on gathering information and knowing 'facts' but on developing a PROBLEM-SOLVING ability. Information and knowledge, important as they are, need to be applied to solving problems, and competencies and tools for this ability need to be developed

'problem' classes. Language classes difficult to teach effectively. The problems may include: the LARGE size of the class; learners of mixed ability in the TL with some of them very poor; unmotivated learners, un-cooperative learner-attitude, unsuitable textual materials.

problem-posing. A LEARNER -CENTRED approach in teaching and training. In it, the teacher may pose an OPEN-ENDED problem relating to a topical issue or a familiar situation. This may be done either verbally or by presenting a visual frame (picture, poster, video clipping, etc.). The verbal or the visual input is administered to stimulate discussion of the problem – its causes, possible solutions, and so on.

Participation in exploring solutions to the problem posed – a meaning-/message-focused, authentic, discourse-generating, activity – is considered to strengthen the learners' communicative competence.

On SL teacher education programmes, problem-posing may lead to REFLECTION(2), and an in-depth discussion and analysis of problems relating to the teaching/learning, and possibly to theorising.

problem-solving. The processes involved in finding solution to a problem. They require cognitive engagement, and lead to DISCOVERY. Engaging in problem-solving activities, esp. in groups, is considered to build up language competence. *See also* SYNECTICS.

procedural knowledge. Knowledge of how to do or operate something. Being a matter of skill, the procedural contrasts with DECLARATIVE KNOWLEDGE.

Procedural knowledge of a language is knowledge acquired through using the language and observing how it is used, rather than through a formal study of the rules. Procedural knowledge is tested through hands-on test, or actual performance.

procedural syllabus. A SYLLABUS that specifies teaching in terms of learning activities/tasks. A procedural syllabus is distinguished from the traditional content or LINGUISTIC SYLLABUSES that are language-items-based. A CONTENT(1) syllabus pre-selects and specifies what the learners should learn and be taught. It is argued by some that there being no LINEARITY between what is taught and what gets learnt, we can only specify in a syllabus activities that the teacher will perform.

A procedural syllabus favours a TASK-BASED methodology. It does not provide for an explicit teaching of form/grammar. The activities in a procedural syllabus are meaning-focused that are intended to engage learners [cognitively] in problem-solving. Language is assumed to be acquired in the process of doing the tasks Procedural syllabuses are associated with NS Prabhu's COMMUNICATIONAL TEACHING PROJECT [Prabhu:1987].

process. *See* PROCESS AND PRODUCT.

process and product. The progression of an activity towards a goal and the outcome of the activity. The reading of a text is the process and the understanding gained as a result, the product.

process approach. The approach in pedagogy that places the means used in learning above its outcome in isolation. Means here include the STRATEGIES, esp. cognitive, that learners employ in the process of LEARNING. *See also* PROCESS WRITING.

Product-focused LT approaches insist, for example, on learners producing ERROR-free language whereas process-focused approaches, viewing the occurrence of language errors as natural, highlight the related learning-effort of which the errors are symptomatic.

processing. Mental activities concerned with information. These include paying ATTENTION, focusing, receiving, storing, and retrieving information.

process of reading. *See* READING PROCESS.

process option. The choice about the how part of teaching. Very broadly, teaching involves two things: what to teach, and how to teach what one wants to teach. About this, one may have several options such as adopting the lecture mode, or the tutorial mode, and so on.

process syllabus. A syllabus that the teacher and the learners jointly evolve as they proceed in the classroom from week to week. Together they decide such modalities as what CONTENT(1) should be taught, how, and in which order. A process syllabus, also known as a negotiated syllabus, is thus different from the usual content or subject syllabuses that specify in advance things like the subject-matter (and books) to be taught and the order in which they will be taught.

process writing. An approach to the teaching of writing in LE. In it the focus is not on a linguistically correct and finished piece of writing that the learner should produce. Rather it is the learners' engagement in the actual process of writing, which is considered to be more significant for learning. Accordingly, in the teaching of the skill a major function of the instructor is to lead the learners through the dough-kneading experience of composing a piece of writing. The dough-kneading experience is one of kicking off with an idea and a make-do sentence, modifying the idea and changing the sentence if necessary, moving on, maybe fitfully, to a working draft. And then, if on a review not feeling happy with it, restructuring and recasting the draft until the learner feels that what has resulted is satisfactory.

In this process learners, under the helping guidance of the instructor, are expected to resource their experience, knowledge, and language to produce a text imperfect though it might appear to be from a professional standpoint. This 'enabling approach' differs from the traditional approaches to writing, which treat it as a means to language practice, its goal taken to be accurate language production.

product. *See* PROCESS AND PRODUCT.

production-based theories of classroom interaction. Theories that say that learners acquire a SL when they attempt to produce it for communication. *Cf.* RECEPTION-BASED THEORIES.

production strategy. The STRATEGY of making use of one's linguistic knowledge in communication – of producing language. The assumption is that if one focuses on producing, one brings into play one's knowledge of the language. And this is a way of enhancing one's competence.

A distinction is drawn between production strategy and 'COMMUNICATION STRATEGY.' The latter is resorted to in order to get over a communication problem. 'Production strategy' does not carry this implication of negotiating a problem.

professional development of teachers. Teachers'[growing] awareness of their role and responsibility as teachers and their awareness about the teaching profession. The awareness includes a knowledge of what effective teaching and learning are. Teachers' professional development is largely autonomous and self-directed. It can be achieved

through various means such as independent reading; conscious analysis of, and critical reflection on one's own teaching experience, observing how learners learn and trying to find ways and means of maximising their learning. *See also* TEACHER DEVELOPMENT.

proficiency in a language. An individual's ability to use the language in a variety of situations, correctly, fluently, and appropriately. Going beyond grammatical CORRECTNESS, proficiency is also a matter of FLUENCY and APPROPRIATENESS. Proficiency could be general or related to special areas/specific skills such as reading and writing. There has been some debate, esp. in the field of language testing, whether language proficiency consists of a single factor (unitary trait) or several distinct subabilities. In this regard, a multi-componential model of SL proficiency is generally favoured. Hence, proficient reading does not necessarily mean that the reader would also be proficient in oral skills.

proficiency tests. Tests that aim at measuring the current level of the test-takers' COMPETENCE (1) in a language. They may have components aimed at testing different skills, or they may be related to one particular skill such as Speaking. Unlike EXAMINATIONS, proficiency tests are not related to any given course of study undergone by the test-takers previously.

proficiency rating scales. *See also* RATING GRID.

profile. A statement of an individual's abilities or TRAITS as a learner or of her scholastic achievements. In some new modes of LANGUAGE TESTING, performance assessment is reported in the form of a profile. *See also* DESCRIPTIVE ASSESSMENT.

prognosis. Prediction of the outcome of a process. Prognosis is also a predictive ASSESSMENT of an individual's future performance.

prognostic tests. Tests designed to make an assessment of the likelihood of the success of some programme of education or training for some individual person.

Prognostic language tests are administered to find out or to predict how well an individual is likely to perform in learning a new language. *See also* APTITUDE TESTS.

programmed learning/instruction (PL). A method of self-instruction assisted by self-learning materials or by teaching machines, popular during 1960s. The mode of instruction and learning is so labelled because in it the course material is carefully analysed into discrete items to be learnt and these items are arranged in a succession of graded and sequenced steps. At each step the learner performs as directed and since there is built-in provision for feedback immediately on completion of each step, the learner knows whether she has performed correctly or incorrectly. In the latter case, i.e., in the case of failure, provision is there for the learner to go back and repeat in order to re-learn the target component.

Though some principles of PL are useful in designing materials for self-learning as in DISTANCE EDUCATION, the theories of language and of learning it is based on are now outdated.

progressive differentiation. In INSTRUCTION, a way of organising information. In it the instructor moves from generalised statements to specific details. *See also* INTEGRATIVE RECONCILIATION.

progressive readers. READERS that gradually introduce new vocabulary items in a planned manner with a view to expanding the learners' VOCABULARY. They may consist of a series graded according to their LEVEL (1). *See* Grade readers. *Cf.* PLATEAU READERS, and SUPPLEMENTARY READERS.

progress test. *See* ACHIEVEMENT TEST.

project. In the context of the language class, an extended TASK-based exercise to be attempted by learner-groups in the classroom. In working on it, learners work co-operatively to gather information and structure it. The work leads to products like a written report, or an oral PRESENTATION (3), a poster session, or a bulletin-board. The teacher coordinates and sometimes may participate in the work.

The important features of project work are:
• Working on a project is an 'authentic learning experience.'
• It engages learners in MEANING-MAKING activities and content-learning
• It is a collaborative group-activity
• The process of working together in learning is as important as the product
• It develops autonomy among learners
• Language, the medium of all the activities, is learnt in relation to its use for generating types of texts and GENRES. *See also* TOPIC METHOD.

pronunciation. Production of speech sounds. It also means the manner of producing speech sounds. *See also* ACCENT (2).

prosody. The suprasegmental system. It includes such features of speech as intonation, stress, juncture, pitch, pitch change, rhythm, stress, syllable duration, tempo. The prosodic features tell us about the speaker – their age, emotional state, social class, geographical provenance, and so on.

prototyping. Associating a word, social class, group, caste with its most typical example. Most people would consider a male to be the referent for manager. Prototyping reflects BIAS(1). Domestic work is typically associated with women, and poverty/simplicity with villagers. Prototyping in teacher-DISCOURSE(2) and teaching-materials can influence learner-attitudes, and create prejudice.

psycholinguistics. An interdisciplinary area combining psychology and linguistics. It studies primarily the cognitive psychology of verbal behaviour, that is, linguistic behaviour in relation to the mental processes that are believed to underlie that behaviour. Some of the sub-areas in psycholinguistics are language ACQUISITION, BILINGUALISM, psychology of reading, and LANGUAGE AND THOUGHT.

psychometric methods. The ways of measuring mental traits and abilities in quantifiable terms – in terms of number, degree, or amount rather than quality. Some examples of TRAITS/attributes are APTITUDE, INTELLIGENCE, language PROFICIENCY and SELF-ESTEEM. The methods use techniques to generate in a careful way samples of behaviour, which are assessed to draw inference about the mental/psychological traits.

puppetry. Dramatising activity using movable doll-like figures representing persons and animals. The figures are attached to strings that are manipulated from behind to simulate action on a makeshift stage. Playback songs, dialogues, pre-recorded or impromptu, accompany the action.

Puppetry can add to the audio-visual in language teaching and make it more effective by dramatising well-known tales or even parts of epics. The dialogues and other stretches of language used [they occur in relevant context] work as COMPREHENSIBLE INPUT. Pupils can be made to create stories, write dialogues, speak or record them to be played in a puppet drama.

purism. *See* CONSERVATISM.

Q

questioning. Teacher(s) asking questions as part of CLASSROOM INTERACTION. Questioning is one of the DIDACTIC FUNCTIONS and is done to promote learner-thinking and learning. *See also* QUESTION TECHNIQUES, and TEACHER QUESTIONS.

questionnaire. An INSTRUMENT for obtaining data by asking oneself or others questions. The questions are usually set out in an organised way on printed sheets (or, in computer files) with space for answers/information to be filled in. A well-designed questionnaire has focused questions, and seeks to elicit focused information. Administering of a questionnaire may accompany or be followed by INTERVIEWS (3) with individual respondents.

Used as an instrument in research, questionnaires have various uses in pedagogical contexts. They can be used to evaluate courses, teacher effectiveness, and teaching materials.

Questionnaires can have a variety of formats. They may have choice-type questions for the respondents to tick the chosen box, or be open-ended ones for the respondents to write out their views and comments. Some make use of ATTITUDE SCALES/INTERVIEW SCALES and ranked questions.

question techniques/Questioning behaviour. Ways of using QUESTIONS in classroom teaching. Some of the purposes for which teachers may put questions to the class, or to the learners they nominate, are: i) to focus learner-attention and keep them from getting distracted; ii) to make them think and find answers and express themselves; iii) to elicit feedback from the learners and to monitor their progress; and iv) to seek contribution to the classroom discourse, and participation in making the class interactive.

The quality of the questions asked, their quantity, and the skilfulness in asking them are related to the standard of classroom teaching.

Many teachers just 'teach' rather monologically and feel no need to ask questions. Some just ask questions routinely, without any planning, and often without waiting for an answer.

Some tips experts offer on questioning are: avoid a stern look when putting questions; let learners feel affectively relaxed; encourage and help them in formulating their answers; when no answer comes forth, rephrase the question comprehensibly/unambiguously; do not let peers make fun of answers wrongly given; praise good answers; distribute the questions over the class; take along weak learners; use patience, WAIT TIME, and create in the class an atmosphere of understanding.

Question techniques also concern language tests and testing. *See also* TEACHER QUESTIONS.

R

range. The area(s) covered. **1.** The range of an item of vocabulary has to do with the different contexts in which it can be used. The word branch has a wider range than one of its synonyms tributary. The criteria of FRQUENCY and range have been used to determine which items should be selected for teaching. **2.** In statistics. The spread of values, scores, etc. over an area. If in a test, the highest score is 92, and the lowest 35, the range is 57.

rapid readers. Books for non-detailed study. In many language curricula, books for RAPID READING are prescribed alongside the TEXTBOOK(s) or the main course-book. The two types of books aim at developing READING approaches, and giving reading experience of two different types. Rapid readers usually consist of full works (novels, plays), often classics.

rapid reading. FAST READING as one does when reading for enjoyment. However, learners often subject their TEXTBOOKS to INTENSIVE READING paying attention to every difficult word and sentence. This they do in order to perform well at the examination, where their knowledge of such items is tested. Consequently, they develop a slow reading speed. In real life one needs to adjust one's reading speed according to the text, and more often one needs to read rapidly rather than closely. Usually there is curricular provision in schools to make learners acquire rapid reading techniques. *See also* RAPID READERS.

rapport. Close correspondence between the teacher and the learners – the state of their being in tune with one another during teaching. For teaching to be successful, it is necessary that there be a rapport between the teacher and the class, and the teacher ensures that the class keep pace with her.

rater. An expert who judges language PERFORMANCE of candidates taking a TEST and awards them GRADES or scores. The expert is a person trained for the job.

rating. Judging the language [and other] performance of candidates and assigning grades, scores, and other evaluative labels. The job of rating involves exercise of objectivity, a clear understanding of the ability [-ies] being judged, the context [the test-takers, the purpose of the test, and so on], and the various levels of performance.

rating grid. INSTRUMENT for CRITERION-REFERENCED judgement of language performance. *See* RATING. Categories of PERFORMANCE are arranged vertically along the grid and their levels horizontally. The following is an **example** of a grid with 5 categories and 5 levels, developed for a test of oral proficiency:

| levels→ | Poor | Fair | Aver- | Good | Exce- |
Categories ↓			age		llent
Grammar					
Pronun-ciation					
Vocabu-lary					
Fluency					
Compreh-ension					

Rating grids are used on DIRECT TESTS of language competence for assigning marks/grades.

rational cloze deletion. *See* CLOZE TEST.

rationalist position. The position that language is innate to humans, and not externally acquired. *See also* ACQUISITION OF LANGUAGE.

readability. A CRITERION of the comprehensibliity of a written text: of whether a particular group of learners are likely to find it easy to read. There are several procedures for judging this. *See,* for example, Cloze procedure, Difficulty level, and Type-token ratio. Though the above-mentioned procedures give us an idea of the difficulty level, they essentially represent rather 'mechanical' procedures and do not take into account reader-cognitive factors. There are other criteria that need to be taken into account. Some of these are: reader-interest; individual LEARNER CHARACTERISTICS, esp. their mental make up and KNOWLEDGE STRUCTURES; their familiarity with the topic of the text and its structure.

read-and-listen exercises. Language-learning activities in which learners listen to the recorded version of a text as they read its printed version. The pedagogical objectives of the exercise are: to establish in the learners' mind the relationship between the written form and its pronunciation; and to teach correct pronunciations and discourage spelling pronunciation.

When the written text is a TRANSLATION of the recorded one, the objective is to train learners in comprehension and in finding the meanings of the TL words.

reader. A book of extracts (sometimes, a complete book) for READING by language learners. The extracts are selected with some objective(s) in mind and according to some principles. An obvious one is to promote learners' competence in the language through reading. For this, carefully designed language tasks and exercises are appended to each extract. The principles guiding the selection relate to the linguistic content and the level of difficulty of the extracts, their suitability to the learners' learning needs, age, interest, level of competence (in the language), etc. *See also* GRADE READERS, PROGRESSIVE READERS, and SUPPLEMENTARY READERS.

reader theory. Theoretical positions that hold the centrality of the reader in literary communication and literary meaning. In these theories, it is the reader who creates the meaning: the text, the authorial intention, and the personal/historic background of the author do not count for much. Reader theory champions the learner-reader role in constructing a personal-response-derived meaning of a text. *Cf.* CLOSE READING.

reading. A complex mental process of deriving, constructing, and synthesising meaning from written/printed text(s). Comprehension is the product of this process. Reading involves not only a knowledge of the language – which includes discourse processing ability – but also an understanding of the context and background of the written text, as also the reader's knowledge of the world in the light of which meaning is created. Thus comprehension results from the interaction between the reader's mind and the text. Reading is a creative process of thinking, relating, imagining and interpreting. *See* CREATIVE READING, READING PROCESS, and READING SKILLS.

reading aloud. Oral reading: reading out a text (saying the words aloud) as different from silent reading. The skill of READING by definition refers to silent reading and teachers are generally advised to encourage it as a cognitive process. However, there is a place in language education for a [dramatized] reading aloud by the teacher of such texts as narratives, poems, and stories. The listening-experience can be spellbinding for learners, specially in lower classes.

Normal reading aloud by the teacher in the class sets an articulated model for learners to perceive and imitate. They can relate the articulation of words to their written form. Similarly, recitation of poems and literary/rhetorical pieces by learners can be an enjoyable experience.

Reading aloud requires an integration of many skills including the ones of taking the meaning into consideration, and paying attention to the punctuation marks. Reading aloud also calls for the use of appropriate INTONATION, ACCENT(1), and RHYTHM. These help listener-comprehension. A preview of the text (by the reader) helps make the reading effective. Oral reading is a good preparatory step to SPEAKING PRACTICE.

Several real-life contexts such as making an announcement, a PRESENTA-TION(3) or addressing a meeting oblige one to read aloud a whole text or portions of it.

Oral reading in the class should be teacher- assisted. Beginning learners gain in confidence by being able to read aloud. Forcing unwilling learners to read aloud, however, may create in them psychological inhibition.

Teachers can make a DIAGNOSTIC use of learner-reading aloud: it can give them an insight into the learner's cognitive processing of the language and the meaning of the text. *See* MISCUE and MISCUE ANALYSIS. Such reading is also a source of information for the teacher on their pronunciation [difficulties, etc.] and on the remedial teaching needed.

Reading aloud is different from loud reading or vocalised reading. The latter is a bad reading habit. It is time-consuming, tiring, and distracts the mind from the meaning.

reading cards. Learning aids in the form of large-sized cards with texts printed on them for EXTENSIVE READING. Along with the texts, illustrations (pictures, maps, charts) may also occur. The texts are followed by questions for the reader's self-feedback. A key is also provided for self-check. The cards, or the texts on them, are GRADED, and deal with a variety of subjects.

reading comprehension. *See* COMPREHENSION, READING, the READING PROCESS, and READING WITH RESPONSE.

reading method. An approach to SL teaching which places the skill of comprehensive READING above the skill of speaking in SL learning. In this method, practice is given in developing

READING STRATEGIES, and the techniques of both INTENSIVE and of EXTENSIVE or RAPID READING are systematically taught. Generally, graded text-materials with controlled vocabulary are used for reading. The use of the MT is not a taboo.

The British educationist, Michael West, working in undivided India, and A. Coleman in USA championed in the 1920s the importance of the skill of reading.

The advocacy of the method is motivated by practical considerations of learner-need, and what they can acquire comparatively easily. Seeds of the notion of LANGUAGE FOR SPECIFIC PURPOSES are to be found here.

M. West argued that reading should be introduced early in SL teaching since learners will have already acquired the skill of reading in their MT when they come to learn a SL. The skill can, therefore, easily be transferred to reading in a SL.

reading miscues. Readers' divergence from the printed text in their oral rendering of it. The divergences are instances of 'unexpected response'. The expected response would be to read out the text as printed. *See also* MISCUE. Miscues reveal the reader's expectation from, and their interpretation of, a text. Even proficient readers use meaning-making strategies leading to miscues. *See also* MISCUE ANALYSIS.

reading process. The process of comprehending/understanding a written/printed text. Reading is a mental process of deriving meaning from the visual cues the text provides. It is an active process of thinking, guessing,

asking questions, imagining, checking, predicting, anticipating and evaluating, and the reader is not a passive recipient of information/meaning, but a participant in MEANING-MAKING.

This process is helped by the reader's knowledge of the language and of the world. and is partly culturally-conditioned.

There are different theories of reading process: The bottom-up or text-driven theories treat the written text as bottom from where the reader lifts the meaning by paying attention to the units – morphemes, words, sentences, etc. – in a linear fashion. [*See also* BOTTOM-UP PROCESSING.]

TOP-DOWN or hypothesis-driven models hypothesise that the reader accesses a text in the light of her assumptions, experience, and background knowledge. ['Top' here is the reader's brain.] According to the interactive process model [*See* the INTERACTIVE APPROACHES TO READING], the reader uses simultaneously different modes of processing in reading. Thus reading becomes an ongoing process of forming hypotheses, modifying them, anticipating/expecting[what would follow], asking questions, checking, interpreting, and arriving at conclusions.

A distinction is drawn between product models and process models of reading. Product models are concerned with the outcome of reading; process models with how the comprehension takes place.

reading skills. Abilities involved in efficient reading. [*See also* 'efficient reading' under Fast reading.]

In READING, one deploys a complex of inter-related skills, the prominent ones of which are linguistic, textual, interpretational, and mechanical & general in nature.

Linguistic skills deploy such abilities as the reader's knowledge of the writing & decoding conventions, and of grammar, that is syntax, vocabulary and IDIOMATIC expressions.

Textual has to do with the ability to perceive how the text is woven as a network of meanings with devices of COHESION and COHERENCE and what its field of discourse, TENOR and GENRE are.

Interpretational skills have to do with the reader's abilities to comprehend – recall, invoke appropriate [mental] SCHEMA, conceptualise, ask questions, generalize, guess, infer and go beyond the surface & the rhetoric to the intended (or the hidden) meaning.

Mechanical and general reading skills relate to the reader's visual perception and discrimination (heeding punctuation marks & capitalisation, blank spaces marking boundaries. They also include the skills of CHUNKING (3), and of silent reading (eye movement, eye sweep, etc.). A skilled reader keeps changing gears, i.e., varying speed and switching techniques – SCANNING and SKIMMING. Such variation depends on reader purpose and the nature of the material being read. See also TEXT-ATTACK STRATEGIES and WORD- ATTACK STRATEGIES.

reading span. The amount of written text that can be perceived within a single FIXATION PAUSE. The size of the text is usually a unit of about five–six words, which would be a phrase, a clause, or a brief sentence. A span is the sequence of words after which we momentarily pause when reading aloud. See also SACCADE, and SENSE-GROUP.

reading speed. See Fast reading.

reading strategies. STRATEGIES that readers adopt or need to adopt to achieve maximally their reading goal without spending more time than is necessary. They involve such pre-reading activities as:
• making up one's mind about the purpose of reading;
• taking a look at the title, index/ references, and graphic materials, if any; at chapter divisions, and the beginning and the concluding part of the larger text;
• identifying the GENRE to which the text belongs; noting the salient features of the text.

Efficient readers adjust their reading according to their purpose and decide whether they need to scan or skim the text or subject it to intensive reading, During-reading strategies involve:
• locating the main idea and the supporting details in successive segments of the text as one reads it on;
• deciding whether one needs to read entire segments or skip certain portions

Discovering the logical structure of the text helps fast understanding . So does noticing text features like topicalization, sub-headings, transition markers, and other discourse devices.

Apart from these text and text-portions-level strategies [see also TEXT ATTACK STRATEGIES], there are word and phrase level strategies used during reading. *See also* WORD ATTACK STRATEGIES.

When reading for academic purposes, the reader may need to highlight key sentences, write down points, make notes and diagrams to analyse the text-content.

A strategy in close reading is to read between the lines in order not to miss inferences and implications, and to discover contradictions, illogicalities, fallacious arguments, deliberate distortions and deceptions. With such awarenesses and strategies, reading does not remain conformist: it becomes critical. [For non-close reading strategies *see also* SCANNING AND SKIMMING.]

Post-reading is the stage of evaluation. The reader may like, at the end, to have another – a critical – look at the text to develop a summative perspective. The review may result in a modification of the impressions formed during the pre-reading stage. *See also* SQ 3R APPROACH. These are equally real and authentic.

reading syndicate. A small group of learners formed with the common purpose of READING collectively certain selected texts/books. The books, selected by the learners themselves or recommended to them, are usually of some distinction and merit. The members of the group read them and then share with other members their individually acquired knowledge and appreciation. The interactive processes of reading, formulating one's impression and evaluating the book, and then sharing it with the group is considered to promote the learners' communicative abilities and enhances their general

LITERACY and AWARENESS.

reading with response. A TOP-DOWN mode of READING in which the reader goes beyond the meaning of the text to reflect on what it says or implies, and to ask questions. Also, the reader tries to see the text in relation to herself, her beliefs and concerns, and look for personal relevance. *See also* CRITICAL READING.

real books. Books not primarily written to be used as textbooks for language learning. 'Real books' are 'whole books:' books that have not been adapted, simplified or retold for pedagogical purposes. *See also* ADAPTATION (1), and Simplification (1) *Cf.* GRADED READERS.

realia. Actual objects teacher bring to the classroom as AUDIO-VISUAL AIDS to teaching. They may include such diverse things as pictures, models, small plants, flowers, balls, sticks. Resourceful teachers can use them in a variety of ways.

received methodology. Language teaching methods (for S/FL teaching) that come from another social, cultural, educational and ideological setting. They may have worked there but may not succeed on a different soil. In the field of language education, esp. of SL education, much theorising has originated in a couple of Western countries. Many other countries have imported and received expertise in the field from there without taking into consideration their own indigenous contexts. *See also* CULTURE-SPECIFIC PEDAGOGIES.

received pronunciation (RP). A prestige, standard, accent of British English. RP has no regional features of accent. Being the variety spoken by the upper classes in England, RP has been seen as a marker of class superiority.

It is the variety extensively described in pedagogical materials for ELT. However, with the decline of colonialism, and the rise in the assertiveness of national and regional – both native and non-native – accents, there are not many supporters today of the PRESCRIPTIVISM associated with RP.

reception-based theories of language learning. Theories that subscribe to the view that learners acquire a SL when they listen to that language being used, or read and understand books/texts in it. comprehension aids the INTAKE of the INPUT(1). The caveat is that the language, i.e., the COMPREHENSIBLE INPUT, should be of a little higher level than the learner's current proficiency level. However, some other writers think that mere comprehension is not enough: it should be accompanied with cognitive effort on the part of the learner so that the input may become UPTAKE (1). *Cf.* PRODUCTION-BASED THEORIES.

receptive skills. *See also* PRODUCTIVE SKILLS.

recitation 1. Reading aloud to an audience a literary piece or saying it from memory. Such performance calls for effective enunciation bringing out appropriate feelings and emotions – feelings and emotions appropriate to the text recited.

Recitation is a curricular activity related to affective factors – the piece and its rendering are usually charged with inspirational elements. *See also* DECLAMATION, and ELOCUTION. **2.** A class

period in which the learners [and the teacher] review what has been taught in the previous class.

recitation teaching. A MODEL(1) of teaching. It is structured around the cycle 'question-response-evaluation [QRE].' Though an improvement on the LOCK-STEP procedure and the teacher-monologue modes, recitation teaching has been faulted for using DISPLAY QUESTIONS and repetition. Teachers questions do not challenge the learners to think hard and critically, although it is possible at the hands of skilful teachers to introduce challenge within the QRE cycle.

recognition test. A language-test or a test item in which the test-taker has to identify the correct answer (key)among a set of answers (key plus distractors). Multiple-choice items are of this type. *See also* SUPPLY TYPE ITEM.

recognition vocabulary. *See* PASSIVE VOCABULARY.

reconditioning. *See* CONDITIONING.

reconstructionism. The ideological belief that man can improve himself and his environment (Clark 1987:14, following Skilbeck 1982). Reconstructionists hold that the welfare of mankind can be 'rationally planned for', and education has a key role in achieving it. Education can help remove social and political injustices, divisions, inequalities, and discriminations.

Reconstructionism seeks to remove elitism in education. Among the things it advocates are common core curriculum and mixed ability classes. Foremost, it seeks to promote 'understanding among people through effective communication' Thus an important reconstructivist agenda is to develop the ability to communicate to achieve understanding and unity among the peoples of the world. For this, the learning of S/F Ls is an important means. *Cf.* CONSTRUCTIVISM.

reduction. A difficulty-tackling device learners adopt when faced with a problem in using a SL. It consists of simplifying to a less complex one the rule relating to the problem. Example: *He go home yesterday.* Here, unable to use the past tense form of the verb 'go,' the learner has used the simple present form.

Reduction is a feature of child language, PIDGIN varieties, and poor learning/learners. Reductive SIMPLIFICATIONS (3) may be phonological, morphological, syntactic, or semantic.

reduction strategies of communication. Devices of REDUCTION in communication. The STRATEGY, taken recourse to during SL use, may consist of avoiding to use the language or of giving up the message the learner wanted to communicate as it involves the use of difficult words and structures or words she fears she does not know. Sometimes, instead of giving up, the learner may switch over to another, easier topic. The use of such devices arises from fear and feeling of linguistic inadequacy. *See also* AVOIDANCE STRATEGY. *Cf.* ACHIEVEMENT BEHAVIOUR and RISK-TAKING.

redundancy. 1. The feature of superfluity. A marker of faulty style, it occurs in language use in the form of words that can be deleted without any loss of meaning, **Example,** *Dying is more preferable to surrendering.* Another, a humorous, illustration: *Help stamp out,* *abolish and eliminate redundancy.* **2.** In linguistics. A built-in feature of natural languages. In the phrase *those three books,* plurality is signalled by three MORPHEMES. PHONOLOG(Y)ical systems too in languages feature redundancy. It helps the listener make out the meaning of the message even when it has been imperfectly conveyed or misheard. In written texts, redundancy, in the form of restatement, may sometimes be useful in helping the reader to understand.

reference skills. *See* STUDY SKILLS.

referential questions. INFORMATION GAP questions as contrasted with DISPLAY QUESTIONS. *See also* TEACHER QUESTIONS.

reflection. 1. In learning, the process of exploring the experience [of learning] and the content of what one has learnt, and evaluating them in relation to one's own feelings about them. **2.** In teaching, the process of cogitation in the teacher's mind: during teaching [reflection-*in*-action], and after it [reflection-*on*-action], the parallel mental process of weighing successes, failures, and their causes. Teacher reflection also explores, among many other things, the other possibilities and the alternative means of achieving teaching goals. Thus reflection in teaching is a process of critically analysing both one's teaching and the performance and participation of the learners during it. The critical review is considered to heighten the teacher's professional awareness and show her the possibilities of modifications and improvements.

reflective learning. A process of

learning in which learners [by concentrating on, and contemplating what they have done, seen, and experienced] generate new ideas and insights for themselves. MEMORISATION as a mode of learning is typically an example of a non-reflective mode of learning. JOURNAL WRITING, on the contrary, is considered to promote reflective learning [among teachers].

reflective practitioner. A teacher who constantly tries to make her teaching more effective by reflecting on her own teaching and its outcome. Some of the modes of reflecting are: evaluating one's teaching critically, SELF-OBSERVATION and SELF-MONITORING; observing others' lessons, writing diaries and journals, [*See also* DIARY KEEPING AND JOURNAL WRITING] sensitively going through learners' journals, and ACTION RESEARCH.

reflective praxis. Practice of teaching informed by the teacher's critical REFLECTION(2) and self-exploration. The reflection could relate to such things as teaching in general, the teacher's own teaching, learning problems of the students, and the classroom environment. *See also* Reflective practitioner.

reform movement. The movement in Europe during 1850–1900 to rationalise language teaching method(s), esp. for the teaching of modern European languages. It arose out of a growing dissatisfaction with the then prevailing GRAMMAR-TRANSLATION METHODS. A number of alternatives with varying emphases were proposed during this period. What emerged finally as most acceptable principles were: primacy of speech and the importance of teaching spoken language; inductive approaches, and avoidance of a formal teaching of grammar, of translation and of the use of the MT in the classroom. These crystallised into what we now know as the DIRECT METHOD.

The Movement was the beginning of the AUDIOLINGUAL approaches that dominated SL teaching through the first six decades of the twentieth century.

refresher course. An instructional programme aimed at updating the knowledge and skills of practising teachers. The selection of the course content and course activities depends on the needs of the participants and the objective(s) of the programme. So does the mode of instruction, which may take the form of one or more of the following: LECTURES, TUTORIALS, WORKSHOPS, SEMINARS, TEACHING PRACTICE, CLASSROOM OBSERVATION, and visits. The duration of the course is fixed in accordance with the above though usually it is not very long.

register. A VARIETY of a language distinguished by its use in social situations, or by the subject matter it deals with. Marked by subject-related vocabulary, registers tend to have their grammatical correlates and other features of STYLE. *Cf.* Genre.

regression. In reading, (the habit of) eyes going back to the last portion of what has just been read, before they (the eyes) move on. Frequent movements back of this kind may be due to the difficulty of the text, or to poor reading skills of the reader.

reinforcement. 1. (The process or procedure of) strengthening what has been taught. The audio-lingual methods, Behaviourist learning theories, and the Structural approaches to SL teaching attach(ed) a lot of importance to reinforcement through practice. Practice follows the initial PRESENTATION(1) of an item of structure. Reinforcement is intended to make learning lasting. In addition to classroom practice, or in place of it, learners themselves could reinforce their learning with the help of practice materials. *See also* REMEDIAL TEACHING. **2.** In Behaviourist psychology, reinforcement means providing a reinforcing stimulus after the learner has made a response. It results in strengthening of the responses made. *See also* STIMULUS-RESPONSE THEORY.

reliability. Dependability of an instrument of measurement, or of a LANGUAGE TEST. A reliable test is consistent: it yields approximately the same results when used again under similar conditions. Reliability is a prerequisite for the VALIDITY of a test. There are various ways of judging the reliability of a test. Reliability could also be a measure of a test-item, or of a RATER.

remedial course. A course designed to raise the learner(s)' level of proficiency to the desired level(s) through further work in speaking, listening, reading, and/or writing. Such courses address identified areas of learner difficulty. *See also* BRIDGE COURSE and REMEDIAL TEACHING.

remedial teaching (RT). Specially arranged instruction to remedy deficiencies in learning. RT follows regular teaching, tests and practice-work. It is essentially a follow-up measure aimed at removing learner difficulties, and is justified by the discovery in their performance of learning failures. RT may also be conducted to improve the learners' general proficiency, particular skills such as reading, or their control of specific areas such as the use of tenses. In many models of language-teaching, remediation is an integral part of, and the final stage in, the process of instruction. Remedying/strengthening of learning has generally been sought through repetition and controlled practice, assuming this to be the key to lasting learning and production of error-free forms/habits.

This approach appears to be a negative one with its obsession with 'failure,' control, and drill, treating language errors as stigmatic, rather than symptomatic of learning effort. The approach may be inhibiting, stifling creativity, and causing unnecessary ANXIETY and STRESS. Instead of it, making available an ACQUISITION-RICH ENVIRONMENT may perhaps be a better course. [*See also* ENRICHMENT.] It has been suggested by Williams and Burden (1997: 78–9, following Denis Lawrence) that Remediation can be more effectively achieved through counselling, encouraging 'a sense of individuality or uniqueness in the learners, and thereby promoting an inner sense of personal worth'. *See also* COUNSELLING.

repetition. The act of saying or writing something again and again. Esp. in SLL, it is one of the ways of practising correct language forms in order to learn them. Learners memorise forms and patterns, **Example**, conjugations of the verb *be*, by repeating them orally, or writing them several times over. *See also* MEMORISATION.

In the BEHAVIOURIST LEARNING THEORY, repetition and PRACTICE are important for an error-free language-habit-formation. Repetition helps CONSOLIDATION.

reporting. Communicating PERFORMANCE-evaluation or test results to pupils/examinees, their parents, employers, etc. Educational institutions periodically do such reporting through 'progress reports.'

reproduction. 1. An exercise in writing in which the learners first read or listen to a selected text such as a story or a description. They are then asked to reproduce it from memory either orally or in writing. Reproduction exercises constitute a variety of CONTROLLED-COMPOSITION-work intended primarily to make learners practise and learn structure and vocabulary. In the process, they may also learn the use of the devices of COHERENCE in discourse. Reproduction exercises are in line with pedagogical models that emphasize learning through PRACTICE, and minimise learner-exposure to language errors. **2.** In the context of education. *See also* REPRODUCTIVE MODEL.

reproductive model of education. The educational order that promotes uncritical transfer and acceptance [rather than transformation] of information as knowledge, and the perpetuation of the existing social order, power structure, and value-systems. *Cf.* CRITICAL PEDAGOGY.

restricted code. A model of speech and L1 use marked by such features as FORMAL(2) simplicity, directness,

frequent use of commands and a rare use of idiomatic or symbolic expressions. Contrasted with ELABORATED CODE/FORMAL CODE, restricted/public code is supposedly the language (MT) used at home by disadvantaged social groups(in Britain). The generalisations about the two kinds of 'code' made by Bernstein (1971) are highly controversial and have been rejected, though they raised the question of the relationship between home background and the attainment of rich linguistic repertoire (in L1).

restricted language. *See* PIDGIN.

restricted vocabulary. In SL pedagogy, a minimal, controlled, vocabulary for a particular purpose, or level of achievement. Such vocabularies have been used for writing teaching materials and SIMPLIFIED TEXTS, though the principle may also be extended to TEACHER TALK and other areas of language use.

restructuring. 1. The process of learners building on, and revising their INTERLANGUAGE. It is hypothesised that learners keep revising their interim grammar rules at successive stages of their development. **2.** A STRATEGY in communication. When a learner is not able to express an idea/message adequately well esp. in a SL, she may try to paraphrase or restructure it to get over the linguistic problem. Restructuring is common in the process of writing or composing. *Cf.* PROCESS WRITING.

retroactive inhibition. *See* PROACTIVE INHIBITION.

retrospective reports. Learners'/teachers' REFLECTION on a learning/teaching event that has taken place.

These are usually written responses to questions focusing on such aspects of the event as difficulties encountered and attempts made to resolve them. Reports may be elicited/written 1) to make one reflect on an event; and 2) to collect feedback for improvement, or to evaluate the effectiveness of a programme or a unit of it.

reverse dictionary. A word finder: a dictionary that helps the user to find the word for the idea in the mind. In it, the user proceeds from the idea she has in her mind to the elusive word (connected with the idea) she is looking for – reverse of what one does when consulting a regular DICTIONARY. A reverse dictionary is similar to a THESAURUS.

reverse interpretation. An exercise in the BILINGUAL METHOD of SLT. In it the learner responds in her MT to a stimulus given her by the teacher in the TL. C.J. Dodson (1967:118) recommends the use of the exercise as, according to him, it reaps double benefit: FLUENCY and ACCURACY in the MT as also improvement of proficiency in the TL. *Cf.* DOUBLE TRANSLATION.

rhetoric. (The art of) persuasive speech or writing, or their study. Courses in rhetoric aim at training learners how to communicate – write and/or speak – with correctness and effect.

rhyme. Sameness of sound between words: words occurring at the end of two or more lines in the stanza(s) of a poem. The nursery rhyme 'Jack and Jill' contains many examples. Young learners enjoy reciting nursery rhymes. Through this they acquire ac-

centual patterns, and develop a sense of rhythm.

Contrived rhymes are used by elder learners as mnemonic devices, and are widely used in teaching and learning. An example of a verb rhyme:

I wrote a letter – the letter was written
To tell the doctor my hand had been bitten.
"Go and lie down," the doctor said.
So all the day I lay on my bed.
The black dog bit it! All day I've lain
On my bed. I won't play with that dog again.

rhythm. The patterned occurrence of strong and weak elements, of ACCENT(1)ed and unaccented SYLLABLES at regular intervals in the flow of sound or speech.

risk-taking. A STRATEGY in SL learning and communication that impels the learner to make a guess, try out a HYPOTHESIS(2), improvise communication without being unduly afraid of making a grammatical error or being made fun of. Risk-taking is considered to be one of the personality factors of good language learners. Timid learners would rather avoid venturing risk. [*See also* AVOIDANCE STRATEGY and REDUCTION STRATEGIES.] Risk-taking is ACHIEVEMENT BEHAVIOUR and facilitates automatization. *See also* CLOSURE-ORIENTED STYLE OF LEARNING.

role play. 1. A language learning/teaching TECHNIQUE. In it, the learners are given a situation and a task. The situation may, for example, be a visit to the airport to meet a friend returning from a holiday abroad. The task may be to greet the friend on his arrival, and carry on appropriate conversation. Role play is basically a SIMULA(TION)ted activity and is usually performed in pairs. By thus using, or attempting to use, meaning-focused and context-appropriate language, learners are expected to develop their communicative ability.

Role play has been criticised for being a form of rote learning – acting out somebody else's script. However, there should be plenty of scope for role players to be creative. In any case, the initial phase, though it may be close to rote learning, is only preparatory to a more free use of language later. Once the learner has acquired the support-

ing linguistic structures, she could use them creatively to express herself.

Role play need not always be scripted. Learners with some fluency can handle unscripted role play, and in the process improvise. **2.** A task in communicative language testing to judge oral proficiency. The candidate(s) is/are assigned a specific role to be performed/simulated.

rote learning. *See* MEMORISATION.

routine. *See* FORMULAIC SPEECH, AND PRACTICE. Classrooms mechanically following the LOCK-STEP procedure or the IRF CYCLE may become routine.

S

saccade. A short, usually involuntary, rapid motion forward of the eyes when reading. During this process, the skilled reader's eyes move, rapidly and successively, from one CHUNK to the next, in a jump-stop-jump-stop kind of rhythm. Each such movement is a saccade. Between each movement the reader's eyes fixate at one point on the page for a very, very brief moment (0.25 sec. or so) during which the mind perceives (or, is supposed to perceive) meaning. *See also* READING SKILLS.

sandwich story method. A bilingual way of teaching SL vocabulary. In it, learners read stories in the MT embedded with TL vocabulary items. It is claimed, **Example**, by Yuhua (2002), that sandwich stories make learning easy. The 'method' is 'based on the assumption that the unknown can be understood only on the basis of what you already know…'. Several considerations operate in choosing the stories and sandwiching them. Some of these are: interest, the learner's chronological and mental age, their proficiency in the TL, and the rate at which the TL items are introduced. *See also* MIXED-CODE READING METHOD.

Sapir-Whorf hypothesis. The proposition made by the American linguist & anthropologist E. Sapir, and furthered by his pupil B.L.Whorf, that the native language affects the way one sees the world. '…we dissect nature along lines laid down by our native languages.' Whorf (1956). The hypothesis has,

however, been disputed.

scaffolded instruction. INSTRUCTION that supports learners' emerging abilities/skills, and seeks to bridge the gap between their current competence and the competence needed to perform a somewhat difficult learning-task. In such instruction, the instructor so devises the learning tasks that they help the learners' developing abilities to mature. This kind of help acts as scaffold, or supporting framework. The help is extended in such forms as teacher-learner dialogue, which embed in them potential learning stimuli. *See also* ZONE OF PROXIMAL DEVELOPMENT.

scanning. Skill in reading that requires the reader to pass quickly through a text in order to locate the specific piece(s) of information she is looking for. Anxious candidates eager to find their name in a long list scan through it. Scanning and SKIMMING are techniques in FAST READING.

schema/schemata(pl.). Knowledge structures: mental frameworks. These structures, abstract and elaborate, serve as guides for interpreting new information. Our experience and knowledge of the world, it is hypothesised, invest our memories with frames of reference in the light of which our minds access new information. **Example**, when we read a description of a wedding ceremony, our minds [tend to] comprehend the description and its language in the light of the marriage-ceremony-related knowledge-structures/schemata present in our minds. Unavailability of appropriate schema (relating to unfamiliar context) causes in-/mis-comprehension. *See also* SCHEMA THEORY.

schema theory. The HYPOTHESIS that human beings organise experience and knowledge-structures/concepts in the form of SCHEMATA, and access new experiences in their light. Further, the schemata undergo modification and expansion as new experiences accrue. Applied to reading, the THEORY claims that a reader tackles the meaning of a text according to her past experience, background knowledge or the existing schemata – according to what she knows of the world, the text, the GENRE it belongs to, and the language system. Thus a text itself does not carry complete meaning: it is constructed by the reader. The schemata that get activated when reading, are of two kinds: content and rhetorical – what a text contains and how what it contains is structured. What applies to reading is generally applicable to listening too.

Scherer-wertheimer study. *See* the COLORADO PROJECT

scholastic aptitude test (SAT). A most widely used test for admission to colleges in USA. A verbal aptitude test is an important part of it. *See also* APTITUDE TESTS, and VERBAL TESTS.

scientific writing. FORMAL(1) writing which includes the writing of reports of studies and experiments in science. Followed in it are certain principles of writing and specific conventions of PRESENTATION (2,3). *See also* TECHNICAL WRITING.

screening test. A test designed to short-list the better-suited persons for jobs and admission to educational and other programmes, and to exclude the less deserving ones.

script.1. The system of writing the alphabet of a language, **Example**, the Roman script. More than one language may use the same script (with minor modifications). **2.** SCHEMATA: the sequence of events and actions related to a particular setting, **Example**, checking in at the airport. In such a schema, familiar expressions like security check assume meanings and procedures perplexing to someone not acquainted with the relevant script.

second language. A language though not native to its users, has some official status in the country, and is used in education and other sectors. An example is that of English in India.

The term is used in two contexts: in the context of language learning, where a major distinction is made between the first acquired language, the MT, and the other learnt language(s). In the discussion of language education, 'L2' is used to imply this contrast. Sometimes the expression 'third language' is used, **Example**, in the context of India's THREE LANGUAGE FORMULA, for the language coming third in the sequence.

The term SL also contrasts with FL. [*See* FOREIGN LANGUAGE.] The use of the latter language, as of Russian in India, is confined to the classroom and some offices.

English has no term to denote a combined SL-cum-FL status or an intermediate one. In this book , the term SL has been used mostly to denote both.

second language acquisition. The process (or, the result) of learning a SL. A SL can be acquired in a formal, taught context as in a school, or it can be acquired informally/naturalistically.

The two are complementary, and there may be opportunities for NATURALISTIC LEARNING within formal teaching/learning settings. Different theories have been put forward of how a SL is learnt/acquired. For some of these, *See also* ACCULTURATION MODEL, BEHAVIOURIST LEARNING THEORY, MENTALIST THEORIES, and MONITOR MODEL.

second language classroom interaction. *See also* CLASSROOM INTERACTION.

selected-response items. Test items that require the test-taker to identify/select the correct answer from among a set of choices given. Such items contrast with CONSTRUCTED-RESPONSE ITEMS, and ESSAY TESTS.

selection. The pedagogical principle of restricting linguistic ITEMs, followed generally in SL education. The principle has been widely applied to the selection of lexical items and sentence patterns/structures. The MATERIALS FOR LANGUAGE TEACHING are often written within the selected lists. The rationale for selecting/restricting is that given the limited time for teaching and learning, and specific learner needs/objectives, it is neither possible nor necessary to include everything for teaching. Another factor is to make the learning of a FL/SL less difficult.

The principle of negative selection relates to the non-inclusion of an item. However, the priority value of an item in specific pedagogical contexts may override other consideration. *See also* CONTROL (2), GRADATION, VOCABULARY SELECTION, and WORD LIST.

selective attention hypothesis. The hypothesis that focusing learners' attention explicitly on features of grammar and structure helps their acquisition of language. *See* Consciousness-raising, and Noticing.

selective listening. Careful listening. According to Billows (1961), it consists of (i.) selecting and listening to the significant in the speech addressed to one; (ii.) not paying attention to noises and unnecessary segments of the speech; and (iii.) monitoring one's response before interrupting the speaker.

self-access materials. *See* SELF-INSTRUCTIONAL MATERIALS.

self-actualization. One of the needs in A.H. Maslow's hierarchical framework of human needs. According to him, human beings turn to their higher needs after they have achieved their basic needs of food, shelter, etc. The highest of these is self-actualization. With the fulfilment of this need, one's full personal potential is actualised. At this level of development, one enjoys independence, autonomy, and 'a general transcendence of the environment.' Need for self-actualizasion acts as a master motive for adults to go on learning.

self-assessment. (S-A). The METACOGNITIVE process of someone, usually a learner, evaluating her own achievement to self-monitor her progress. It may also be done at the beginning of a new course to judge one's readiness to undertake it. Such evaluations are different from tutor evaluation.

The process usually follows a course or sub-course of [self-]learning, and is DIAGNOSTIC in nature, as through it one can diagnose one's weaknesses and seek remedies. S-A is usually done with the help of QUESTIONNAIRES , and is widely used in OPEN LEARNING and on SELF-INSTRUCTIONal programmes. Though mostly used by learners, S-A can also be done by teachers and others. *See also* ASSESSMENT.

self-development. *See* SELF-ACTUALIZATION.

self-direction in learning. Taking control of one's own learning: not being dependent on guidance from outside. A self-directed learner has the confidence and competence to identify and set up goals for her learning. She knows the ways of achieving them, of MONITORING and evaluating her progress in learning. *See also* SELF-MONITORING.

self-esteem. The high or low image one has of oneself. Self-esteem is related to one's appraisal of one's ability to achieve. Low self-esteem, a discouraging factor, is related to poor achievement in language learning. It is a negative trait that not only makes one [teacher or learner] feel inferior but also act inferior. Positive self-image gives one confidence and encouragement.

self-evaluation. *See* SELF-ASSESSMENT.

self-image. One's view of oneself and one's capabilities, esp. relating to the ability to learn. *See also* SELF-ESTEEM.

self-instruction. *See* SELF-(MANAGED) LEARNING.

self-instruction materials. Specially written lessons/LEARNING MATERIALS for self-learning. (*See* Learning materials for self-managed learning.) The materials need not always be in printed form. They could also be audio- or video-recorded to be used in combination with print materials or independently. Along with the contents to be learnt, the lessons contain directions for the learners giving them advice and guidance on how best to use the material. A lesson may comprise one Unit or more than one. Each unit is a structured entity. It usually begins with a statement of the AIMS (of the unit), followed by an INTRODUCTION and LEAD IN. There may be an activity to help the learner develop suitable cognitive frames to facilitate access to the lesson-content. The unit usually has sub-sections, each with an activity, a discussion point, questions, and practice tasks, esp. the last mentioned in the case of lessons dealing with language skills. The lesson content is supported and enriched with graphics and illustrations. S-I materials are the main body of support DE institutions extend their learners. *See also* LEARNER SUPPORT.

self-(managed) learning or self-instruction. Learning in which the learner takes charge of her learning. Such learners may use SELF-INSTRUCTION MATERIALS, epecially when enrolled as distance learners. Self-learners are usually adults with a high degree of motivation and goal orientation. Learners' confidence in their capacity to learn and their positive self-image help them to achieve their goals.

self-monitoring. SELF-OBSERVATION and evaluation. New thinking about teachers' professional growth expects them to take charge of their own development through self-monitoring and critical REFLECTION(2) on their professional behaviour. There are many ways in which teachers can self-monitor. They can keep a diary to write in what they felt about their teaching. Such a record, objectively analysed, and in retrospect, may indicate the strengths & weaknesses in their performance, and also directions for future modifications and improvements. Triangulation of feedback from other sources such as from students and independent observers may put the monitored performance in perspective. *See also* DIARY-KEEPING, DIARY STUDIES, and SELF-OBSERVATION.

self-observation. A form of SELF-MONITORING by teachers. For this, usually a self-observation CHECKLIST is used. This facilitate the teacher's [critical] observation of their own performance and helps them self-rate its various aspects. Self-observation is claimed to make teachers feel affectively secure as it develops in them a feeling of self-responsibility. It is also considered to be a better procedure than evaluation by others such as the PEERS or by supervisors during training,. Further, it is asserted that self-observation leads to reflectiveness, and PROBLEM-SOLVING – a kind of ACTION RESEARCH. *See also* REFLECTION (2).

self-rating. *See* SELF-ASSESSMENT.

semantic approaches to language teaching. Approaches in which the emphasis is on teaching & learning how to communicate meanings rather than on producing grammatically correct forms (phrases, sentences, etc.). Accordingly, the meanings (notions & functions) are the organising principles of the SYLLABUS-content rather than grammatical units or sentence structures, though in effect the two may not be very different. *See also*

NOTIONAL-FUNCTIONAL SYLLABUSES, and GRAMMATICAL SYLLABUSES.

semanticising. The process of noticing and understanding meaning. H. Palmer (1921) has used the term to mean associating chunks of sounds or syllables[or, structure] with their meanings. Semanticising constitutes memorizing by which Palmer meant acquiring language. *See also* CATENIZING, and MEMORISING.

semantic knowledge/semantic memory. Knowledge *not* unique or personal to an individual but shared in common with others. Knowledge of the world in general is semantic knowledge. Narrowed to language knowledge, semantic knowledge would be meanings of words, idioms, proverbs, and so on in a language commonly shared by most speakers of that language and those others who know it. Much language teaching consists of imparting semantic knowledge or of enabling learners to acquire it.

Language testing usually targets this kind of knowledge. Semantic knowledge is context-free. It is contrasted with EPISODIC KNOWLEDGE, which is context-sensitive.

semantic map. *See* CONCEPT MAP.

semantics. A discipline concerned with the study of MEANING and meaning relationships.

semi-direct tests. Tape-mediated tests of ORAL PROFICIENCY/LISTENING-comprehension. In them, pre-recorded instructions, questions, and texts relating to them are administered to the test-takers and their responses recorded for RATING.

semilingualism. The phenomenon

or the state of a person knowing two or more languages but not being so proficient in any as to use it as one uses one's MT. Semilingualism results from a person being placed or operating in two (sometimes more than two) linguistic environments such as at work and at home, or from moving between countries a great deal during one's early years. A consequence of this is the attainment of limited proficiency in the languages. Semilingualism could also be a consequence of learners developing negative ATTITUDES towards both their own CULTURE and that of the other language or languages.

seminar. A theme-based paper-reading and discussion session [or a series of them] in a small group, in which the participants present written papers/ make oral presentations related to the theme.

seminar strategies. Skills and strategies that make one an effective participant in a SEMINAR or discussion. One of them is LISTENING. Some others are: prefacing and introducing a topic, directness, brevity, clarity, relevance, and absence of CIRCUMLOCUTION in making a point and in asking and answering questions; asking for repetition and clarification; expressing agreement & disagreement. These do not include skills required for writing seminar papers, and making presentations. *See also* ACADEMIC SKILLS.

semiology. The study of the system of communication that uses non-linguistic signs. Examples of such systems are road signs and semaphore. Coded messages are signalled by the signs in the system. 'Semiology' is now used synonymously with SEMIOTICS.

semiotics. The study of signs and symbols and their use in human communication. Semiotics treats language as a SYSTEM of signs like other systems.

semivowel. *See* VOWEL AND CONSONANT.

sense. The general meaning of a word, sentence or an utterance. Sense is an integrated complex of impressions aroused in our minds by a word. Following Paulhan, Vygotsky (1962) distinguishes sense from meaning. He says, 'a word acquires its sense from the context in which it appears: in different contexts it changes its sense.' Meaning remains stable throughout the changes of sense.

In the context of literary interpretation, I.A. Richards (1929) defines sense as the paraphrasable meaning of a poem. The other components of meaning according to him are feeling, tone and intention.

sense-group. A sequence of words that are grammatically closely related and form part of a running text. In speech, and in giving DICTATIONS, the words are generally said together, and there is a brief pause between two sense-groups. *See also* CHUNK, and SACCADE.

Teacher's **sense of plausibility.** 'A teacher's subjective understanding of what learning is like and what kind of teaching can best promote it.' N.S. Prabhu (1995). This sense, a product of the teacher's REFLECTION, is a dynamic and developing understanding nurtured by her insightful perception of learners' learning and by her own professional growth. This recognition of the teacher's understanding is an assertion of the importance of the teachers' own experience, knowledge and belief, and a rejection of externally formulated solutions and methods.

sentence. The largest grammatical UNIT(1) of a language. It may consist of one word or phrase or more than one; one clause or more. The occurrence of the units in a sentence, meaningfully related, is controlled by the rules of grammar. The oral production of a sentence is controlled by the rules of PHONOLOGY, and the written by those of orthography. *See also* SYNTAX.

sentence completion task/test. A measure to test LINGUISTIC ability. The task consists of supplying appropriate words in appropriate grammatical form to complete a sentence. Completing a sentence bound in a longer DISCOURSE(1) is considered to be a pedagogically better procedure than completing sentences torn out of context.

sentence method. An approach to the teaching of reading in the MT. In this approach, learners begin reading whole sentences rather than single letters or words. In the beginning the sentences to be read are simple and short – as short as even two-word sentences. Learners' familiarity with the spoken form supports their reading.. With such beginnings, learners gradually move to larger texts in reading which they are aided by the context, illustrations, and familiarity with the subject matter. Early reading of extended texts is supposed to promote in the learner-reader fluency and speed.

The method is closer to the word or WHOLE WORD method [than to the ALPHA-

BETIC METHOD] because they are meaning-oriented. The names of the various approaches to the teaching & learning of reading give the impression of their being exclusives. In actual classroom practice, teachers have often used a mix.

sentence structure. Meaningful arrangement of words forming a SENTENCE. The arrangement follows rules of SYNTAX. STRUCTURES represent grammatical PATTERNS. The structure *John plays tennis* represents the *SVO* [*subject+verb+object*] pattern.

sequence of development. *See* DEVELOPMENTAL SEQUENCE and ORDER OF DEVELOPMENT.

sequencing. Arranging ITEMS in a particular order according to pre-specified criteria. An example of it is the alphabetical ordering of entries as in a dictionary.

Sequencing or grading is a specific procedure in the STRUCTURAL APPROACHES to SL pedagogy. The items selected [for teaching] are put in groups, and those within a group are then sequenced. (Mackey, 1965). *See also* GRADATION, GROUPING, and STAGING.

setting. The environment in which something exists. The environment could be spatial, social, historical, cultural. Often the expression 'context' is used to mean setting. One could refer to the classroom setting, or in a wider frame, talk of curricular/pedagogical setting.

severity of errors. *See* ERROR GRAVITY.

sexism. Prejudice and discrimination based on sex. Sexism in language system refers to the use of grammatical and lexical choices in a language that connote prejudice [about women]. Users of many languages, including English, it is said, discriminate between sexes by selecting options that carry their BIAS(1)ed attitudes. **Example**, In the sentence *a manager should ensure that his men in the factory... .* , the choice of the pronoun his for 'manager' expresses partiality to men as it suggests that only men can hold the [superior] position of a manager. As English does not have an epicene pronoun in singular number, it has developed alternative usages to avoid gender-marked references. *See also* GENDER AND LANGUAGE, and GENDER BIAS.

sheltered instruction/programmes. Language instruction programmes meant for special groups [in USA]. These may be groups of learners who are physically or otherwise challenged. The programmes are designed to provide compensatory assistance. Sometimes programmes for non-native learners in a native speaking country are called, unjustifiably though, 'sheltered.' The learners are taken aside to be taught separately.

shipboard language teaching. Instructional programme for migrating adults to impart them a rudimentary knowledge of the language and culture of the country of destination. Such programme was used in 1950s for the benefit of non-English-speaking Europeans migrating to Australia. They were taught English on board the ship. The mass-teaching methodology used was memorisation and choral drill-based.

short-term memory. *See* MEMORY.

sight method. *See* WHOLE-WORD METHOD.

sight vocabulary. Large-lettered words in elementary books for beginning learners: words that children can read quickly on sight. The words have relevant pictures juxtaposed. The principle is the same as that of the WHOLE-WORD APPROACH. Instead of saying B A T = BAT, learners begin learning the words directly. *See also* PHONICS. *Cf.* ALPHABETIC METHOD.

signification and value. The literal meaning of a word, word group, or sentence in isolation, and its meaning in context/use. The contrast, drawn by H. Widdowson (1978), points to the importance of students learning to look for the ' value' aspect of the meaning.

sign language. A language based on gestural communication using manual-visual signs. Used by the deaf, it has an elaborate grammatical system of communicating meaning with hands held in different positions and combinations. Like natural languages, different sign languages have their own system of using signs in place of speech sounds.

silent period. The period of listening and assimilation preceding the learners' readiness to produce speech. Some learners have been observed to take rather a long period before they are ready to begin speaking.

silent way. A method of F/S L teaching. The basic principles of the method involve use of learner-centric approaches that facilitate learners' application of their cognitive-creative faculties in learning. The method contrasts with the teacher-centred practices in which it is the teacher who speaks most of the time and the learners are passive.

The method devised by Caleb Gattegno in 1970s, is called the Silent Way because the teacher in the class does not speak much. Nor does she repeat at all. This makes learners pay full attention to what the teacher says and associate its meaning with the accompanying action performed by the teacher in the classroom. The typical action the teacher performs is to use coloured wooden sticks as pointers to point at words and pictures in different colours in a chart. The method is mainly used for elementary level teaching.

simplification. 1. (The process of) making a text suitable for learners [usually SL learners] to read and understand by applying the principle of CONTROL(2). This is done by writers of instructional-materials by rewriting or adapting a text to make it less complex/difficult. The difficulty may relate to the language and the allusions used in the text, the ideas it deals with, or the way it is organised. Thus simplification involves working on the vocabulary, the sentence structure, the discourse structure, and the subject matter by using the devices of addition, omission, and replacement/rewriting. *See also* SIMPLIFIED TEXT.

M.L. Tickoo (1993) distinguishes between LINGUISTIC simplification and PEDAGOGIC simplification: the former makes the language less complex, and the latter 'smoothens' the process of teaching. The pragmatics of classroom teaching and the theoretical perspec-

tives on simplification, however, may differ. An instance of the latter is H.G. Widdowson's (1978) view that simplification may not necessarily facilitate communication, and the simplified version may 'lose the communicative facility and character of the original.' Also, a simplified text becomes a different discourse. **2.** The teaching strategy of modifying teacher speech. It has been noticed that teachers in SL classrooms use a simplified variety of the TL. It includes additionally modifications in the features of speech – slightly exaggerated accentuation and intonation, slower delivery of speech, and repetition. **3.** A feature of the language of elementary-level learners. The language they produce in the beginning is marked by structural and semantic simplification. *See also* REDUCTION. **4.** An essential characteristic feature of PIDGINS/restricted languages. **5.** A deliberate process in creating 'artificial' languages to make them simple. *See also* ARTIFICIAL LANGUAGE, and BASIC ENGLISH.

simplified text. A text, for LL, with its content, length, vocabulary, and sentence structures deliberately controlled with the intention to match it to the learners' cognitive and proficiency levels. Such attempts are based on the assumption that the 'difficultness' of a text is the function mainly of the words and structures in it, that the simpler the words used in it, and the shorter the sentences are, the easier it would be to read the text. *See also* ADAPTATION (1).

simulation. Mimicking real life situations. In language teaching, simulations are used as techniques, in which learners act someone else, as in a drama. Simulation tasks involve learners in ROLE PLAY. Simulating persons are assigned problems such as negotiating a deal with a prospective buyer. Their performance is later analysed. For example the 'negotiation' in the above-mentioned 'problem' may be analysed for how natural-looking the simulating persons and their performance were during the simulation, and how accurate, appropriate and effective their language use was in terms of persuasiveness, salesmanship, and so on.

Ken Jones (1982) distinguishes simulation from role play. According to him, in simulation there is 'reality of function, not pretence.' It is 'an act in which the participants really function their roles as judge or lawyer... .' *See also* ROLE PLAY (1), specially the point of role play as rote learning, and Pretence in language teaching.

simultaneous bilingualism. BILINGUALISM in which two languages have been learnt as L1 simultaneously.

situation. 1. A complex of circumstances – events, objects, persons and patterns of relationships among them, and location – at a given point of time. In more general terms 'at the airport,' 'in the restaurant,' etc. are examples of situations – situations, among other things, of language use. They may be used as contexts for pedagogical utilisation. **2.** In classrooms, teachers often create situations to demonstrate the meaning and/or the use of a particular item of learning. For **example**, to demonstrate the use of the present continuous tense, the teacher may draw the learners' attention and ask them to watch him walking to the window and then opening it. When doing so, she may audibly utter, 'I'm walking to the window.' 'Now I'm opening the window.'

SIMULATION and DRAMA TECHNIQUES for language learning create make-believe situations for providing near-authentic context

situational decision-making. An approach in the teachers' handling of ever-new exigencies arising in the everyday classroom. In this approach the teacher does not depend on, or look for guidance from labelled methods or what researchers say. Rather, depending on her own resources, insights, and judgement and keeping the CONTEXTUAL FACTORS in mind, she takes a decision on the spur of the moment in the best interest of the learners and learning. Such decision-making is an integral part of REFLECTIVE practice.

situational method. A method of SL teaching based on a SITUATIONAL SYLLABUS. *See also* SITUATIONAL TEACHING and ORAL-SITUATIONAL APPROACHES

situational syllabuses. SYLLABUSES organised around various situations of language use – **Example**, at the airport, in a hairdresser's saloon – situations the learner is likely to be in: situations where the learner may need to use the TL. The rationale given for such syllabuses is that language is used in social situations, and the choice of language [to be] used depends on the context of its use. It is axiomatic that language is not used as isolated and context-independent grammatical forms. *Cf.* CONTEXTUAL SYLLABUS

situational teaching. Introducing/teaching language items (words, structures), or presenting meaning with the help of a SITUATION (2). The situation provides a natural-like context in which the target item would typically fit. Situational teaching, which often accompanied the STRUCTURAL APPROACH, uses meaningful [i.e., coherently linked] dialogues built round pre-selected and graded items. Situational teaching imitates MT learning. Billows (1961) recommends, 'All actual teaching of new language material must be done in relation to the situation of the classroom and the familiar home surroundings'.

When an appropriate situation is not readily available in the classroom, it may be created. The situation created/ acted by the teacher is a kind of dramatisation, which helps contextualise/illustrate the target item/meaning, and makes it easy for the learners to understand . In Situational teaching, appropriateness of the utterance to the situation takes precedence over mere correctness of form.

Situational teaching is both useful and feasible in elementary classes. In higher classes, where the learners have a greater cognitive maturity and richer SCHEMATA, situationalisation becomes, laborious, time-consuming, and therefore unnecessary.

Situational teaching may also be teaching language according to a SITUATIONAL SYLLABUS.

skill. Ability to do something well, **Example**, to speak or write: ability acquired through meaningful practice, i.e. mind-applied-practice.

The term skill is variously used in LT contexts. Generally it refers to the

four modes language is used in: listening, speaking, reading, and writing [LSRW]. Each of these comprises a number of micro- or sub-skills.

Sometimes, specially in the context of PRACTICE(1)-based models of teaching SLs, a distinction is drawn between 'knowledge' and 'skill', the former being METALINGUISTIC in nature, and the latter referring to the practical ability in using the language.

skills-based teaching. LT aimed primarily at developing the learners' skills in using the language for communication. Skills-based LT contrasts with pedagogical practices preoccupied with the explication of the subject-content of the prescribed textual material, in which the main role of the students is to listen. *Cf.* CONTENT-BASED LANGUAGE INSTRUCTION.

skill-learning model. A theory of LL which, while recognising the important role of COGNITION in the ACQUISITION OF LANGUAGE, does not reject the role of PRACTICE(1) in honing language skills.

skills of reading. *See* READING SKILLS.

skimming. A skill in FAST READING. Its use involves judiciously paying attention to relevant parts of a text in order to form a general idea of what it contains. In the light of the impression thus formed, the reader may decide whether she wishes to read the text more closely, or not read it at all. In skim-reading what the reader will pay attention to or ignore will depend on factors like the reader's purpose, interest, and the available time. Skimming is a different process from SCANNING, in which we look through a text for specific information.

Skinner box. An apparatus designed by the American psychologist BF Skinner for conducting experiments. It mainly consists of a device meant for the experimental subject to manipulate. It is like a bar, or lever. Its manipulation by the subject sets in motion the delivery of REINFORCEMENT (food, etc.). *See also* OPERANT CONDITIONING and THORNDIKE PUZZLE BOX.

slang. Highly informal language (words, phrases, usages) avoided in formal/standard speech and writing. **Example**, *moke* is a British English slang for a donkey.

social class. A division of a SOCIETY. The members of a class generally belong to one major socio-economic stratum. They are also characterised by identity, ATTITUDES, and system of VALUES distinct to themselves, and different from those held by the members of the other class(es). Among other things, education and social class correlate with each other.

social communication approaches to language teaching and testing. Approaches that teach a SL for communication in social contexts, and design language tests that test the related abilities. To a large extent, these are similar to the communicative approaches in general. It is to be noted that SL teaching and testing may address language-learning and language-use-needs not related to social communication. For **example**, the social communication approach emphasises oral communication competence, which may not be of much importance in SLT for developing competence in reading.

social constructivism. The cognitive view that knowledge is created through interaction with others, which may take place in family, neighbourhood, with peers, in the classrooms, and the outside world.

Interaction in the social context, it is claimed, promotes successful employment of cognitive processes. *See also* CONSTRUCTIVISM.

social distance. An abstract concept relating to the learners' ATTITUDE to the target language COMMUNITY and CULTURE, and the TL group's attitude towards the learners' community and culture. The greater the degree of congruity and compatibility between the two, the narrower the "distance," and greater the ease in ACCULTURATION and in acquiring the TL. The concept derives from Schumann (1978).

social learning theory. Theory that says we learn from observing other people, the social world. In this process are involved both the external reinforcement and the internal cognitive interpretation. The theory in a way bridges the behaviourist and the cognitivist theories. Learning is the result of 'a continuous reciprocal interaction of personal and environmental determinants'. (Bandura, 1977).

social strategies. Learning STRATEGIES that prompt learners to interact with others in order to learn. Asking a PEER to help with the meaning of a difficult word is an instance of social strategy. *See also* LEARNING STRATEGIES.

society. A group of persons, usually very large, distinct by its CULTURE and institutions which it shares in common. The members of the group have a sense of unity and belonging, and usually inhabit one geographical area.

sociolinguistic competence. Knowledge and application of socio-cultural rules in language use. It has to do with contextual appropriateness. Whereas people [naturally] acquire these in their MT through socialization processes, SL learners need to learn them to be communicatively competent in the TL. The need is highlighted in view of most SL teaching concentrating on imparting LINGUISTIC COMPETENCE.

sociolinguistics/the **sociology of language**. 'The study of society in relation to language' – the field that studies language choice in relation to SOCIETY and its structure. Some of the areas it deals with are how in multilingual societies certain languages acquire a more important position than others, how languages adapt to social needs and pressures, how they are maintained or given up, how they suffer loss and die. The sociology of language is not concerned with analysis or study of the linguistic structure of languages.

sociopragmatic. Relating to the APPROPRIATENESS of (second) language use to the social context. For example, it would generally be considered a sociopragmatic mistake to use an imperative in a context where a polite/request form is expected. Such infelicities in L2 may result from LANGUAGE TRANSFER(1) or a literal translation. It is axiomatic that sociopragmatic norms vary from society to SOCIETY.

sound discrimination test. Test to judge whether a learner/test-taker can aurally distinguish between PHONEMES. The test is often used for PROGNOSTIC purposes. Good discrimination is considered to be a good predictor of success in LL. Prognostic tests are in line with the ACCURACY-dominated paradigms of SL learning.

source language (SL). (especially in CONTRASTIVE STUDIES) The learner(s)' MT.

spacing. Allowing time gap between two cycles of the teaching of an ITEM/SKILL in order to let the learning in the previous cycle get consolidated.

The concept relates to the PRACTICE and habit-REINFORCEMENT-based approaches to teaching. One of its slogans in such approaches was 'spaced, controlled, meaningful repetition' of the target learning item.

speaking. Producing orally language that is contextually meaningful, and intelligible. SPEECH, the product of speaking, is usually addressed to a listener or listeners – the audience.

speaking practice. Practice in oral skills. An important activity in much SL instruction is making learners practice the ability to speak the TL correctly. Much SL pedagogy emphasises ACCURACY – GRAMMATICAL and PHONOLOGICAL though in recent times equal importance is being accorded to the COMMUNICATION of meaning. Accuracy-based practice work is mostly MODEL(2)-controlled, and the meaning-based one spontaneous. Model-controlled activities include PATTERN DRILLS, and model dialogues, i.e., conversation appropriate to the given occasion. Besides formal accuracy, a number of other learning points such as socially appropriate utterances are modelled through them. Model dialogues suffer from the limitation of being 'closed' units and permit no scope for NEGOTIATION OF MEANING so characteristic of real life conversation.

special education. Education of persons with special needs, such as the handicapped and the aged. Children with emotional, social, physical or mental problems are known as special children, and education to them is imparted by teachers specially trained for the purpose. *See also* INCLUSIVE SCHOOLING; and SHELTERED INSTRUCTION.

specific practice. Language practice to specifically learn/master a particular item, skill or subject. The principle of specific practice implies that, for example, in order to improve one's skill in speaking one may have to practice specifically correct production of problem CONSONANT clusters. 'Specific practice' becomes marked in the context of the predominance of a generalised teaching of languages which mostly consists of the teaching of general rules of word usage, sentence-formation, and pronunciation.

speech. Coherent, meaningful language produced orally in communication. Speech is the product of SPEAKING, one the four major SKILLS of language.

speech accommodation. INTERLOCUTORS' variation or maintenance of their speech styles within the course of a conversation. Depending on her attitude to the addressee, the speaker may either bring her own speech style close to the speech style of the addressee or make it different. She may also choose not to bring in any change. The nature of accommodation gives a clue to the social-psychological attitudes of the speakers towards each other. *See also* STYLE SHIFTING.

speech act theory. A THEORY about the UTTERANCE-function, the speaker's meaning and intention, and the effect of the speech on the listener. Philosophers Austin (1962), and Searle (1969, 1976) have the credit of authoring the theory. It postulates types of acts: one of them the Indirect speech act, is an oblique/polite way of asking. An **example** is the utterance 'It's rather cold in here.' It may be an indirect way of asking the listener to shut the window, or to serve a hot drink, or, to switch the heater on.

Locutionary act is the utterance itself, what we say and its literal meaning. However, in saying something there is some purpose, **Example**, to remind, request or caution someone. The act of saying, according to Austin, is performing the Illocutionary act, and the intended meaning of the utterance its Illocutionary force. The result/impact of the utterance on the listener is termed perlocutionary effect.

The theory has been of considerable influence on language pedagogy in making the LINGUISTIC aspects of utterances as important as their functions and meanings.

speech and writing. Modes of expression using language. Speech is generally considered to be the primary mode, and writing its representation through graphic symbols. Almost every human learns to speak but not all can write[or, read]. Children begin using language with listening and speech, and writing follows, if at all. This led many theoreticians on language teaching to assert in SL teaching the primacy of speech over writing.

speed reading. *See* FAST READING.

speed test. A language test that imposes constraint of a maximum time allowed to the candidates to answer the questions. *Cf.* POWER TEST.

spelling. The way the letters of an ALPHABET are used to represent the spoken word. The degree of correspondence between sounds and letters varies from language to language.

spelling pronunciation. Pronouncing a word as it has been spelt. The lack of full correspondence between the SPELLING of a word and its prevailing pronunciation often leads learners to make mistakes both of spelling and of pronunciation.

spoken language. Language used in SPEECH. It is usually marked by features that contrast with those of the written language. For **example**, spontaneous spoken language is marked by such features as false starts, pauses, and gap-fillers. Spoken language is usually informal in tone [unless it is a prepared presentation for oral delivery]. It presupposes an INTERLOCUTOR. It is dynamic in the sense that it is shaped from moment to moment according to the interlocutor's/listener's response and feedback. In most speech-events the interlocutors share knowledge of the context, references to which are mutually unambiguous. The TENOR of the speech is governed by the mutual relationship between the interlocutors and the subject(s) they are talking about.

SQ 3R approach/method. A procedure of READING/study recommended as effective – effective in the sense of reading with a high degree of COMPREHENSION. The steps in the procedure are: survey the text to be read; raise in the mind questions on the subject dealt with; read attentively; recite the main points; and finally, review your reading. *See also* READING STRATEGIES.

staging. Division of the content of learning into stages, i.e., into ordered phases. As the teaching process in the institutional setting extends over sessions, semesters and years, the course of study is organised in such a way that it is introduced to the learners in stages. The ordering of stages follows principles of priority, SPACING, relative difficulty, relative importance.

Staging relates to the assumption that language learning is a linear process, that it can be neatly organised, managed and controlled, and that there is a symmetrical relationship between teaching and learning. The assumptions are questionable on theoretical grounds. Yet, staging facilitates 'organization' in the practical business of teaching. *See also* SEQUENCING.

standard. 1. A level of excellence. The LEVEL(1) may be used as NORM(2). Levels are set up or recognised in different fields, and these levels serve as bases of comparison. Standards may apply to teachers, students, quality in teaching, and to academic programmes including teacher-education programmes. In language education, a recognise degree/level, or attainment of proficiency considered adequate is used as the norm in measurement or a norm in making evaluative judgements. **2.** 'Standard' is also the label attached to a particular DIALECT or LANGUAGE VARIETY. *See also* STANDARD VARIETY, AND CANON.

standardised test. A language test that has been developed following the norms for it. The norms include those of RELIABILITY and VALIDITY. The TOEFL is an example of a standardised test.

standard variety. The VARIETY of a language used by its educated speakers, used in books and writing, and taught in schools. *See also* ACCENT (2); and DIALECT.

stereotype hypothesis. The hypothesis that children and adults tend to behave according to the stereotype they are categorised into (*See* Stereotyping.). M. Halliday (1978:23) citing Fredrick Williams 1970, who tested the hypothesis in the US, says that if the teacher believes that the pupils belong to a particular stereotype, **Example**, the 'deficient social dialect'-speaker- stereotype, she would 'predispose' them to linguistic failure.

The hypothesis has implications for teacher ATTITUDE, learner SELF-IMAGE and learner performance. *See also* DEFICIT HYPOTHESIS, and DIFFERENCE HYPOTHESIS.

stereotyping. Representing someone or something, often unfairly, in a fixed image. That is, showing them as possessing certain qualities, habits, manners etc. because they belong to a particular class, race, community, or sex. In textual materials the grandmother is almost always shown as kind but conservative, old-fashioned and feeble. Such stereotyping develops fixed notions in learner-readers. Edward Said (1978) has shown how the colonial representation of the East in the Western discourse is stereotypical, i.e. prejudiced, often deliberately.

stimulus-response theory. The BEHAVIOURIST LEARNING THEORY that seeks to explain learning in terms of the connection between the stimuli and the responses (S-R). Basically, the THEORY sees BEHAVIOUR a result of CONDITIONING. *See also* CLASSICAL CONDITIONING. In its POSITIVE focus on external behaviour (that can be observed) to the exclusion of the processes of the human psyche, the theory has serious flaws.

story method. A story-listening-based technique of WHOLE LANGUAGE teaching for young learners. Though the key activity is listening, the approach involves all the skills, and no discrete and overt linguistic points relating to grammar, usage, morphology, phonology and such other things are taken up for special treatment. This makes the approach HOLISTIC. The overall goal of the story-focused method is to lead the learners to FLUENCY.

The stories are carefully selected for their interest, textual quality and SCHEMATIC level. Familiar folk tales make a good choice in the beginning. Learners may also select and narrate their own stories.

Modes of the traditional art of storytelling may be used. Visual support to aid listening comprehension may be provided through blackboard work and/or printed illustrations when the story selected is from an illustrated book. Pre-recorded stories with individual [professionally trained] voices for different characters, and with songs and music create a better impact on learners and involve them in listening fully.

The 'method' has no set procedure. The following are some of the activities that may follow the teacher narration of the story: learners in pairs retelling it to their partners in their own words or in words they remember from their listening; learners performing particular roles either extempore or from scripts; and learners performing the story on stage.

There may be a warm-up activity in the beginning, repeat of the story-reading or narration; and post-listening activity. The last may have a covert reinforcement purpose. Reinforcement may include (further) reading and writing work. Follow-up writing-work extending from the technique appears to be a better procedure than story REPRODUCTION(1).

A major advantage of the technique is that when applied well it has in grip the learners, ever inquisitive to follow the storyline. They are fully involved in listening, and feel affectively relaxed – a condition conducive to language acquisition.

strategic competence. One of the components of communicative competence. Canale and Swain (1980) in their componential model of COMMU-NICATIVE COMPETENCE include strategic competence as the third component. According to Canale (1983), who places it as the fourth component in his framework, strategic competence is the ability to cope with, and to make up for any COMMU NICATION shortcomings caused by such factors as unintended faulty sentence-construction, imprecise choice of words, fatigue, and forget-fulness. Strategic competence involves mastery of VERBAL and non-verbal com-munication STRATEGIES to compensate for any breakdown in communication or to enhance its effectiveness.

In certain situations, it might include the ability to guess what the speaker/writer means to communicate over-looking slight linguistic or referential inaccuracies.

strategic reading. Reading a TEXT using flexibly and in conjunction with one another a wide variety of STRATE-GIES. These may vary from SCANNING, SKIMMING, close reading to CRITICAL READING, evaluating one's own pur-pose in reading, and questioning the author's hidden agenda(s), if any, in writing. Strategic reading is trainable, i.e., it can be taught and learners can benefit from the awareness-raising in-struction and practice. *See also* READING STRATEGIES.

strategies of communication. *See* COMMUNICATION STRATEGIES.

strategies of learning. *See* LEARNING STRATEGIES.

strategies of reading. *See* READING STRATEGIES.

strategy. A cognitive attempt to achieve something such as comprehen-sion. Originally a word used in military contexts, the term has come to signify non-competitive and non-combative devices/TECHNIQUES(2) employed by the users of a language. They may use strategy for different purposes – com-municating, learning, reading, teaching. Thus a strategy is an action, performed consciously or unconsciously, to deal with a problem. LEARNERS use them all the time. Pedagogical TECHNIQUES(1) are teaching strategies.

Apart from the language-education contexts, such expressions as 'strategy,' and 'strategy deployment' are used in more general learning contexts. An example is the expression HEURISTIC strategies.

streaming. Placing, for the purpose of language instruction, members of one class into different groups according to their level of proficiency. This means that learners with comparable prior knowledge of the language and ability in it are put together in one group, and learners with low proficiency are segregated from those possessing higher proficiency. The division is usually made on the basis of a proficiency test or on the basis of the marks obtained at the preceding public examination. Streaming is often proposed, and sometimes practised, as a solution to the problems of teaching a class of learners with greatly varying levels of ability. It has, however, been pointed out that streaming may cause psychological damage to the learners branded weak/poor. Maybe, mixed ability classes call for a more appropriate handling than crude streaming. *See also* ABILITY GROUPING.

street learning. Learning a SL through exposure to it in natural contexts, not through school or formal instruction. Street learning usually leads to limited proficiency and oral fluency related to immediate contexts of language use.[*See* in this context Restricted code.] It is to be noted here that NATURALISTIC (LANGUAGE) LEARNING of the MT is not street learning.

stress. A psychological state of panic (with its possible physical correlates such as thirst and sweating). It is caused when one faces an intimidating or challenging situation called 'stressor'. Teachers going to face, or facing, a difficult class, a LARGE CLASS, or an unfamiliar/foreign set of students, and teachers with unprepared lessons may develop the fear of underperformance, and run into bouts of stress. A similar feeling of panic may cause stress to a teacher teaching a difficult topic or facing students feared to be of a higher standard. Teachers giving PRACTICE TEACHING lessons in the presence of a supervisor and PEERS, typically suffer from stress.

Teacher stress has its parallel in LEARNER ANXIETY. Like anxiety being debilitating or facilitating, stress could be either positive or negative. Some positive stress acts as spur though a complete lack of stress, or a feeling of overconfidence may be a negative trait.

structural approaches. Primarily, AURAL-ORAL ways of teaching SLs, also known as SOS(Structural, Oral, Situational) approaches. In these, the learners(usually beginners), are initially given intensive oral practice in using TL sentence-patterns/structures introduced to them in a graded manner. Learning of vocabulary is secondary to the mastery of SENTENCE STRUCTURES. Skills of literacy – reading and writing – are taken up after foundation-level grammatical ability has been orally 'created' in the learner.

The relatively greater emphasis and time given to a particular item of structure for practice would draw justification from CONTRASTIVE ANALYSIS tenets.

The principles underlying the structuralist approach are derived from the perceptions of the pre-1940 linguists in USA. It was pioneered in 1940s by neo-Bloomfieldians, prominent among them being Charles Fries and Robert Lado. Later, the approach developed into a methodology labelled audio-lingual.

The British version of the aural-oral way that became known as Structural-situational approach was developed by Harold Palmer and A S Hornby, but it carried a Firthian influence, and included along with most of the principles mentioned above, the principle of 'contextualisation,' and SITUATIONAL TEACHING. *See* Context 3

In India, a massive 'reform' movement, The MADRAS ELT CAMPAIGN, was begun in 1955. It was influenced more by the British model and become popular with the name STRUCTURAL APPROACH. The Boards of Secondary Education in India designed their class IV–VI to class VIII syllabuses on 'structural' lines.

The main features of the structural approach as promoted and practised in India are: 1. The syllabus consists of carefully selected, graded, and sequenced items of structure; the sequencing operates across the three or four years' teaching (of English) at the post-primary level. 2. At convenient points, provision is made in the syllabus for 'reinforcing' the patterns already taught. [*See* Reinforcement.]. 3. The vocabulary to be introduced to the learners is controlled and graded.

4. The teaching of the items in the beginning is entirely oral, drill-based, and sentence-based. 5. Emphasis in the teaching is on the learners producing accurate form and pronunciation. The teacher models these for the learners to imitate and repeat. 6. The introduction of new items to the class follows techniques of PRESENTATION(1), of which the principle of CONTEXTUALISATION is an important component. 7. It is important to adhere to the sequence of the prescribed structures, and make the learners 'overlearn' them through contextualised repetition and drill. This stage of classroom work is called ESTABLISHMENT/CONSOLIDATION(2). 8. Reading and writing are introduced after the learners have achieved orally basic structural-grammatical competence. The textual materials for reading and writing are organised on structural principles. 9. Establishment of structures in the learners' mind should ensure that they do not go wrong in handling them: that the possibilities of error are ruled out. Also, learners should never be exposed to language errors. 10. The establishment-stage is followed by testing, which provides the teacher FEEDBACK on whether remediation is needed. REMEDIAL TEACHING, where needed, follows in the form of more PRACTICE, oral and written. 11. Use of the learners' MT and explications of the formal rules of grammar of the TL are to be avoided. 12. The entire process is teacher-controlled.

Despite the above pedagogical principles of the approach as conceived by curriculum planners during the 1950s and 1960s in India, actual classroom practices have varied from teacher to teacher. Many learners are introduced to all the four skills of language simultaneously.

structural drills. Exercises in sentence PATTERNS, intended to rid learners of errors in SYNTAX or to forestall them. A typical drill would consist of a CUE intended to ELICIT from learners response in which the target structure figures. Feedback is provided in case of flawed responses. PRACTICE(1) in the correct form follows. There could be variations on this routine. For example, the cue could be a sentence or a dialogue with the target structure highlighted in it as MODEL(1). A variety of forms could be the targets for elicitation. Form-focusedness of the drills during 1960s gradually accommodated meaning-focus with the coming in of new ideas on language acquisition.

structuralism. A set of theoretical approaches to analysing things such as art-forms, cultural practices, mind, language, and social institutions. It sees the subject of its study as a network of interrelated elements that constitute a system, and considers significant the pattern in which the elements are structured and organised. *See also* STRUCTURE (1). Structural linguistics is a method of analysing language structure, of segmenting and classifying utterances.

structural readers. *See* GRADED READERS.

structural-situational. *See* 'THE BRITISH VERSION' under STRUCTURAL APPROACHES.

structural syllabuses. Syllabuses, esp. for SLL, that specify the content of teaching in terms of discrete items of grammatical structure. These items of STRUCTURE are first short-listed for each term or semester's teaching, and then graded according to how easy or difficult would they be for the learners to learn (and teachers to present). Perception of DIFFICULTY is usually based on the surface complexity of the item. Thus, *this is a book* is a simpler structure than *this is the book that....* The items of structure so graded are arranged in a sequence for teaching. This hierarchic progression is maintained across the syllabuses for successive classes. The teacher is expected to 'introduce' each item in the class in the order they are prescribed, the assumption being that the learner would learn them in that sequence. A structural syllabus insists or insisted on the sequence being followed.

Introduction of the items of vocabulary and phrases, pre-selected according to the considerations of FREQUENCY, usefulness, etc. goes hand in hand with the introduction of items of structure. Structural syllabuses form the backbone of what is broadly categorised as AUDIO-LINGUAL APPROACHES. Such syllabuses are based on a concept of language and its learning which is pre-Chomskyan and pre-'communicative.' However, despite later insights into the nature of language and its learning, the underlying structure of much SLL syllabuses and materials continue to be structural or grammatical in nature.

structure. 1. Interrelated units so patterned and ordered as to form a whole, as words form a sentence. The constituent units of the configuration could also be structures in their own right. Thus, a SENTENCE has its structure; and within a sentence, groups and clauses have their own. Words have morphological structure. Structure also means the way the elements are networked/patterned. **2.** The word 'structure' is used in a variety of other contexts – brain structure, social structure, structure of a lesson, thought structure, administrative structure, and so on. In all these contexts, however, the core conceptual element is that of an intrinsic, systematic, organization. **3.** In Piaget's theory of cognitive development of the child, structures are the characteristic modes of thought as the child, in a dynamic interaction with the environment, passes from one stage of cognitive development to the next.

structure tables. *See* SUBSTITUTION DRILLS.

structure words. *See* FUNCTION WORDS.

student-teacher. Pupil teacher; a person undergoing training to become a teacher. A student teacher is a prospective teacher.

studial methods. The practice of learning a SL approached through formal study and conscious attention to rules and meaning, and through reading and writing exercise. The expression has been used by Harold Palmer (1921a) who contrasts it with the 'spontaneous' way of acquiring 'speech'. The studial 'method' or approach is one of deliberate effort and involves such practice as ANALYSING(1), SYNTHESISING and using METALANGUAGE.

Decades later, Stephen Krashen, among some others, drew the dichotomous and rather controversial distinction between acquisition and learning. Later a slightly modified distinction was drawn between INSTRUCTED and NATURALISTIC LEARNING. Interestingly, Palmer also pointed out that the 'spontaneous powers' and the 'studial powers' are 'complementary' to each other; 'both have their place in a well conceived programme of study'.

In his recognition of 'studial powers,' Palmer anticipates the present day acknowledgment of the role of AWARENESS RAISING, and of the cognitive in language learning.

study approaches. Learner motives for, and approaches to, study. Learners, esp. adult learners, have been noted to be impelled by one of the following major goals, which also determines the approach and the STRATEGIES they adopt to achieve them: 1. *Surface motive*: to pass the examination with good grades so that it becomes easy to secure a job, or admission to the next higher class. With such extrinsic MOTIVATION the approach to be adopted is most likely to be that of surface study, and the adoption of such strategies as MEMORIZATION, selective study, and concentration on expected exam-questions. 2. *Deep* or intrinsic motives: to achieve personal development. It leads the learner to look for personal meaning, satisfaction and fulfilment in study. Thus the study strategy adopted is to seek meaning in what is studied and relate it to one's own experience. Deep learning occurs when learners engage in the construction of knowledge for themselves. 3. The motive to achieve excellence drives one to adopt achieving strategy.

It involves persistent hard work and a highly systematic approach to study.

study centre. (Specially in DE) Place where learning materials, facilities and services are made available to DE learners. Learning facilities may include, among other allied things, a library, an AUDIO-VISUAL room, and study room(s). Learning services may include academic support in the form of periodic individual and group TU-TORIALS and personalised COUNSELLING service. Study centres link the learners with the supporting organisation (the Board/Institute/University, as the case may be).

study skills. The strategies deployed by learners in study. They are deployed by learners in order to keep pace with the demands of study and to make their learning effective, efficient, and economical in terms of time and effort. Essentially mental in nature, the STRATEGIES relate to gathering, storing, and retrieving knowledge/information independently. The skills do not come naturally and learners may need training in using them.

Used in a narrow sense, study skills may just mean reference skills – making an efficient use of dictionaries, encyclopaedia, atlases, thesauri and such other tools. In an extended sense they include those learning resources & techniques (used esp. in formal learning contexts) that support the development of ones listening, speaking, reading, and writing abilities. *See also* NOTE MAKING, AND NOTE TAKING.

style. The characteristic features of language -use by individuals, writers and speakers. The choice of vocabu-lary, sentence-construction, and use of figurative language are some of the features that mark style. Style is vari-ously labelled according to its features, **Example**, formal, conversational, liter-ary, pedantic. Style is so individual to a language user that it can be recognised like one's voice, but not defined com-prehensively enough for all contexts. **2.** Style is also used in relation to the ways of learning and of teaching. *See* LEARNING STYLE, and TEACHING STYLE.

styles of language teaching. *See* LANGUAGE TEACHING STYLES.

styles of learning. *See* LEARNING STYLE.

style shifting. Variation of speech style. The syntax, vocabulary, and pronunciation of speakers vary depend-ing on how careful they are about their speech. It may be casual in the com-pany of friends and careful in a formal context. The two styles are also known as vernacular and careful styles.

styles vs. strategies. Broad approach-es (to doing something) versus specific steps, actions or behaviours. A distinc-tion is generally made between styles and strategies of learning. Styles are general characteristics, predilections and propensities of individual learn-ers. STRATEGIES are specific techniques of dealing with problems in learning. *See also* LEARNING STRATEGIES.

stylistics. The study of the use of lan-guage in literary and other TEXTS. [*See* Style.] Use of language may include choices of the language forms and VARIETIES made in creating the text/ DISCOURSE and of its field, MODE, and TENOR. Linguistic stylistics is more concerned with the description of the choices and distribution of the LINGUIS-TIC forms in a text/discourse. Literary stylistics is closer to literary criticism in its concern with interpretation. *Cf.* TEXTUAL STUDY.

subjective. That which is internal to a person's mind, is not available for verification, and based on the person's view and judgement. *See also* OBJEC-TIVE1.

subject knowledge. Disciplinary knowledge: knowledge relating to a branch of learning gained through study. *See also* PEDAGOGICAL KNOWL-EDGE and TEACHER KNOWLEDGE.

submersion. The educational setting in which L2 learners of a language are students along with its native speakers. *See also* IMMERSION EDUCATION.

subordinate bilingualism. *See* CO-ORDINATE BILINGUALISM.

substitution drills. Language learn-ing exercises in which learners have to supply grammatically acceptable items to fit blank space(s) in a sentence. *See also* SUBSTITUTION FRAMES.

Typically the sentences are iso-lated ones, and not occurring in a DIS-COURSE(1). The drills are intended to consolidate the learning of a structural PATTERN that has been the focus of the teaching based on a structurally graded syllabus a slightly different form of substitution drills require learners to generate [correct] sentences from a table, instead of just supplying them. *See* SUBSTITUTION TABLES. Substitution drills have been a part of the practise of the STRUCTURAL APPROACHES to SL teaching. In keeping with their theoreti-cal underpinnings, they were intended to AUTOMATIZ(ATION)e through DRILL and

PRACTICE learner production of gram-matically correct patterns/sentences.

substitution frames. Sentences with one of their elements deleted. **Exam-ple**: *Ram ... books.* In this FRAME(1), a number of items (**Example**, reads, writes, likes) can suitably fill the blank space. Substitution frames are used in language teaching for making learners practise grammar and vocabulary. They are also used in language tests and examinations.

substitution tables (STs). Grids with columns offering choices of elements to be combined to form correct sen-tences. See the example below. Each column has one or more exponents of the elements of the structure of a sen-tence. The columns are arranged in the sequence in which the elements they contain should occur in the sentence – the target PATTERN for learners to practise and learn. By combining the elements picked from each column in the sequence they are arranged in the table, learners can generate a number of [grammatically] correct patterns/ sentences. The table below is intended to be used for giving learners practice in forming sentences in the Present Perfect Continuous tense. There

Subject	Auxiliary	Main verb	Adverb
I	have been	singing	all day.
He		playing	all night.
The boys	has been	working	

may be built-in constraints to be taken care of. In this table the constraint is that of concord.

The table can be made complex by

putting plain infinitives in the fourth column instead of the *–ing* form, and asking the learners to produce complete sentences changing the infinitive into the present perfect continuous tense form. They may also be asked to frame sentences from the table, supplying new verbs of their own.

STs are a product of the era that held the occurrence of language errors in learner output as learning-failures, and believed in practice and HABIT-FORMATION as the essentials of the process of learning. However, they are still useful as foundational support for primary level learners. They can also be used as remedial tools in LARGE CLASSES.

subtractive bilingualism. *See* ADDITIVE BILINGUALISM.

sub-vocalization. Moving lips and tongue and producing whisper when reading – considered to be a faulty habit.

suggestopedia. A dialogue- and music-therapy-based approach to LT. The approach was developed by the psychiatrist G. Lozanov in 1970s. The basic premise in it is that one learns fast when one is free from psychological hurdles. Hence, in this approach the classroom ambience and arrangement receive very careful attention – soft music playing, dim lighting, cushioned chairs arranged in a semi-circle, pictures and charts on the walls, and other things that go with these.

The key technique in the approach is to suggest to the learners that they can learn easily. Any fears they may have in their minds about their ability to learn, are removed. Thus Suggestopedia approaches learning through lower-

ing the learners' AFFECTIVE FILTER, and strengthening their self-confidence.

summarising/summarisation. Presenting in clear and COHEREN(CE)t language the main points of a TEXT (statement/narrative). [*See* Summary.] Keeping out the less important/ unnecessary details, and re-tailoring the essentials of a discourse demands both linguistic proficiency and semantic knowledge – the ability to see through the web of words and discern the link(s) between ideas.

Often needed outside pedagogic contexts, summarizing is a higher order skill practised by learners as study-aid and a learning STRATEGY/TASK. *Cf.* PRÉCIS-MAKING.

In LANGUAGE TESTING it may be used as a test of ACHIEVEMENT or of PROFICIENCY. When summarization is intended to test only COMPREHENSION in the TL, there may be a case for the summary to be produced in the learner's L1.

summary. A shortened version of a written or spoken text. It contains the main ideas of the original TEXT, presented systematically and coherently in IDIOMATIC prose. Summaries are brief statements, but there is no insistence on a fixed length for them, although in the context of an examination the question-task may specify the word limit.

Apart from written texts, audio-recorded/spoken texts are also used for learners/examinees to write summaries of. Summaries may also be presented orally.

Making summaries is an INTEGRATIVE language task that brings into play a range of abilities: reading-/listening-comprehension, judging main points, and putting them together in the form of a coherent composition. When orally presented, it additionally tests the ability to compose and present a summary orally either with the help of notes or independently. *See also* SUMMARY CLOZE, and SUMMARISING.

summary cloze. A form of CLOZE TEST which consists of supplying deleted words/phrases in a SUMMARY of a text the learner/test-taker has read or listened to. A variety of response-formats can be dovetailed: the learner may be asked to construct the response or select the correct one from the choices given.

In scoring summary close, generally a simple system of one mark for each acceptable response is followed. This, however, does not appear to be satisfactory as supplying responses vary in their difficulty and complexity.

summative evaluation. Evaluation carried out at the end of an educational or curricular programme to evaluate its success. Contrasted with FORMATIVE EVALUATION, summative EVALUATION is applied to projects to judge their outcome, response, cost and expenses, and long term benefits.

sunburn method. The method, or more appropriately the educational environment, that provides learners intensive and comprehensive exposure to the TL. This could be through residence and education in the TL community, or instruction in all subjects through the medium of the TL, or through providing an ACQUISITION-RICH ENVIRONMENT. *Cf.* IMMERSION EDUCATION.

superordinate. Holding a higher rank in a HIERARCHY. The term superordinate refers to such hierarchies as those of linguistic UNITS, meaning-relationships, and LANGUAGE VARIETIES/dialects. In sentences we may have a superordinate clause and subordinate clause(s). The word cutlery is a superordinate term for such items as knives, forks, and spoons. The STANDARD dialect of a language may be the superordinate one.

supervision. Guidance in teacher education. *See* MENTORING.

supplementary readers (SRs). Curricular reading materials for extensive reading to be used in addition to the MAIN COURSE-BOOK. SRs (also called RAPID READING materials) are books meant for developing FAST READING skills among learners, esp. of SLs,. The rationale given for supplementary reading is that (at least in the Indian context) quite often the only reading learners do is of school TEXTBOOKS. And they are subjected to intensive reading with the result that the learners do not develop in them general, authentic reading skills. Nor do they read for pleasure. [*See also* NON-DETAILED READING, and *Cf.* EXTENSIVE READING.]

M. West (1950), talking about SLT/ELT, says that SRs (simplified, abridged, and vocabulary-controlled texts) serve many purposes: they give learners extra practice in reading, and afford them occasion to review & fix the vocabulary they have already learnt. Through encountering the words in different/new contexts, learners discover the [greater] width of their meaning. And, finally, the learner's discovery of what she can do with what she has already learnt, boosts her confidence and encourages her to go on to other readable materials. Much, however, depends on the pedagogical treatment of the SRs, learner perceptions and initiatives, and general educational practices.

SRs are, in such cases as envisaged by West (*op. cit.*), simplified versions often of classics. Questions have been raised about the AUTHENTICITY of such texts as they do not truly represent the original. [*See also,* in this context, SIMPLIFIED TEXT, and SIMPLIFICATION (1)]

Champion (1937) was of the view that since the reading of the so-called SRs afforded learners the real experience of reading, it was rather misleading to call them supplementary.

Many SRs are constructed on the principles of GRADE READERS, and many carry in them comprehension questions for the guidance of the readers.

supply-type items. Test-items that require test-takers to supply the target answer. Fill-in-the-blanks type questions are of this type, also known as completion type.

supportive feedback. *See* F-MOVE.

suprasegmental. *See* PROSODY.

surface structure. *See* DEEP STRUCTURE.

surrender value. The value or utility that a pupil derives from an uncompleted course of instruction. A pupil who is not able to complete a course, **Example**, in English or arithmetic, has nevertheless learnt something that she can benefit from. 'Surrender value' is the benefit derived from that knowledge. Michael West (1926/1960) used the expression metaphorically drawing an analogy from Life Insurance policies that provide for the payment of some money 'to an insurer who decides to discontinue premiums of his policy'. Whereas in reading, West said, 'the learner gets a very high and very early Surrender Value', in speech 'he will soon forget what he has learnt'. 'With a [reading] vocabulary of as little as seven hundred and fifty words, he can go on learning by himself even if he leaves school by then.'

sustained-content language teaching (SCLT). An approach to LT. In it the primary focus is on the exploration of a single content area, **Example**, biology or international law. Although CONTENT learning and LL take place in tandem, SCLT (or SC-based LT) is closer to the former. In it, the learning centres on a single, content-related, text rather than an anthology of short pieces dealing with a variety of subjects. *See also,* CONTENT-BASED LANGUAGE INSTRUCTION.

syllable. A unit of speech that consists of at least a VOWEL (or, DIPTHONG) *SOUND*. The interjection 'oh,' pronounced 'o' is a syllable. Syllables usually have one or more consonant sounds in them.

syllabus. Specification of the content of learning and teaching [(sub-)skills, names of recommended texts, etc.] during a course of study, and what the evaluation of learner-achievement will be based on. A syllabus is usually a written statement, often indicating OBJECTIVES(3). It may also include such specifications as the division of the content of study in terms of the time (a week, a term, a semester), weight to be assigned in the exam to the components of the course, the nature of examining – oral, written, type of questions to be asked – and the examination plan.

Some hold the view that a language syllabus determined in advance of teaching is not only a constraint but also an imposition insensitive to the dynamics of classroom teaching – an open-ended process. *Cf.* CURRICULUM.

Writers on LT syllabuses have classified them according to what is planned prospectively to be taught and learnt, and retrospectively, what gets taught and learnt. Most documented syllabuses are of the former kind, syllabuses that specify in advance and thus become reference points for teachers, learners and examiners. They are also classified according to the nature of the content specified. *See also* GRAMMATICAL/STRUCTURAL SYLLABUSES, NOTIONAL-FUNCTIONAL SYLLABUSES, and SITUATIONAL SYLLABUSES, ANALYTIC SYLLABUSES.

syllabus design. Selecting instructional content and arranging it in the order in which its elements would be taken up for teaching. The job requires considerable expertise, and a theoretical framework. In language pedagogy, the design conforms to the designers' theory of what LANGUAGE is and how it is learnt, and how it should be taught. During the pre-1970 decades when language-learning was viewed mainly as the learning of STRUCTURES(1), syllabuses consisted of an inventory of selected & graded sentence-structure types/grammatical PATTERNS. [*See* Structural syllabuses.]

In 1970s when the focus shifted from form/usage-based teaching to communicative functions-based teaching, many syllabuses were (re)designed with FUNCTIONS and notions at their centre. [*See also* NOTIONAL-FUNCTIONAL SYLLABUSES.] With the conceptualisation of learning as primarily PROBLEM-SOLVING and DISCOVERY, TASK-BASED SYLLABUSES have come in vogue.

Some other models of syllabus design are content-topics-based, skills-based, and SITUATIONAL SYLLABUSES.

syllabus reform. Syllabus renewal. Though SYLLABUS-specification is only a first step in the process of LANGUAGE EDUCATION, improvement in it has often been sought through only changing/improving the syllabus-prescription, expecting change in teaching and examaminations to follow as corollaries. *See also* CURRICULUM DEVELOPMENT/RENEWAL.

syncopated approach. An approach to pedagogy in which variation is introduced by de-stressing such things as SYLLABUS, METHODS, and learner-groups that have traditionally received attention and by introducing new areas, TECHNIQUES, and goals consonant with the new contexts. The term syncopate is derived from the field of music where it means 'to modify a musical rhythm by shifting the accent to a weak beat of the bar.' Applied to LT, the approach calls attention to adopting a new set of priorities such as developing pedagogies suited to disadvantaged learners and their needs, combining with LL skills newer skills such as those related to information and communication technology.

synectics. A technique for generating ideas in a group and making its members think creatively in order to solve problems. Developed by William Gordon (1961), it has been applied to foster creativity among pupils through group exercises. One way of this is making metaphorical comparisons and analogies. For example, a task in Joyce and Weil (1986, p.160) to compare/analogise a poem to an automobile led to the following response 'it takes you on a trip, a word trip', 'and you have to have the road in your imagination.' Synectics can be used in higher-level language classes to develop FLUENCY, vocabulary, and imagination. *Cf.* BRAIN STORMING.

syntactic frames. *See* SUBSTITUTION FRAMES.

syntax. The rule-governed arrangement of words in a SENTENCE. Syntax is also the study of the rules/the branch of grammar and linguistics that studies the rules of how words and phrases combine to form sentences. It is axiomatic that the elements of a sentence are related to each other in a meaningful and rule-governed manner. The study of syntax i.e. of sentence structure, along with that of MORPHOLOGY, or word structure, has traditionally formed part of the study of grammar. A fuller study of grammar and LANGUAGE would include PHONOLOGY and SEMANTICS also.

synthesis. A combination of the various constituent UNITS that form a whole. Synthesising is the LL task of combining correctly the given words/ phrases/clauses to form a sentence, or of combining jumbled sentences to form a paragraph. In doing this, one needs to pay attention to the constrains of meaning and form – to the rules of word-formation, sentence-formation, and DISCOURSE organisation. These may entail deletion, or rephrasing of the units, or some addition to them.

A task like synthesising into one brief objective report the coverage of a sensational even by different newspapers could be a demanding one requiring higher order skills.

synthetic syllabuses. *See* ANALYTIC SYLLABUSES.

system. A network of interrelated and interacting units. The units may have their sub-systems, each functioning in a patterned manner in the larger system. The grammar of a language is a system of sub-systems. The verb-system of English has a sub-system of auxiliaries, within which modal auxiliaries form one sub-system different from the non-modal ones. It is characteristic of a system that it allows for choices, which may be finite or unlimited.

systemic grammar. A model of describing the GRAMMAR(1) of a language. In it the notion of SYSTEM is the central explanatory principle.

system revision. The expansion of the learner's [restricted] INTERLANGUAGE when further input is assimilated. The concept of system revision is very close to that of ACCOMMODATION (1) and ASSIMILATION (1) – -two complementary processes. Together, they aid the learning process of ADAPTATION.

systems approach. An approach to PROBLEM-SOLVING which takes into account all the aspects, the entire set-up, or the whole organization and not just a part of it in isolation.

T

taboo. In language, an expression that has offensive CONNOTATIONS, is considered vulgar, or refers to something unpleasant. Such expressions are avoided in polite conversation and formal writing.

tabula rasa. Latin phrase meaning 'blank tablet.' The expression has been used in the argument that human beings are born without any innate knowledge, *i.e.,* with a mind that is a blank tablet, and that all learning is acquired from the environment. *See also* LANGUAGE ACQUISITION DEVICE, and UNIVERSAL GRAMMAR.

tact. Social intelligence; the perception of the right thing to do or say in a particular situation. In language use, it is a factor related to APPROPRIATENESS, and COMMUNICATIVE COMPETENCE.

talk. Contextually relevant, purpose-oriented, information-carrying, spoken language addressed to an INTERLOCUTOR/ interlocutors or an audience. The important elements of the CONTEXT include the audience profile, and the occasion. As 'talk' may occur in a variety of social contexts, it belongs to different GENRES such as gossip, chat, TEACHER TALK, LECTURE. Each of these follows rules relating to LANGUAGE VARIETY/ REGISTER, CODE MIXING, audience role, participation rules, TURN-TAKING, and turn length (short turns/long ones), which the participants in the talk are expected to follow. Many of these rules are language-, CULTURE-, and context-specific. Native speakers generally acquire them socially though the rules of 'talk' in FORMAL(1) contexts may have to be learnt. For the learners of a SL beyond the elementary level, it may be a necessity to learn the rules of performing 'talk' in the TL.

tandem learning. *See* LANGUAGE EXCHANGE.

target language (TL). The language, Second or Foreign, that a learner is trying to learn. Use of this term often implies a contrast with the GRAMMAR, PHONOLOGY, and meaning system of the learner's MT, or the Source language. A TL is also the language into which one is TRANSLATING.

task. 1. Broadly, an assigned piece of work in LL, or work done voluntarily to practice language. In the context of new perceptions of the nature of (second)LL, tasks are now conceptualised as meaning-focused and structured learning-activities that involve using language as it is used in real life. Writing an application for a job, or composing a fax message is a task, but filling the blanks in a sentence is just an exercise done for language practice. A 'task' is communication-purpose-oriented. Performing tasks, it is held, activates the processes of (S)LA. LL tasks may be oral or written, or a combination of both. They are so designed that they cannot be done mechanically: there is an element of cognitive CHALLENGE in them. However, not all tasks need to be AUTHENTIC. LL is equally well promoted by PEDAGOGIC TASKS. They are a pedagogical necessity. *See also* ASSIGNMENTS, AND TASK-BASED-TEACHING. **2.** In LANGUAGE TESTING, a piece of work intended to test the test takers' knowledge or skill.

task-based language teaching. *See* TASK-BASED TEACHING.

task-based learning (TBL). A model of LEARNER-CENTERED curriculum for SLL which assigns a pivotal role to structured learning tasks. In it, learning is expected to take place collaboratively through INTERACTION, and PROBLEM-SOLVING. (*See also* COLLABORATIVE LEARNING.) TBL encourages learning through DISCOVERY, and puts a premium on the use of authentic texts, TL use, and encourages learners to express their views, feelings, experiences, and so on. *See also* TASK-BASED TEACHING.

task-based syllabus. A MODEL(1) of SL SYLLABUS-design organised around learning activities and TASKS. The activities/tasks to be included in the syllabus are selected on the basis of a NEEDS identification, which determines the real-world tasks the learners will be expected to perform in the jobs they are preparing for. The tasks so identified are categorised into task-types. In a course for hotel receptionists, for example, the various tasks related to dealing with arriving guests, face to face as well as telephonic enquiries, and room allotments may be categorised into one or more task-types. Further, these are arranged in a SYLLABUS very different from those that contain a list of items of grammar and structure. *See also* TASK-BASED TEACHING.

task-based teaching (TBT). A model of SL teaching built round a series of graded TASKS. It follows a TASK-BASED SYLLABUS. TBT tasks are designed to suit the age, proficiency level, and interest of the learners. AWARENESS-RAISING tasks and activities figure in it prominently.

TBT intends to keep to the minimum learner-dependence on teachers, although designing the task itself requires a lot of instructional resource. A contrast to the LOCK-STEP method, TBT marks a departure from the traditional teacher-centred, grammar-rule-based and vocabulary-based teaching.

taught mother language. The formal variety of one's MOTHER TONGUE treated and recommended as STANDARD(2). *Cf.* Language varieties, MT and Vernacular tongue. The hegemony of the 'taught mother tongue' over the other varieties has been viewed critically by some.

tautology. *See* REDUNDANCY (1).

teachability. 1. Feasibility and amenability of an ITEM to classroom teaching, usually of SLs. Teachability has been a criterion in the SELECTION of items for pedagogical purposes. In addition to its application to the selection of items of VOCABULARY and STRUCTURE, teachability is a criterion applied to the amenability of grammatical and phonetic forms. If the form is in the learners' ZONE OF PROXIMAL DEVELOPMENT, its learning can be mediated. Conversely, if a MT phoneme has got entrenched in the learners' INTERLANGUAGE phonology, the teachability of the correct TL sound may be difficult. **2.** Relevance. In contexts where the constraint of time, teaching-purpose, learning objectives and goal prevail, usefulness and relevance of an item may outweigh the considerations of feasibility and amenability.

teacher as facilitator. A concept of

teacher-role vis-à-vis learners in contrast to the traditional BANKING CONCEPT. The latter, though widely accepted, is dependence-breeding and suppressive of learner role and initiative in learning. Facilitating learner-learning and enabling them to learn is considered a better role than that of 'telling' and coercing. CONSTRUCTIVIST insights validate this reappraisal of teacher-role.

teacher as researcher. The teacher empowered to work out solutions to her teaching-related problems in the light of her own experience and research. Some of the procedures teachers may use for this are: critically evaluating their own teaching process; collecting data on their own classes and analysing them; exploring own thinking and beliefs; keeping a DIARY/JOURNAL, seeking feedback from learner-diaries; observing PEERS teaching; making CASE STUDIES – in short doing ACTION RESEARCH.

A teacher who becomes autonomous in this way is not controlled in matters of teaching by external factors such as prescriptions by experts on how to teach. The redefined role of teacher as researcher comes in the wake of several developments in recent times. Some of them are: rejection of top-down approaches, failure of the Method as solution to the problems of SL teaching, and the cognisance of the role of ACTION RESEARCH or 'insider research'.

It should not be assumed, however, that every teacher can do research. In order to take professional decisions the teacher has to have some experience, needs to know well such things as the CONTENTS of teaching, the learners &

their profile, principles of pedagogy, the instructional context and constraints. Above all, the teacher has to understand what action research is. See also Teacher empowerment.

teacher beliefs. Teachers' normative beliefs about such matters as learning and teaching, about their pupils, the language they teach, and their own competence. Held whether consciously or not, the belief-systems are conditioned by the teachers' knowledge, their AFFECTIVE FACTORS, experience of the world, experience of teaching, views on education, political persuasion, and social and cultural influences. Being of psychological and sociological significance, the belief-systems influence teachers' attitude and approach, and may be reflected in their classroom practices. An understanding of TEACHER KNOWLEDGE and belief-structures is of value in research on the teacher and on teaching, and can help plan better the content of TEACHER EDUCATION. *See also* LEARNER BELIEFS.

teacher development (TD). The process of preparing teachers to take responsibility for their own DEVELOPMENT, i.e., their professional-personal growth. TD also implies the state of a teacher having achieved such competence and level of maturity. Such a stage comes after the teacher has acquired performing-skills and knowledge-base, and is able to adopt an investigative and REFLECTIVE approach to teaching. *See also* PROFESSIONAL DEVELOPMENT OF TEACHERS, and TEACHER AS RESEARCHER.

teacher education (TE). The process of preparing those who intend to take up a teaching career and become knowledgeable and efficient teachers. It involves giving such theoretical knowledge of concepts as relate to principles of education, its purpose, process of learning, and the art of teaching. An important part of the process is supervised PRACTICE TEACHING [of which PEER TEACHING(1) may be part] , done with the purpose of heightening awareness of what teaching is and what its practical problems are. Many TE courses also impart [content-] knowledge of the subject one is preparing to teach.

A distinction is made between pre-service, i.e. initial TRAINING, and in-service EDUCATION programmes. The latter are organised for practising teachers with the primary purpose of updating them and ensuring their continued DEVELOPMENT.

Going beyond the concept of TRAINING as a once for all exercise, the term education is a reminder that education is a process that develops the subjects' minds, enables them to think critically, to solve problems, and, when needed, to apply these abilities to pedagogical issues.

teacher educator. A person who imparts or helps in imparting professional education to teachers, or to those preparing to become teachers. Some of the designations used for teacher educators are: teacher trainers, (course-) tutors, developers, MENTORS, supervisors, though each of these has a slightly varying meaning-accent. *See also* TEACHER EDUCATION.

teacher effectiveness. Teacher competence to achieve successful teaching in terms of its goals. Though difficult to define 'successful teaching,' one may posit factors that contribute to it.

These include the teacher's:
• academic and professional training,
• knowledge of the subject/content,
• understanding of the dynamics of the classroom, i.e., of the processes of learning and teaching,
• homework preparatory to teaching,
• positive attitude towards the learners, the subject matter, and the profession.

teacher empowerment. Equipping teachers with decision-making ability and power. The TRAINING concept of preparing teachers implicitly expects them to perform the role of technicians. They are not prepared/'educated' – and therefore not expected – to take professional decisions and exercise 'power' in curricular matters, although the very context of teaching provides teachers opportunities, and therefore expects them to take decisions and use the 'power' that belongs to them.

teacher-initiated curriculum. CURRICULUM emerging from the classroom practice, experience, and the REFLECTION of teachers. Such curricula are considered to be better aligned to LEARNER-CENTRED pedagogy. The fluidity and open-endedness of such curricula, it is claimed, allow for teacher-initiative, innovation, and creativity in the classroom. The concept is a response to the closed nature, the rigidity, and the insensitivity (to learner preferences, characteristics, needs, etc.) of the imposed curricula.

teacher knowledge. What teachers know about their teaching and about what they teach. In other words, their SUBJECT KNOWLEDGE and professional or PEDAGOGICAL KNOWLEDGE of which the teachers' PERSONAL-PRACTICAL KNOWL-

EDGE is part. Significant also are the teachers' own beliefs and experience and their knowledge of self. Self knowledge consists of one's objective awareness and evaluation of oneself – of one's educational IDEOLOGY, purpose of teaching, what one likes doing, what one can do well, and what one cannot do so well. *See also* TEACHER BELIEFS.

teacher preparation. *See* TEACHER EDUCATION, AND TRAINING.

teacher questions. Questions teachers put to learners in the process of classroom teaching. They are of different types. D. Barnes has analysed questions teachers ask into the following categories:

1. *Factual* ('What?' questions)
   (i) naming
   (ii) information
2. *Reasoning*('How' and 'Why' questions) DISPLAY QUESTIONS, etc.
   (i) 'closed' reasoning - recalled sequences
   (ii) 'closed' reasoning - not recalled
   (iii) 'open' reasoning
   (iv) observation
3. *'Open' questions not calling for reasoning*
4. *Social*
   (i) control ('Won't you...?' questions)
   (ii) appeal ('Aren't we...?' questions)
   (iii) other

See also CLOSED QUESTIONS, and REFERENTIAL QUESTIONS. For further discussion, *See* QUESTION TECHNIQUES.

teacher reflection. *See also* REFLECTION (2), and REFLECTIVE PRACTITIONER.

teacher research. Teacher initiated action to find solutions to the problems they face in teaching. *See also* ACTION RESEARCH, and TEACHER AS RESEARCHER

teacher self-observation. *See* SELF-OBSERVATION.

teacher talk. The language used by teachers in the classroom. Esp. in the context of SL teaching, TT is an important source of input for learners, and has a key-role in generating INTERACTION. Being the medium of pedagogic-discourse, TT is marked by certain features. **Example,** SL teachers are known for adjusting their language in order to make it comprehensible. *See also* CLASSROOM INTERACTION, AND DIDACTIC FUNCTIONS.

teacher training. *See* TEACHER EDUCATION, and TRAINING.

teaching. (with ref. to classroom LT). Basically, a process of helping and enabling learners to learn. For this the teacher in the classroom employs a repertoire of strategies too many to be mentioned here. Formal teaching is part of a curricular framework of which the course of study, the learners admitted to the course through formalised procedures, the classroom setting, the administrative set-up, and the evaluation system are important part. At the centre of all this is the CLASSROOM, the teaching arena, which has traditionally been teacher-controlled. This dominant MODEL(1) of teaching is very close to the concept of it as INSTRUCTION – the pedagogy of telling and directing, though new perceptions are bringing in change. Noteworthy in them is the view of teaching as a dynamic, learner-centred, process – a process of an on-going negotiation in which the learner's role is crucial, and learning occupies the centre stage. Accordingly, teaching, a product of TEACHER-KNOWLEDGE, is a negotiated series of professional decisions, all aimed at facilitating learning. Teaching is also effected through other modes than the classroom-centred one. **Example**, DISTANCE LEARNING.

teaching aids. *See* AUDIO-VISUAL AIDS.

teaching-induced errors. *See* INDUCED ERRORS.

teaching language to the disadvantaged. 1. Addressing the needs of those SL learners who come from (remote) rural areas or from the socially and/or economically disadvantaged sections of the society – from ACQUISITION-POOR ENVIRONMENTS. In MT learning, there may be some disadvantage in the form of difficulty in mastering the STANDARD VARIETY. *See also* DEPRIVATION, COMPENSATORY EDUCATION, and *cf.* INCLUSIVE SCHOOLING. **2.** SPECIAL EDUCATION for learners with cognitive deficiencies or learning handicaps. *See* LANGUAGE DISABILITIES, and SPECIAL EDUCATION.

teaching materials. *See* MATERIALS FOR TEACHING LANGUAGE.

teaching practice. *See* PRACTICE-TEACHING.

teaching style(s). Any set of coherent principles and procedures of TEACHING. As there are no labelled 'styles,' the meaning of the expression depends on the context of its use. In the context of SL teaching, 'style' may refer to a particular METHOD of teaching such as the DIRECT or the AUDIOLINGUAL Or else, it may refer to an APPROACH, which un-

der a unified guiding principle such as COMMUNICATIVE, may include practices from different method. **Example**, using grammar-translation activities communicatively is more a matter of using a teaching style than a Method. Very broadly, the choice of a DEDUCTIVE or an INDUCTIVE approach in teaching could also be a matter of style.

Classroom instruction employs a variety of formats: TUTORIALS, LECTURES, discussions, group discussions, lecture-discussions, DEMONSTRATIONS, BRAINSTORMING, ROLE PLAY, GROUP WORK. These formats also distinguish styles of teaching. With the demise of the 'Method' concept in SL teaching, it seems appropriate to call a set of classroom procedures 'style.' [*See* POSTMETHOD CONSTRUCTS.] Styles could be ranged on a teacher-centred/LEARNER-CENTRED continuum.

A particular style, specially in the case of adult learners, may be classified as didactic (teacher-centred), Socratic (enquiry-questioning-based), facilitative (learner- centred).

teaching to the test. *See* EXAMINATION-ORIENTED TEACHING.

team teaching. More than one teacher teaching together in the same classroom. In the context of SLT, particularly in LANGUAGE FOR SPECIFIC PURPOSES-teaching, the subject teacher and the language teacher may team-teach collaboratively and simultaneously. In this format, the learning and teaching of the special subject (**Example**, engineering, medicine) does not remain isolated from the learning and teaching of the SL. This helps the language teacher grasp the conceptual structures embedding the subject, and the subject teacher to understand how language is used to represent those structures.

In some contexts, as in FL classes in Japanese schools, team teaching may consist of teaching by the homeroom teacher and a foreign teacher (the Assistant Language teacher) working together. The presence of the homeroom teacher makes available MT assistance, if needed.

In TE contexts, when apprentice teachers/teacher internees observe the team working together, team teaching becomes teaching-cum-demonstration.

technical writing. Writing specifically related to the jobs of engineers, technical personnel, and executives. Though the basic principles of writing are the same as for good writing in any other area, TW has to follow GENRE-specific conventions of formatting, organisation and structuring. The vocabulary has a high incidence of terms belonging to the particular REGISTER. In that context, the terms are used with precise reference. Some of the [writing] jobs in TW are writing proposals, reports, specially project reports, feasibility reports, minutes, instructions and manuals. *See also* 'SCIENTIFIC' WRITING.

technique. 1. The means/devices used for pedagogical purposes such as to explain. The device could be one of demonstrating, **Example**, for explaining how to produce the sound/w/. Making students practice this is also using a technique. 'Technique' covers a wide range from blackboard work to dealing with special learners.

A narrower concept than that of METHOD, a technique is not necessarily method-specific. **2.** In general, technique is the skilful way in which one handles a task, **Example**, READING.

telegraphic speech or stage of language acquisition. The early stage when the child produces two word utterances or short utterances consisting of CONTENT WORDS and no grammatical/ functional markers or inflections.

tenor. The degree of formality/ informality carried by the language in a discourse, written or spoken. The tenor of a TEXT/DISCOURSE follows the relationship between the participants – speaker/writer and listener/reader: the relationship determines the tenor. The choice of linguistic items such as vocabulary, sentence forms, and sentence length contribute to the tenor. *Cf.* TONE.

tenor. (=**T**eaching **E**nglish[or a foreign or classical language] for **no o**bvious reason). The acronym 'TENOR' represents a compulsory teaching of a second language for some unspecified future need. As part of school-curriculum, learners are often made to learn languages without their knowing why though the motivating factors in prescribing the learning are considerations of inculcating value systems and developing desired attitudes, preserving heritage, giving comprehensive schooling, or preparing learners for their future education needs. Such teaching has often been a failure because in the absence of any 'obvious reason,' learners have felt highly demotivated.

terminal behaviour. EXIT BEHAVIOUR or what a typical/average learner has/ will have learnt and is/will be able to do at the end of a course of study.

The 'behaviour' is specified in terms of knowledge, skills, and abilities. There are MEASUREMENT procedures to assess/quantify the behaviour. The reference point is either the ENTRY BEHAVIOUR, or the desired terminal behaviour specified in advance. The information helps in evaluating the[degree of] success/suitability of the instructional programme and/or such other related things as the textbooks/materials used on the programme. The information is also of use in designing courses & curriculam.

TESOL. Teaching/teachers of English to speakers of other languages. *See also* ENGLISH LANGUAGE TEACHING.

test. A tool or procedure used for measuring the test-takers' abilities pertaining to some field of knowledge. *See also* LANGUAGE TESTS.

test analysis. Evaluation of test items and tests: procedure(s) to judge the extent to which they DISCRIMINATE, and are RELIABLE and VALID. The analysis is based on the data gathered from the trialling or administration of a TEST. The analysis may also indicate how easy a TEST ITEM or a test is for the target population. Statistical procedures are used in the analysis.

test anxiety. [*See* Anxiety]. AFFECTIVE REACTION to a TEST one is going to take. It could be caused by the test-taker's fear that the tasks/questions will be difficult and she may not be able to answer them correctly. Test anxiety affects performance at the test and may lead to results that reflect poorly the real competence of the test-taker.

Test examination. A test of LINGUISTIC COMPETENCE rather than of information-knowledge. M. West (1952) drew this distinction when emphasising the need for the examinations [in English] to test students' LANGUAGE SKILLS AND ABILITIES. Though the expression sounds quaint today, it points to the need in much SL teaching for prioritising proficiency-development.

testing. *See* LANGUAGE TESTING.

test item. An ITEM [independent or forming part of a larger test] the test-taker responds to by producing an answer as specified. Test items have different formats and are scored in different ways. *See also* CONSTRUCTED RESPONSE ITEM, DISCRETE POINT TESTING, FORCED CHOICE TEST ITEM, OBJECTIVE 2, and RATING.

Used in a general way, a test item is an examination-task that directs the test taker to do something on the basis of which judgement would be made of her ability.

test method. The way in which a test chooses to elicit from the test-takers responses that would reflect their knowledge of the language. Language testing offers a variety of techniques and devices for this ranging from INDIRECT TESTS TO DIRECT TESTS and from face-to-face to the machine-based.

test method effect. *See* METHOD EFFECT.

test purpose. The objective in measuring what a LANGUAGE TEST intends to measures. It could be to assess and evaluate: what a test taker knows at the time of taking the test (PROFICIENCY TESTS); what she has learnt over a period of instruction (ACHIEVEMENT TESTS); what deficiencies she has (DIAGNOSTIC TESTS), and what promise she holds for doing well on a new language course (APTITUDE, and PROGNOSTIC TESTS). The purpose determines the nature of a test and its content though a particular TEST ITEM may be suitable for more than one test-type. *See also* PLACEMENT TESTS.

test-taking strategies. Techniques used by test-takers to ensure that during the test/examination they work fast answering (correctly & well)as many questions as needed. Among other things, this may involve time-management, and advance practice in the form of rehearsals using dummy tests. *See also* TEST-WISENESS.

test type. For some major types, *see,* TEST PURPOSE.

test usefulness. The inclusive or overall quality of a LANGUAGE TEST that makes it comprehensively useful. Bachman and Palmer postulate the following as constituting together test usefulness: RELIABILITY, CONSTRUCT VALIDITY, AUTHENTICITY, impact, and PRACTICALITY.

test-wiseness. A test taker's prior familiarity with such things as the test, its structure, items, rubrics. The 'wiseness' also includes her experience and preparation in relation to the test. *See also* METHOD EFFECT.

text. A piece of authentic spoken or written/printed language. It can be of any length, short or long. Sometimes 'text' is used interchangeably with DISCOURSE(1). In recent literature on the subject, however, a distinction is drawn between the two terms: 'text' is treated as product, a linguistic entity, and 'discourse' a dynamic process by which meaning is realised.

It may be noted that many authors restrict the meaning of text to the written discourse.

text-attack strategies. STRATEG(Y)ies employed by readers in comprehending a[written]TEXT. They include previewing the text, locating the TOPIC SENTENCE or the main idea in each PARAGRAPH, taking a quick glance at the key words and the linking words in it, and the first and last sentences of the paragraphs. In the case of a book, reading the blurb, the contents page, the lists of illustrations, figures, and appendices prepares the reader better to approach the text. *See also* READING STRATEGIES.

textbook (TB). The main course-book(s) prescribed in the syllabus. The exam questions (or a major section of them) are based on it. Most language-learners and many teachers have traditionally identified the content to be learnt/taught with what the TB contains, and to an extent textbooks do pre-determine the course of teaching. This underscores the role and the responsibility of the TB(in the language curriculum). M. West (1960) called attention to this [in the context of ESL] when he said, 'A textbook is the teacher's tool.' Even with bad textbooks resourceful teachers can achieve good results.

A well-planned and executed TB, no doubt, carries many advantages for the average learner. It is a convenient, systematic, compact, economical one-volume package ready for use. However, some educationists view with concern the privileging of the TB to the exclusion of wider reading and other sources of knowledge. They find unhealthy the over-dependence of teachers and learners on the TB (howsoever good in itself) as the sole source of knowledge. A TB is no predictor of the quality of teaching. Ultimately, it is what teachers and learners make of it that matters. *See also* TEXTUALISM.

text grammar. The 'grammar' of UTTERANCES longer than a sentence. Traditionally GRAMMAR has been the study of SYNTAX and MORPHOLOGY, which generally do not go beyond the level of sentence. Text or DISCOURSE(1) grammar, however, studies relationships between sentences in larger units of speech and writing. The relationship can be of such nature as of restriction, AMPLIFICATION, and modification.

text type. Genre. TEXTS of one type or GENRE usually have similar content and structure.

textual competence. The ability to produce TEXT, written or spoken. A competently produced text is COHEREN(CE)tly organised following such principles as that of UNITY and CONSISTENCY (1), and it presents information and content systematically. The competence also include the (critical) ability to analyse and interpret text.

textualism. The system that upholds the POWER and authority of the CANONical literary texts [in the lang.-litt. curriculum]. This means, among other things, privileging the written word as the sole source of knowledge to the exclusion of other GENRES and sources. It further means suppressing texts that carry VOICES (2a) of the marginalised groups.

Underlying textualism is the belief that the canonical literary texts carry benevolent moral values and cultural content. In line with this, much formal education [in India, for example] has been written material- and textbook-based, and any reading beyond it is not much encouraged. Further, exams have been textbook-centred.

Thinkers critical of textualism question the processes by which texts are constructed, interpreted (treating meaning as determinate) and allowed to be read which creates 'textual authority', and justifies dominant positions.

textual study. Linguistic analysis of a TEXT [for LT purposes]. Textual study, deriving from the practice in France of *explication de texte,* is a forerunner of linguistic STYLISTICS, which became popular in 1950s and 1960s. Though the French tradition puts a text to a comprehensive, in depth treatment, some language teachers elsewhere have used the analytical technique as instruments for imparting/acquiring linguistic and METALINGUISTIC KNOWLEDGE.

theories of language learning. *See* LANGUAGE LEARNING THEORIES.

theories of learning. *See* LEARNING THEORIES.

thesaurus. A reference source that lists word groups but does not give their meanings. The words are listed as groups of alternative expressions having semantic relationship of close to distant synonymy. *Cf.* DICTIONARY, and REVERSE DICTIONARY.

theory. An abstract set of claims relating to some phenomenon, **Example,** language, language learning. An **example** of a theory is Schumann's 'ACCULTURATION HYPOTHESIS,' which is a theory of SL acquisition.

thinking. The process of mental activities related with ideas, CONCEPT-formation, MEMORY, PROBLEM-SOLVING, and a host of other intellectual engagements. The word covers a very wide field and is difficult to define comprehensively and precisely. The word 'cerebration' is an apt synonym for the process of thinking but it does not take one far if one wishes to know what exactly the process involves. The following are some entries (in this volume) related to 'thinking': Convergent thinking, Critical thinking, Divergent thinking, Lateral thinking.

thinksheet. A kind of WORKSHEET based on assigned reading of a key text/article/paper dealing with a particular topic with pointed questions designed to make learners/trainees reflect on the issue and think out solutions. Thinksheets may be collaboratively worked through by two or more learners usually adults at advanced levels of study.

The sheets may have pre-reading questions to prepare the ground for THINKING. They may form the base for further oral and/or written work.

Thorndike-Lorge list. *See also* LORGE-THORNDIKE LIST.

Thorndike puzzle box. A laboratory apparatus designed to study learning. The apparatus was designed by E.L. Thorndike in 1930s for the study of operant behaviour. It consists of a box in which an animal is trapped. It has to perform certain operations to be rewarded with food when the performance is successful. *See also* SKINNER BOX, AND OPERANT CONDITIONING.

thought. *See* THINKING.

three language formula. A policy for the teaching of languages in a multilingual country. It accommodates in a patterned way the OFFICIAL LANGUAGE(s) of a country, its regional languages, and the other MTs.

The formula was adopted in India during 1960s as the official policy for the teaching of languages in schools following the recommendation made by the Education Commission-1964–66. *See also* LANGUAGE PLANNING, and LANGUAGE POLICY.

three Ps of SLT. PRESENTATION, PRACTICE, and Production. They form the traditional framework of SL classroom INSTRUCTION. The Audiolingual and STRUCTURAL APPROACHES generally follow this framework. The would-be teachers in training are generally recommended this framework. Penny Ur sees them as the three major parts of the 'teaching process', albeit using 'Tests' in place of 'Production'.

threshold. The minimum quantity or LEVEL that would be sufficient for some purpose. In LE-related-parlance, 'threshold' is an extension of the meaning of a doorway, a point of entry. *See also* THRESHOLD LEVEL SPECIFICATIONS.

threshold level specifications. Details of the content and learning-objectives for adult SLL. The specifications are intended to ensure adequate COMPETENCE in the language for social communication, exchange of information, and expressing opinion on everyday matters. 'in a relatively straightforward way and to conduct the necessary business of everyday living when abroad with a reasonable degree of independence.' [Preface to *Threshold*, CUP, 1998.] It has been found that this takes two years. *See also* UNIT-CREDIT SYSTEM, and WAYSTAGE.

Thurston-type scales. Instrument for measuring ATTITUDES [named after the American psychometrician, LL Thurstone]. It consists of a number of statements reflecting particular attitudes with reference to some topic, **Example**, 'the teaching of grammar'. An example of a 'statement' is "there should be no explicit teaching of formal grammar in elementary classes". The subject indicates her response by choosing one of the stimuli ranging, for example, from 'most strongly disagree' to 'agree totally'. The stimuli are separated by equal steps. For this reason the technique is also known as the 'method of equal-appearing intervals.' *See also* ATTITUDE SCALE.

time-on-task. The length of (instructional) time devoted to a learning job/ undertaking. The HYPOTHESIS that the gain in learning something (**Example**, a language) is in proportion to the time spent on it has not been found sustainable. *See also* OVERLEARNING.

tolerance level. The acceptable limit: the extent to which something can be tolerated. If the limit is exceeded, negative consequences may follow. Learner writing [in a SL] may have language errors within the tolerance limit [of the reader] or exceed it. When exceeded, incomprehension follows. Even when comprehensible, the speech of foreigners or dialect speakers may sound jarring because of the unacceptable deviations in it. *Cf.* TOLERANCE OF AMBIGUITY.

tolerance of ambiguity. i. Learners' willingness to tolerate ideas that do not conform to their own belief systems and SCHEMA. This extends to their willingness to tolerate and accept the parametric properties of the TL. (*See* PRINCIPLES AND PARAMETERS.) A high degree of tolerance presages success in learning. **ii.** In Psychology: the degree to which people can be comfortable with ambiguity in a situation. Poor tolerance level is considered to be a negative trait. *Cf.* CLOSURE-ORIENTED, and FIELD (IN)DEPENDENCE.

Tomatis method. A method of auditory [aural and oral] training in FL education. It consists of stimulating and training the learners' ear muscles to help them with their listening problems. [An **example** of the problem is the/l/and/r/confusion the Japanese learners of English face.] Through raised confidence and accurate listening achieved through the method, the learners improve their oral skills The method is also claimed to help those learners who have disabilities and psychological problems.

The method is named after a French ENT specialist, Dr Alfred Tomatis (1920–2001), and is premised on his theory that every language has a different frequency span. The use of the method (aided with electronic devices such as headphones) enhances the learners' familiarity and sensitivity to the phonetic features – sounds, rhythm, etc. of the target FL. To achieve this, the devices have to exaggerate a little the unique [phonetic] features of the language.

tone. 1. In writing. The manner in which writers convey their ATTI-

TUDE(2) towards the subject they are writing on. Tone is conveyed through the style(1) of the writer – the way language is used: choice of words and sentences, for example. Some of the labels that characterise tone are ironic, enthusiastic, humorous. The criterion of tone is equally well applicable to SPEECH. There exists a thin distinction between tone and TENOR. Whereas 'tenor' relates to the speaker/writer attitude towards the audience, 'tone' relates to the speaker/writer attitude towards the subject of the DISCOURSE. **2.** Tone of voice, often described in such terms as warm, kind, discourteous. **3.** The phonetic feature of PITCH variation. *See* Intonation.

tone group. *See* INTONATION.

top-down. 1. A mode of information processing in which the focus is on the whole meanings rather than the component elements. In this approach, it is the reader's/listener's previously acquired knowledge and experience that play an important role in the understanding and construction of meaning. Top-down approaches hold the reader/listener above the TEXT. The meaning is not what the text contains: it is what the reader/listener constructs in the light of her knowledge structures. *See also* BOTTOM-UP 2, and Bottom-up processing.

Top-down and bottom-up approaches are also called 'conceptually driven' and 'data driven.' The terms are applied to the processing of information in READING and LISTENING. The 'top' here is the reader/listener's brain, and the 'bottom', the text/discourse. 'Top-down' and 'bottom-up' represent an either-or approach. An approach that

harmonises the two is an interactive approach where the processing person's brain [with its cognitive structures] processes meaning in interaction with the text/discourse. There is interaction in a slightly different sense also. The hypotheses made initially by the reader/listener in the light of their existing SCHEMATA may have to be modified in the course of further processing. Interactive approaches have emerged as favoured STRATEG(Y)ies in reading and listening. *See also* BOTTOM-UP PROCESSING. **2.** In a general sense, 'top-down' implies movement from above – for example, from the bosses to the subordinates. Top-down process is an authority- or power-driven process. Top-down models of teaching are teacher-dominated following a methodology in which the teacher causes[supposedly] and controls learning. Thus, Method-based approaches to language teaching are considered to be top-down.

'Bottom-up' are approaches to teaching in which the teachers' own initiative and understanding of what actually works determine the course of teaching, and what have precedence over teaching are the learner and learning.

topic. (In linguistics). The information shared by or assumed to be known to the INTERLOCUTORS and therefore selected to be talked about, expanded, or commented upon.

In the sentence *the students came very late,* 'the students' is the topic, and what follows is comment or new information not shared yet between the interlocutors. Topic and comment go together. In the example above, the topic also happens to be the grammatical subject in the sentence. Usually, though not always, the subject of the sentence is the topic. Generally speaking, subject-predicate, topic-comment, and theme-rheme refer to the same constituents of a sentence. *Cf.* TOPIC SENTENCE.

topic method. A 'method' of instruction, especially on TE programmes, in which pupil-teachers/learners collaborate to work on a major 'topic' or PROJECT to produce a comprehensive document arrived at by gathering relevant information, organising it systematically with illustrations and supporting details. Topic method, a kind of ACTIVITY METHOD, encourages and enhances learner participation in [self]learning and learning through doing.

topic sentence. The sentence that introduces a paragraph's main theme. The other sentences of the PARAGRAPH (typically in EXPOSITORY writing) usually expatiate on it. As different from a topic sentence is the topic idea – the immanent topic of descriptive and narrative paragraphs.

TPW. Think, Plan, and Write: a formula for writing. Think in advance who you are writing for, what its purpose is, and what you are going to say. Plan the 'beginning': the TOPIC SENTENCE, how you will amplify it – with the help of examples, by drawing a comparison, and so on, and how you will conclude. Write and then look at the written product again. You will need to revise it. More than one draft may have to be written before you have the final version. *See also* PROCESS WRITING.

total physical response (TPR). A method of teaching SLs developed during the 1960s by James Asher, a professor of psychology in USA. The main activity consists of learners listening to commands in the TL while they respond to them by physically performing the action. Simultaneously, the teacher also performs the action. Thus the skills emphasised in this method are those of listening, i.e., understanding the message/command. TPR draws its rationale from the observation that children, even before they are ready to speak their MT coherently, acquire the ability to listen [and comprehend] and in the beginning, much speech directed at them is in the form of commands.

In teaching according to the method, the commands are varied and gradually made more complex. Later, the learners issue their own commands. Underlying these activities is the acquisition of grammatical structures and vocabulary.

The listening in the beginning is followed by speech production, and speech production is followed by reading and writing.

Action provides fun and enjoyment, and keeps learners affectively relaxed – one of the key principle in HUMANISTIC APPROACHES. *See also* The Comprehension approach and Language through actions.

tower of babel. A confused mixture of languages, words, and noises. The Biblical story in the Book of Genesis narrates the building of a tower to reach heaven, frustrated by God by making its builders speak different languages. The resulting confusion and mutual incomprehension led to the failure of the venture.

The expression is used in the general sense of a medley of unintelligible and meaningless words, i.e., noises. This kind of chaos can result from people shouting and talking at cross purposes using different languages.

tracking. *See* ABILITY GROUPING.

training. (In the context of LE). The process of imparting novices the skills of teaching. In TEACHER EDUCATION, the notion of 'training' suggests practice-based learning to carry out set procedures, and is often distinguished from the more inclusive expressions 'education', and 'development.' Training is skills-specific, and aims at imparting fixed outlooks to deal with a limited range of problems, often predictable. It may not develop the ability to find out one's own solutions to new problems through analysis and REFLECTION. Teaching being a dynamic process, dealing with ever-active human learners and their minds, needs teachers who are prepared to tackle unforeseen problems and situations as and when they arise. Mere training may not develop this competence in the pupil-teacher. *See* also Teacher development.

trait. A particular ABILITY of an individual reflected in her language performance. The language PERFORMANCE of the individual is externalisation of implicit ability/abilities. In LANGUAGE TESTING, performance is elicited so that inference about the ability may be drawn for EVALUATION.

transcription. 1. A written representation of spoken words or linguistic units, usually in a phonetic script, in which each symbol represents precise values, i.e. the quality and quantity[length] of the language sound. [*See* The International phonetic alphabet (IPA)]. A transcription represents how words were actually spoken on some occasion, or how they are generally articulated, or how they should be articulated.

Transcriptions could be broad or narrow. The former are usually PHONEM(E)ic and use symbols that are sufficient to convey appropriate distinctions. The latter include precise phonetic information. *Cf.* Transliteration.

Customarily, in transcription, phonemic symbols are put between slanting lines, **Example,**/p/and phonetic symbols in square brackets, **Example,** [ph]. **2.** An elementary-level writing activity. It consists of writing down or transcribing phrases and sentences already learnt. Transcription is intended to fix the patterns [of the learnt sentences] in the learner's mind.

transfer. Generally, the process whereby the experience of doing one kind of activity influences, either in a positive or negative manner, the performance of another kind of activity done later. Past learning [of language] is considered to have transfer effect on present learning. Transfer is generally a positive process of extending and applying knowledge and experience acquired in one setting to solving problems in other similar settings. In certain contexts, however, transfer may have a negative effect. *See* LANGUAGE TRANSFER.

transfer of skills. Concept relating to the hypothesis that skills of language acquired in one language/the MT have pay off value in a SL. For example, it has been claimed that proficient readers in the MT acquire skills that make them good readers in another language provided they possess a minimal level of competence in that language. *See also* CROSS-LINGUISTIC INFLUENCE, INTERFERENCE, and LANGUAGE TRANSFER.

transfer of training. Transfer of learned skills from one situation to another. *See also* TRANSFER OF SKILLS. Whereas 'transfer' can have either facilitating or lessening effect, the expression 'transfer of training' generally indicates that knowledge of skills acquired in one context results in increased performance in another context.

transformation. 1. In grammar and linguistics, a rule, also known as transformational rule, applied to convert sentences of one type into another, **Example**, to convert active voice sentences into passive voice sentences. **2.** A type of language exercise. In it the learner is asked to change a sentence from one form into another. **3.** Transformation as an aim of education. *See* REPRODUCTION (2), and TRANSFORMATIVE PEDAGOGY.

transformational generative grammar (TGG). A MODEL(1) of grammar originally proposed by the American linguist A. Noam Chomsky (1928–). It has a set of rules for mapping deep structures on a surface form. Deep structures represent the underlying meaning. *See also* GENERATIVE GRAMMAR, and TRANSFORMATION (1).

transformative pedagogy. CRITICAL PEDAGOGY: pedagogy that creates socio-political awareness among learners and enables them to fight inequalities, domination, and oppression. Since Paulo Freire talked of such pedagogy in 1970s, a number of other writers and thinkers on education have highlighted the transformative and empowering role of education.

transitions. Connecting devices that link sentences in a paragraph, and paragraphs in longer discourse. Words and phrases like also, consequently, furthermore, in addition, nevertheless mark transitions. This function may sometimes be served by a full sentence: **Example**, *We now come to the functions of language.*

transitional competence. A learner's competence in a SL as reflected in her interim grammar of the language. *See* APPROXIMATIVE SYSTEMS, and INTERLANGUAGE GRAMMAR

translation. The rendering of a message/text from one language into another. Translation has traditionally been used as a learning activity in LE, and is an essential component of the 'GRAMMAR TRANSLATION METHOD'. Translation could be from the MT to the TL, or vice versa.

Translation, essentially a mental activity, focuses on meaning. It requires both COMPREHENSION and expression abilities – first to comprehend the text to be translated and then to express it appropriately in the other language.

Though disfavoured during much of the twentieth century as a F/S LL activity, translation may be of pedagogical value as it cognitively engages the learner with interpretation of MEANING, and draws her attention to meaning-form relationship. *See also* DOUBLE TRANSLATION.

transliteration. Representing the words, sentences, or longer pieces of one language through the script/writing system of another. As the letters of two different ALPHABETS do not always have exact phonetic equivalence, transliteration has conventionally resorted to approximation in using TL letters that phonetically resemble the letters in the SL. *Cf.* TRANSCRIPTION.

transmission approach to teaching. An approach to LE in which the teacher 'transmits'/passes on to the learner information and knowledge in the belief that receiving information and knowledge is learning the language. A teacher-centred approach, the transmission mode considers learners' minds empty vessels to be filled with the transmitted information. The approach does not conceive of learners' minds playing any role in creating knowledge.

transposition error. An error caused by swapping the positions of two elements in a word or sentence. **Example**: perfe̱c̱t̲ – perke̱ft̲; pressure cooker – cooker pressure.

treatment of learner errors. *See* CORRECTION and FEEDBACK (1a).

triadic dialogue. The three move exchanges typically occurring in classroom discourses, also known as the IRF CYCLE. The moves are *initiate - respond – evaluate/feedback/follow up* A move initiated by the teacher, **Example**, a question asked, is responded to by the learner, and this is followed by the teacher's evaluation of the response (**Example**, 'good') or FEEDBACK/FOLLOW UP on it.

turn-taking. Participants in a conversation/transaction taking turns to speak. Turn-taking usually takes place in an order, and follows norms that are culturally determined. For **example**, in a conversation no one speaks all the time, and when one person speaks, the other(s) listen(s). When the speaker has finished, she listens to the other participant(s). In the classroom context, the teacher has the authority to nominate pupils [to speak, or answer questions] and assign turns.

tutorial. A format of face to face, interactive, small-group teaching as part of a student's higher education course. In it the tutor and the student(s) discuss the latter's written assignments and study-problems. In some instructional modes, tutorials can be taken electronically. Outside the mainstream, privately-run coaching classes may also arrange tutorials.

two cultures in ELT. Two different VALUE- and belief-systems and the concomitant sets of practices in EL education. It has been observed that much theorising and prescribing in the field of SL education has emerged from what is known as BANA countries, but chiefly from UK and USA. These constitute the domain of culture 'One.' The generalisations derived from it are based in, and applicable particularly to its own [unique] social and cultural milieu.

The other culture embraces learners, teachers, and schools in what is popularly known as the III world countries. They have their own indigenous assumptions and pedagogical practices that go back to the times before Culture

One started talking about reforming LT methodologies. Today, Culture 2 are the recipients of the curricular formulations of culture 1. When applied to, and practised in the social and classroom cultures of this other world, they lead to anomalous results, and 'tissue rejection.' [expression used by Adrian Holliday (1994)]. As an approach to understanding the problem(s) and seeking remedy, a plea has been made for an ecological and ethnographic study in-context of the local conditions. *See also* APPROPRIATE METHODOLOGY, CULTURES OF THE CLASSROOM, and CULTURE-SPECIFIC PEDAGOGIES.

type-token ratio (TTR). The ratio of the number of particular class/types of words or utterances to the number of times their examples or tokens appear in a CORPUS of language. For example, in the last three words of the preceding sentence *corpus of language*(noun, prep., noun), there are 3 word tokens but 2 word types. The ratio indicates verbal diversity in the corpus. The notion of 'type' is a flexible one. Instead of basing it on parts of speech as in the example, one could use abstract and concrete or other categories of types.

typology of languages. The study of language types on the basis of structural similarities.

U

unfavourably circumstanced schools. In the ESL context, schools without acquisition-enriching facilities. (*See also* ACQUISITION ENRICHED ENVIRONMENT, and ENRICHMENT.) According to M. West (1960), such schools have large classes, congested classrooms, untrained teachers, teachers not proficient in the language [English], grammar and translation-based teaching, examination-result-oriented teaching, and high rate of dropouts. West was of the view that teachers should be trained to understand the difficulties of less fortunate schools, and to acquire methods which can be used under those conditions.

unit. 1. A single thing complete in itself but forming part of a larger thing. For example, a MORPHEME is a unit of a word just as a WORD is a unit of a SENTENCE. **2.** One of the segments into which a textbook or a teaching programme may be divided. Lessons and chapters are well known divisions of [text]books. Often they are organised in a sequence of blocks known as units. A unit may be constructed around a theme, a situation, a topic of interest, or a language point (form or function). The sub-sections of a unit consist of learning activities and tasks involving different skills.

unitary-trait hypothesis. The HYPOTHESIS(1) that there is a single TRAIT of intelligence underlying language proficiency. However, a multiple-trait hypothesis seems to have replaced it.

The hypotheses have implications for LANGUAGE TESTING.

unit-credit system. A system of dividing a course of study into UNIT(1)s and assigning each of them specific weighting/credit. The learner earns the credit on successfully completing/ learning the unit. The system was initiated by the Council of Europe for their Threshold Level course. In this system, units represent the objectives, or specifications of learning points. The system is associated with van Ek(1976). *See also* WAYSTAGE.

unity. The quality of the elements of discourse such as sentences in a paragraph working together to support the main idea [COHERENTly and CONSISTENTly]. A unit of discourse achieves unity when it deals with one central idea and avoids contradictory statements.

universal grammar (UG). A set of basic grammatical principles assumed to be fundamental to all natural languages. It is hypothesised that children bring their knowledge of the principles, abstract in nature and innate to them, to the task of learning language(s). *See,* in this regard, PRINCIPLES and PARAMETERS.

universals, linguistic. Linguistic features that are common to all natural languages. For **example**, all languages will have devices for indicating the doer of an action, the action and its modalities. Similarly, antonymy, synonymy and other meaning relationships are universal to the semantic structure of all languages though their surface realization may differ from language to language.

uptake. 1. A linguistic item that a

learner has learnt and can use fluently. Uptake is distinguished from. INPUT, the language a learner is exposed to. In the terminology of theorists, input becomes INTAKE when the learner comprehends it, and uptake when she can use it communicatively. **2.** The meaning/message intended by the speaker/writer or the meaning actually understood by the person addressed.

usage. Choices of linguistic-forms in using a language: how a language is actually spoken/written as different from what its grammar prescribes. Grammar books usually present general rules whereas usage [by the users of the language] may consist of acceptable deviations. Since a language offers a PRAGMATICS-related choice of forms at every point, and one chooses the forms that suit one's meaning and particular disposition, the pragmatics and STYLE of language usage may vary to some extent from one individual to another. *See also* USAGE and USE.

usage and use. Accuracy and appropriacy as distinguished by Widdowson (1978) in the context of priorities in (S)LE. According to him, *usage* has to do with the grammatical ACCURACY of an UTTERANCE, and use with its (communicative) APPROPRIATENESS to the context. In this contrasted pair, usage has a slightly different meaning from what it carries in the phrase 'grammar and usage.' *See* USAGE. Widdowson's distinction highlights the importance in SLE of teaching 'use' neglected in the STRUCTURAL APPROACHES.

use. *See* USAGE and USE.

utterance. A sample of AUTHENTIC speech (or writing). It may be as short as a few words or a longer DISCOURSE(1).

V

valid. Conforming to principles. The adjective 'valid' is used with reference to something [**Example**, argument, conclusion, inference, reasoning, score, test] about which a statement is being made. Something (**Example**, an argument) is valid if it has followed proper procedure, a principle, or a theory.

validation. Determination of VALIDITY. Validation of a LANGUAGE TEST is a procedure to find out whether the test is RELIABLE, and whether it measures what it sets out to measure. For, a test may achieve reliability and yet may not measure the right thing or be valid for a particular use. Validation may also try to ensure that the test meets other requirements. Some of these are that it looks face-valid, that the scores on it do not violate expectation, and that it predicts more general performance. To validate a new Test, often correlations are obtained between test-takers' scores on it and on test (s) already validated and established.

validity. The property of being VALID. In logic, an argument or conclusion is valid if it has followed the principles of logic.

Validity, in relation to language Tests is the quality and CRITERION that a test evaluate/measure the TRAIT it professes to test. Validity of a test can be of different types. Some of these are: CONCURRENT, CONSTRUCT, CONTENT, CONVERGENT, CRITERION-RELATED, and PREDICTIVE.

value. 1. *See* SIGNIFICATION and VALUE. **2.**

Weighting/numerical quantity assigned to a test-question.

values. Standards of social and ETHICAL behaviour that develop over a period, and are dearly upheld by a SOCIETY as desirable goals. Value systems may vary from CULTURE to culture.

value judgement. A SUBJECTIVE evaluation of such things as a person, principle, object, institution, and viewpoint made in such terms as of good, bad, proper, improper. Non-value judgement is objective and descriptive.

variability. The nature (and degree) of language features/samples differing from each other. Variability is a natural feature of living languages. There always exists variation in pronunciation and phonology, rules of sentence construction and word connotations across time, social classes, and geographical spaces and boundaries. Attitudes to such change vary. Whereas linguists accept variability as natural, purists frown on it. Linguistic CONSERVATISM believes in upholding a CANON.

variety. *See* LANGUAGE VARIETIES.

verbal. Characteristic of, or expressed in words (as different from gestures), often orally. Verbal skill relates to the ability to use language in speech and writing.

verbal routines. Typical structure(s) of conversational INTERACTIONS between two persons. In most cases, the routine begins with greetings, followed by enquiries and responses to them, and ends with the expression of thanks or good wishes. Many elements in the routine are phatic in nature.

Whereas learners naturally acquire in due course the culturally determined forms used in the routines in their MT, they need to learn it in a SL.

verbal tests. Tests of language knowledge and VERBAL skills.

verb-form frequency count. A count of how frequently [certain specified] forms of verbs occur in a given/selected corpus of NS use of the language. Such counts [products of a particular phase in the history of theorising on SLT] were carried out in 1960s in the belief that a high or low incidence of a verb-form [**Example**, the simple present form eat/eats] would be an index of its usefulness. This information about the relative frequencies of occurrences, it was asserted, should be useful in prioritising and SEQUENCING of ITEMS in SYLLABUS-framing, materials construction and in teaching. H.V. George carried out such a study [of English] in India *circa* 1960, and reported that in a set of 4 form-categories – forms like play, plays and played – occurred more frequently than to play and playing. Further, within these, certain, usages were more frequent than others. *See also* WORD LISTS.

verbiage. (Also, verbalism, verbosity). UTTERANCES that consist of the use of CLICHÉ, hackneyed expressions, unnecessary words and roundabout language but lack in meaningful substance. *See also* BABOO VARIETY, and CIRCUMLOCUTION.

vernacular. [Used both as noun and adjective]. An indigenous language used by the 'native' or the local people. In the context of education, the word has come to mean the MOTHER TONGUE of the people as contrasted with the

language of their colonial rulers. In India, 'vernacular press' refers to the journalists and newspapers in Indian languages as different from the journalistic publications in English. *See also* VERNACULAR TONGUE.

A distinction is made by some sociolinguists between the vernacular or the native speech and MOTHER TONGUE. Native speech, according to Khubchandani (1977), is 'the first speech acquired in infancy, through which a child gets socialised.' It has a formative role in the CONCEPTual and PERCEPT(ION)ual development of man in society. (Pattanayak 1984, after Illich and Labov). MT is often the homogenised, urban, cultivated, variety also known as the STANDARD VARIETY. It is the latter which plays a role in formal education, not the vernacular. There may be a wide gap between the two. Khubchandani (*ibid.*) says 'Thus the acquisition of literacy in languages like Hindi, Urdu, Punjabi, Marathi, Tamil becomes more like learning a second language'. In such contexts the *MT* is a 'second language', and its learning is not as smooth and easy as the learning of the native language is thought to be. *See also* Taught mother tongue.

vernacular style. Casual style as contrasted with CAREFUL STYLE.

vernacular tongue. The speech variety of everyday use. Ivan Illich who uses this term, describes VT as the unbound and ungoverned speech in which people actually live and manage their lives. Using the term in the context of the PRESCRICTIVISM of STANDARD/standardised forms, Illich contrasts it with 'TAUGHT MOTHER TONGUE'.

violence. Hurtful behaviour an example of which is (corporal) punishment meted out to students for making language errors. Violence motivated by prejudice and AUTHOREITARIAN attitudes may be inflicted verbally and/or behaviourally. These may relate to gender, caste, creed, colour and such other sensitive matters. Reverse violence in the form of booing and jeering teachers, and student-student violence also occur.

virtual classrooms. Simulated classrooms. Usually, CLASSROOMS are located in educational institutions. Virtual classrooms can be any physical location such as home or office. And students can participate in the learning process (as they would in actual classrooms) from across different places – places they happen to be located at. From there they can interact with tutors or peers using learning MODULE(1)s and electronic gadgets. Virtual classrooms offer interactive and self-paced learning. The learning process is assisted by sounds, visuals and graphics, animation, text and other aids. The software is so designed as to introduce interactive learning. *See also* OPEN LEARNING, and VIRTUAL UNIVERSITY.

virtual university. A university 'without walls.' It is an extension of VIRTUAL CLASSROOMS. In it, almost all instructional and related functions take place electronically over digital links and networks. Though printed texts are used, much instruction is multi-media-based through disk-based digital storage techniques. Learning programmes may additionally be delivered via the satellite. *See* also OPEN LEARNING, and OPEN LEARNING SYSTEM.

visual aids. *See* AUDIO-VISUAL AIDS.

vocabulary. **1**. The words used in a language. **2**. The words that one knows. *See* ACTIVE VOCABULARY, and PASSIVE VOCABULARY. The distinction is utilised in prioritising the teaching of words in a SL. **3**. The vocabulary of a branch of knowledge. When used in this sense, it refers to the terminology, and a qualifier is used before the word, **Example** medical vocabulary.

vocabulary control. *See* CONTROLLED VOCABULARY.

vocabulary selection. Making a list of relevant and useful words for specific purposes (such as teaching a SL at the secondary level), according to specific criteria, such as FREQUENCY. [*See* Selection.] Michael West (1953) specifies the following other considerations he adopted for the GENERAL SERVICE LIST (GSL): 1. ease or difficulty of learning(=cost), 2. necessity, 3. cover, 4. stylistic level, and 5. Intensive and emotional words.

This is not to suggest that these criteria are absolute. Vocabulary selections are purpose-related, and it is the stated purpose that governs the criteria for selection. In this context, the usefulness of an item for/in teaching, and its usefulness for the learners may be a consideration overriding that of relative frequency.

vocabulary teaching. Activity aimed at developing learners' knowledge of new words, esp. of a SL. It has traditionally been done by giving learners a PARAPHRASE or an MT equivalent of the target word. Vocabulary has sometimes been taught as an independent module, not dovetailed with the textual materials.

Many learners think that knowing a word and its meaning ensures that they can use the word [correctly] when needed. However, new LT practices follow CONTEXT(3)-based approaches, and the learners are encouraged to use strategies of comprehension to discover word-meanings.

Current SLT theories do not attach much importance to the BEHAVIOURIST beliefs regarding LINEARITY and LINEAR SEQUENCING in teaching-learning. These latter follow the principles of SELECTION, and GRADING of the vocabulary-items and their PRESENTATION to the class in a pre-determined sequence.

vocabulary test. A tool for assessing an individual's knowledge of words. For doing this, there are different techniques and formats each testing an aspect of the knowledge, from simple recognition of a word to the ability to supply it, and further to use it appropriately. The level of the knowledge tested varies from test to test.

vocal cords. Vocal folds: the two muscular folds of flexible tissues in the larynx. They rapidly open and close setting up the vibration pattern for voicing. *See also* VOICE (1).

vocational course. A programme of study/instruction aimed at preparing the learner for a specific job she can take up to earn a living. In such courses, the stress is on practical skills, and the language is taught for instrumental purposes.

voice. 1. The SPEECH-sound(s) resulting from the vibration of the VOCAL CORDS. **2. (i).** One's personal philosophy, beliefs, and concerns: one's individual way of thinking, and looking at things. **(ii)** The speaking consciousness.

vowel and consonant. Traditionally the two major classes in which speech sounds are divided. Vowels are 'frictionless,' and 'prolongable' in their articulation whereas consonants do not have any appreciable duration in the speech continua. A third category consists of 'semivowels' such as [w] and [j], which, though articulated like vowels, function as consonants in the structure of a SYLLABLE.

A distinction needs to be made between the vowel 'letters' in the ALPHABET used by a language and the vowel sounds it uses. *Cf.* DIPHTHONGS.

255

W

wait time. The time a classroom teacher allows a learner to answer a question. Teachers are known for asking questions and not waiting for an answer. Whereas the teacher may have rehearsed her questions, learners need time to formulate their answers. Similarly, many teachers do not have the patience to wait till the learners have completed their answer. Often the answering is interrupted. Teachers may be well advised to be patient and wait till the learner is ready to answer. *See also* QUESTION TECHNIQUES.

wall charts/pictures. Graphic materials dealing with a topic or theme, used as illustrative aids in classroom language-teaching.

washback. *See* BACKWASH.

Watsonian. (After the American behaviourist psychologist, JB Watson (1878–1958). Theory and approach characterised by BEHAVIOURISM. Watsonians i.e., faithful behaviourists hold that all behaviour, even breathing, is learned. Learning is caused by chance and experience. They believe that animal- [man included] behaviour is formed through conditioning, its two kinds being – CLASSICAL and OPERANT CONDITIONING. Cognitive experiences such as THINKING and feeling have no place in the theory. Environment is responsible for individual differences. In behaviourist experiments only objective and publicly verifiable methods are considered valid.

Waystage. Intermediate level proficiency in a SL. *Waystage* is a publication that describes the competence to be achieved by SL learners [of English] at this level. The course objectives and specifications have been worked out by van Ek and Trim (1991, 1998) for the Council of Europe These objectives and specifications [arrived at after careful deliberation] can be used as guidelines in planning an intermediate level course in a SL. *See also* THRESHOLD LEVEL SPECIFICATIONS.

Wernicke's aphasia. A form of language disorder. *See* Aphasia. The symptoms are incoherence and volubility without meaning-content. *See also* WERNICKE'S AREA.

Wernicke's area. (After Carl Wernicke, a German doctor). Part of the brain in its left hemisphere involved in the understanding of speech. The left hemisphere is hypothesised to be the language area. *See also* BROCA'S AREA

whole books. *See* REAL BOOKS.

whole language approach. A children's- literature-based approach to LL and LT. In it language is not seen as fragmented into skills. Teaching done in a NATURALISTIC setting aims at whole language development. Learning in the classroom extends to the whole life of the learner. *See* LANGUAGE EXPERIENCE APPROACH, and HOLISTIC APPROACHES.

whole-word approach. *See* LOOK-AND-SAY (METHOD), SIGHT READING, and WORD METHOD. *Cf.* SENTENCE METHOD

Whorfian hypothesis. *See* SAPIR-WHORF HYPOTHESIS.

wide-band procedures. Procedures in testing and evaluation that are wide-tuned and subjective. Unstructured interviews are an example.

word. the smallest UNIT(1)of a language that can stand alone – a free MORPHEME. The word 'word' represents a concept that almost everyone understands intuitively but few can define it to everyone's satisfaction. According to one definition, a word is a FORMAL grammatical UNIT, meaningful and rule-governed. Its combinations form phrases and SENTENCES. *Cf.* LEXEME.

word association. Mental connection between words: a vocabulary-expansion task based on this. 'Rose,' 'beauty' and 'flower' are words that are mentally associated. How people recall other words at the mention of a particular word is a matter of interest for psychologists, semanticists and language teachers. *See also* WORD CHAIN, AND WORD GAME.

word-attack strategies. A related group of STRATEG(Y)ies [in reading]dealing with the GUESSING of the meanings of words in a text with the help of contextual, semantic, grammatical and morphological clues.

Awareness of how clues are often implied or built into the text may help learners discover them. *See* also READING STRATEGIES, and TEXT-ATTACK STRATEGIES.

word blindness. *See* ALEXIA.

word-building test. A test or task in which the test-taker is asked to form as many words as possible from a given set of disconnected letters. *See also* ANAGRAM.

word chain. A language learning game. In it a chain of words is created with each link having the same kind of addition, deletion, or alteration. The following is an example of a chain

created by adding. The second part of a compound word begins the next link, and so on: *box-office, office-boy, boy-servant, servant-girl, girl-friend, friendship, ship-load.*

The players in the game have to give the next word by turns. Thus a sequence is made. The game has several variations. *Cf.* CHAINING.

word count. A systematic count of the FREQUENCY of the occurrence of words in a given CORPUS.

word game. A LL activity in the form of a game. Forming nouns from verbs is an example. A game is designed to make learners practice, or learn new items. The element of quiz, puzzle, competition with prize or reward makes the game interesting. *See also* LANGUAGE GAMES, and WORD CHAIN.

word lists. *See* WORD COUNT. A word count leads to a word list. *See also* A GENERAL SERVICE LIST OF ENGLISH WORDS, and LORGE-THORNDIKE LIST. Word lists are useful tools for writers of teaching materials for SL learners.

word method. A method of teaching reading, also known as the WHOLE WORD, or the LOOK-AND-SAY METHOD. In it learners are taught to begin reading by reading words and not the discrete ALPHABETS that constitute them. *See* the ALPHABETIC METHOD. As in the Alphabetic so in the PHONICS, learners are taught to begin with individual letters/sounds. In favour of this method it is argued that L1 learners being already familiar with the words in speech, and SL learners with reading and writing also [in their MT], it makes more sense to them to begin with reading whole words. *See also* the LANGUAGE

EXPERIENCE APPROACH, and the SENTENCE METHOD.

word-play. Handling in a rather clever way the meanings or sounds of words for humorous effect. To deliberately pronounce *letter-box* as *litter-box* is word play. Note the play in the following:

When is a cook bad?

When he beats an egg!

workbook. Teaching material for language use-/practice. The work-book material usually follow the order of the lesson-units in the MAIN COURSEBOOK. The items of teaching introduced and highlighted in a lesson-unit are taken up for consolidation in the workbook.

worksheet. Paper with tasks on them designed by tutors for learners to work through. *See also* THINKSHEET.

workshop. A group activity in which the participants work collectively or in groups on a PROJECT or a TASK(1). A workshop may be part of an instructional programme in which the participants learn[practically] doing something under supervision. It may also be the working together of a select group to discuss a problem and propose solution(s).

On TE programmes, MENTORS and teachers in training often adopt the workshop way.

writing. One of the four major language-SKILLS, traditionally classified along with 'speaking' as an 'active' skill. 'Writing' refers to a range of abilities from the elementary level GRAPHICS and secondary level COMPOSITION-writing to the advanced level ability of creating DISCOURSE(1). Writing involves a great number of subskills from the mechanics[punctuation, capitalization] to sentence construction [of various types] to paragraph writing, and further on to the production of longer texts. Advanced-level writing may need to take in view, among others, AUDIENCE [AWRENESS], COHERENCE, COHESION,CONSISTENCY 1, STYLE 1, TEXTUAL COMPETENCE, and UNITY.

written language. *See* SPOKEN LANGUAGE.

Y

yerkish. An ARTIFICIAL LANGUAGE or Chimp language: According to the Microsoft Encarta Dictionary, it is a 'language of visual symbols created for experimental communication between chimpanzees and humans.'

Z

Zhang Sizhong method. A pedagogical approach to FL teaching popular in China and associated with the Chinese teacher, Zhang Sizhong (1930–). Sizhong was originally a teacher of Russian as a FL and developed his approach now widely applied to the teaching of English in China, from his experience of teaching Russian as a FL. The approach consists of (i) grouping mixed ability-class-learners according to their proficiency and skill in the TL; (ii) emphasis on rapid vocabulary learning; (iii) focused teaching of grammar, and (iv) reading of texts in the TL.

In accordance with point (i) above – a very important principle in the approach – the bright students [in the mixed-ability class] are allowed to work at their pace rather independently and the teacher concentrates instruction on the weaker ones. Sizhong found that such skill-based grouping into fast moving and slow moving tracks resolved the problem of classroom indiscipline.

Other principles characteristic of the approach are; moving from simple to complex, repetition and REINFORCE-MENT(1). Students are asked to work in pairs, and produce one minute speeches. (Sinorama, 2001)

zone of proximal development (ZPD). A developmental level in a child's cognitive development, posited by Vygotsky (1978). At this level, a child cannot solve a problem independently but she can do so under guidance and in collaboration. ZPD relates to the distance between what the learner can do on her own and what she can achieve in co-operation with others. For Vygotsky, learning and development are interrelated processes and cognition develops as a result of social interactions. *Cf.* ACTUAL DEVEL-OPMENTAL LEVEL. It may be noted that in language testing we measure what the learner can do at a given point of time but do not consider what she can achieve through interaction with others. *See also* CONSTRUCTIVISM.

References

Abercrombie, D., 'Teaching Pronunciation', *English Language Teaching,* Vol. 3, 1949.

Alatis, James A., 'Towards a LAPSE Theory of Teacher Preparation in English as a Second Language', *ELT Journal, 39/1,* 1974.

Alexander, L.G., *Guided Composition in English Language Teaching,* London: Longman, 1971.

Austin, J.L., *How to do Things with Words,* Oxford: Clarendon Press, 1962.

Ausubel, D.P., 'The Use of Advance Organizers in the Learning and Retention of Meaningful Verbal Material', *Journal of Educational Psychology,* 51, 1960, pp. 262–72.

Ausubel, D.P., *Educational Psychology: A Cognitive View,* New York: Holt, Rinehart & Winston 1968.

Bachman, L.F. and A. Palmer, *Language Testing in Practice,* Oxford: Oxford University Press, 1996.

Bandura, A., *Social Learning Theory,* Englewood Cliffs, NJ: Prentice Hall, 1977.

Barnard, Helen, 'A Test of PUC Students' vocabulary in Chota Nagpur', *Bulletin of the Central Institute of English* 1, 1961.

Barnes, Douglas, 'Language in the Secondary Classroom', in Barnes, et al., 1969/1971.

Barnes, D., James Britton, Harold Rosen and the L.A.T.E., *Language, the Learner and the School,* Harmondsworth: Penguin Books Ltd., 1969, Revsd. Edition. 1971.

Bellack, A.A., H.M. Kliebard, R.T. Hyman and F.L. Smith, *The Language of the Classroom.* New York: Teachers College Press, 1966.

Bender, Byron W., 'Pretence in Language Teaching', *ELT 19/.1,* 1964.

Bernstein, Basil, *Class, Codes and Control. Theoretical Studies Towards a Sociology of Language,* Vol. 1, London: Routledge & Kegan Paul, 1971.

Bialystok, Ellen, *Bilingualism in Development: Language, Literacy, and Cognition.* Cambridge: Cambridge University Press, 2001.

Billows, F.L., *The Techniques of Language Teaching,* London: Longman, 1961.

Block, J.H. (ed.), *Mastery Learning: Theory and Practice,* New York: Holt, Rhine & West, 1971.

Blcom, B.S. (ed.), *Taxonomy of Educational Objectives,* New York: McKay, 1956.

Brisk, M.E., *Bilingual Education: From Compensatory to Quality Schooling,* Mahwah, NJ: Erlbaum, 1998.

Brooks, N., *Language and Language Learning* (2nd edition), New York: Harcourt, Brace and World, 1964.

Brumfit, C.J. and K. Johnson (eds.), *The Communicative Approach to Language Teaching,* Oxford: OUP, 1979.

Brumfit, C.J., 'Accuracy and Fluency: A Fundamental Distinction for Communicative Teaching Methodology', *Practical English Teacher*, 1/3, 1981a.

Brumfit, C.J., 'Notional Syllabuses Revisited: A Response', *Applied Linguistics* 2(1), (1981b): 90–2.

Bruner, Jerome, *On Knowing: Essays from the Left Hand*, NY: Atheneum, 1966.

Bruner, J., *Actual Minds, Possible worlds*, Cambridge, Ma.: Harvard University Press, 1986.

Burt, M.K., Dulay, H.C. and Finocciaro, M. (eds.), 'Viewpoints on English as a Second Language', New York: Regents, 1977.

Canale, M., 'From Communicative Competence to Communicative Language Pedagogy' in Richards, J. and R. Schmidt (eds.) *Language and Communication*, London: Longman, 1983.

Canale, M. and Swain, M., 'Theoretical Bases of Communicative Approaches to Second Language Teaching and Testing', *Applied Linguistics* 1-1, 1980.

Catford, J.C., 'Intelligibility', *English Language Teaching*, Vol. 5, 1950.

Champion, H., *Lectures on Teaching English in India*, London: Humphrey Milford for Oxford University Press, 1937.

Chapman, L.R.H., *Teaching English to Beginners*, London: Longmans Green & Co. Ltd., 1958.

Chaudron, Craig, *Second Language Classrooms: Research on Teaching and Learning*. Cambridge: Cambridge University Press, 1988.

Coleman, A., *The Teaching of Modern Foreign Languages in the United States*, New York: Macmillan, 1929.

Connelly, F.M. and D. Jean Clandinin, *Teachers as Curriculum Planners: Narratives of Experience*, New York: Teachers College Press and Ontario: OISE, 1988.

Corder, S. Pit., 'The Significance of Learners' Errors', *IRAL*: Vol. 5, No. 4, 1967.

Crystal, David, *English as a Global Language*, Cambridge: Cambridge University Press, 1997.

Cummins, Jim, 'Cognitive/academic Language Proficiency, Linguistic Interdependence, the Optimal Age Question and Some Other Matters', *Working Papers in Bilingualism.* 19, 1979.

Curran, Charles A., *Counselling-learning in a Second Language,* Apple River, Ill.: Apple River Press, 1976.

Cutts, Martin, *The Plain English Guide,* Oxford/New York: Oxford University Press, 1995.

de Bono, Edward, *Parallel Thinking,* London: Viking, and Penguin Books. http://www.edwdebono.com

Dodson C.J., *Language Teaching and the Bilingual Method,* London: Sir Isaac Pitman & Sons Ltd., 1967.

Dulay, H.C. and Marina K. Burt, 'You can't Learn without Goofing: An Analysis of Children's Second Language Learning Strategies' in Richards 1974.

Dulay, H.C. and Marina K. Burt, 'Remarks on Creativity in Language Acquisition' in M. Burt, H. Dulay and M. Finnochiaro (eds.), 1977.

Dunkin, M.J. and B.J. Biddle, *The Study of Teaching,* New York: Holt, Rinehart, & Winston, 1974.

Fairclough, N., *Critical Discourse Analysis: The Critical Study of Language,* London: Longman, 1995.

Feuerstein, R., P.S. Klein and A.J. Tannenbaum, *Mediated Learning Experience; Theoretical, Psychological and Learning Implications,* London: Freund 1991 [as discussed in Williams and Burden (1997)].

Forrester, Jean, 'Demonstration Lessons', *ELT Journal, 29/1,* 1974.

Fowler, H.W., *A Dictionary of Modern English Usage,* London: Oxford University Press, 1926, 2nd edition Revised by Ernest Gowers 1965.

Friere, Paulo, *Pedagogy of the Oppressed,* Harmondsworth: Penguin Books, 1972.

Frohlich, M., N. Spada and P. Allen, 'Differences in the Communicative Orientations of L2 Classrooms', *TESOL Quarterly, 22/3,* 1985.

Fry, Edward, *Teaching Faster Reading: A Manual,* Cambridge: Cambridge University Press, 1963.

Galyean, Beverly, 'A Confluent Design for Language Teaching', *TESOL Quarterly* 11, 1979: 143–56.

Gardner, R.C., *Social Psychology and Language Learning: The Role of Attitude and Motivation,* London: Edward Arnold, 1985.

Gardner, R.C. and Lambert, W.E., *Attitudes and Motivation in Second Language Learning,* Mass.: Newbury House, 1972.

Gattegno, C., *Teaching Foreign Languages in Schools: The Silent Way,* New York: Educational Solutions, 1972.

George, H.V., *101 Substitution Tables for Students of English,* Cambridge: Cambridge University Press, 1967a.

George, H.V., *101 Substitution Tables for Students of English: Teachers' and Advanced Students' Guide,* Cambridge: Cambridge University Press, 1967b.

Gingras, R.C. (ed.), *Second Language Acquisition and Foreign Language Teaching,* Arlington, VA.: Centre for Applied Linguistics, 1978.

Girard, D., *Linguistics and Foreign Language Teaching* (Translated from French and edited by R.A. Close), London: Longman, 1972.

Girard, D., 'Audio-visual Methods and the Training of Teachers', *ELT Journal* 29/1, 1974.

Goodman, Kenneth S., 'Reading: A Psycholinguistic Guessing Game', *Journal of reading specialists,* 6, 1967: 126–35.

Goodman, Paul, *Compulsory Miseducation,* Vintage Books, 1964.

Gordon, William J.J., *Synectics,* New York: Harper & Row, 1961.

Govt. of India, *Report of the Education Commission, 1964–66, Education and National Development,* New Delhi: Manager of Publications, 1966.

Gowers, Ernest (Sir), *The Complete Plain Words,* London: HMSO, 1954.

Grice, P., *Logic and Conversation,* 1967/1975, reprinted in Cole, P. and J. Morgan (eds.), 1975.

Gurrey, P., *Teaching English as a Foreign Language*, London: Longmans, 1955.

Halliday, M.A.K., 'Categories of the Theory of Grammar', *Word*, 17, 1961: 241–92.

Halliday, M.A.K., Angus Mcintosh and Peter Strevens, *The Linguistic Sciences and Language Teaching*, London: Longman Group Ltd., 1964.

Halliday, M.A.K., *Learning How to Mean: Explorations in the Development of Language*, London: Edward Arnold, 1975.

Halliday, M.A.K., *Language as Social Semiotic: The Social Interpretation of Language and Meaning*, London: Edward Arnold, 1978.

Hargreaves, Andy, *Changing Teachers, Changing Times*, New York: Teachers, College Press, 1994.

Hawkins, E., *Awareness in Language: An Introduction*, Cambridge: Cambridge University Press, 1984.

Hill, L.A., *Selected Articles on the Teaching of English as a Foreign Language*, London: Oxford University Press, 1967.

Holliday, Adrian, *Appropriate Methodology and Social Context*, Cambridge: Cambridge University Press, 1994.

Howatt, A.P.R., *A History of English Language Teaching*, Oxford: OUP, 1984.

Hymes, Dell, 'On Communicative Competence' in Pride and Holmes, 1972.

Illich, Ivan, *Deschooling Society*, New York: Harper & Row, 1971, [also Penguin Books, 1973].

Illich, Ivan, 'Taught Mother Tongue and Vernacular Tongue', in Pattanayak, D.P. 1981.

Jenkins, Jennifer, *The Phonology of English as an International Language: New Models, New Norms, New Goals*, Oxford: Oxford University Press, 2000.

Jones, Ken, *Simulation in Language Teaching*, Cambridge: Cambridge University Press, 1982.

Joyce, Bruce and Marsha Weil, *Models of Teaching*, Boston: Allyn and Bacon, 1972, 1986.

Kachru, B.B., *Indianisation of English: The English Language in India.* Delhi: Oxford University Press, 1983.

Khubchandani, L.M., 'Language Ideology and Language Development', in *The International Journal of the Sociology of Language*, 13, 1977.

Knowles, M., 'Andragogy: An Emerging Technology for Adult Learning', in Tight, M. (ed.), *Education for Adults*, Vol. 1. London: Croom Helm, 1983.

Krashen, Stephen D., *Second Language Acquisition and Second Language Learning*, Oxford: Pergamon Press, 1981.

Krashen, Stephen D., *Principles and Practices in Language Acquisition*, Oxford: Pergamon Press, 1982.

Kumaravadivelu, B., 'Towards a Postmethod Pedagogy', *TESOL Quarterly* 35, 2001: 537–60.

Kumaravadivelu, B., *Beyond Methods: Macrostrategies for Language Learning*, New Haven and London: Yale University Press, 2003.

Larsen-Freeman, D., 'Chaos, Complexity, Science, and Second Language Acquisition', *Applied Linguistics, 1997,* 18/2.

Lee, W.R. (ed.), *ELT Selections 1,* London: OUP, 1967 (a).

Lee, W.R. (ed.), *ELT Selections 2,* London: OUP, 1967 (b).

Lukmani, Y.M., 'Motivation to Learn and Learning Proficiency' in *Language Learning,* 22, 1972.

Mackey, W.F., *Language Teaching Analysis,* London: Longman, 1965.

Mackey, W.F., 'Shipboard Language Teaching' in Lee, W.R. (ed.), *ELT Selections 2.*

Maley, Alan and Alan Duff, *Drama Techniques in Language Learning,* Cambridge: Cambridge University Press, 1978, 1982.

Markee, Numa, *Managing Curricular Innovation,* Cambridge: Cambridge University Press, 1997.

Maslow, A.H., *Motivation and Personality,* New York: Harper & Row, 1954/ 1970.

McKay, S., 'Literature in the ESL Classroom', *TESOL Quarterly,* 1982, 16/4.

Mercer, N., *The Guided Construction of Knowledge: Talk Among Teachers and Learners,* Cleveland: Multilingual Matters, 1995.

Mellows, D., 'Non-linearity and the Observed Lesson'. *ELT Journal,* 56/1, 2002.

Morris, John, 'Creative Reading', *ELT Journal,* 26/3, 1972.

O'Neill, Robert, 'Why Use Textbooks?' *ELT Journal* Vol. 36, No. 2, 1982.

Oxford, Rebecca, *Language Learning Strategies: What Every Teacher should Know,* Boston: Heinle and Heinle. 1990.

Palmer, H.E., *The Scientific Study and Teaching of Languages,* George G Harrap & Co., 1917 [reprinted at London by Oxford University Press, 1968].

Palmer, H.E., *The Principles of Language-study,* London: Harrap, 1921a. (Republished at London in 1964 by Oxford University Press).

Palmer, H.E., *The Oral Method of Language Teaching,* Cambridge: Heffer, 1921b.

Palmer, H.E., 'That will Come in Handy', in Lee, W.R., *ELT Selections 1.* London: Oxford University Press, 1967.

Pattanayak, D.P., *Multilingualism and Mother Tongue Education,* New Delhi: Oxford University Press, 1981.

Pattanayak, D.P., *Proceedings of AILA, Brussels,* Vol. V, plenary papers, 1984.

Paulston, C.B., 'Notional Syllabuses Revisited: Some Comments', *Applied Linguistics* 2(1) 1981: 93–5.

Piaget, Jean, 'On Developmental Psychology' in Gruber, Howard E. and J. Jacques Vonèche (eds.), 1977.

Prabhu, N.S., *Second Language Pedagogy,* Oxford University Press, 1987.

Prabhu, N.S., *Attempting Educational Change,* Vallabh Vidyanagar: HMPIETR, 1995.

Prabhu, N.S., 'Acquisition Through Comprehension' in Singh, Rajendra (ed.), 1997.

Prabhu, N.S., 'Ideation and Ideology' in Chaudhari, S.C. (ed.), *Teaching English in Non-native Contexts*, Chennai, 2002.

Pride, J.B. and J. Holmes (eds.), *Sociolinguistics: Selected Readings*, Harmondsworth: Penguin Books, 1972.

Richards, Jack C. and Theodore S. Rodgers (II ed., 2001), *Approaches and Methods in Language Teaching*, Cambridge: Cambridge University Press, 1986.

Rivers, W., *Teaching Foreign Language Skills*, Chicago: University of Chicago Press, (1968/1981).

Rogers, C.R., *On Becoming a Person*, Boston: Houghton-Mifflin, 1961.

Rosenblatt, L., *The Reader, the Text, the Poem*, Carbondale: Southern Illinois University Press, 1978.

Rubin, J. 'What the "Good Language Learner" can teach us', *TESOL Quarterly*, 9/1, 1975.

Rutherford, W., *Second Language Grammar: Learning and Teaching*, Longman: London, 1987.

Said, Edward, *Orientalism*, 1978, (3rd edition) Penguin: Harmondsworth, 1991.

Scherer, G.A.C. and Wertheimer, M., *A Psycholonguistic Experiment in Foreign Language Teaching*, New York: McGraw-Hill, 1964.

Schon, D., *The Reflective Practitioner: How Professionals Think in Action*, New York: Basic Books, 1983.

Schumann, J.H., 'The Acculturation Model for Second Language Acquisition', in Gingras, R.C. (ed.), 1978.

Searle, J.R., *Speech Acts: An Essay in the Philosophy of Language*, Cambridge: Cambridge University Press, 1969.

Searle, J.R., 'A Classification of Illocutionary Acts', *Language in Society*, Vol. 5, No. 1, 1976.

Selinker, Larry, 'Interlanguage', *International Review of Applied Linguistics*, Vol. 10, 1972.

Sinclair, J.Mc H. and R.M. Coulthard, *Towards an Analysis of Discourse*, London: Oxford University Press, 1975.

Singh, Rajendra (ed.), *Grammar, Language, and Society*, New Delhi: Sage Publications, 1997.

Sinorama, 'The ABCs According to Zhang Sizhong', Sept. 14, 2001. www: Sinorama.com.tw

Skilbeck, 'Three Educational Ideologies' in T. Horton and P. Raggat (eds.) *Challenge and Change in the Curriculum*, Sevenoaks: Hodder and Stoughton, 1982.

Skinner, B.F., *Verbal Behavior*, New York: Appleton-Century-Crofts, 1957.

Skutnabb-Kangas, T., Multilingualism and the Education of Minority Children', in Skutnabb-Kangas, T. and J. Cummins (eds.), 1988.

Skutnabb-Kangas, T. and J. Cummins (eds.), 'Minority Education: From Shame to Struggle', Cleveland (UK): Multilingual Matters, 1988.

Stern, H.H., *Fundamental Concepts of Language Teaching*, Oxford: Oxford University Press, 1983.

Stevick, Earl E., *Images and Options in the Language Classroom*, Cambridge: Cambridge University Press, 1986.

Tickoo, M.L. (ed.), *Simplification: Theory and Application*, Singapore: SEAMEO Regional Centre, 1993.

Titone, R., 'A Psycholinguistic Description of the Glossodynamic Model of Language Behaviour and Language Learning', *Rassegna Italiana di linguistica applicata*. Vol. 5, 1973.

Titone, Renzo and Marcel Danesi, *Applied Psycho-linguistics: An Introduction to the Psychology of Language Learning and Teaching*, Toronto: University of Toronto Press, 1985.

Tripp, D., *Critical Incidents in Teaching*, London: Routledge, 1993.

Tudor, Ian, *Learner-centeredness as Language Education*, Cambridge: Cambridge University Press, 1996.

Tudor, Ian, *The Dynamics of the Language Classroom*, Cambridge: Cambridge University Press, 2001.

Tyler, R., *Basic Principles of Curriculum and Instruction*, Chicago: University of Chicago Press, 1949.

Ur, Penny, *A Course in Language Teaching*, Cambridge: Cambridge University Press, 1996 (6th reprint 2000).

van Ek. J.A., *The Threshold Level*, Strasbourg: Council of Europe, 1976.

van Ek, J.A. and J.L.M. Trim, *Waystage 1990*, for Council of Europe, UK: Cambridge University Press, 1991.

Van lier L., 'Observation from an Ecological Perspective', *TESOL Quarterly* 31, 1997: 783–87.

Vygotsky, L.S., *Thought and Language*, Cambridge, Ma.: MIT Press, 1962.

Vygotsky, L.S., *Mind in Society. The Development of Higher Psychological Process*. Cambridge, Ma.; MIT Press, 1978.

West, Michael, *Bilingualism (with Special Reference to Bengal)*, Calcutta: Govt of India, Central Publication Branch (Occasional Reports No. 13), 1926.

West, Michael, *Learning to Read a Foreign Language: An Experimental Study*, NY: Longman, Green & Co., 1926.

West, Michael, *The New Method English Dictionary*, London: Longman, 1935.

West, Michel, 'Types of Exercise in Language Teaching' in Lee (ed.), *English Language Teaching*, (1947), Republished 1967a.

West, Michael, 'Simplified and Abridged' (1950), *English Language Teaching*, republished in Lee (ed.), 1967a.

West, Michael, 'Examinations in a Foreign Language', *English Language Teaching*, 1952, republished 1967a.

West, Michael, *A General Service List of English Words*, London: Longmans, 1953.

West, Michael, 'Factual English', In *English Language Teaching*, Vol. 12, No. 4, 1958.

West, Michael, *Teaching English in Difficult Circumstances,* London: Longmans, 1960.

West, Michael, *An International Reader's Dictionary,* London: Longmans, Green & Co. Ltd., 1965.

Whorf, B.L., *Language, Thought, and Reality: Selected Writings of Benjamin Lee Whorf,* (ed.) J.B. Carrol, Cambridge, Mass.: MIT Press, 1956.

Widdowson, H.G., *Teaching Language as Communication,* Oxford: Oxford University Press, 1978.

Widdowson, H.G., *Learning Purpose and Language Use,* Oxford: Oxford University Press, 1983.

Wilkins, D.A., *Linguistics in Language Teaching,* London: Edward Arnold. Cambridge, Mass.: The MIT Press, 1972.

Wilkins, D.A., *Notional Syllabuses,* Oxford: Oxford University Press, 1976.

Wilkins, D.A., 'National Syllabuses and Concept of a Minimum Adequate Grammar', in Brumfit, C.J. and K. Johnson (eds.), 1979.

Williams, Frederick (ed.), *Language and Poverty: Perspectives on a Theme,* Chicago: Markham, 1970.

Williams, Marion and Robert L Burden, *Psychology for Language Teachers: A Social Constructivist Approach,* Cambridge: Cambridge University Press, 1997.

Willis, Jane, *Teaching English through English,* Harlow: Longmans, 1981.

Woodward, Tessa, *Models and Metaphors in Language Teacher Training: Loop Input and other Strategies,* Cambridge: Cambridge University Press, 1991.

Yuhua, Ji, 'English Through Chinese: Experimenting with Sandwich Stories', in *English Today* Vol. 18, No. 1, Jan., 2002.